The OMRI Annual Survey of Eastern Europe and the Former Soviet Union
1996

The OMRI Annual Survey
of Eastern Europe and the Former Soviet Union 1996

Forging Ahead, Falling Behind

With an Introduction
by J. F. Brown

Open
Media
Research
Institute

Routledge
Taylor & Francis Group

LONDON AND NEW YORK

First published 1996 by M.E. Sharpe

Published 2015 by Routledge
2 Park Square, Milton Park, Abingdon, Oxon OX14 4RN
711 Third Avenue, New York, NY 10017, USA

Routledge is an imprint of the Taylor & Francis Group, an informa business

Library of Congress Cataloging-in-Publication Data

Open Media Research Institute.
The OMRI annual survey of Eastern Europe and the former Soviet Union :
1996—forging ahead, falling behind / by the Open Media Research Institute.
    p.   cm.
Includes bibliographical references (p.) and index.
ISBN 1-56324-925-1 (alk. paper)
1. Europe, Eastern—Politics and government—1989–   .
2. Former Soviet republics—Politics and government.
3. Europe, Eastern—Economic conditions—1989–   .
4. Former Soviet republics—Economic conditions.
5. Post-communism—Europe, Eastern.
6. Post-communism—Former Soviet republics.
I. Title.
DJK51.068   1996
320.94—dc20
96-19263
CIP

ISBN 13: 9781563249259 (hbk)

Contents

List of Tables and Figures

Tables

Figures

PREFACE

This is the second annual survey of political developments in the twenty-seven countries of the former socialist bloc from the Open Media Research Institute (OMRI). It was produced in rather difficult circumstances, since in November 1996 OMRI's joint founders, the Open Society Institute and Radio Free Europe/Radio Liberty, announced that funding for the institute would be radically curtailed. But, despite the closure of OMRI's Research and Analysis Department, it was decided to proceed with the publication of a 1996 survey using materials already written for publication in the OMRI magazine *Transition* or as program briefs for Radio Free Europe, updated wherever possible with the best available data estimates for 1996.

As reader response to last year's publication of the 1995 survey has generally been positive, it is hoped to continue the publication of an annual survey with M.E. Sharpe in future years. Although the countries of the region have become more diverse with the passage of time since the collapse of communism, it is probably still useful to have concise information about key political and economic developments gathered together in a single volume.

The original articles were written under the direction of Jiri Pehe, head of OMRI's Research and Analytical Department, with country clusters supervised by Pat Moore (South East Europe), Michael Shafir (Eastern Europe), Liz Fuller (Transcaucasus and Central Asia), Peter Rutland (Russia), and Jiri Pehe (Central Europe). Thanks must go to the authors for producing excellent material under extraordinary pressure, and to the editorial and archival staff for their meticulous and dedicated work. Particular assistance in putting this volume together was provided by managing editor Josephine Schmidt and production editor Pete Baumgartner.

Peter Rutland

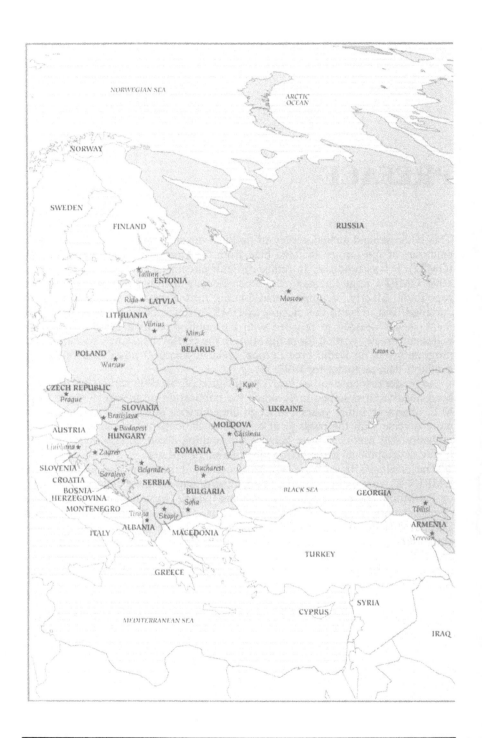

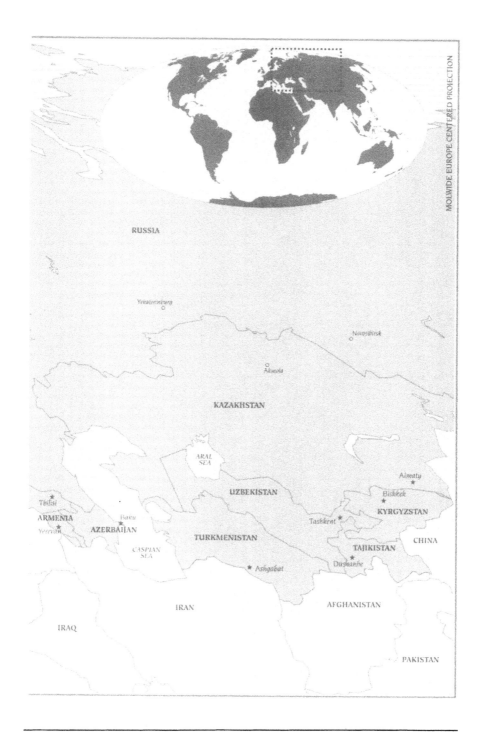

MOLWIDE EUROPE CENTERED PROJECTION

RUSSIA

Yekaterinburg

Novosibirsk

Akmola

KAZAKHSTAN

ARAL
SEA

Almaty

UZBEKISTAN

Bishkek

KYRGYZSTAN

Tbilisi

Baku

ARMENIA

Tashkent

AZERBAIJAN

TURKMENISTAN

TAJIKISTAN

CHINA

Yerevan

CASPIAN
SEA

Dushanbe

Ashgabat

IRAN

AFGHANISTAN

IRAQ

PAKISTAN

INTRODUCTION

I

A Year of Productive Discontent

—*Elections*

—*Dangers*

—*Balkan Developments*

—*East–West Relations*

Introduction

A YEAR OF PRODUCTIVE DISCONTENT
by J.F. BROWN

Elections matter. They are not the be-all and end-all of democracy: civil society, political culture, and rule of law are also definitive. But free and fair elections, with results accepted as final, are the bedrock of the constitutionalism on which democracy depends.

Free and fair elections assume a special significance in post-communist Eastern Europe. Under communism, elections were used to affirm and legitimatize power. In pre-communist Europe (interwar Czechoslovakia apart), they were, much more often than not, ritualistic charades aimed at producing foreordained results. Thus, for practically the whole of Eastern European history, elections have been a travesty, recognized as such by successive generations. But since 1989, they have been what they were always supposed to be: the exercise of individual choice and the reflection of constitutional values. Electoral practices are still far from perfect; political brigandage is alive and kicking. But a watershed has been passed, and progress will quicken.

The right to choose is more important than the eventual choice; the process takes precedence over the result; the constitutional aspect outweighs the political. Those truisms are worth remembering. In the West, they are easy to forget. Fair elections are mostly taken for granted there (although it is not all that long since "vote early and vote often" was the battle cry of many a ward heeler). But in Eastern Europe, the very novelty of a clean contest should give elections a landmark luster.

Not that results are not important. Democratic elections can produce catastrophic results. One such produced Hitler in 1933. But as political maturity develops, and if nationalist passions can be contained, a decent electoral process should generally put in power decent democratic leaders. Not necessarily the ablest, but, as Henry Campbell-Bannerman, one of the most decent of all British ministers, said at the beginning of this century: "Good government could never be a substitute for government by the people themselves."

AN ELECTION HARVEST

Nineteen ninety-six was a year of elections—presidential, parliamentary, or local—in Albania, Bosnia-Herzegovina, Bulgaria, the Czech Republic, Lithuania, Macedonia, Moldova, Romania, Russia, Serbia, and Slovenia.

The process was still patchy. In Albania, President Sali Berisha seemed to doubt his government's powers of political persuasion, and his "take no chances" electoral conduct earned a sharp reproof. In Russia's hinterland, there was hocus-pocus galore, though not apparently enough to have affected the result overall. And in Serbia, clear opposition victories in key local elections were officially annulled, causing a massive, spectacular, and sustained outburst of defiance. Elsewhere, too, knavery was dying hard. But generally, 1996 was a year of real progress toward democratic practice—a year when the level of political culture moved up noticeably.

The results, too, were encouraging. Take the less spectacular ones: Slovenia, Western by preference and performance, is beginning to look increasingly like post-World War II Austria or prewar Czechoslovakia—not democracy at its most bracing, perhaps, but democracy nonetheless. In the Czech Republic, there were elections to the Chamber of Deputies and to the new Senate, both well-conducted and both producing stable results. Could a two-party system be emerging there, of all places? Generally, the Czech situation still looks very promising. But President Vaclav Havel's health—he had surgery for lung cancer in December—gives everyone cause for concern. A couple of years ago, he seemed in danger of being politically marginalized, especially by the more aggressive and ideologically modish Prime Minister Vaclav Klaus. But Havel's character and historic stature refused to be marginalized, and it is a tribute to the Czech majority that it has realized how crucial he is. Democracy does not exclude leadership, especially of the sort Havel provides. As for Klaus, his political standing has been buffeted considerably, in the country as a whole and inside his own party. He seems to exemplify another lesson of democracy: the public doesn't like leaders who let their brains go to their head.

But the most encouraging election results were those that reflected a swing of the pendulum away from "post-communists" and back toward the "democratic forces." A swinging pendulum (steady, not crazy) is another democratic essential, and those changes were good in themselves. They also give the "democratic forces" an early chance to do better this time. That goes especially for many intellectuals among them, who, the first time around, preached democracy better than they practiced it. It should also force more ex-communists throughout the region to think and act like social democrats. Many have already genuinely changed their spots, but more need to do so for democracy to feel safer.

The election results in Lithuania were, therefore, welcome. So were the presidential results in Bulgaria. There, the ex-communists, with some exceptions, have been particularly slow to change, particularly incompetent, and particularly corrupt. But before the election, President Zhelyu Zhelev had become a perfectly innocent casualty of the electoral process: he lost the "primary" (will this become a feature of Eastern European democracy?) for the presidential nomination and had to stand down. The democratic victory, therefore, could turn out to be a Pyrrhic one if Zhelev is permanently lost to public life. Steadfast and moderate, he is a democrat through and through, a heroic anti-hero, a European figure, and a Bulgarian giant.

But the most encouraging and dramatic election results were in Romania.

They produced both a change of government and a change of president—a clean sweep, the most significant change in Romanian politics since the execution of Ceausescu. The new prime minister, Victor Ciorbea, and the new president, Emil Constantinescu, could now bring Romania international respectability and internal progress. Both need to keep the Romanian political elite looking firmly forward. Leapfrogging backward may be a physical impossibility, but it is also a great psychological temptation. The new leaders must resist it. As for Ion Iliescu, the defeated president, his role over the last six years may be criticized but not belittled. Almost in spite of himself, he became the key figure in the transition toward democracy, and history might judge that, while it was good for Romania that he left office in 1996, it was not necessarily bad that he took it in 1990.

In the former Romanian, later Soviet, province that is now Moldova, the presidential-election results could bring a real problem. The election was won, fair and square, by Petru Lucinschi, a member of the last Soviet Politburo and Secretariat. However token his membership may have been, it obviously meant something: since Moldovan independence, Lucinschi has advocated closer relations with Russia. The question is, "How close?"

All elections matter, but some elections matter more than others—not in principle, but in terms of their impact at home and abroad. By that reckoning, it was obviously the Russian presidential election in June 1996 that was the most important. It was the most dramatic, too, with the heroics centering on President Boris Yeltsin and his epic battle to save his presidency and his own life. Yeltsin was global Man of the Year in 1996. If there is a Valhalla, or a celestial Hall of Fame, for power politicians, there will eventually be no keeping him out of it. And, in view of Russia's economic and political circumstances, his induction should be later rather than sooner. Even a Pollyanna would find those circumstances daunting. So much, therefore, depends on Yeltsin's health, strength, nerves, luck—and ability to pay the army. Admittedly, this doesn't sound much like democracy, and Yeltsin himself is no democrat, either by instinct or upbringing. But, warts and all, he is the best bet Russia has for a democratic future and the most likely person to pry the door to a civil society open.

NOT DOUBTS, BUT DANGERS

Last year, therefore, was a good one for political progress—probably the best since 1989. What has been achieved, politically as well as economically, can hardly be reversed. But it can be threatened or even warped by several dangers. Three internal dangers in particular are worth stressing.

The first points up the inextricable link between politics and economics. Western economic institutions of repute—such as the OECD, ECE, and EBRD, to name a few of the best alphabetically known—agree that there has been general Eastern European progress (the Soviet Union's successor states partly excluded) in the macroeconomic sector. Some countries are doing better than others, but even the laggards (Bulgaria now excepted) have agreeably surprised. The progress has largely been due to the inevitability of the reforms that produced it and to the good sense of the successive governments, whether "democratic" or "post-communist," that realized reforms were inevitable. The latter were elected on the assumption that they would ease the pain involved. But one of the reasons for the partial swing against them in 1996 was disappointment at their not taking enough shock out of whatever shock therapy was being applied.

But now that the macroeconomic revolution is well in motion and building a solid foundation, it is time for microeconomic revolution, or "structural reform." Two of the biggest components of structural reform will be a drastic slimming of the welfare state and the dismantling of many of the leviathans, the surviving huge state enterprises. That is when real pain, or still greater pain, is going to begin for many people, including many of the more helpless members of society.

Eastern Europeans want to have their cake and eat it too. We all do. But what many Eastern Europeans liked about socialism (at least, they like it in retrospect) was the treadmill security that must be watered, even melted, down. And what they like about capitalism is unattainable for most of them. What many are now getting is nothing but those freedoms that they need a full stomach to enjoy.

Rarely will the situation be as stark as this. Some measure of protection will be afforded, and, as the Eastern European economies become more buoyant, capitalist opportunities will become more evident and more widespread. But the wait may be very long for many people, and, in the meantime, it is essential for governments, political elites, and Western states and institutions to act responsibly and knowingly. The need is to balance political savvy, genuine concern, and economic necessity. Western Europe and the United States are, of course, facing some of the same problems, but the comparisons should not be pushed. Most Western democracies have what is politically, economically, socially, and culturally needed to face the severity of whatever reorientations are required. The Eastern European democracies are unproven, and the reorientation they must make is deep, wide, and urgent. The encouraging thing is the resilience that the new democratic order, with all its imperfections, has already acquired, a resilience manifest both at close hand and from afar. It stems largely from the rigors of history and is something personal and indefinable. It has withstood the rotting inroads of the "real existing socialism" that those nations have recently endured.

The second danger is mounting crime, a way of life that in some of the democracies could easily become a way of death for them. The constant threats to life and property that confront most citizens are the form of crime most discussed and most consciously feared. Government corruption, too, is rarely off the front pages anywhere and only shores up popular cynicism. But potentially more dangerous than either of those is organized economic crime and its interaction with politics.

Organized crime has three, usually interconnecting, causes: war, or the impact of it, as in the Balkan countries; mass "nomenklatura" privatization, mainly in Russia, but also in Ukraine, Bulgaria, throughout most of the Balkans, and to some degree in several East-Central European countries; and the "robber baron" mentality of many members of the new capitalist elite, whose self-enriching zeal far exceeds whatever laws exist to control them.

That kind of crime exists in the state of nature that still dominates large parts of state and society in Eastern Europe. The tactics used to succeed or survive in this state of nature are becoming more violent, more organized, and more spectacular. Last year, a leading political opponent of the Ukrainian prime minister was gunned down at the Donetsk airport; the prime minister himself narrowly escaped assassination. An American hotel owner was murdered in broad daylight in Moscow, and a former Bulgarian prime minister suffered a similar fate in Sofia. Those were just a few of the more "newsworthy" cases of the prevailing gang-crafted violence and the growing mafia mentality. And, perhaps after allowing for the inevitable exaggeration and conspiracy theorizing, it is clear that a large number of active politicians are mafia-linked or -controlled. Many people, too, are entering politics not out of any sense of public duty, but solely to serve their economic ambitions.

That situation threatens a growing democracy—and, if there were the will to change it, then the means used could also threaten democracy. Still, complacency is the worst response of all. In the West, the seriousness of the problem is often grossly downplayed. "We have the same in New York City" is how one American luminary dismissed the subject.

The third internal danger is less spectacular but could be just as profound: governing institutional confusion and impotence, the need to fix precedence, powers, and relationships among presidencies, executives, and legislatures. That need has been discussed by theorists and wrangled over continuously since 1989. Southern European and Central American analogies (analogies at least on paper) have been cited to prove or disprove the virtues of one or the other system. In Eastern Europe, as elsewhere, the personal dimension—the character, strength, and adroitness of the personalities involved—is also playing a dominant role: in the cases of Havel, for instance; ex-Polish President Lech Walesa; and, most meaningfully of all, President Kiro Gligorov in Macedonia.

In 1994, President Berisha of Albania tried to increase his presidential powers by referendum, but he was rebuffed. In 1995, relations between President Walesa and the Polish government nearly broke down on several occasions. Political differences, Walesa's personal pretensions, and his ingenuity in playing fast and loose with the law were the main causes of those disputes. In the Czech Republic, the political association between President Havel and Premier Klaus has, in the words of one commentator, often resembled a Punch and Judy show, though the rivalry is more personal than political. In Slovakia, Prime Minister Vladimir Meciar's feud with President Michal Kovac has assumed a much more serious character. In Russia, Yeltsin has been on a war footing with the State Duma for much of the time (though his powers as president are so great that what the Duma says amounts to little). In Ukraine, presidential relations with the government have often been dangerously strained. During 1996 in Bulgaria, President Zhelev, who enjoyed the distinction in his time of being besieged by successive "democratic" and "post-communist" governments, spoke out strongly for strengthening the presidency. So did President Aleksander Kwasniewski of Poland. As a parliamentarian and former government minister, he had been strongly against this, but now the view from the Belvedere is clearly different.

To put it mildly, there is a need for regulation through clearly worded constitutions, made as impervious as possible to chicanery and shysterism. Changes in presidential powers could, legitimately and effectively, be the subject of national referenda. The sooner those at the top stop fighting over turf, the sooner those below will lose their cynicism of both them and the institutions they purport to champion. Of course, democratic means don't assure democratic ends: Belarus's Alyaksandr Lukashenka even managed to have himself voted dictatorial powers.

HOPES AND FEARS IN THE BALKANS

Keeping the peace is one thing, ensuring it is another. The NATO-led Implementation Force (IFOR) was remarkably successful in its immediate task in Bosnia-Herzegovina and handed over its responsibility to a Stabilization Force (SFOR) half its size, with a mandate to stay 18 months. But peace alone is not enough. Dayton demanded free parliamentary and local elections, the building of common Bosnian institutions, the return of refugees to their original places of abode, the arrest and sending for trial of accused war criminals, respect for human rights, and the control of weapons. Of those, only the first—parliamentary elections—has taken place. Local elections were delayed to this year. The rest of the requirements have not only not been met, but have been cynically disregarded.

IFOR allowed the requirements to be disregarded, pleading the narrowest interpretations of its mandate. SFOR might try to be broader in its outlook. But a crucial year has passed since Dayton, and whether its initial momentum can be regained is doubtful. What might happen is that not only will Dayton's provisional nature become cruelly exposed, but so also will its basic contradiction: the attempt to re-inject ethnic unity into a society and state that had become irretrievably divided. Dayton is in danger of being remembered less for its achievements than for the institutional absurdities inherent in the new "Bosnia and Herzegovina." Take, for example, the fact that this new state creation, though having a Foreign Ministry and endowed with international responsibility, has neither a Defense Ministry nor a defense capacity. Defense is vested in its two "entities," intensely hostile to each other. The illogicality is unprecedented, grotesque, and dangerous. It also reflects the Dayton peacemakers' lack of real belief in what they claimed to be doing.

The immediate danger could be Brcko, the town that dominates the Posavina corridor, the space linking the two parts of Republika Srpska. Formerly mostly Muslim and Croat, Brcko was ethnically cleansed with customary savagery by the Serbs and then resettled by them. The spirit and the letter of the Dayton accord dictate that Brcko revert to its former citizenry, but that would cut Republika Srpska in two, and the Serbs insist that the corridor's remaining in their hands is a matter of survival. The crisis reflects and dramatizes the whole Dayton predicament. The peacemakers there have closed their eyes to Brcko and hoped for the best. They left it for settlement by international arbitration at a later date. The Serbs, though, refuse to recognize or participate in such arbitration, while Washington has insisted that it must proceed. A tough one for Madeleine Albright.

Recently, though, it has been the Serbs in Serbia itself, most notably in Belgrade, on whom the world's attention has been riveted; and just before that it was Franjo Tudjman's democratic delinquencies in Croatia. What has happened is clear enough. What it might mean is not.

The demonstrations in Belgrade will be seen, in historical perspective, as the beginning of the end for Slobodan Milosevic. (And for Mirjana Markovic as well: the last Balkan "double bed" dictatorship—following the Hoxhas and the Ceausescus—is not far from being heaved into history.) But some of the leaders of the Belgrade demonstrations still don't inspire much confidence. Is Serbia in an uproar not because the war was started but because the war was lost?

Serbia is bankrupt and seething with economic and social discontent. Several hundred thousand refugees from Croatia and Bosnia compound the bitterness and fuel a potentially explosive situation. And the ethnic and international impact of an upheaval in Belgrade could range far and wide. It could further unsettle Vojvodina; the Muslims of the Sandzak are becoming more assertive; Montenegro is fed up with being taken for granted. Results have already been seen in Bulgaria, as demonstrators there emulate the Serbian movement.

But it is in Kosovo that the biggest explosion by far could (finally) occur. (And if it were to do so, the reaction of the Belgrade opposition would be instructive. Is Kosovo still the Serbian Jerusalem?) Nor, probably, would an explosion in Kosovo end there. It would spread across the Albanian areas of Macedonia, threatening the existence of Macedonia itself, the weakest state in the region, but whose survival is the strongest hope for peace. At the end of the 20th century, Macedonia could again become the apple of discord it was at the beginning. Apocalypse? Not necessarily, but perhaps edging a little closer.

Milosevic is undoubtedly intoning "Après moi" to anyone still willing to listen. The question is whether, or how much, his departure would affect stability in the southern Balkans. The political question becomes a moral question, and moral questions easily become emotional. How much injustice is preferable to the disorder that is often the only alternative to it? That is a dispute that is sure to go on—and not only in the southern Balkans. In the meantime, it is worth remembering that some problems simply cannot be solved. They can only be contained or managed. And in the Balkans, even that can only happen if there is real and observable commitment on the part of the West. And that means mainly the United States.

Amid all those forebodings, it is pleasant to recall that the Hungarian-Romanian state treaty was signed and finally ratified by both parties toward the end of 1996. It was not the most satisfactory treaty, and as much mistrust as trust emerged from its text. Nationalists in both countries opposed it. It was either a sellout to, or of, the Hungarian minority in Transylvania, depending on which nationalists looked at it. But in the end, it was a victory for common sense, compromise, and courage. And most of the Hungarian minority in Romania thought it was better than nothing. A good example of a problem by no means solved but at least contained.

GOING WEST

The Hungarian-Romanian treaty also reflected Western influence. Western acceptance (or, more likely, Western rejection) concentrated the minds wonderfully. But, in a case like that, Western follow-up is essential. Romania must be kept true to the promises it has made. Agreements under international pressure are often broken once the pressure is relaxed. Slovakia is a case in point: it signed its treaty with Hungary to ingratiate itself with the West and then ditched the concessions to its Hungarian minority when it thought the world had stopped looking.

In general, there were no dramatic breakthroughs in East-West relations during 1996, either collectively or singly. But progress toward breakthroughs was made in several contexts, especially on NATO enlargement. The whole field of East-West relations post-1989 is complex, even arcane. It makes the Cold War look easy. But there are three simple topics about this current phase of relations in particular that should be considered in the coming year.

There is much talk of simultaneous NATO enlargement and "partnership" with Russia. Many advocates of NATO enlargement don't give two hoots about partnership with Russia. Those who do should look up what partnership means— and then forget it. The notion is both infeasible and insulting.

The European Union presents such a degrading scene of division, doubt, pettiness, and churlishness that some Eastern Europeans might begin wondering whether this is still the club they so desperately want to join. Who can blame them?

The Eastern European states will never be taken very seriously by the West or by each other until they themselves make some real effort at regional and subregional cooperation. They all need help and must get it. But, in the end, they must pull their own chestnuts out of the fire.

CENTRAL EUROPE

II

Czech Republic

Slovakia

Hungary

Poland

Czech Republic _____

Population:	10,331,206
Capital:	Prague (pop. 1,215,000)
Major cities:	Brno (pop. 391,000), Ostrava (pop. 331,000),
	Plzen (pop. 175,000)
Area:	78,864 sq. km.
Major ethnic groups:	Czech 94%, Slovak 3%, Romani 2.4%
Economy:	GDP growth: 4.4%
....	Inflation rate: 8.8%
....	Average monthly income: $374
....	Unemployment rate: 3.5%

MAVERICK CZECH REFORMERS GET BOGGED DOWN

by JIRI PEHE

As evidence mounted that the express train of Czech reform could use a few course corrections, Czech politics hit a deadlock. Parliamentary elections produced a weak minority government, Prime Minister Vaclav Klaus seemed unable to accept the lessons voters gave him, and President Vaclav Havel—the only figure with the authority to moderate between the ruling coalition and the strengthened opposition—fell into ill health.

The Czech Republic, which a year earlier had been considered by many the undisputed reform leader of the post-communist world, lost much of its luster in 1996. The elections to the lower and upper chambers of the parliament resulted in a political stalemate. Macroeconomic indicators remained impressive, but at the same time the country was rocked by a series of scandals uncovering serious problems in the banking industry and the privatization process. And politicians appeared to be unsure about how to deal with a mounting foreign-trade deficit.

Prior to the general elections, held on 31 May and 1 June, opinion polls had indicated that the right-of-center coalition headed by Prime Minister Vaclav Klaus and his Civic Democratic Party (ODS) would sweep the elections. Instead, the elections changed the country's political landscape (see Table 1). Klaus and his coalition allies lost their parliamentary majority, owing mainly to the strong showing by the Social Democratic Party (CSSD), led by Milos Zeman, which placed second, only three percentage points behind the ODS. The coalition gained only 99 seats in the 200–seat lower chamber, while the CSSD, the Communist Party (KSCM), and the extreme-right Republican Party (SPR-RSC) took the other 101 seats.

The CSSD was the real winner of the elections; it managed to more than quadruple its popular support from some 6 percent in 1992 to 26 percent in 1996. Although the overall vote for the left did not increase significantly when compared with the 1992 elections, Zeman's achievement was remarkable. He managed to consolidate the democratic left, creating a strong opposition force that speaks, above all, for those who have not benefited from Klaus's reforms. The CSSD, while acknowledging the overall relative success of the Czech Republic, had emphasized that the country needed to deal with such outstanding problems as corruption, crime, housing, and the badly functioning education and health-care systems.

Opinion polls after the elections indicated that many people who had cast their votes for the CSSD had not done so in support of that party, but as a protest against the ODS. Before the elections, the ODS—and Klaus in particular—had been accused of increasing arrogance and overconfidence. Confident of their

Table 1. General (Chamber of Deputies) Elections			
	Support in 1992	Support in 1996	Seats in 1996
Civic Democratic Party	29.73%	29.62%	68
Social Democratic Party	6.53%	26.44%	61
Communist Party	14.05%	10.33%	22
Christian Democratic Union	6.28%	8.08%	18
Republican Party	5.98%	8.01%	18
Civic Democratic Alliance	5.93%	6.36%	13

Source: Lidove noviny, 4 June 1996.

victory, the coalition parties had spent much time both before and during the election campaign challenging each other rather than the opposition parties.

President Vaclav Havel emerged as a key political figure after the elections. During difficult negotiations, he brokered an agreement under which Klaus and his coalition allies—the Civic Democratic Alliance (ODA) and the Christian Democratic Union-Czechoslovak People's Party (KDU-CSL)—formed a minority government, while Zeman took the post of parliament chairman.

FIRST-EVER SENATE ELECTIONS

Political observers believed that the stalemate produced by the June elections would make leading parties more conciliatory. But neither the ODS nor the CSSD changed its style after the elections. Confrontation rather than consensus-seeking prevailed over the summer, as the country prepared for its first-ever elections to the new upper house of the parliament, the Senate. After four years of governing virtually unopposed, the ODS found it difficult to search for compromises; the CSSD, on the other hand, repeatedly showed it was more interested in humiliating its main political rival than in the country's stability. Moreover, acrimonious conflicts between the two parties often took the shape of personal conflicts between Klaus and Zeman, who are known for intensely disliking each other.

Under pressure from the strengthened opposition, scandals broke out concerning the banking industry and privatization, suggesting that beneath the veneer of impressive macroeconomic indicators, all is not well with the Czech economy. It became clear that rules governing the transparency of the privatization process, and the rule of law in general, had been neglected during the rapid economic transformation of the previous four years. Instead of accepting responsibility for such failures and promising a remedy, the ODS showed little willingness to implement changes. In July, Foreign Minister Josef Zieleniec, an ODS deputy chairman, called for the party to be less arrogant and more open, but the debate prompted by his call quickly subsided.

The Senate elections, previously seen as potentially unexciting, were billed as

Figure 1. Senate Elections

TOTAL SEATS: 81

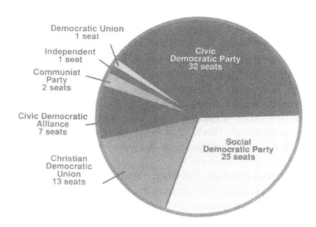

Democratic Union
1 seat

Independent
1 seat

Communist
Party
2 seats

Civic Democratic
Alliance
7 seats

Christian
Democratic
Union
13 seats

Civic
Democratic Party
32 seats

Social
Democratic Party
25 seats

a way of breaking the political deadlock. Many of the same politicians who had previously besmirched the Senate as a redundant institution began portraying it as a stabilizing force and an important check on the Chamber of Deputies. Some politicians did not hide their hope that their party's resounding victory in the Senate elections could be used to trigger early elections in the lower chamber.

But the two-round elections, held on 15–16 and 22–23 November, failed to break the deadlock. Based on a majority system and held in 81 small districts, the elections were marred by an abysmally low voter turnout (35 percent in the first round and 30 percent in the second round). Although the ODS won 32 seats— seven more than the CSSD—the low turnout made it impossible for Klaus to claim that the political pendulum had returned back to his camp; it was not clear what the mood was of the two-thirds of voters who did not cast their votes.

With three ODS candidates elected and 76 ODS candidates leading in their districts in the first round, a broad anti-ODS alliance formed before the second round. In many districts, supporters of the two junior coalition allies of the ODS banded together with CSSD and Communist supporters to defeat ODS candidates (see Figure 1). As a result, the coalition—in which the ODS had dominated its two junior parties—appeared rather shaky.

In many ways, the elections represented a victory for the KDU-CSL, whose leader, Josef Lux, had repeatedly warned before the second round against a monochromatic Senate. Shortly before the elections, Lux accused the Czech Intelligence Service (BIS) of following him. Lux's accusations triggered a scandal uncovering serious problems in the BIS, and Stanislav Devaty, the ODS's choice as BIS chairman, was forced to resign.

Opinion polls taken after the elections indicated that the main reason for the low voter turnout was the electorate's dissatisfaction, or even disgust, with the country's politics in general—and in particular with the low level of political culture. Another reason was that the Senate was a new institution, which few people trusted. It surely also didn't help that the Senate had long been described as redundant by leading politicians across the political spectrum.

HAVEL'S ABSENCE FELT

Still recovering from the disappointing Senate elections, the Czech Republic had to grapple with more problems in December. President Vaclav Havel underwent surgery for lung cancer on 2 December, and his recovery was complicated by pneumonia. Havel's sudden departure from active political life brought it home to most Czechs that there is no one ready to replace the president—not only is there no one as popular as Havel, but more important, no other politician has enough authority to bridge differences between the deadlocked coalition and opposition.

Havel's absence was painfully felt when Czech and German media published the text of a long-awaited joint Czech-German declaration in mid-December. The contents of the document, designed to put to rest mutual Czech-German grievances arising from their common past, immediately galvanized radicals on both sides of the border into action. Without Havel's moderating influence, the fate of the Czech-German declaration hung in the balance. A number of opposition deputies—upset that the Czechs would express regret over the expulsion of some 3 million Sudeten Germans from Czechoslovakia after World War II—indicated that they might want to amend the declaration, a move that would invalidate the document.

Klaus was re-elected chairman of his party at the ODS congress on 7–8 December, but the congress failed to convince political observers that the party has learned from its mistakes and that Klaus can again assume a pivotal role in Czech politics. Delegates called for more openness and agreed to a change of style, but the leadership of the party remained virtually the same. The ODS parliamentary caucus chairman, Milan Uhde, and several other delegates criticized Klaus for his lack of critical self-reflection. Analysts agreed that that failing will make it extremely difficult for his party to fulfill most of the promises for change made at the congress and to stop the decline in its popularity ratings.

At year's end, serious cracks appeared in the ruling coalition. In light of the Senate-election results, both the KDU-CSL and the ODA realized that being seen as allies of the ODS may not always be to their advantage. Relying on CSSD support, the KDU-CSL overcame staunch ODS opposition to have its candidate—Petr Pithart, Czech prime minister in 1990–1992 and a former political rival of Klaus—elected to the post of Senate chairman. Both junior coalition partners also warned they would vote against the 1997 budget unless the ODS agreed to their demands. In the end, the two parties backed down, but the coalition was shaken. On 19 December, Klaus threatened to take his party out of the ruling coalition.

Meanwhile, ODA Chairman Jan Kalvoda resigned from his government posts and gave up his deputy mandate, admitting that he had regularly appended the title "Dr." to his name although he had never earned such a degree. (Like several deputies who had earlier admitted to the same error, Kalvoda had finished his studies but never submitted a dissertation, and thus earned a slightly lower-rank degree.) Kalvoda's sudden resignation—suggesting he had been threatened with exposure—sent tremors through Czech politics and left the coalition further weakened. It was clear that finding a replacement for Kalvoda as ODA chairman would be a daunting task, as he had held together the smallest parliamentary party's two competing wings.

In a great success for the minority government, the parliament on 13 December approved a state budget for 1997. That was made possible by two CSSD deputies' decisions to vote for the budget despite having been threatened with expulsion from the party. (One day after the vote, the two were indeed expelled.) However, the balanced budget was a compromise almost no one liked.

Perhaps the most important criticism came from Defense Minister Miroslav Vyborny of the KDU-CSL, who argued that the budget severely underfunds the army. The lack of willingness on the part of the government to give more money to the army had previously prompted some Western politicians to express wonder about the Czech Republic's preparedness to join NATO.

While the questions of NATO and European Union membership were high on Czech politicians' foreign-policy agenda, at home not much discussion or political effort was devoted to those issues. Opinion polls have repeatedly shown that only one-third of Czechs support NATO membership (with one-third undecided and one-third in favor) and about 50 percent support EU membership. Changing those unfavorable opinion trends and actively preparing the country for membership in both organizations may be the most important task for Czech politicians in the next few years.

At the end of 1996, housing, banking, the health-care system, and the energy sector remained the areas yet to be tackled. Given the decision-making paralysis produced by the elections, it was not clear that solutions could be found quickly. The coalition advocated a gradual deregulation of rents and energy costs, as well as the privatization of the largest banks. The CSSD and other opposition parties either opposed such solutions or were in favor of more cautious approaches.

The coalition did not appear to have any solution for the mounting foreign-trade deficit, which reached more than 150 billion crowns ($3.5 billion) by the end of 1996. Suggestions by some experts that the crown be devalued and that import tariffs be introduced were rejected. Coalition economists apparently hoped that exports would increase faster in 1997 than in 1996, in light of expected improvements in the German economy and the competitiveness of Czech products. The government's approach to the issue perhaps best characterized the country's overall situation in 1996: it appeared to be running out of steam while the government's ability to address serious problems was seriously weakened, and the commitment of Czechs to radical reforms was clearly waning.

Sidebar: CZECH SECRET SERVICE SCANDAL—A STORM IN A TEACUP?

by STEVE KETTLE

The November firing of the head of the Czech secret service, Stanislav Devaty, can be seen as a settling of long-outstanding accounts among the three parties in the coalition government, and as a confirmation that frictions among them continued to be significant. The junior coalition partners—who, along with some parts of the opposition, had been calling for Devaty's head for almost two years—effectively forced him out, demonstrating the changed balance within the government since the May/June parliamentary elections.

Devaty, a dissident under communism and a founding member of Prime Minister Vaclav Klaus's Civic Democratic Party (ODS), was appointed interim head of the Security and Intelligence Service (BIS) when it was created in late 1992 as the Czech successor to the former Czechoslovak federal secret service. He remained "interim" leader for almost four years; although he resigned from the ODS on taking up his appointment, the BIS under Devaty's direction was consistently accused of acting to further ODS interests.

In early 1995, Deputy Prime Minister Jan Kalvoda, the leader of the Civic Democratic Alliance (ODA), publicly accused the BIS of illegally collecting information on him and other political leaders. Those accusations were never publicly substantiated, but the more astute Josef Lux, Agriculture Minister and leader of the Christian Democratic Union-Czechoslovak People's Party (KDU-CSL), bided his time and then prompted Devaty to resign by making similar allegations just one week before the Senate elections.

Lux charged that the BIS kept tabs on him in 1993–1994, and then covered up their activity by removing mention of it from a report to the parliamentary committee charged with overseeing the BIS. Devaty's version was that a BIS agent in the Agriculture Ministry was not spying on Lux but on one of his advisers, Antonin Moravec, the former director of a bank that crashed in 1993 with up to 500 million crowns ($18.5 million) missing. Moravec's bank was also involved in a scandal over more than 50 million crowns lent to Kalvoda's party before the 1992 elections and not repaid years later.

Klaus and other ODS ministers, including Interior Minister Jan Ruml, came out strongly in support of Devaty; but after a reportedly stormy cabinet session in which Klaus was bitterly at odds with Lux and Kalvoda, the government accepted Devaty's resignation. Opposition leader Milos Zeman joined in the attacks on Devaty and his agency, alleging that the BIS and the Interior Ministry had set up groups of agents to spy on political parties and leaders. Devaty later sued Zeman, the speaker of parliament, for 5 million crowns ($185,000) for those remarks, which had implied that he had attempted to restore a totalitarian police state.

The specter of a ubiquitous and efficient secret service operating in murky waters and serving one particular political party is still easy to raise just seven years after the fall of communism. But it hardly gels with Czech media reports following Devaty's resignation that he himself had spent more time at the head of the BIS completing his law studies than running the agency, and that the BIS is an incoherent organization on the verge of collapse.

The allegations against Devaty and the BIS also hardly compare with secret-service scandals in neighboring countries: the overt use of the Slovak Information Service by Prime Minister Vladimir Meciar's Movement for a Democratic Slovakia, particularly its alleged role in the kidnapping of President Michal Kovac's son; or the findings of a Sejm commission made public this week that a former Interior Minister and the State Security Office illegally gathered and published materials accusing former Polish Prime Minister Jozef Oleksy of spying for the Soviet Union and Russia.

But the role and control of the BIS had never been fully defined, due to an ODS-dominated government allowing the BIS to act however it wanted, and the ineffectuality of the parliamentary oversight committee (again, ODS dominated). These factors started to change after the parliamentary elections. The appointment of a minister without portfolio with direct responsibility for overseeing the BIS—the minister, Pavel Bratinka, is another former dissident and an ODA member—was designed by the ODA and KDU-CSL to bring the BIS finally under tighter political control.

Sidebar: COLLAPSE OF CZECH KREDITNI BANKA TURNS CRIMINAL—AND POLITICAL

by BEN SLAY

The collapse of Kreditni Banka (KrB), one of the Czech Republic's leading investment funds in the summer of 1996 embarrassed the Czech financial authorities, created new political problems for Prime Minister Vaclav Klaus's minority government, and showed that the Czech financial system's problems were not confined to the business pages.

The Plzen-based Kreditni Banka was a frequent news item in the summer of 1996, especially following the 8 August decision of the Czech National Bank (CNB) and the Finance Ministry on to revoke KrB's license. Kreditni Banka's losses stood at an estimated 12 billion koruny ($450 million), and KrB's collapse generated a political firestorm. At issue was not only the question of who was responsible for the alleged embezzlement and fraud that brought Kreditni Banka down, but who would pay to clean up the financial mess—a question of particular concern to Ceska Pojistovna, Kreditni Banka's majority shareholder and the

Czech Republic's largest insurance company. The question of how and whether the political opposition would benefit from these events was also at issue.

Milos Zeman, head of the leading opposition party, told a Czech TV audience on 1 September that Finance Minister Ivan Kocarnik was personally responsible for KrB's failure. Zeman's Social Democrats had expressed varying degrees of opposition to the government's plans for partially privatizing the large Czech banks through attracting foreign investors, and the Social Democrats repeatedly called for a parliamentary investigation of Kreditni Banka's collapse. President Vaclav Havel also expressed his concern that no one seemed to be held accountable for the bank's collapse.

These developments were followed by the arrest on 13 September of five business executives. While three were from Kreditni Banka itself, the two other arrestees were both high-ranking officials of the Motoinvest investment fund, one of the largest shareholders of Ceska Pojistovna and, therefore, indirectly the partial owners of KrB. The KrB and Motoinvest officials were suspected of using their position to embezzle 288 million crowns ($109 million) from Kreditni Banka. Also, KrB's economics director allegedly received a 3 million crown "golden handshake" upon leaving his post in August—after the bank's license had already been revoked by the Czech authorities.

However, despite this aura of scandal and financial malfeasance, the authorities released Motoinvest director Jan Dienstl on 16 September. Motoinvest President Pavel Tykac insisted that the fund had done nothing wrong, and told Czech TV on 14 September that, "It was necessary to throw a victim before the public . . . and the people at Motoinvest are a very good catch."

To President Havel and many others, the investigation and arrests of the KrB and Motoinvest officials would seem to mean that, finally, something is being done about the Czech Republic's most serious financial scandal to date. There is another side of the story, however. Motoinvest has acquired the reputation of being one of the Czech financial system's leading "bad boys." Following its appearance on the Czech financial scene last year, Motoinvest has portrayed itself as a crusading friend of the small investor, ready to do battle with the large banks and investment funds that dominate Czech finance and, critics claim, are responsible for the Czech financial system's opaqueness and inefficiency. Motoinvest clearly made some enemies within the Czech financial and political elite.

Sidebar: CZECH PARTIES' VIEWS OF THE EU AND NATO

by JIRI PEHE

The seven parties that were leading contenders in the May-June parliamentary elections differed widely in their attitudes toward the European Union and NATO.

NATO

The three coalition parties that formed the government—the Civic Democratic Party (ODS) of Prime Minister Vaclav Klaus, the Civic Democratic Alliance (ODA) of Deputy Prime Minister Jan Kalvoda, and the Christian and Democratic Union (KDU) of Deputy Prime Minister Josef Lux—all favored the Czech Republic's speedy admission to NATO, with the rights and duties of a full member. The ODS described achieving NATO membership as its main foreign policy goal in its election program and claimed that the Czech Republic was politically and economically ready for such a step. The ODA, in addition, emphasized the need for the continued presence of US troops in Europe. The three parties were currently opposed to holding a referendum on NATO membership.

The Social Democratic Party (CSSD), the main opposition group, is in favor of NATO membership but was opposed to the presence of foreign troops and nuclear weapons on Czech territory. It stressed in its election program that Russia's interests must be taken into account. The party favored a referendum on NATO membership, despite the fact the Czech Constitution does not provide for holding referenda.

The extreme-right Republican Party (SPR-RCS), the far-left Communist Party of Bohemia and Moravia (KSCM), and the reform-communist Left Bloc (LB) were all opposed to NATO membership. The Communists called instead for dissolving NATO and replacing it with a new system of collective security. The Left Bloc proposed a military alliance with other post-communist states, including former Yugoslavia. All three parties favored for a referendum on NATO membership.

THE EUROPEAN UNION

All three coalition parties were in favor of EU membership but differed in emphasis. The ODS was the most cautious of the three parties. Its election program said that under the ODS leadership the Czech Republic would take all legislative and economic steps necessary for EU membership. At the same time, the party opposed increasing the powers of EU institutions and the supremacy of EU laws over national ones. The ODS program repeatedly talked of "defending Czech national interests." Vaclav Klaus said he is opposed to a single European currency and common European taxes, and suggested he may be in favor of a referendum on EU membership because questions of "national sovereignty" are involved.

The ODA was less cautious about increasing the powers of EU institutions. Kalvoda attacked Klaus in 1995 for making statements that, in his opinion, repeatedly cast doubts on the Czech Republic's resolve to join the union. The KDU generally favored EU membership but provided no details in its program.

The Social Democrats were unambiguously in favor of EU membership, claiming that their own policies were fully "anchored in the policies of the EU." The CSSD sees the EU as "implementing the system of social justice" and favors European laws' supremacy over national ones. It accepts all principles on which the EU is built. The party was in favor of holding a referendum on EU membership.

The KSCM, the SPR-RCS, and the LB were all critical of the government's efforts to join the EU. The LB's program said that it is a mistake to think EU membership will increase the standard of living in the Czech Republic and that the country needs to rely on its own policies. The LB argues that the Czech Republic should form an economic union with other post-communist countries. All three parties demanded a referendum on EU membership.

Slovakia

Population:	5,324,632 (1993)
Capital:	Bratislava (pop. 448,785)
Major cities:	Kosice (pop. 238,886); Presov (pop. 90,963), Nitra (pop. 86,679)
Area:	49,036 sq. km.
Major ethnic groups:	Slovak 86%; Hungarian 10.7%; Romani 1.6%; Czech, Moravian, and Silesian 1.1%; Ruthenian, Ukranian 0.6%
Economy:	GDP growth: 6.9%
	Inflation rate: 6%
	Average monthly wage in industry: $273
	Unemployment rate: 12.8%

SLOVAKIA HEADS TOWARD INTERNATIONAL ISOLATION

by SHARON FISHER

The year 1996 in Slovakia was one of continued political polarization and international disappointment. Slovakia's ruling coalition disregarded repeated warnings from the West and continued policies that have divided society since the fall 1994 elections

Throughout 1996, Slovakia's ruling coalition—led by Prime Minister Vladimir Meciar—continued in its efforts to grasp control of Slovak society. In 1994 and 1995, focus was placed on controlling parliamentary and other state organs, privatization, and the electronic media. In 1996, the coalition went a step further, with attacks on local administrations, foundations, universities, and cultural institutions. Meanwhile, warnings from Western representatives that the government must change its ways if it hopes to gain membership in the European Union and NATO were largely ignored.

The investigation into the abduction of President Michal Kovac's son was the most polarizing and controversial issue in Slovakia in 1996 and served as a backdrop for much of the political conflict throughout the year. Michal Kovac Jr. was kidnapped in August 1995 and dumped in Austria where he was arrested based on an international warrant issued in November 1994 by a Munich prosecutor. The warrant demanded that Kovac Jr. testify in a $2.3 million fraud case involving the Slovak trade firm Technopol.

One and a half years after the kidnapping, the state administration remained unwilling to bring the kidnapping case to its resolution. The Slovak Information Service (SIS), led by Meciar's close ally Ivan Lexa, was widely suspected of orchestrating the kidnapping in an effort to discredit the president, who was involved in a long-running feud with Meciar. Three police officials were fired in fall 1995 after declaring such suspicions, and additional evidence was found by the opposition media and by an independent investigation team led by a former interior minister. However, the official investigation was closed in May, with police saying they could not determine whether a real kidnapping had taken place or if Kovac Jr. had organized his own abduction, as government allies had argued. After being temporarily reopened, the case was adjourned inconclusively a second time in late August.

On 20 February, a Vienna court rejected Germany's request for Kovac Jr.'s extradition, ruling that Kovac Jr. had been brought to Austria illegally and his human rights violated. The court also noted that testimony indicated the involvement of Slovak state organs in the abduction and that Slovakia had neither asked Austria for Kovac Jr.'s return nor protested the kidnapping. Slovakia's Constitutional Court on 4 September ruled that the Slovak Foreign Ministry's inactivity constituted a violation of Kovac Jr.'s right to free entrance to Slovak territory. Slovak border guards confiscated Kovac Jr.'s passport as he was trying to travel to Germany to testify in June, officially to prevent him from evading the Slovak police's own investigation of the Technopol case.

Warning signals went out on 29 April, when former police officer Robert Remias was killed in a car explosion. Remias had been the closest friend of former SIS agent Oskar Fegyveres, a key witness in the Kovac Jr. case who admitted to participating in the kidnapping. Although police initially said Remias's accident was caused by mechanical failure, opposition figures called his death "political murder." It was not until September that police admitted that Remias's death was "most probably" caused by explosives. Still, the case was closed on 15 October for "lack of evidence." That same day, another case was also closed involving a taped phone conversation between Lexa and Interior Minister Ludovit Hudek that was full of hints about interference in the police investigation of the kidnapping. Although independent analyses of the conversation confirmed the tape's authenticity, police investigators said the voices were not unambiguously proved to be those of Hudek and Lexa.

The Kovac-Meciar battle hit a high in late May, when Kovac filed charges against the prime minister for misuse of power, slander, and defamation of the head of state. Kovac was reacting to Meciar's radio interview of 24 May, when he accused the president of involvement in the Technopol fraud, of knowing about preparations for his son's kidnapping but failing to intervene, and of influencing the investigation of the Technopol case. A Bratislava prosecutor on 5 August suspended Kovac's complaint, saying there was no suspicion of criminal activity.

In late August, Meciar held his first meeting with Kovac in over a year to discuss a ministerial reshuffle involving three key ministers—interior, foreign affairs, and economy—all of whom were members of Meciar's Movement for a Democratic Slovakia (HZDS). Despite his persistent feud with Kovac, Meciar was obliged to consult with the president, who has a constitutional right to appoint and dismiss cabinet members. The ministerial changes were seen as an attempt to improve Slovakia's image abroad. However, Hudek—the most controversial of the three dismissed ministers—was replaced by Gustav Krajci, a former physical-education teacher with no police experience. The other replaced ministers were Foreign Minister Juraj Schenk, who was seen as partly responsible for Slovakia's poor international image, and Economy Minister Jan Ducky, who oversaw a skyrocketing trade deficit.

COALITION CONFLICT

Foreign affairs and privatization were the subjects of coalition conflict in 1996. A controversy over the Slovak-Hungarian treaty continued from the previous year, with the Slovak National Party (SNS)—a junior coalition partner—finally agreeing on 13 January to support the treaty's ratification in exchange for the approval of several highly controversial laws. Those included a penal-code amendment on "the protection of the republic" prescribing prison terms to people who organize public rallies "with the intention of subverting the country's constitutional system, territorial integrity, or defense capability" and to those who "spread false information" that could damage Slovakia's interests. Ethnic Hungarian political leaders and opposition journalists and politicians were widely seen as potential targets of attack.

The Slovak parliament finally ratified the treaty on 26 March, more than one year after its signing, but only after approving the penal-code amendment. Following a presidential veto and strong criticism from the West, the amendment was put aside. A somewhat milder but still controversial version of the law was approved by the parliament on 17 December.

An embarrassing dispute over privatization triggered a month-long conflict in June between the HZDS and its junior coalition partners—the SNS and the Association of Workers of Slovakia (ZRS). The controversy, the biggest since the coalition was formed, began with an SNS revolt after the party realized it would be excluded from the privatization of the lucrative insurance firm Slovenska poistovna. To attract Meciar's attention, SNS chairman Jan Slota called for a number of steps that had long been demanded by opposition parties, including giving them representation on the boards overseeing the SIS and the National Property Fund.

With SNS and ZRS support, the opposition came close to gaining representation on the control organs; however, through skillful political maneuvering, Meciar managed to outwit his opponents and take full control of the situation. One representative of the ex-communist Party of the Democratic Left (SDL) managed to gain a spot on the parliamentary organ overseeing SIS, but the opposition remained shut out of the property fund.

By 1 July, the coalition parties were back to their old tricks, overriding a presidential veto of a restrictive law on foundations. Later, the parliament overruled presidential vetoes on territorial administration and higher education laws. The former was widely seen as a way to increase HZDS control and allowed the party to appoint all eight new regional heads. The opposition also fears the law is the first step toward changes in the electoral law from a proportional to a majority system, which could help bring the HZDS an overwhelming victory in the next elections. Meanwhile, in late summer and fall, Culture Minister Ivan Hudec launched an attack on state-sponsored cultural institutions, replacing top officials with government loyalists.

The opposition used the seventh anniversary of the 17 November "velvet revolution" to organize a series of "Save Slovakia" rallies in 20 cities around the country to protest Meciar's style of governing. The first and biggest protest, held on 14 November in Bratislava, was attended by nearly 20,000 people. The opposition was joined by representatives of the church, universities, nonprofit organizations, actors, and trade unions in calling for political change.

In an effort to present a more united front, three opposition parties formed the center-right "blue coalition" on 29 October. Cooperation between the "blue coalition" and the ethnic-Hungarian opposition parties strengthened in the last months of the year as Hungarian politicians' calls for autonomy for minorities became less frequent. The coalition's relations with the SDL remained troubled, however, as that party preferred to follow its own course as an "independent opposition party."

Although there were some calls for early elections, the opposition remained generally opposed, demanding instead that Meciar serve out his full four-year term and suffer the consequences of any unpopular decisions. Despite all the scandals and controversies, the HZDS remains by far the country's most popular party. Still, Meciar apparently remained afraid that some HZDS deputies would desert and join the opposition in dismissing him from office, as had occurred in March 1994. On 4 December, one month after dissident HZDS deputy Frantisek Gaulieder abandoned the party's parliamentary caucus, the parliament voted to strip him of his mandate and replace him with another HZDS candidate. The opposition warned that the move was unconstitutional since it was made against Gaulieder's will and there is no provision in the constitution or other legislation allowing the parliament to cancel a deputy's mandate.

'ECONOMIC MIRACLE' FALTERS

Despite continued high gross-domestic-product growth and low inflation (see box, p. 21), Slovakia's "economic miracle" was faltering by mid-1996. Unemployment remained high, at 12.3 percent in September, and cumulative foreign investment since 1990 had reached only $808.4 million by June (a tiny fraction of the amounts invested in the Czech Republic, Hungary, and Poland). Most alarming, Slovakia's trade balance, which had been in surplus the previous year, shot up to a 48.8 billion crown ($1.5 billion) deficit by November 1996. Trade with Russia accounted for a large portion of the deficit.

Slovak exports continue to be dominated by semifinished goods that are sensitive to changes in the world economy. Meanwhile, Slovakia's advantage of comparatively low wages started to be exhausted, with statistics in certain sectors showing wages increasing significantly faster than productivity. Many analysts criticized the fact that Slovakia had yet to make efforts toward diversification of resources. In 1996, Slovakia continued to depend almost entirely on raw-material and energy imports from Russia.

The June coalition crisis seemed to confirm critics' allegations that the main concern of the three ruling parties regarding privatization was not the future of Slovakia but financial gains for themselves. Throughout 1996, the coalition came under heavy criticism for the way privatization was carried out: through secretive direct sales to domestic supporters at cheap prices. Sporadic media reports linked coalition officials and their relatives with key firms.

Controversy also emerged with the launching of the government's bond scheme that replaced the second wave of coupon privatization. Arguing that not everyone had benefited from coupon privatization, the government issued five-year, 10,000 crown bonds in exchange for citizens' 1,000 crown coupons. When bond trading began on 5 August, many citizens rushed to get rid of them; however, there were few buyers willing to pay the 7,500 crown minimum price set by the government. A black market soon emerged, with bonds selling for as little as 2,500 crowns.

ATTACKS ON THE MEDIA

Although the print media remain largely free, economic and other indirect pressure was used against opposition papers in an effort to force them into line. One such case concerns the daily *Narodna obroda*. The paper's publisher and editor in chief, Tatiana Repkova, aimed to turn it into a nonpartisan, economic-oriented daily. Those aims appeared threatened, however, when the steel giant VSZ—which has close ties to the government—gained 100 percent of the shares in *Narodna obroda*'s publisher. VSZ management initially vowed that it would not interfere in Repkova's work, but it later went back on its word, and Repkova was fired from all of her posts at *Narodna obroda* on 15 November. At least 10 of the newspaper's journalists quit in protest.

On 6 November, the opposition daily *Sme* lost a libel case and was ordered by a Banska Bystrica District Court to apologize to all 18 cabinet members for an article published on 14 May. The court also demanded that *Sme*'s publisher pay each minister 400,000 to 500,000 crowns ($13,000 to $16,000). The article in question quoted a speech by *Sme* journalist Peter Toth at Remias's funeral, stating that "these are the first victims of a political cold war that the government is waging against Slovak citizens." The newspaper planned to appeal.

Throughout 1996, state-run Slovak Television continued its biased, pro-government reporting. It lost a number of libel suits, including several involving Kovac Jr. and his associates. At the recommendation of Slovak Television's supervisory board, the parliament voted on 10 December to replace director Jozef Darmo. But his replacement, Igor Kubis, was also said to be a strong HZDS supporter and a key player in the production of programs slandering Kovac Jr.

In late August, Slovakia got its first private terrestrial television channel—Markiza. Providing a more objective view of the domestic situation, the channel almost immediately became the most popular in Slovakia, despite the fact that it reaches only 60 percent of the country's territory. In radio, the private Bratislava-based Radio Twist continued to broadcast programs with impressive investigative journalism.

TROUBLED INTERNATIONAL TIES

Although the Slovak government, at least in rhetoric, remains committed to EU and NATO integration, its controversial domestic policies were seen by the West as a major obstacle. In 1996, the international community, clearly frustrated with the Slovak government's lack of response to its repeated warnings, more or less rejected the country as a first-round candidate for Western integration. Meanwhile, leaders of EU member countries—most notably German Chancellor Helmut Kohl—avoided meeting with Meciar. At the same time, mutual ties with Russia were tightened through a series of bilateral meetings.

Pavol Hamzik, a career diplomat who became Schenk's replacement as foreign minister, did not have an easy job. By December, when the parliament removed Gaulieder's mandate, the EU's patience with Slovakia was wearing thin. In a parliamentary address on 11 December, President Kovac warned that the ruling coalition was leading Slovakia to international isolation. The follow-ing day, the European Parliament approved a resolution on Slovakia concerning the Gaulieder affair, pointing to Slovakia's pledge in its EU association agree-ment to respect human and minority rights, democracy, and the rule of law.

Sidebar: SLOVAK GOVERNMENT CLAMPS DOWN ON CULTURE

by SHARON FISHER

In July, Culture Minister Ivan Hudec launched an attack on Slovak theaters, particularly the Slovak National Theater (SND). The controversy began on 22 July when Hudec replaced SND stage director Peter Mikulik with actor Lubomir Paulovic. The firing of Mikulik was said to be connected to plans to merge the SND with Bratislava's Nova scena theater, a move against which theater employees—including Paulovic—had signed a petition earlier that month. SND staff immediately protested Paulovic's appointment, saying he was supported "neither by the SND's general director Dusan Jamrich nor by a single actor." SND dramaturg Martin Porubjak complained that Hudec took the step during the theater's summer break, when actors would be unable to stage a protest. Several famous actors announced they would leave the theater. In early September, when the theater's angry staff returned to Bratislava, Paulovic an-nounced his resignation. Meanwhile, Jamrich warned that the theater was experi-encing "the darkest period in its history, including the Fascist era."

Following Mikulik, further casualties of Hudec's theater policy have included former actress Olga Salagova, who was dismissed from her position as Culture Ministry state secretary in early September after she criticized Hudec. Early in October, Hudec also fired the Slovak Philharmonic chief and Trnava Theater's director. Meanwhile, Hudec scorned contacts with actors. Speaking with the pro-government *Slovenska Republika* in late July, he said they were behaving like "privileged children of the revolution."

In fact, Slovak and Czech actors played a key role in the November 1989 revolution that brought down the communist government, and they continue to hold high respect among the population. A poll showed 68 percent of respon-dents thought the actors were justified in their actions. Although the Slovak opposition expressed solidarity with the theater employees, two attempts to dis-miss Hudec during the September parliamentary session failed.

The theater community's protest intensified after 1 October, when Hudec replaced Jamrich with Miroslav Fischer, SND opera director and a candidate of the ruling Movement for a Democratic Slovakia (HZDS) in the last elections. The following day, some 10,000 protesters gathered in Bratislava, demanding Hudec's dismissal and announcing an indefinite strike beginning on 3 October. Popular actor Ladislav Chudik, one of the key figures in the protest, said there would be no public performances until Mikulik is reinstated and a proper competition is held for the post of director that would include actors on the selection committee. SND employees have not held a strike since the time of the November 1989 revolution.

During an HZDS rally on 3 October, Prime Minister Vladimir Meciar joined Culture Minister Ivan Hudec in his attack on SND employees, stressing that "we will not allow the transformation of the National Theater into a workplace of the opposition against the government. Not for state money." Hudec said striking actors will not be paid, while Meciar indicated that they would be replaced with their colleagues from regional theaters.

Sidebar: SLOVAK PRIME MINISTER LISTED AS ONE OF TEN "WORST ENEMIES OF THE PRESS"

by SHARON FISHER

The U.S.-based Committee for the Protection of Journalists (CPJ) on 2 May presented its list of the ten "worst enemies of the press," which includes Slovak Prime Minister Vladimir Meciar in tenth place. Meciar is in the company of (in order of ranking): Abu Abdul Rahman Amin, leader of the Armed Islamic Group of Algeria; Chinese leader Deng Xiaoping; Nigerian President Sani Abacha; Turkish Prime Minister Mesut Yilmaz; Tajik President Emomali Rakhmonov; Indonesian President Suharto; Cuban President Fidel Castro; Saudi Arabian King Fahd bin Abdulaziz Ibn Saud; and Kenyan President Daniel arap Moi.

The CPJ made the following statement in connection with Meciar's listing:

> In his latest assault on press freedom, the thin-skinned prime minister pushed through parliament an amendment to the Criminal Code that would imprison journalists and others found guilty of "spreading false information abroad." Since Meciar dismissed all but one of the 18 members of the state radio and television supervising councils in November 1994, the Slovakian broadcasters have become mouthpieces and apologists for the prime minister's increasingly autocratic rule. This backslide into repression bodes ill not only for Slovakia but for all of post-communist Central Europe.

Since the last parliamentary elections, held in fall 1994, steps taken against the independent media have included the following:

November 1994
- replacement of 17 of 18 members of the boards overseeing Slovak Radio and TV; replacement of SRo Director Vladimir Stefko with Jan Tuzinsky, a parliamentary deputy representing Meciar's party, the Movement for a Democratic Slovakia (HZDS) (Tuzinsky later gave up his parliamentary seat)

December 1994
- replacement of STV Director Ivan Stadtrucker with Jozef Darmo; dismissal of chairman and five other members of the nine-member Board for Slovak Radio and Television Broadcasting
- appointment of pro-government *Slovenska Republika* journalist Erika Vincourkova as head of "Radiozurnal" program at SRo
- replacement of TASR Director Ivan Melichercik with Dusan Kleiman
- cancellation of three popular TV political satires by Darmo

February 1995
- proposal by HZDS deputy Jan Fekete during a session of the parliamentary Committee for Education, Science, Culture, and Sport, that VAT be raised on all commercial publications and radio and TV broadcasts with a foreign capital share above 30 percent (The proposal is rejected.)

March 1995
- Finance Ministry removes license of investment firm PSIS, which owns a majority of shares in the publisher of the opposition daily *Sme*

April 1995
- bill on ethics in journalism drawn up by three deputies from the ruling coalition

May 1995
- pro-government dailies *Slovenska Republika* and *Hlas ludu* given funding by the Culture Ministry to publish supplements aimed at ethnic minorities although few minorities read the two papers

October 1995
- private printing press Concordia suddenly refuses to continue printing *Sme*, allegedly for political reasons

January 1996
- pro-government daily *Nova Smena mladych* begins publication with the help of some 50 million crowns of state budget subsidies

March 1996
- parliament approves controversial criminal code amendment on the protection of the republic
- controversial media bill approved by the government's legislative council

While Meciar cannot be personally held responsible for all of these steps, he could have stopped at least some of them from happening. Meciar and his government have received a number of warnings from Western leaders, diplomats, and media-watch groups; however, little concrete action has been taken to rectify the situation.

The government's unwillingness to change its behavior is particularly puzzling in that it remains extremely sensitive to criticism; Meciar's appearance on the top-ten list sparked a wave of protests in Slovakia. The government office protested Meciar's inclusion on the list, noting that "since 1989 no case of persecution, imprisonment, or violent death of a journalist because of his journalistic activities has been recorded in Slovakia." The HZDS responded by blaming "the current opposition, headed by President Michal Kovac." Meanwhile, Anna Malikova of the Slovak National Party (SNS), a junior coalition partner, noted that "the SNS considers the listing of Meciar among the worst enemies of the press not only as a gross insult to Slovakia but also as proof of the incompetence and lack of professionalism of the CPJ."

Hungary

Population:	10,277,000 (January 1994)
Capital:	Budapest (pop. 1,996,000)
Major cities:	Debrecen (pop. 218,000), Miskolc (pop. 190,000), Szeged (pop. 179,000)
Area:	93,030 sq. km.
Major ethnic groups:	Hungarian 90%, Romani 4%, German 2.6%, Slovak 1%
Economy:	GDP growth: 0.5%
	Inflation rate: 20%
	Average monthly income: $360
	Unemployment rate: 10.5%

A YEAR OF SCANDALS AND RESIGNATIONS IN HUNGARY

by ZSOFIA SZILAGYI

In 1996, Hungary's Socialist-led government tried to soften the reform plan it had committed itself to in 1995, casting doubts on its efforts to stabilize the economy. Meanwhile, the public witnessed a series of major political scandals pointing to widespread corruption in the state administration.

The year 1996 marked major anniversaries of two pivotal events in Hungarian history: the settling of Hungarian tribes in the Carpathian basin 1,100 years ago and the 1956 revolution against the Soviets. The year, however, will be remembered more for economic hardship, political scandals, an increase in extremist rhetoric, growing corruption, and a further widening of the gap between the nouveaux riches and lower classes.

During the year, several major disputes surfaced between the two members of the ruling coalition, the ex-communist Hungarian Socialist Party and the liberal Alliance of Free Democrats. They confirmed the fundamental ideological differences between the two parties, strengthened divisions within the massive Socialist Party caucus, and led many to believe that the coalition would break up. Meanwhile, public confidence in the country's leadership was significantly shaken by allegations of high-level corruption and the government's apparent inability to cut down on increasing organized crime and black-market trading. Nevertheless, the coalition held together, but its popularity suffered a significant drop.

Although Prime Minister Gyula Horn promised a government of experts during his Socialist Party's 1994 election campaign, he had to let five ministers go in 1996. The resignations of Finance Minister Lajos Bokros and Welfare Minister Gyorgy Szabo and the dismissal of Agriculture Minister Laszlo Lakos were mainly related to the government's difficulties implementing the comprehensive austerity program it had launched the previous year. The resignation of Trade and Industry Minister Imre Dunai and the dismissal of his successor, Tamas Suchman, (who was responsible for overseeing privatization as well) were associated with political scandals. The police's inability to fight growing internal corruption and tackle organized crime—blamed for a series of murders and grenade bombings toward the end of the year—prompted Interior Minister Gabor Kuncze to fire the country's four top police officials in November.

Following Western criticism of the government's July declaration supporting autonomy for Hungarian minorities in neighboring countries, Hungary signed a bilateral friendship treaty with Romania in the fall. The long-negotiated pact, which both Budapest and Bucharest had sought to present as a step toward overcoming past tensions and animosities, was welcomed by Western leaders but was fiercely criticized by opposition parties in both countries.

Hungary's opposition was particularly concerned about the inclusion of an interpretive footnote specifying that the treaty's reference to Council of Europe Recommendation 1201 would not provide for collective rights or territorial autonomy for the ethnic Hungarian minority in Romania. Despite the opposition's accusations that the government was trading minority rights for Western recognition, the treaty's ratification was never in question, as coalition deputies held a 72 percent majority in parliament. During 1996, ties with Brussels were strengthened and preparations for joining the European Union and NATO continued to be given strong emphasis. However, public support for membership in those two organizations remained below 50 percent, with skepticism about the EU growing and an increasing number of people supporting neutrality over NATO membership.

SLOWING ECONOMIC REFORMS

Approval of a $387 million loan by the International Monetary Fund in March and membership in the Organization for Economic Cooperation and Development in May showed that the government was earning international respect for its welfare-cutting, stabilization-oriented economic program. At home, however, frustration grew as the government failed to meet its pledges to stabilize inflation and halt the decline of real wages.

The first major political event of 1996 was the resignation in February of the economic pragmatist Bokros and his replacement with Peter Medgyessy in March. Although Medgyessy pledged to continue his predecessor's rigorous stabilization program, the Finance Ministry did not make major headway in economic reforms, and as a result, the economy showed signs of stagnation. While inflation remained around 24 percent, annual growth in gross domestic product was only 0.5 percent, much lower than the growth rates of other countries in the region.

Medgyessy's focus seemed limited to promoting a pleasant-sounding "anti-inflation" package, which involved a sizable reduction in state expenditures as well as cuts in personal-income-tax rates. But few concrete measures were implemented, and plans for comprehensive state-budget reform were not finalized. Pressure from trade unions and the government's involvement of various interest groups in the decision-making process—so-called "interest coordination"—bogged down reforms.

The softening of economic policy went hand-in-hand with a noticeable increase in "socially sensitive" rhetoric. Although the country's bloated social-welfare system and high foreign debt had brought calls for reforms for more than a decade, the remodeling of the health-care and pension systems proceeded very slowly. The Welfare Ministry was under pressure to cut its spending as the social-security deficit widened to three times the 1996 target of 17.8 billion forints ($112 million). But the cost-cutting measures it took—including phasing out 10,000 of the country's 93,000 hospital beds and suspending certain lifesaving operations—were more of the "lawn mower cuts" variety than components of a comprehensive reform program. Demonstrations for wage hikes and protests against hospital closures kept the health-care system in the spotlight the whole year.

FRACTURED POLITICAL SCENE

The political scandals, the socialist-liberal government's unpopular stabilization program, and Horn's inconsistent governing style helped two opposition parties—the Smallholders and the Young Democrats—grow significantly stronger. At the same time, extraparliamentary parties on the extreme left and right also increased in popularity; the communist Workers' Party's platform included fierce protests against Hungary's ambitions to join NATO, while the radical right played the traditional nationalist-populist card.

Overall, Hungary's political scene remained highly fractured and conspicuous for its lack of a strong center-right political force. The former ruling party, the Hungarian Democratic Forum, split in two in March under pressure from its nationalist and liberal wings. The two splinter parties' popularity ratings both hovered around the minimum 5 percent of the vote needed to win seats in parliament. Support for the seventh parliamentary party, the Christian Democrats, remained similarly low.

Although the coalition parties held a majority of the parliamentary votes, disagreements between them and divisions within the Socialist Party delayed the passage of high-priority legislation, including a new constitution and a law on conflicts of interests for public officials. The coalition partners were continually at odds over the latter. A group of five deputies from opposition and coalition parties submitted a proposal that would limit the jobs that deputies can hold in addition to their legislative duties and require stricter reporting by deputies of their outside incomes. The current law only covers political conflicts, forbidding, for example, those holding elected office from becoming public prosecutors or judges. The main dispute between the parties revolved around whether the law should apply to current parliamentary deputies.

Relations between the coalition parties deteriorated in June, when Socialist deputies obstructed the adoption of a conceptual outline for a new constitution. The outline was meant to provide a framework for the final text of a new basic law to replace the country's dated 1949 constitution. Although five parliamentary parties, including the coalition parties, had previously agreed to support the constitutional outline, the Socialist leadership did not support it during the parliamentary vote. The Socialists wanted the new constitution to include references to social rights (to read that the Hungarian Republic is a "social state"), to spell out that the president is to be elected directly, and to make "interest coordination" compulsory for governing parties. The reworked concept, which was eventually passed in December, contained all the Socialists' suggested elements. Many constitutional lawyers fear the new outline paves the way for a constitution that could block any future economic-stabilization program.

In July, the parliament finally passed a revised law on screening public officials who had worked with Hungary's communist-era secret police. Hungary's parliament had been working to replace the country's screening law since the one adopted by the previous parliament was annulled by the Constitutional Court in 1994 as being too vague. The amendment of the law stirred considerable controversy in parliament—and especially between the governing parties—over who was to be screened.

In the end, the number of officials to undergo screening was narrowed from about 5,000 to about 600. Only those public officials who are required to take an oath before parliament or the president are to be screened. Although the new law was considered far more constitutionally sound than its predecessor, it remained a subject of criticism from the committee charged with its implementation, who argued that its scope is too narrow to make public life clean.

POLITICAL SCANDALS

In 1996, the State Audit Office discovered irregularities in several major privatization deals concluded during the Horn cabinet's tenure, while the bank-consolidation process and other deals that aroused suspicions of corruption were given significant attention by the press. Several serious accusations were brought against top government officials, while press and parliamentary investigations showed that billions of state forints had landed in private hands through the shady dealings of government-connected circles. In one of the largest scandals, a number of top officials, including former Industry and Trade Minister Imre Dunai and his predecessor, Laszlo Pal, were accused of using their influence to help favored companies obtain contracts related to Russia's repayment of its state debt to Hungary.

Dubbed "oilgate" because it was initially believed that Russian oil shipments to Hungary were part of the suspicious deals, the scandal involved several Socialist Party members who held business interests in companies that happened to come out as favorites in closed ministry tenders. The implicated ministers called the allegations a series of lies and mudslinging, but they could not present any credible counterevidence. On the opposition's initiative, a parliamentary probe was launched into the affair, but certain documents related to the probe were given an 80–year stamp of secrecy by the Socialist minister without portfolio in charge of the secret services.

The "oilgate" scandal was followed by a privatization scandal involving the State Privatization and Holding Company's payment of a hefty fee to an outside consultant under an irregular contract. Revelations about the privatization company's corrupt conduct and mismanagement prompted Horn to dismiss the entire privatization leadership, including Minister of Industry, Trade and Privatization Tamas Suchman. The affair put into question the fairness of the privatization process and created the biggest political scandal of contemporary Hungary. The governing parties were especially embarrassed when many political scientists and newspapers suggested that the record-high fee was probably destined for party election coffers. Although the "oilgate" and privatization fiascoes will undoubtedly have a negative impact on the governing parties' 1998 electoral performance, neither seemed to undermine the confidence of foreign investors.

But according to leading analysts, the scandal signaled that the country faces a deep-rooted crisis of state administration and that its inefficiency and inclination to corruption has reached such a level that it cannot be solved by the dismissal of a few officials. As the privatization scandal unfolded, tension between and within the coalition parties increased. The Free Democrats faced a huge political dilemma: whether to stay in the coalition with the Socialists or leave it for a position in the opposition, where none of the other opposition parties could be expected to show much cooperation toward them.

Despite the growing public mistrust, the ruling parties appear determined to continue their joint governing until the 1998 general elections, and for that purpose both seem able to tolerate the ever more diverging views of their coalition partner. For 1997, more cure-all rhetoric is expected from the government, while the opposition's anti-government propaganda is likely to further intensify.

Sidebar: HUNGARIAN MINORITY SUMMIT CAUSES UPROAR IN SLOVAKIA

by SHARON FISHER *and* ZSOFIA SZILAGYI

An ethnic Hungarian minority summit, held on 5–6 July in Budapest, strained relations between Slovakia and Hungary. The conference, entitled "Hungary and Hungarians beyond the borders," was organized by the prime minister's office and the Office of Hungarians Beyond the Borders. Summit participants—including representatives of the Hungarian government, all Hungarian parliamentary parties, and 11 ethnic Hungarian organizations from neighboring countries—called for establishing local governments and autonomy in line with the Western European practice.

The final statement of the conference was endorsed by all delegates with the exception of the representatives of the Democratic Union of Vojvodina Hungarians [in rump Yugoslavia]. The signatories made it clear in an 11–point document that "the establishment of local governments and autonomy, in line with the current European practice and the spirit of international norms, is vital to preserving the identity of Hungarians beyond the borders, their survival and development as a community in their native land." The declaration also mentioned the Hungarian government's constitutional responsibility towards the Hungarian communities beyond the borders. Further, it specified that a coordinated support would be granted to the autonomy aspirations of those communities and a fixed quotient of the annual Hungarian budget will be put aside for them.

The participants also agreed that for the future of the Hungarian nation, the country's earliest possible accession to the Euro-Atlantic organizations is of decisive importance. "It is in the interest of every Hungarian living in the Carpathian Basin, and it is also a chance for Hungarians to come together." The declaration also expresses support for the NATO and EU membership of all Hungary's neighbors, "in the belief that in the countries concerned, through the fulfillment of the conditions of accession and in addition to the undisturbed operation of the institutions of democracy and market economy, the endeavors of the Hungarians communities to achieve special legal status will also succeed, in accordance with the positive practice of the EU member states."

SLOVAK REACTIONS

Bratislava-based Coexistence chairman Miklos Duray, who attended the summit, argued that "the spirit of the declaration" is included in the Slovak-Hungarian basic treaty. However, Slovak ruling coalition representatives were of the opposite opinion. Foreign Ministry State Secretary Jozef Sestak stressed on 8 July that mentioning the word "autonomy" in the conference's final document could be a violation of the basic treaty. Meanwhile, Augustin Marian Huska, deputy chairman of the Slovak parliament, stressed that Hungary had clearly breached its international obligations and its pledge not to support irredentism and separatism.

Slovak Foreign Minister Juraj Schenk on 9 July read a government statement expressing "surprise and concern" over the summit's declaration, which the government regards as "a step against the trend of positive development of mutual relations" marked by the ratification of the bilateral treaty. The government stressed that the "key demand" of the summit—the creation of autonomy and self-government on the territory of other states where Hungarians live—has not been adopted by the Slovak government or by international organizations, such as the Council of Europe and the OSCE. Since there is "no relevant international document" that codifies the idea of ethnic autonomy, it is "misleading" to talk about "the spirit of international norms," Schenk stressed.

Hungarians argue that at least two international documents support the idea of autonomy for minorities. The first is the "Document of the Copenhagen Meeting of the Conference on the Human Dimension of the CSCE," adopted on 29 June 1990 at a conference attended by representatives of all CSCE states, including Hungary and Czechoslovakia. Article 35 of the document says:

> The participating States note the efforts undertaken to protect and create conditions for the promotion of the ethnic, cultural, linguistic, and religious identity of certain national minorities by establishing, as one of the possible means to achieve these aims, appropriate local or autonomous administrations corresponding to the specific historical and territorial circumstances of such minorities and in accordance with the policies of the State concerned.

Another international document mentioned by Hungarians is the Council of Europe's Recommendation 1201, which was included in the Slovak-Hungarian bilateral treaty. The Recommendation was prepared in 1993 and is described as "an additional protocol on the rights of national minorities to the European Convention on Human Rights." The controversial clause is Article 11, which reads:

In the regions where they are in a majority the persons belonging to a national minority shall have the right to have at their disposal appropriate local or autonomous authorities or to have a special status, matching the specific historical and territorial situation and in accordance with the domestic legislation of the state.

Both of these articles are rather vague, and because of the reluctance of many West European states to put such policies into practice, Slovakia has tried to evade them, calling instead for a common standard of minority rights that will be adopted by all European countries. Since the signing of the bilateral treaty with Hungary in March, Slovak representatives have repeatedly stressed that they are resolutely against the creation of autonomous regions based on ethnic principles or the allowance of collective rights for minorities.

HUNGARY DEFENDS THE DECLARATION

In reaction to the Slovak uproar, Hungarian Foreign Ministry spokesman Gabor Szentivanyi said that although the wording of the final document refers to autonomy and not "autonomous authorities"—as in Council of Europe Recommendation 1201—the declaration does not go beyond the spirit of 1201. He added that autonomy cannot be identified with the misleading meaning that nationalist politicians abroad have given to the concept. According to him, the document should be interpreted as a reflection of the conference's collective thinking and not as a legally binding international document.

Still, the Slovak cabinet on 10 July accused Budapest of trying to "destabilize the region." Foreign Ministry State Secretary Jozef Sestak summoned Hungarian ambassador to Slovakia, Jeno Boros, to explain the conference's "motives and conclusions" and Hungary's views on the further development of bilateral relations.

Meanwhile, Hungarian Foreign Minister Laszlo Kovacs told *Magyar Hirlap* that an "ethnic-based territorial" autonomy was out of the question and reiterated that the statement did not violate either European norms or the Hungarian-Slovak basic treaty. He attributed Bratislava's heated response to mistrust, lack of understanding, and domestic political considerations in that country. The minister recalled that the Hungarian government had made it clear in its 1994 program that it would support the autonomy aspirations of Hungarian minorities in line with [Western] European norms.

However, independent analysts say, that—to some extent—the Hungarians can be blamed for the tension. Knowing Slovakia's sensitivity to demands of autonomy for ethnic Hungarians, the summit participants might have been more careful. Relations between Slovakia and Hungary were starting to improve as the bilateral treaty calmed fears of Hungarian irredentism. Within Slovakia, cooperation between the Hungarian coalition and the other opposition parties had strengthened in some areas.

The Hungarian government's firmer stance on ensuring minority rights abroad could be attributed to a 15 June meeting of the World Congress of Hungarians in Budapest, where Prime Minister Gyula Horn was booed and whistled while explaining that the government is not planning changes in its foreign minority policy. Earlier, nationalist circles and the opposition have blamed the government for "trading" minority rights for the Slovak-Hungarian basic treaty. Addressing the gathering of ethnic Hungarians from abroad, Horn asked Hungarian minority representatives to make clear their autonomy concepts and distance themselves from separatist declarations.

Hungary's rather nationalistic opposition was satisfied with the declaration's contents, saying the current conference was the first step towards restoring a foreign policy consensus which was disrupted over Hungarian minorities and regional ties two years ago. They called the statement significant since it declares that Hungarian minorities form part of the Hungarian nation. At the same time, the opposition voiced concern that a clause providing Hungarians beyond the borders with the right of veto over interstate treaties had been left out of the document. They also regretted that a autonomy council to coordinate future cooperation had not been set up.

Sidebar: HUNGARY COMMEMORATES 40TH ANNIVERSARY OF 1956 REVOLUTION

by ZSOFIA SZILAGYI

On 23 October, Hungarians commemorated the 40th anniversary of the crushed 1956 revolution that left 25,000 dead. For the past few years, 23 October—the anniversary of the day the revolution broke out—had gradually been losing its significance as a national day for ordinary Hungarians. At the same time, it increasingly became the subject of historians' debates, a day that political parties abused, and a time when extremist manifestations and anti-government rallies were most frequent.

Although an end to a 33–year silence on the crushed revolution stirred up survivors' emotions and historians' interest, several elements that might make 23 October a true national day in contemporary Hungary were missing. Government rhetoric on 1956 was often puzzling, and its dispensation of "historical justice"—that is, punishing the criminals of 1956—rather spotty.

The fall of communism in Hungary was closely associated with the legacy of the ill-fated 1956 uprising. In spring 1988—with Janos Kadar losing political control—the relatives and survivors of the crushed revolution established a Committee for Historical Justice. In January 1989, the government announced that it had decided to allow the exhumation, identification, and decent reburial of the remains of 1956's executed leaders. A Communist Party subcommittee was established to "re-evaluate the last 40 years." Soon afterward, Imre Pozsgay, a reformer within the party, pronounced that 1956 was not—as had been previously maintained—a "counterrevolution" but rather a "popular uprising."

The turning point for the socialist regime in Hungary was the reburial of Imre Nagy on 16 June 1989, just a year after opposition activists held a demonstration on the anniversary of Nagy's execution and were violently dispersed. Nagy was prime minister in Hungary's reform government in 1956 and was executed in 1958 by the Soviet-backed Hungarian government.

Seeking to make up for the failure of 1956 and to replace the memories of those tragic days with positive ones, the Communist Party leadership chose 23 October 1989 to proclaim the state a republic. Ever since, 23 October has been a politically charged date. In a recent article in *Beszelo,* historian Gyula Kozak discussed reasons why the revolution has not become part of the Hungarian general thinking as a positive value and why Hungarians, in fact, prefer to forget 1956. According to Kozak, the revolution in retrospect has not appeared as a "uniting" but rather as a "divisive" historical element. The revolution was initiated by reformist communist circles and did not produce a hero that people could identify with. Nagy was, after all, a communist, and the freedom fighters—who were portrayed by the international media of the time as the heroes of the revolution—were too low-class for Hungarians to identify with, he writes.

When the socialist-liberal coalition took office in 1994, the debate took a new turn, and most people became even more uncertain of how to judge the 1956 events. The successor to the former Communist Party became the main coalition party, holding 54 percent of the seats in parliament. The government's political will to tackle "historical justice" remained in question, as Prime Minister Gyula Horn's role in the militia unit that crushed the revolt (a role he admitted in 1990) made the issue particularly sensitive for the government. In an attempt to distance themselves from their predecessor, the Socialists in May pushed through a bill honoring the memory of Nagy. The bill stirred an emotional debate in parliament and was strongly criticized by the anti-communist opposition and the liberal coalition party, the Alliance of Free Democrats. "One could say that this move was a Socialist action *against* the memory of the revolution," wrote Kozak.

The 1995 anniversary of the 1956 uprising was marked by the release of crucial documents that rekindled the long-debated issue of whether Radio Free Europe/Radio Liberty broadcasts at the time instigated Hungarian freedom fighters, promising Western assistance. It was hoped that the documents would answer some crucial questions regarding the U.S.-funded broadcaster's role, but, as memoranda revealed at an October conference in Budapest show, they have thus far failed to provide an unequivocal answer. Historians are still at odds over whether the RFE Hungarian Service's broadcasts could be held responsible for prolonging the fight. Some conference participants said the broadcasts did have an impact on the revolution, but few thought they were decisive.

Poland

Population:	8,600,000
Capital:	Warsaw (pop. 1,638,300)
Major cities:	Lodz (pop. 825,600), Krakow (pop. 745,400), Wroclaw (pop. 642,700)
Area:	312,685 sq. km.
Major ethnic groups:	Polish 97.6%, German 1.3%, Ukrainian 0.6%, Belarusian 0.5%
Economy:	GDP growth: 6%
	Inflation rate: 19%
	Average monthly income: $318
	Unemployment rate: 13.6%

WITH THE LEFT IN CHARGE, THE POLISH RIGHT PREPARES FOR 1997

by JAKUB KARPINSKI

With Aleksander Kwasniewski as president, the leftist ruling coalition gained firm control of the Polish state, ending years of battle between the president and government. The political center-right, led by the Solidarity trade union, consolidated in hope of toppling the current coalition in the next parliamentary elections.

In 1996, Polish President Aleksander Kwasniewski had only partial success delivering on his campaign promise the previous fall to unite the divided Polish electorate. Chairman of the ex-communist Social Democracy of the Republic of Poland (SdRP) from 1990 until his election in November 1995, Kwasniewski had promised a "normal" presidency—contrasting himself to his combative and unpredictable predecessor, former Solidarity leader Lech Walesa. Kwasniewski's election signaled a new era of cooperation between the presidency and the government, which has been controlled since 1993 by a coalition of the SdRP-dominated Democratic Left Alliance (SLD) and the Polish Peasant Party (PSL).

Although as president Kwasniewski usually earned approval ratings of more than 50 percent, many Poles refused to reconcile themselves to his victory. When Kwasniewski was sworn in on 23 December 1995, Walesa did not attend the ceremony. And just before leaving office, Walesa and his ally, then-Internal Affairs Minister Andrzej Milczanowski, left behind a political bomb for their left-wing opponents that would make headlines for much of the following year.

On 19 December 1995, three days before the end of Walesa's term, Milczanowski deposited a motion in the Warsaw military prosecutor's office demanding an investigation of evidence that Jozef Oleksy, prime minister since March 1995, provided confidential information to Soviet and later Russian intelligence officers from 1983 to 1995. The scandal forced Oleksy to step down on 24 January—although his colleagues in the SdRP showed their continuing support for the former prime minister by electing him party chairman on 27 January.

After the names of two officers he allegedly had contacts with were disclosed, Oleksy admitted to having had a social relationship with the first, a Soviet and later Russian intelligence officer active in Poland on various posts from 1981 until December 1995, and to knowing that agent's successor, a Russian officer active until October 1995. Oleksy denied, however, that he knew they were intelligence officers. The crucial problem with the case against Oleksy was the lack of clear evidence that he had knowingly given confidential information to foreign intelligence agents.

Finding no convincing evidence of crime, the Warsaw military prosecutor formally dropped the investigation against Oleksy on 22 April. However, a special Sejm commission continued to investigate the role of the secret services in the affair, presenting a report in December that said Milczanowski "may have violated the law" in connection with the proceedings against Oleksy. Over the rest of the year, various documents relating to the case were published, providing detailed information on the functioning—or ill-functioning—of the Polish security services.

The Oleksy affair cast a shadow on both sides of the Polish political spectrum. Supporters of Walesa accused the left of having close contacts with Moscow that could prove detrimental to Poland's security, portraying the Oleksy case as merely an example of a widespread tendency of very friendly relations that current Polish left-wing politicians had formed with Soviet officials during the communist era. The left accused Walesa's supporters in the Internal Affairs Ministry and especially the State Security Office of having trumped up the allegations, basing their calls for a formal investigation on thin, hastily gathered evidence and a large dose of wishful thinking and jumping to conclusions. Impartial observers tended to agree that both sides had their points.

CHANGES IN GOVERNMENT

Oleksy was replaced as prime minister on 7 February by Wlodzimierz Cimoszewicz, a former head of the SLD parliamentary caucus and justice minister from 1993 to 1995. Although Cimoszewicz was a member of Poland's communist party—the Polish United Workers Party—from 1971 until its dissolution in 1990, he did not join its successor, the SdRP. As a left-wing candidate for president in 1990, he received 9 percent of the votes.

The government had already changed significantly in December 1995, with the end of Walesa's presidency and the semi-constitutional institution of three "presidential ministries"—defense, foreign affairs, and internal affairs. According to the so-called "little constitution" of 1992, the heads of those ministries had to be appointed "after consultation with the president." Walesa imposed his interpretation of that clause to give the president the decisive voice in those ministers' nominations. In that way, Walesa created a presidential mini-government within the government, which was often independent from the prime minister (the most extreme example being Milczanowski's collection of information against Oleksy). With the end of Walesa's term on 22 December 1995, all three of his appointees to the "presidential ministries" resigned, and the institution was no longer mentioned.

A draft of a new constitution approved by the parliament's Constitutional Commission in June would significantly reduce the president's powers, eliminating the obligatory consultation with the president on appointments to the "presidential ministries" as well as the president's current right to nominate the chief of the General Staff and to veto the budget. Those moves are clearly rooted in the experience gained by politicians and the public during the five years of Walesa's stormy presidency. However, quarrels over other issues, including territorial administration, the Sejm majority needed to override the president's veto, and whether so-called "social rights" (to housing, education, and health care) should be guaranteed in the constitution, delayed the commission's adoption of a final draft. After that, the draft must be approved by two-thirds of the National Assembly (that is, the Sejm and Senate in joint session) before the new constitution can be adopted in a national referendum.

In June and August, the Sejm adopted a packet of laws significantly reforming the government structure. In October, the Privatization Ministry was abolished, replaced by the newly created Treasury Ministry and its subordinate Privatization Agency. Also at that time, the State Security Office, a part of the Internal Affairs Ministry, was subordinated directly to the prime minister, and the new Committee for European Integration, with Cimoszewicz as chairman, started its activities. The main part of the reform was implemented on 1 January 1997: the Internal Affairs Ministry was expanded into the Internal Affairs and Administration Ministry, taking over some of the local administration duties of the now-defunct Government Office (with the remainder of the latter's duties going to the Prime Minister's Chancellery). The ministries of foreign economic cooperation and industry and trade were abolished, with their functions being taken over by the Treasury Ministry and the new Ministry of the Economy. The Central Planning Office was replaced by the Center for Strategic Studies.

Along with the restructuring came a shuffling of ministerial posts. The PSL's Miroslaw Pietrewicz became the new treasury minister, while former Privatization Minister Wieslaw Kaczmarek took on the expanded economics portfolio. Leszek Miller moved from the Government Office to the Internal Affairs and Administration Ministry, while former Internal Affairs Minister Zbigniew Siemiatkowski became a minister without portfolio overseeing the State Security Office on behalf of the prime minister.

The reform strengthened the prime minister's powers with respect to other ministers, the president, and other high-ranking officials. The prime minister gained the power to nominate "task ministers" (ministers without portfolio, such as Siemiatkowski) to supervise particular domains in the government's purview. When the government resigns, high-ranking government and local officials—state secretaries, undersecretaries, provincial governors, and deputy governors—are now obligated to offer their resignations to the next prime minister.

FIRM WESTERN ORIENTATION

Kwasniewski's first visits abroad made clear that his presidency would bring no change in the Western orientation of Poland's foreign policy. In January, he visited Germany and France and was received at NATO and European Union headquarters in Brussels. Polish-German-French cooperation in the "Weimar triangle" was confirmed at a meeting of the three countries' foreign ministers in Warsaw on 19 December. At a meeting on 7–8 June in southeastern Poland with the presidents of eight other Central European countries (Austria, the Czech Republic, Germany, Hungary, Italy, Slovakia, Slovenia, and Ukraine), Kwasniewski described expanding the EU and NATO as a natural move crowning the integration process that started after the fall of the Iron Curtain.

Poland's good relations with its neighbors were shadowed only by Belarusian

President Alyaksandr Lukashenka's anti-democratic policies (but Kwasniewski visited even Lukashenka). Poland was active in developing the 20 November joint Polish-Lithuanian-Ukrainian presidential statement expressing the three countries' concern over the situation in Belarus.

The bulk of Polish trade is with the EU, with Germany leading the list of Poland's trade partners since 1990. But unregistered trade—and in particular, private visits by "commercial tourists" from Poland's eastern neighbors—also play an important role. About 10 million Ukrainians, Belarusians, and Russians visit Poland each year, and more than a million people from ex-Soviet countries are in Poland on any given day.

Several macroeconomic indicators showed Poland's good performance in 1996. Gross domestic product was up an estimated 6 percent, compared with 7 percent in 1995 and 5.2 percent in 1994. Inflation in 1996 was reported to be 18.5 percent, down from 21.6 percent in 1995 and 32.2 percent in 1994. Unemployment also continued to decrease (to 13.2 percent in October). Foreign direct investment was estimated at $5 billion in 1996.

The distribution of mass-privatization vouchers was completed in November, with 26 million Poles—95 percent of those eligible—claiming vouchers. The vouchers, distributed at a cost of 20 zloty ($7), were priced at 150 zloty on the stock exchange. They could also be exchanged for shares in any of 15 investment funds managing some 500 enterprises. In recognition of its economic performance, on 11 July, Poland was admitted as the 28th member of the Organization for Economic Cooperation and Development (the Czech Republic and Hungary had also recently been admitted).

One of the main respects in which the leftist coalition that has ruled since the 1993 Sejm elections differs from the Solidarity-linked governments of 1989–1993 is in its unwillingness to grant the Catholic Church an influence in matters regulated by law. A concordat with the Holy See signed in July 1993 has not been ratified by the Sejm; on 3 July, the Sejm decided to delay its ratification until a new constitution was adopted. On 24 October, the Sejm overrode a Senate veto and liberalized Poland's formerly restrictive law on abortion, allowing abortions to be performed in the first 12 weeks of pregnancy if the woman is in a difficult social or financial situation. Those decisions aggravated already strained relations between the Vatican and current Polish authorities. One sign of how tense those relations were was the fact that Kwasniewski—who as president made frequent official visits abroad and received numerous heads of state—was not received by Pope John Paul II in 1996.

In an attempt to meet the demands of the Catholic Church hierarchy, the Constitutional Commission decided during the fall to adopt a compromise version of the preamble of its draft constitution: the preamble refers to God as a source of values for believers, but adds that nonbelievers share similar values without a theological background.

The ruling coalition successfully imposed its control over state-television programming, acting through the supervisory and managing boards of Polish Television (TVP). A series of personnel changes in TVP's top management were followed by the canceling of programs that left-wing politicians and commentators considered overly critical of the communist era. Current-affairs programs considered antagonistic toward the ruling coalition were also removed from the air.

In a long-awaited move—postponed since September 1995—the Polish Radio and Television Broadcasting Council in October issued two licenses to private television broadcasters. The council assigned a network in northern Poland to TVN—a company one-third-owned by Central European Media Enterprises, which operates television stations in several other Central European countries. A network in central Poland was allocated to Nasza Telewizja, organized by Polish businessmen apparently supported by the co-ruling SLD. The private station Polsat has become slightly more popular than the TVP's second channel, while TVP's first channel remains by far the country's most popular.

In the print media, *Rzeczpospolita* continued to be the most impartial and informative of Warsaw's daily newspapers, while *Gazeta Wyborcza*, the most popular, displayed loyalty to and support for the centrist Freedom Union. In April, a change of ownership in the previously right-of-center *Zycie Warszawy* prompted 29 journalists to resign and launch a new daily, *Zycie,* in September. The new paper, which immediately established itself as conservative and critical of the ruling coalition, will probably play a role in the 1997 parliamentary elections.

CONSOLIDATION ON THE RIGHT

The Polish political scene changed radically in 1996 with the creation of two new political formations on the right side of the political spectrum. The Movement of Poland's Reconstruction (ROP), created after the 1995 presidential election by former prime minister and presidential candidate Jan Olszewski, received 16 percent of the public's support in opinion polls in mid-1996, just ahead of Solidarity's 14 percent. Later, the ROP's support dropped to around 10 percent, owing mainly to competition from another new political formation: Solidarity Electoral Action (AWS), formed on 8 June by the Solidarity trade union and more than two dozen right-of-center political parties.

As a coalition, the AWS received a bonus for unity, a value widely appreciated by the Polish electorate. By the end of the year, the AWS was getting around 26 percent of support in polls and had clearly established itself as the SLD's main rival. According to public-opinion polls, public support for the SLD remained above 20 percent throughout 1996, ending the year at about 26 percent (compared with the 20 percent the SLD had received in the 1993 Sejm elections). Support for the PSL hovered around 12 percent, somewhat down from the 15 percent it took in the 1993 elections. The centrist Freedom Union (UW), combining liberal, Christian-democratic, and socialist factions, had around 10 percent support (under the name of the Democratic Union, it had received 11 percent in 1993), and the leftist, secular Labor Union had 8 percent (up from 6 percent in 1993).

The AWS intends to present common electoral lists in the parliamentary elections scheduled for fall 1997. In December, Solidarity leader Marian

Krzaklewski established a draft allocation of votes among the coalition's member organizations, with Solidarity getting half and other groups splitting the remainder according to their various strengths. According to Krzaklewski, the AWS will work "like a shareholder company."

The AWS was not the only actor on the Polish political scene preparing for the parliamentary elections. Besides preparing coalitions in order to present common electoral lists and avoid the wasting of votes on numerous marginal parties unable to garner the 5 percent of the vote that is required to enter the Sejm, some politicians and commentators began discussing the possibilities for a new governing coalition after the elections. The polls led to the conclusion that unless public opinion changed radically in 1997, at least three political parties will be needed to form the next government. Even with the addition of the Labor Union, a leftist coalition built around the SLD and PSL would probably not have a majority. Commentators considered a center-left coalition of the SLD, the PSL, and the UW less probable than a center-right coalition of the AWS, the ROP, and the PSL. The versatile PSL and ROP seem to be ideologically closer to the AWS than the liberal and internally divided UW. The PSL has often shown its distance from the SLD, which some interpreted as a signal that the PSL might be willing to replace its current coalition partner with a center-right coalition.

There were a number of opportunities for political education of Poles during 1996, and a few of those lessons were quite well taken. The left showed that it could be as Western-oriented as its Solidarity predecessors. The left probably learned from the Oleksy affair that having close friends in Moscow, so valued under communism, can be quite dangerous today. The right learned that unity is useful in politics and that only a united political formation has a real hope of competing with the SLD. Applying that lesson could well change the governing team in Poland in 1997.

Sidebar: ABORTION LAW EASED BY THE POLISH PARLIAMENT

by JAKUB KARPINSKI

On 30 August, the Sejm, the lower chamber of the Polish parliament, voted in favor of amending the abortion law—amidst heated polemics and arguments that usually accompany this issue. The amendment broadened the conditions under which abortion is legal. The current law of 7 January 1993 allowed for abortions only if the pregnancy poses a threat to the woman's life or health, if it results from rape or incest or if the fetus is irreparably damaged. Any person who performs abortions in other cases faces a prison term of up to two years, but the woman is not subjected to punishment. The 1993 law was a compromise between a radical ban on abortion (as advocated by the Catholic Church) and a right to abortion on demand (perhaps only limited by the duration of pregnancy).

Deputies from the Labor Union (UP) and the ruling Democratic Left Alliance (SLD) moved on 1 March to change the 1993 law. The amendment would allow a woman to have an abortion until the twelfth week of pregnancy if she cannot afford to have a child or has other personal problems. An earlier bill easing the 1993 law was vetoed by former president Lech Walesa. The amendment was passed on 30 August by 208 to 61 with 15 abstentions, in a vote which split the ruling coalition, the SLD backing the amendment, while the deputies from the co-ruling Polish Peasant Party (PSL) either voted against or, like many other deputies, left the Chamber in the hope that a quorum of 230 deputies would be prevented.

Public opinion polls taken since 1990 show that—in overwhelmingly Catholic Poland—18–26 percent of Poles favor legalization of abortion with no restrictions, 34–37 percent—favor legalization with some restrictions, 21–26 percent are for a ban with some exceptions, 11–14 percent favor a total ban. Contrary to the stereotypes, younger people, below 24 years of age, and women are less likely to favor legal abortions. Only a total ban on abortion is consistent with the Catholic Church's teachings and the Church's legislative proposals, while some Protestant churches tolerate abortion.

Voting on the 30 August amendment was preceded by a heated debate in the Sejm. The Supreme Court President and former presidential candidate Adam Strzembosz said that hardships should not be a sufficient cause for abortion. Izabela Sierakowska from the Democratic Left Alliance (SLD) defended women's right to choose. Izabela Jaruga-Nowacka from the Labor Union (UP) also supported the amendment, saying that the current regulation is "hypocritical." The SLD's Danuta Waniek said, "Liberalization does not prevent believers from living according to their religious principles."

After the voting, Pope John Paul II condemned the amendment out of hand, saying on 1 September in Castelgandolfo that "A nation that kills its own children is a nation without hope." The Polish Catholic hierarchy, with Poland's Primate Jozef Glemp, was also critical. Primate Glemp said on 1 September that the law was a "general license to kill, aimed at children." Polish President Aleksander Kwasniewski, for his part, said on 2 September: "Liberalizing the law on abortion is a means of fighting hypocrisy which unfortunately emerged in Poland in recent years." On 3 October the Senate voted down the Sejm's amendments by 52 to 40, but the Sejm overrode the Senate veto on 24 October, and President Kwasniewski signed the bill into law.

EASTERN
EUROPE

III

Lithuania

Latvia

Estonia

Belarus

Ukraine

Lithuania

Population:	3,709,100
Capital:	Vilnius (pop. 575,700)
Major cities:	Kaunas (pop. 415,300), Klaipeda (pop. 202,800)
Area:	62,500 sq. km.
Major ethnic groups:	Lithuanian 81.3%, Russian 8.4%, Polish 7%,
	Belarusian 1.5%, Ukrainian 1%
Economy:	GDP growth: 4.0%
. . . .	Inflation rate: 13.1%
. . . .	Average monthly income: $173
. . . .	Unemployment rate: 6.2%

THE POLITICAL PENDULUM SWINGS BACK IN LITHUANIA

by SAULIUS GIRNIUS

The triumphant return of the first post-communist head of state, Vytautas Landsbergis, and his party was the year's most important political event. Things were calmer on the international front, although relations with Latvia worsened over disputed sea borders. Crime and widespread corruption continued to worry citizens, but the economy improved.

The Homeland Union (Conservatives of Lithuania) [TS (LK)], led by Vytautas Landsbergis, scored a crushing victory in the fall parliamentary elections and returned to power. Its triumph not only ended four years of rule by the Lithuanian Democratic Labor Party (LDDP) but signaled the LDDP's demise as a serious force in Lithuania's political life.

The LDDP, the first ex-communist party to return to power via the ballot box after the revolutions of 1989, was also the first to be voted out. In the 20 October and 10 November elections, the TS (LK) captured 70 out of 137 seats, while its Christian Democratic (LKDP) allies won 16 mandates; the LDDP got only 12. Voter turnout, however, was only 53 percent, which compares badly to the 75 percent turnout in 1992.

POST-COMMUNIST OLD GUARD RETURNS

Several factors contributed to the stunning victory of the Conservatives. During their four years in opposition, they matured and toned down much of the harsh rhetoric that had irritated a substantial part of the electorate, while their emphasis on individual responsibility and initiative appealed to many younger voters. Nonetheless, the decisive cause was an unprecedented decrease in LDDP supporters, falling from 817,000 in 1992 to 131,000 in 1996. Voters were dissatisfied with the LDDP's inability to reverse the decline in living standards and improve the economic situation and, more importantly, by its toleration of corruption.

The fate of the LDDP was probably sealed in January 1996, when the party failed to react adequately as evidence of unethical conduct by Adolfas Slezevicius—the prime minister and party chairman—was revealed. The revelation that Slezevicius had withdrawn his personal savings—on which he had been receiving higher-than-normal interest—from the Lithuanian Joint-Stock Innovation Bank before the decision to suspend its operations was announced prompted calls for resignation, but he weathered the initial storm because of his party's and President Algirdas Brazauskas's support. Continuing protests, however, forced Brazauskas to change his stance and call for Slezevicius's ouster. On 8 February, the Seimas voted by an overwhelming majority—94–26, with four abstentions—

to dismiss the prime minister. Slezevicius was replaced by Mindaugas Stankevicius, a technocrat who was not even a formal member of the LDDP. But the damage had already been done, and the LDDP's popularity plummeted irretrievably.

Many leading figures of the Sajudis government of 1990–1992 resumed their former duties after the elections. Landsbergis became the new Seimas chairman, and Gediminas Vagnorius prime minister; a post he had held from January 1991 to June 1992. LKDP Chairman Algirdas Saudargas returned to the job of foreign minister, which he had occupied in 1990–1992. Ceslovas Stankevicius, who was deputy chairman of parliament during the same period, was put in charge of the Defense Ministry. The TS(LK) had agreed to a coalition with the LKDP prior to the elections and maintained it even after winning a majority of Seimas seats. The LKDP, the second-largest party with 16 seats, was given three ministerial portfolios, including the important posts of foreign and defense ministers.

In an important and unexpected move, the TS(LK) offered two ministerial posts to members of the Center Union. The third largest party in parliament accepted the offer. And although no formal coalition agreement was signed, the Center Union was expected to support the government more firmly than it would have done without the ministerial posts. Moreover, the invitation indicated that the Conservatives have overcome the insularity that contributed greatly to their defeat four years earlier.

In early October the TS(LK) had signed an economic memorandum with the Confederation of Industrialists. Continuing the policy of cooperation, Vagnorius offered the post of the new Economy Ministry to Vincas Babilius, the confederation's vice president. The decision to offer three ministries to parties and organizations that do not belong to the ruling coalition was unexpected and shows its desire to seek broader support. It also makes political sense. With support of the 13 members of the Center Union faction, the coalition would have 99 votes and is in a position to pass any legislation, including amendments to the Constitution, that it wishes.

TROUBLED WATERS WITH LATVIA

There were no major foreign-policy developments in 1996 other than a further deterioration in relations with Latvia because of the dispute over the demarcation of sea borders (see "A Year of Consolidation in Latvia"). Lithuania's chief foreign-policy goals remained entry into the European Union and NATO. Although the chances for admission by the year 2000 are almost nil, Lithuania continued to argue its case vigorously. Vilnius urged the EU to begin negotiations on membership simultaneously with all 10 associate members from Central and Eastern Europe, with the proviso that membership should be granted according to a country's ability to fulfill the EU criteria. Lithuania also argued that NATO should announce which countries will be granted eventual membership without necessarily specifying the date of entry. It seems that the EU will indeed begin negotiations at the same time, but no new members are likely to be admitted until 2002 or even later. NATO has not officially responded to the "who, not when" proposal, but U.S. Defense Secretary William Perry has stated that the

Baltic countries are not yet ready for membership (see "US Acts To Sooth Baltic Concerns").

The Lithuanian government is eager to show its willingness to assume the burdens of NATO membership. Lithuania is a very active participant in the Partnership for Peace, and its soldiers are serving with Stabilization Force troops in Bosnia. The defense budget was increased substantially in 1996, and Lithuania is acquiring weapons systems that meet NATO standards.

In preparation for EU membership, the Lithuanian parliament amended the constitution in June to permit foreigners to purchase land and approved the so-called European agreement. The three Baltic states also finally signed a free-trade agreement on agricultural goods. That pact is considered an important step on the road to the EU, for it demonstrates an ability to cooperate and solve the kinds of issues that are a central component of EU activity.

Despite the free-trade agreement and military cooperation, ties among the Baltic states are not as good as they could be and are not considered a priority item by the respective governments and parliaments. In 1996, the meetings of the Baltic Assembly and the Baltic Council of Ministers were quite perfunctory. Lithuania's ties with Latvia seriously deteriorated because of possible oil deposits in a disputed area of the Baltic Sea. Lithuania's relations with Estonia are correct, rather than warm. Trade among the three Baltic states remains modest.

The program of the new Lithuanian government emphasized the country's ties with Poland. Relations between the two countries are already excellent, and a joint peacekeeping battalion is expected to become operational this year. During Brazauskas's visit to Poland in September, President Aleksander Kwasniewski guaranteed Poland's support for Lithuania's membership in the Central European Free Trade Association, and both leaders expressed hope for rapid ratification of the bilateral free-trade agreement between their countries.

Lithuania continued to maintain good relations with Russia. Significant progress was made in negotiations concerning the delimitation of borders, and an agreement seems imminent. After the Conservatives' victory in the elections, Landsbergis went out of his way to emphasize his desire for good relations with Russia. On 7 November, Vagnorius met with Leonid Gorbenko, the new governor of Kaliningrad Oblast, and suggested further development of trade and economic relations.

ANXIETY OVER ECONOMY AND CRIME

Fear of crime and uncertainty concerning the economy weighed heavily on Lithuanians in 1996, contributing greatly to the protest vote that removed the LDDP from power. During the first 10 months of the year, 55,533 crimes were registered—a 10.5 percent increase over the same period in 1995. Crimes related to narcotics, burglaries, and robberies increased sharply, but the number of murders and rapes decreased. A relatively high percentage of cases has been solved—41.1 percent—during this period, but the random and brutal nature of the more gruesome acts of violence caused general anxiety.

Corruption also seems to be spreading. Like Slezevicius, Romasis Vaitekunas—

then interior minister—had also withdrawn his savings from the Lithuanian Joint-Stock Innovation Bank in time and had received much higher interest rates than normal. It was also learned that leading officials of the suspended bank were allowed to deposit most of their salaries into special accounts at 80 percent monthly interest rates (interest income is not taxed in Lithuania). Judges, police officers, and influential lawyers have been caught taking or giving bribes, while the prosecutor-general and his chief deputies awarded themselves bonuses several times larger than their annual salaries. Despite universal outrage, few public officials have been tried and even fewer convicted.

The economic situation in Lithuania stabilized in the course of the year. Gross domestic product grew during the years 1993–96, although at a modest 2 percent to 4 percent. Industrial sales increased by slightly less than 2 percent in 1996. Genuine strides were made in the fight against inflation—it was reduced from a rate of 35.7 percent in 1995 to 13.1 percent in 1996. The currency remained stable, and Lithuania managed to weather the banking crisis that loomed so menacingly at the beginning of the year. Not all the news was good. Lithuania's foreign debt continued to climb sharply along with the foreign-trade deficit, while foreign direct investment remained much smaller in per capita terms than Latvia's or Estonia's.

The majority of the population did not see many tangible benefits from favorable macroeconomic results, however. The standard of living remains substantially below the 1989 level. The benefits of economic transition were distributed unequally. Many savings had been wiped out, and large holes emerged in the social-security net. Health care was no longer free, while the pension system was tottering. Thus, it is not surprising that many Lithuanians were still dissatisfied with their lot and that political apathy had increased. The Conservatives benefited from the protest vote in 1996, but, if their efforts to reduce crime and increase welfare fail, they could easily become the next victims of unhappy voters in 2000.

Sidebar: NEW LITHUANIAN GOVERNMENT PRESENTS PROGRAM

by SAULIUS GIRNIUS

On 10 December the Lithuanian parliament (Seimas) voted 87 to 21 with 13 abstentions to approve the government program of Prime Minister-designate Gediminas Vagnorius. The vote also confirmed the appointment of the new

17–member cabinet. After the vote, Vagnorius and the ministers were formally sworn in as the eighth Lithuanian government since the re-establishment of independence.

The new government's program was quite optimistic in tone, placing particular emphasis on economic and law-and-order issues. The program predicted that the GDP will grow at an annual rate of 7 percent to 9 percent. Average salaries and pensions will grow more modestly. The average monthly wage should increase from the current level of 710 to 960 litai ($240) in 1998 and to 1,150 litai in 1999. It called for promoting business reform and combating the flourishing shadow economy. The tax system would be restructured by such measures as ending the taxation of interest on profits, and dividends redirected into investments. The value-added tax will be reduced from the current 18 percent to 15 percent, but the property tax increased from 1 percent to 1.5 percent. The program promises reduction of the state budget deficit and lower inflation to 7 percent by 2000. The conclusion of free-trade agreements with the other members of the Central European Free Trade Association and membership in the World Trade Organization will help encourage Lithuanian exports. The functions of the central bank would be increased, and the pegging of the litas to the dollar would be gradually removed by linking it with the German mark and later the new European currency.

The new Lithuanian government committed itself to aggressively fighting against corruption. All law-enforcement institutions, including the customs department, police, prosecutor's office, and tax-inspection office, would be subject to supervision by government watchdog agencies. The government program did not devote much space to foreign policy, in part because there was a general consensus that integration into the EU, NATO, and other structures of collective security is the main goal of Lithuanian foreign policy. The program did, however, specify that priority would also be given to ties with Poland. A new European Affairs Ministry was established to promote integration into the EU.

Latvia

Population:	2,485,400
Capital:	Riga (pop. 820,577)
Major cities:	Daugavpils (pop. 117,835), Liepaja (pop. 97,917), Jelgava (pop. 70,943)
Area:	64,610 sq. km.
Major ethnic groups:	Latvian 54.8%, Russian 32.8%, Belarusian 4.0%, Ukrainian 3.0%, Polish 2.2%, Lithuanian 1.3%, Jews 0.5%
Economy:	GDP growth: 2.5%
	Inflation rate: 13.1%
	Average monthly income: $179
	Unemployment rate: 7.2%

A YEAR OF CONSOLIDATION IN LATVIA

by SAULIUS GIRNIUS

1996 was relatively quiet for Latvia—a year of consolidation after the banking and political crises of 1995. The new coalition government proved more stable than many observers had expected, and the economy picked up. Latvia settled its long-standing dispute with Estonia over fishing rights, but the disagreement with Lithuania over the delimitation of their sea border intensified.

The Latvian government, approved by the Saeima on 21 December 1995, has been backed by a coalition of six parties covering the political gamut from the moderate left to the radical right. Andris Skele, a businessman with no political affiliation, became prime minister as a result of a compromise after both the right and left failed to win majority support for their candidates. Skele handled quite successfully the difficult task of keeping the diverse coalition together. At the end of 1996, not only was his government in place, but not a single party had left the ruling coalition. That is not to say that harmony prevailed. Disagreements were frequent, but Skele managed to resolve all of them.

On 6 May, the prime minister dismissed Alberts Kauls, chairman of the leftist Latvian Unity Party (LVP), from the post of agriculture minister because of disagreement over agrarian policy. The LVP, supported by former directors of Soviet industrial plants and collective farms, urged the government to grant substantial subsidies to Latvian agriculture and impose import tariffs on food products. International financial institutions, such as the International Monetary Fund (IMF) and the World Bank, objected to the protective measures, as did other coalition parties. After Kauls was fired, the LVP announced immediately that it was leaving the government. But after three weeks, it reconsidered and named Roberts Dilba as Kauls's replacement.

A more serious challenge was launched indirectly by Ziedonis Cevers, the ambitious leader of the Democratic Party Proprietor (DPS). Cevers, who believes he should be prime minister because his party received the most votes in the elections, has been openly expressing his dissatisfaction with Skele. He has criticized the prime minister for not consulting with the ruling-coalition parties. Cevers opposed the re-election of Guntis Ulmanis as president, partly because he had appointed Skele, and on 21 October he resigned his post as deputy prime minister. He apparently hoped that his party would follow his lead and leave the government. It did not.

Paradoxically, what appears to be the main source of the government's weakness is actually a stabilizing factor. The very breadth of the ruling coalition—originally holding 70 of the 100 seats in the parliament—ensures that even the withdrawal of the largest party would not bring down the government, for the remaining five would retain a majority in parliament. Two other factors also play a stabilizing role. First, ministries have been apportioned among the coalition partners, and the parties are free to manage them almost at will. Second, although Latvia's electorate is very volatile, a constant in the last two elections was that ruling parties have done very poorly. Thus, rather than risk losing ministries and mandates in parliament by calling early elections, the ruling-coalition partners have opted to gloss over their differences.

The policy of conciliation has its downside, particularly the avoidance of difficult and controversial decisions. As Skele's confidence grew, however, he began to take bolder steps, proposing the elimination of some ministries and supporting legislation that would allow foreigners to buy land in Latvia.

On 18 June, the Saeima re-elected Guntis Ulmanis as president of Latvia. Ulmanis received 53 out of 97 votes cast. His closest rival, Saeima Chairwoman Ilga Kreituse of the DPS, received 25 votes. During his first three-year term, Ulmanis displayed formidable political skills and a popular touch as he transformed the presidency from a primarily symbolic institution into one of genuine political influence.

SETTLEMENT WITH ESTONIA, TROUBLE WITH LITHUANIA

Latvia, like its Baltic neighbors, has made integration into Western economic and security structures its major foreign-policy objective, but the European Union and NATO have given few encouraging words regarding the country's early membership. In September, U.S. Defense Secretary William Perry explicitly stated that the Baltic countries are not yet ready for NATO. While welcoming U.S. efforts to allay Baltic security fears by announcing the Baltic Action Plan in late August and an enhanced Partnership for Peace plan in November, Latvian officials insisted that neither of the plans could be considered a substitute for full membership in the Atlantic alliance.

Although the EU has indicated that new members are unlikely to be admitted before 2002, Latvia continued its efforts to ensure that its laws are in accord with EU norms. The Saeima took an important step in that direction on 5 December, when it passed laws that increased the number of categories of individuals and firms that are permitted to buy land, although foreigners still have to seek the approval of local governments. Similarly, the Constitutional Court held its first session on 11 December and elected an acting chairman. However, cases will not be heard until 1997, because not all of the judges have been confirmed by the Saeima. The court will have seven judges, serving 10–year terms, and will have the right to annul legislation it finds unconstitutional.

Relations with Russia improved slightly during the course of the year. Moscow criticized Latvia's treatment of its Russian minority less vociferously, but it occasionally repeated the line about violations of the human rights of Russian speakers. In November, a Russian representative at the United Nations accused Latvia and Estonia of blatant violations of human rights, but the relevant UN committees and the UN General Assembly dismissed the charges. The right-wing For the Fatherland and Freedom Union's failure to secure enough signatures in January and February for its proposal to organize a referendum calling for a more restrictive citizenship law also improved interethnic relations.

Negotiations concerning the delimitation of borders with Russia have been deadlocked for some time. Latvia, like Estonia, has insisted that Russia recognize the validity of its 1920 peace treaty with Latvia and that that agreement be used as the starting point in negotiations. Russia categorically rejected the proposal because, under the treaty, the Abrene region—now part of Russia—is considered Latvian territory. Three rounds of negotiations ended in a stalemate. But after Estonia abandoned its demand for mentioning the validity of its 1920 treaty with Russia in November, Skele let it be understood that Latvia would do the same. That concession should eliminate the major stumbling block in the negotiations.

Latvia's ties with its northern neighbor—Estonia—improved, while its relations with its southern Baltic neighbor—Lithuania—worsened. On 12 July, Estonia and Latvia signed a treaty demarcating the sea border between the two countries, putting an end to a dispute that had re-emerged in March 1993. The fish-rich waters near the island of Ruhnu in the Gulf of Riga had been the main bone of contention.

Oil—rather than fishing rights—has fueled the Lithuanian-Latvian dispute. Although the sea border has not been demarcated, the Latvian government signed an offshore-oil-exploration agreement with the U.S.-based Amoco and the Swedish OPAB in October 1995. Efforts to resolve the dispute have been unsuccessful. On 24 October 1996, Latvia's parliament ratified the agreement, ignoring vehement Lithuanian protests and appeals. Negotiators have not even succeeded in determining an agenda for discussion. Lithuania insists that the border question must be resolved before negotiations on the potential sharing of the projected oil revenues commence, while Latvia believes that both issues must be treated simultaneously. The position of both countries hardened during the course of the year.

Their dispute, however, did not prevent Latvia and Lithuania from signing a free-trade agreement regarding agricultural products with Estonia in June, and it did not hinder their close cooperation in military matters. Latvia also continued to maintain its excellent ties with the Scandinavian countries and strengthened its relationship with the Central European states.

CRIME, THE ECONOMY, AND POPULATION DECLINE WORRY THE PUBLIC

Crime, the shrinking population, and the state of the economy were among the issues that held the attention of the public. Although the number of crimes committed in 1996 was lower than in 1995, anxiety about personal safety remained widespread. The population continued to decline. In the first nine months of 1996, deaths exceeded births by 10,694, and emigration surpassed immigration by 5,619 people. Since 1990, the population has shrunk almost 7 percent, from 2,668,000 to 2,485,400.

The economy improved at a moderate rate as it emerged from the shock of the 1995 banking crisis. During the first nine months, gross domestic product grew by 2.5 percent, a modest gain in light of the 1.6 percent drop in 1995. The budget deficit—90 million lati ($165 million) in 1995—was forecast to be reduced to 60 million lati in 1996, but the target deficit was subsequently lowered to 40 million lati at the IMF's urging. In December, the Saeima passed a balanced budget for 1997. The negative trend in foreign trade, manifested by the record trade deficit—$500 million in the first eight months—will surely figure high on the government's agenda this year.

Sidebar: U.S. ACTS TO SOOTH BALTIC CONCERNS OVER NATO ENLARGEMENT

by SAULIUS GIRNIUS

U.S. Defense Secretary William Perry wrote a letter to his Baltic counterparts, dated 3 October 1996, in which he assured them that they were "fully eligible" for NATO membership. The letter, received by Lithuanian Defense Minister Linas Linkevicius, was printed in the daily *Lietuvos rytas* on 9 October. Its purpose was clearly to reassure the Baltics that the United States had not intended to relegate them to a gray area of security between NATO and Russia.

In the letter, Perry expressed regret that the media had focused on the negative aspects of his comments and not stressed the U.S. pledge to help get the defense capability of the Baltic states up to NATO standards. To counter charges of possible Russian interference against Baltic NATO membership, the letter stated: "In particular I reject—and the U.S. rejects—any idea that the Baltic countries are excluded a priori or that any non-NATO country has a veto over their aspirations—whether de jure or de facto."

Perry's letter was prompted by the desire to quiet Baltic fears raised by his remarks at a press conference on 27 September in Bergen, Norway, that the Baltic states would not be among the first new members admitted to NATO. That comment was a great surprise, since American and other NATO officials had previously followed a common policy of saying that no decision had yet been made on when and to what countries invitations to join NATO would be issued. A conference was scheduled for Madrid in July 1997, at which it was expected that the first countries eligible for membership would be named. It was commonly accepted that Poland, Hungary, and the Czech Republic would be among the first new NATO members. Perry noted that the Baltic states were not ready for NATO membership since their military forces were unable to fulfill the responsibilities of Article Five, which include the ability to respond with force to an armed attack on any member country. Perry said that the Baltic states were working very hard to get that capability and that "the Nordic nations and the United States are working with them to help make that happen. That is why I want to emphasize it is not 'no'; it is 'not yet.' " But his remarks were overshadowed by the feeling that some unofficial agreement had been made with Russia's Defense Minister Igor Rodionov, giving Russia what amounted to veto power over new memberships. Defense ministers from the 16 NATO states had just concluded two days of talks with Rodionov, and Perry had made the optimistic comment that NATO and Russia will work so closely together that Moscow will no longer view NATO as a threat.

The reaction of the Baltic states to Perry's comment was immediate. The Baltic presidents issued a joint statement the next day (28 September) in which they promised to do whatever was necessary to meet NATO standards. They reaffirmed their determination to join NATO and said they would intensify diplomatic efforts to achieve that goal. Evidently feeling that too high standards were being set, Estonian Foreign Minister Siim Kallas even inquired, "What country besides the United States has the capability of defending NATO single-handedly?"

The Baltic leaders sought clarification of the meaning of Perry's remarks. Lithuanian Foreign Minister Povilas Gylys took a more determined step by even traveling to Washington on 8 October to hold talks with Deputy Secretary of State Strobe Talbott. The choice of Talbott was probably determined by his being the author of the Baltic Action Plan that is intended to determine U.S. assistance to the Baltic states. In the meeting Gylys reaffirmed that Lithuania wanted to retain the same status as other Central European countries in joining NATO and the European Union. Talbott responded by saying that Lithuania had earned the right to be part of the Western world and would not end up on the other side of a dividing line, as the U.S. would not allow Lithuania to become "the victim of any political games by major powers," as had occurred earlier. He said that the first wave of NATO memberships would be followed by a second and perhaps a third. Talbott's remarks and Perry's letters were intended to assuage Baltic fears that they will be abandoned.

Estonia

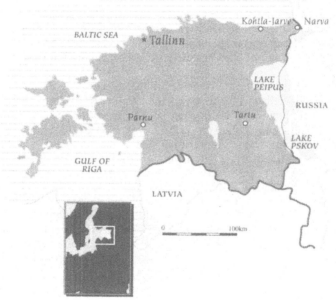

Population:	1,466,900
Capital:	Tallinn (pop. 434,763)
Major cities:	Tartu (pop. 104,907), Narva (pop. 77,770), Kohtla-Jarve (pop. 55,415)
Area:	45,000 sq. km.
Major ethnic groups:	Estonian 64.2%, Russian 28.7%, Ukrainian 2.7%, Belarusian 1.5%, Finnish 1%
Economy:	GDP growth: 3.5%
	Inflation rate: 14.8%
	Average monthly income: $246
	Unemployment rate: 5.6%

ESTONIA PROVES ITSELF

by JOHN B. TAHT

Although Estonia experienced some political instability in 1996, it also saw strong improvement in the economy and took steps toward a compromise on the Russian minority problem.

Estonia continued to make great progress in transforming its political and economic institutions. Arguably, it had made more progress than any other nation in Eastern Europe or the former Soviet Union since the collapse of the Soviet Union. Indeed, in 1996, the United States Agency for International Development decided it would no longer send aid to Estonia to promote democracy and a market economy. In a letter to mark the occasion, U.S. President Bill Clinton said that the agency's work in Estonia was done. Estonia was the first nation in Eastern Europe or the former Soviet Union to be so honored.

Economic success was not, of course, the only news of 1996. Political instability, a slight improvement in Estonia's acrimonious relations with Russia, and various social strides and struggles also made the headlines.

POLITICAL SQUABBLING

While 1995 had been characterized by frequent political scandals, most notably a wiretapping incident that brought down the government, 1996 was less tumultuous. Still, with the re-election of President Lennart Meri in September and the breakup of the ruling coalition in late November, it was eventful. As in 1992, Meri's challenger in the 1996 presidential election was Arnold Ruutel, deputy speaker of the parliament. In August, the first round of elections failed to produce a candidate with the required minimum of 68 votes. The decision then fell to the electoral college, which consists of members of parliament and various local politicians. Five candidates took part in the election, including Ruutel, but they were no match for Meri, who won easily in the second round.

Though generally quite popular, Meri was the target of numerous attacks during the campaign. Politicians and journalists alleged that Meri had collaborated with the KGB. Clearly, however, the issue did not harm Meri's re-election bid.

Then, in late November, the government collapsed. The ruling coalition consisted of a brittle alliance between Prime Minister Tiit Vahi's Coalition Party and Rural Union (KMU)—which includes the Coalition Party, which Vahi heads, and several small rural parties—and the Reform Party, led by Foreign Minister Siim Kallas. Vahi's signing of a cooperation agreement with Center Party Chairman Edgar Savisaar precipitated the collapse. As the Center Party had had an earlier alliance with Vahi, he was probably only trying to revive that connection. But the Reform Party had been told nothing of the agreement. Although neither Savisaar nor Vahi had suggested that the Center Party join the ruling coalition, the Reform Party demanded that Vahi denounce the agreement. Vahi refused to do so, and on 20 November, six Reform Party ministers resigned. The situation is even more complicated since Vahi also signed an agreement with the Progress Party, which had earlier split from the Center Party and refused to cooperate with it again.

Instead of forging an alliance with Savisaar and the Center Party, Vahi decided to form a minority government. Estonia's ambassador to the United States, Toomas Hendrik Ilves, became the new foreign minister.

SOCIAL STRIDES

The crime rate in Estonia, which had skyrocketed in 1995, decreased in 1996. The first eight months of 1996 saw an 11 percent decrease in the overall crime rate compared with the same period the previous year. The number of violent crimes decreased by 20 percent during that period.

Considerable efforts were made to improve the lives of the Russian minority in Estonia. In January, the government decided to grant alien passports to the 300,000 or so Estonian residents who carried Soviet passports, which were to expire on 12 July. But there was hardly an onslaught of applicants. So few had applied by the beginning of July that Vahi had to extend the validity of the old passports until many eligible applicants had received new ones.

The Estonian government had long been unwilling to grant residence permits to retired Soviet officers and their families. But on 10 December, the government decided to issue alien residence permits to approximately 10,000 ex-Red Army personnel. There are about 20,000 such people in Estonia, many of whom have adopted Russian citizenship. The practice of denying residence permits to retired officers is now seen as discriminatory. In another effort to improve the lot of the Russian minority, the parliament amended the local election law. In December, a fact-finding mission representing the Russian Foreign Ministry visited Estonia and found that Russians there weren't being treated as badly as was previously thought.

BORDERS AND FISH

Estonia's foreign-policy successes included a free-trade agreement with Ukraine, a free-trade agreement on agricultural goods with the other Baltic states, and a sea-border agreement with Latvia. That last, a long-standing dispute, concerned fishing rights in the Gulf of Riga. Estonia wished to maintain fishing rights in the herring-rich waters around Ruhnu Island, which belongs to Estonia. But the island is located in the Gulf of Riga, and Latvia considers the gulf to be exclusively its own. The dispute was still simmering in early May when Estonian border patrols forced five Latvian trawlers out of a fishing area in the Gulf of Riga, enraging Latvian officials. Shortly thereafter, the president of the European Parliament, Klaus Haensch, warned the two governments that the dispute could endanger their admission to the European Union. Within days, the dispute was settled, and on 22 August, both countries' parliaments unanimously ratified the agreement. Far from hailing the agreement as a swift end to diplomatic gridlock, however, Estonian and Latvian fisherman expressed disappointment. Estonia, especially, seemed concerned that too many kilometers of sea around Ruhnu Island had been conceded. But clearly Haensch's threat had created an environment in which an agreement, however flawed, had to be reached without delay.

Relations with Russia remained strained throughout the year, although the border dispute, long the most visible sign of discord between Russia and Estonia, came close to resolution. On 5 November, the two foreign ministers approved a draft border agreement that avoided the main issue of contention. Estonia had been insisting that Russia recognize the Tartu Peace Treaty of 1920—in which Russia had agreed never again to violate Estonia's borders— before any border agreement could be signed. Meri had called the Tartu Treaty a sort of "birth certificate" for Estonia. Russia alleges that the treaty never was violated because, it claims, Estonia willingly joined the Soviet Union. But the November agreement was of a technical nature and dealt only with the border between the two countries, a matter about which there were few disagreements.

The quest to join NATO remains Estonia's most important foreign-policy objective. But it seems unlikely that the country will be admitted in the first wave of NATO expansion. U.S. Defense Secretary William Perry said as much in late September. He said the Baltic states still lacked minimum defensive capability and that they were not sufficiently militarily compatible with other members of the alliance. He did say, however, that the Baltics were working hard to achieve those aims and that they might be admitted at a later date.

On the other hand, Estonia will most likely become a full member of the European Union. It is that goal, coupled with its dream of joining NATO, that dominated Estonia's foreign policy in 1996. When it appeared that the sea-border dispute with Latvia might endanger membership in the EU, a solution was found within days. Many Estonian politicians also attribute the draft border agreement with Russia to a desire to appease the EU and to show NATO countries that Estonia can have neighborly relations with Russia.

Relations with Russia will probably improve in 1997 with the signing of a border agreement. The alarmingly low birth rate among Estonians makes the integration of Russians into Estonian society all the more imperative. Estonia's remarkable economic success will also continue, although many fear the consequences of an excessively liberal and unfettered market economy. Undeniably those policies have helped Estonia to prosper like no other erstwhile state-run economy, but social ills have also emerged, especially in rural areas, in the struggle to become the ideal market economy.

Sidebar: **MERI RE-ELECTED ESTONIA'S PRESIDENT**
by SAULIUS GIRNIUS

The Estonian electoral college on 20 September re-elected incumbent president Lennart Meri in the second round. Meri received 196 votes, parliament deputy speaker and Chairman of the Country People's Party Arnold Ruutel 126 votes, with 44 abstentions and six invalid ballots.

Estonia has a complicated presidential election system. The president is elected indirectly. He can either obtain a two-thirds majority (68 votes) in the 101–member parliament or—when that is unsuccessful—gain a majority of votes cast by a special electoral college. The college consists of 374 persons, the 101 parliament deputies and 273 representatives of local councils. The parliament holds three ballots and the electoral college two, with the last ballot in both cases being reduced to the two candidates receiving the most votes in the previous ballot.

The presidential contest between Meri and Ruutel had become a tradition. In 1992 although Ruutel had outpolled Meri in the popular elections (42.7% to 28.8%), the parliament elected Meri president by a vote of 59 to 31. This year Meri and Ruutel were also the only candidates in three rounds of elections in the parliament on 26 and 27 August. Meri clearly defeated Ruutel in these elections, obtaining 45, 49, and 52 votes to Ruutel's 34, 34, and 32, respectively, but failed to gain the needed 68 votes.

According to the Estonian Constitution adopted on 28 June 1992, Estonia's president has very limited powers and is intended to be primarily only a representative head in international relations. Meri, however, was not content with this and took a more active role, most notably by signing an agreement with Russian President Boris Yeltsin in June 1993 for the withdrawal of Russian troops from Estonia without getting prior approval of the government or parliament. This agreement was criticized for allowing too many Russian military retirees to remain in Estonia. Many parliament deputies also thought that Meri had paid too little attention to the parliament, appearing at its sessions only four times in four years.

Another matter that was also brought up in the days before the vote was the claim heard already in 1992, but never satisfactorily settled that Meri had cooperated with the KGB. The accusers charge that Meri, the son of a diplomat exiled to Siberia, could only have been allowed to study and to travel abroad with the KGB's approval. Meri responded to these charges on 8 September on Estonian television by reading the text of the oath of conscience he took in 1992 and 1996 in which he denied collaborating with any organizations that persecuted people.

Estonian parliament deputies Villu Muuripeal of the Country People's Party and independent Eldur Parder, and the editor of the *Kultuur ja Elu* cultural magazine, Juri Estam, however, filed an application on 17 September to the

Tallinn City Court asking that the issue of Lennart Meri's past ties with KGB be clarified. Estam alleged that Meri actively cooperated with VEKSA, the Society for Cultural Relations with Estonians Abroad, that was directly subordinate to the KGB. BNS revealed the next day that Center Party Chairman Edgar Savisaar had sent a letter to Meri on 16 September suggesting that he should withdraw his presidential candidacy because of his past ties with KGB. Savisaar also allegedly reminded Meri that he never fulfilled his promise in 1992 to organize an international investigation of allegations against him through Council of Europe institutions. The Tallinn court on 19 August turned down the application saying that it did not have the authority to handle the case.

The electoral system's requirement to have a two-thirds parliamentary majority for president seems unnecessarily difficult. In Estonia, political opinion is too varied and personal ambitions too great to achieve such a great consensus. While the first round showed that Meri did not have the support of the majority of the delegates, he was able to gain enough support in the second round. In fact, some delegates may have even voted for him simply to end an electoral process that had gone on too long and created unfavorable publicity for their country. The next presidential elections will be in five years and there is a good possibility that the presidential electoral system will be changed before then.

Belarus

Population:	10,279,000
Capital:	Minsk (pop. 1,693,000)
Major cities:	Homel (pop. 383,000), Vitsebsk (pop. 297,000),
	Mahileu (pop. 290,000)
Area:	207,600 sq. km.
Major ethnic groups:	Belarusian 77.9%, Russian 13.2%, Polish 4.1%,
	Ukrainian 2.9%, other 1.9%
Economy:	GDP growth: 3.0%
	Inflation rate: 39%
	Average monthly income: $88
	Unemployment rate: 4.0%

BELARUS CHOOSES DICTATORSHIP
by USTINA MARKUS

After being paid scant notice by the international community in its first four years of independence, Belarus stepped into the limelight in 1996. Unfortunately, most of the attention it drew was negative. Two and a half years after Belarusians adopted a new, post-Soviet era constitution, they replaced it in a national referendum. The initiative for a new constitution came from President Alyaksandr Lukashenka, who felt he did not have sufficient powers under the 1994 constitution. Since coming to office, Lukashenka had been at odds with parliament over his economic and domestic policies. Starting in 1995, parliament began bringing his decrees to the Constitutional Court for review; 17 of them were declared unconstitutional. In addition, Lukashenka was at odds with parliament over some of his official appointments. In February, parliament refused to approve his choice for the head of the National Bank of Belarus, Tamara Vinnikau. Parliament had also been in dispute with the president since 1995 over his removal of the editor-in-chief of the parliamentary newspaper *Narodnaya hazeta*. In 1996, Lukashenka reorganized the newspaper into a joint-stock company, causing more conflict with the legislature.

The disputes over policy and parliament's constant criticism led Lukashenka to conclude that he could not rule under the 1994 constitution and a new basic law emasculating the legislature would have to be adopted. In July, he announced his intention to hold a national referendum to change the constitution. Under the 1994 constitution, the president had the right to call a referendum and parliament was legally obliged to set a date for it. Rather than holding the plebiscite on 7 November (the day of the Bolshevik anniversary) as Lukashenka wanted, parliament decided it would be held on 24 November to coincide with parliamentary by-elections. At the same time, parliament decided to counter the president by placing its own questions on the referendum, including a version of an amended constitution that would emasculate the presidency.

REFERENDUM CONTROVERSY

Over the following months, the charges and countercharges between the president and legislature reached a new low. One result of Lukashenka's attacks against parliament was an unprecedented alliance against the president between a number of political parties across the entire political spectrum, ranging from nationalists to hard-line communists. Deputies began to discuss initiating impeachment proceedings against Lukashenka.

The political stakes were high, and Lukashenka did everything he could to ensure passage of his referendum. He announced bonuses for students, pensioners, veterans, and other voters. He banned funding for the by-elections. Two weeks before the referendum was to take place, he fired the chairman of the Central Electoral Commission, Viktar Hanchar. Lukashenka set up his own regional commissions to organize and oversee the referendum, ignoring the electoral commission.

The president also used the state-controlled media to promote his referendum and denounce parliament. The head of state radio and television, Hryhor Kisel, was even fined for failing to publicize parliament's activities. Kisel also had individual cases filed against him, including one by Parliament Speaker Syamyon Sharetsky, for denying him airtime. Under the law, the speaker should have had unlimited access to state media. The bias in state-television reporting was so obvious that parliament eventually voted to bar it from covering its sessions.

Parliament pinned its hopes of blocking the referendum on the Constitutional Court. Under the 1994 constitution, a referendum could be held on amending the basic law, but not on replacing the constitution with a new one. On 4 November, the court ruled that the two competing draft constitutions were effectively new constitutions, and not just amendments. Therefore, the court declared, the results would not be legally binding. Lukashenka immediately denounced the court's ruling. Two days later, he issued a decree making the results of the referendum legally binding. Prime Minister Mikhail Chyhir resigned in protest.

The referendum conflict raised fears of political instability. Russia was particularly concerned and tried to mediate. Russian Prime Minister Viktor Chernomyrdin and other Russian officials flew to Minsk on 22 November and brokered an 11th-hour compromise. The deal called for Lukashenka to repeal his decree making the constitutional referendum binding and for parliament to withdraw its request to the Constitutional Court to start impeachment proceedings against the president. The compromise collapsed the next day because parliament did not ratify the agreement. Lukashenka blamed parliament for failing to ratify the accord, while Sharetsky charged Lukashenka with sabotaging the vote in the legislature so that the referendum would proceed.

On 24 November, 84.1 percent of the Belarusian electorate turned out to vote on the referendum and gave Lukashenka a sweeping victory on every question. Lukashenka's new constitution passed with 70.5 percent in favor. Only 7.9 percent backed parliament's draft constitution. In addition, voters chose to change the national holiday from 17 July, when the republic declared independence, to 3 July, when the Red Army liberated Minsk from the Germans. They did not support the free sale and purchase of land, effectively ruling out private land ownership in the country. They did, however, favor the death penalty, which will probably prevent Belarus from being accepted into the Council of Europe. Voters also rejected electing local administrations by direct popular vote and having all bodies of state power funded directly from the budget.

Hanchar and other opponents of the president said the results were faked.

Several independent observers claimed there were violations in voting procedures, and even the new acting head of the electoral commission appointed by Lukashenka, Lidziya Yarmoshyna, admitted there had been some irregularities. In addition, there were virtually no international observers. The United States, European Union, and the Organization for Security and Cooperation in Europe (OSCE) denounced the referendum, and Lukashenka was snubbed at an OSCE summit in Lisbon that took place in December, just days after the referendum.

Critics of the referendum did not succeed in exerting any influence over its consequences. Deputies loyal to the president dissolved the old legislature after the referendum results were announced and regrouped as the lower house of a new bicameral parliament. The old parliament continued to meet under Sharetsky and refused to recognize the authority of the new legislature, but it had no impact on the governing of the country. In addition, five of the 11 Constitutional Court justices, including Chief Justice Valeryi Tsikhinya, resigned, opening the way for Lukashenka to appoint his own people to the court.

INTEGRATION WITH RUSSIA

On New Year's Day 1996, Lukashenka announced that he had spoken with Russian President Boris Yeltsin over the phone and the Russian president had agreed to a "zero option" on mutual debts. The news seemed surprising since most of the money Belarus owed Russia was owed to the Gazprom company, and the monopoly had been making it plain that it was not interested in political deals as payment for gas supplies. In February, Lukashenka visited Russia, and the two Slavic presidents signed a number of agreements, including the "zero option," canceling Belarus's $1.27 billion debt to Russia for gas and credits in exchange for Belarus's canceling Russia's $914 million debt for ecological damage caused by Russian troops in Belarus, troop-stationing costs, and compensation for valuable materials in nuclear weapons removed from Belarus. Later in the year, the Russian oil company Lukoil participated in several projects in Belarus in which it was the majority shareholder, indicating that Minsk had signed away shares in its oil refineries and other assets to Russian energy suppliers when it signed the "zero option."

As the Russian presidential-election day neared, the integration process picked up speed. Lukashenka made every effort to prevent the opportunity from being derailed. On 29 March, the leaders of Kazakstan, Kyrgyzstan, Russia, and Belarus met in Moscow and signed an agreement on furthering economic and humanitarian integration within the context of the CIS—effectively, a customs union. The agreement contained loose wording, and its signing was interpreted as having been prompted by short-term political considerations rather than a real intention to integrate. A few days later, on 2 April, Yeltsin signed an even more comprehensive agreement on integration with Belarus, called the Treaty on the Formation of the Community. His commitment to it, however, was doubtful. Many felt the signing was just a publicity stunt to woo the conservative Russian electorate during the presidential-election campaign.

While Lukashenka was making sure that an integration agreement was signed, nationalist forces in Belarus began to stir. On 24 March, 40,000 people demonstrated in Minsk. The demonstration was largely peaceful, although toward the end a few protesters were reportedly beaten by security troops. Trying to quash any further protests, Lukashenka issued an arrest warrant for the leader of the nationalist opposition Belarusian Popular Front, Zyanon Paznyak, and for the party's spokesman, Syarhei Naumchyk. The two went into hiding and later fled the country. Eventually, they made their way to the United States, where they applied for political asylum in July. In a blow to Lukashenka, Paznyak and Naumchyk became the first individuals from any of the western republics of the USSR to be granted political asylum because of the regime in their home country.

The integration treaty sparked considerable controversy. Proponents hailed it as the first step toward uniting Russia and Belarus. Opponents in both countries denounced it as detrimental to their country's interests. On the day it was signed, another demonstration, this time of 30,000 people, was staged in Minsk in protest. Yet despite the strong emotions the accord evoked, the document itself was little more than a declaration of intent on the part of Russia and Belarus to integrate. The exact nature of integration was unclear, as there were a number of contradictions in the text. In addition, the treaty did not provide the Supreme Council set up to implement the process with any binding powers. Decisions were to be made on the basis of unanimity. Given the conflicting interests of Russia and Belarus on so many major issues, the council would only be able to reach agreement over the most mundane matters. In addition, as the chairmanship of the Supreme Council was to be rotated between Russia and Belarus every two years, it was difficult to imagine that Moscow had agreed to allow the chairman any overriding power.

Problems with implementing the accord were soon apparent. A month after Yeltsin's re-election, Lukashenka began heaping criticism on Russia for not implementing the customs-union agreement and for failing to cancel the energy debt. By October, six months after the treaty was signed, Chernomyrdin complained that the community treaty was nothing more than ink on paper.

FOREIGN RELATIONS

While Lukashenka focused his foreign-policy efforts on integration with Russia, relations with other countries suffered. The spring protest demonstrations and Paznyak's and Naumchyk's applications for political asylum in the United States led the U.S. State Department to express concern over the human-rights situation in Belarus. Further concern arose over the mass arrests that followed a rally on the 10th anniversary of the Chornobyl nuclear accident. In addition, relations with Ukraine became strained because seven Ukrainians were among those arrested. Despite Kyiv's attempts to mediate and secure the release of the Ukrainians, the seven were sentenced to prison terms ranging from one year to two and a half years.

Relations with Poland also suffered following the May arrest of four leading members of Poland's Solidarity union for allegedly organizing an illegal gathering outside of Minsk. The four were deported several hours after their arrest, and

Solidarity leader Marian Krzaklewski was ordered to stand trial for interfering in Belarus's internal affairs.

By the end of the year, the European parliament had condemned Lukashenka's regime and urged a suspension of all EU aid to Belarus except for projects promoting democracy and freedom of the press. In addition, the political committee of the parliamentary assembly of the Council of Europe recommended that Belarus's observer status in the organization be suspended. International financial institutions were unwilling to release credits to Belarus because of its poor track record in implementing market reforms.

SECURITY ISSUES

At the end of November, the last nuclear warheads were removed from Belarus to Russia. Of the republics that had been left with nuclear weapons when the USSR broke up, Belarus was the last to become nuclear-free (with the exception of Russia).

At a public banquet in November, just before the referendum, Lukashenka unceremoniously fired Defense Minister Leanid Maltseu for drunkenness. There were rumors that Maltseu had in fact been doped and his drunken behavior used as an excuse for his dismissal. First Deputy Defense Minister Alyaksandr Chumakau was named acting Defense Minister.

Sidebar: BELARUSIAN OPPOSITION LEADERS APPLY FOR ASYLUM
by USTINA MARKUS

On 30 July the leader of the Belarusian Popular Front (BPF) Zyanon Paznyak, and BPF spokesman Syarhei Naumchyk, applied for political asylum in the United States. The two had been in exile since March when they learned that President Alyaksandr Lukashenka had issued a warrant for their arrest for their part in organizing demonstrations against the president and his policies. Although Paznyak and Naumchyk were the most prominent Belarusians to date asking for asylum, there have been other cases of journalists and individuals involved in politics fleeing the country.

In the latter part of 1994 and first half of 1995, the nationalist BPF had been the most active opposition to the president against his plans for integration with Russia and other policies. In April 1995, eighteen opposition deputies, including Paznyak, staged a hunger strike in parliament in a last-ditch effort to derail Lukashenka's plans to hold a referendum on closer integration with Russia. Lukashenka had security troops storm the parliament building and forcibly remove the deputies that same night. Several were beaten during the operation. Paznyak, who had been a rival for the presidency against Lukashenka, viewed the use of troops against the non-violent protest by people's deputies as a new low in Lukashenka's regime. In August he set a new precedent in his disrespect for the legislature when he arrested deputy Syarhei Antonchyk for his role in organizing a strike of transport workers. Under the constitution, deputies are immune from arrest. Lukashenka circumvented this obstacle by issuing a decree lifting deputies' immunity.

When a new parliament was elected after four rounds of voting in December 1995, neither Paznyak, nor Naumchyk, nor a single BPF member succeeded in winning a seat. Nonetheless, a new opposition, united less by nationalist principles than by their resistance to Lukashenka's increasingly dictatorial rule, was represented in the new legislature. Despite its less nationalistic platform, this opposition was dedicated to maintaining the country's sovereignty.

Starting on 24 March 1996, a series of political demonstrations against Lukashenka's policies were staged. Two of the demonstrations ended in mass arrests of demonstrators. Most detainees were released after serving short sentences of 1–2 weeks. Two prominent leaders of the BPF, Yuriy Khadyka and Vyacheslau Siuchyk, were held on the more serious charges or organizing, rather than just participating in, the demonstrations. They faced up to three years in prison. The two staged a hunger strike which lasted over two weeks. They were released and received probationary sentences after their health was seriously endangered.

The protest rallies drew international attention to the opposition to Lukashenka, and the president resorted to increasingly hard-line tactics in breaking it up. Not only were participants arrested, journalists had camera equipment confiscated and were physically intimidated by security troops. This obstruction of the press was not limited to domestic media. Journalists from Russia, Poland, and the West were subject to the same treatment. The most serious case of straightforward intimidation of the media was that of RFE/RL correspondent Yuriy Drakokhurst. While he was out of town, three men broke into his apartment and beat his wife.

After leaving Belarus in March, Paznyak and Naumchyk made their way from Ukraine, to the Czech Republic, to Poland, and Britain, before arriving in the United States on 7 July, where they were eventually granted asylum. Given Lukashenka's disregard of the law, his hostility toward any opposition, and the intimidation those who have criticized his regime have had to face, there was good reason for Paznyak and Naumchyk to fear for their safety. The security troops in Belarus now number over 120,000 (outnumbering the 70,000 strong regular armed forces). Since the break-up of the Soviet Union, most western states have come to regard at least the western republics of the former USSR as democracies, so that people wishing to leave those countries have a slim chance of seeking political asylum in the West. Lukashenka may have changed that for Belarus.

Sidebar: CENSORSHIP IN BELARUS

by USTINA MARKUS

Under President Alyaksandr Lukashenka's rule, Belarus has distinguished itself as the least democratic European country when it comes to the freedom of the press. On 2 May the Belarusian Association of Journalists issued a statement condemning Belarusian authorities for their intimidation of journalists. Polish, Russian, and western journalists lodged similar complaints. These were made in connection with the 26 April and 1 May demonstrations during which journalists had equipment confiscated by security forces, and some were even jailed. As the journalists were merely reporting on events, and not inciting riots, their treatment would be considered harsh under West European (even Russian and Ukrainian) standards.

This strong-arm policy against the press began within a few months of Lukashenka's election as president. In December 1994 papers appeared with big blank spots where articles on a report charging corruption in the president's administration were slated to appear. In January 1995 a new law on the press and other media was passed. It failed to lay out legal protections for journalists and instead increased state control over publications by reducing the circulation of periodicals which require official registration from 1,000 to 100, and providing a variety of reasons for which a periodical could be suspended. In addition, several state bodies were appointed to supervise the media. These include: the Permanent Committee of the Supreme Council on Freedom of Speech, Mass Media, and Human Rights; the Ministry of Culture and Press; the Department of Social and Political Information of the Presidential Administration; and the National State Television and Radio Company.

In April 1995 the Cabinet of Ministers passed a decree "On Newspapers and Magazines Founded and Co-founded by the Cabinet of Ministers." Essentially the decree placed the major papers *Respublika, Belaruskaya niva, Znamya yunosti,* and *Zvyazda* under its jurisdiction. Soon after, Lukashenka removed the chief editors of *Znamya yunosti* and *Respublika.* During the 1995 parliamentary elections candidates were allotted such a pittance for their campaigns (600,000 Belarusian rubles or $50) that almost no mention of candidates, parties, and their campaigns appeared in the national press. Only local papers carried such information.

Having gained control of the state media, Lukashenka turned his attention to the independent press. In October 1995, the independent newspapers *Beloruskaya delovaya gazeta*, *Imya*, and *Narodnaya volya* were ordered closed by the president's office, and the main publishing house was forbidden from printing the papers. Two of the papers began printing in Lithuania. Lukashenka retaliated by forbidding the Belarusian postal service from delivering newspapers not printed in Belarus, and ordering border guards to confiscate printed material being brought in by vehicles from neighboring states. His then spokesman, Uladzimir Zamyatalin, also criticized the Russian press for ridiculing the Belarusian president and threatened to ban *Komsomolskaya pravda* and other Russian papers from being sold in Belarus if they continued to deride Lukashenka.

The censorship policies continued into 1996. Just before the signing of the controversial 2 April agreement on the formation of a community between Russia and Belarus, Lukashenka fired the new editor-in-chief of *Narodnaya hazeta*, ostensibly for allowing articles critical of the agreement to appear in the paper. Following the 26 April demonstrations and arrests, state television and radio banned journalists from broadcasting the events live. Programming was also to be strictly regimented until 9 May, and Radio 2 was forbidden from recalling the 26 April events, except to criticize them. Indeed, the Belarusian television correspondent reporting on the events referred to protesters as "drunken students, idle pensioners, and other loafers." He went on to say they behaved like "wild animals" who had forgotten they were human beings.

Censorship of state media is also evident by what is not reported. For example, the Constitutional Court decision finding several decrees issued by Lukashenka in late 1995 unconstitutional was not mentioned by Belarusian radio or television. The decrees in question demanded that all state structures comply with the president's decrees, including decrees found unconstitutional by the court. Since spring 1995 Lukashenka had been at odds with the court and repeatedly said he would like to see it disbanded. As the Belarusian president was not been able to bring the Russian press under his control, however, Russian agencies reported on the Constitutional Court's rulings, and on the April and May demonstrations.

Document: DEFENDING THE "SACRED CAUSE" OF RUSSO-BELARUSIAN INTEGRATION

Belarusian President Alyaksandr Lukashenka addressed the Russian State Duma on 13 November 1996. Although 70 deputies walked out of the hall in protest, the Communist- and nationalist-dominated audience that remained, repeatedly interrupted Lukashenka's speech with enthusiastic applause. The following excerpts from Lukashenka's lengthy address were published by Sovetskaya Rossiya *the following day.*

The Russian Federation President's illness has unfortunately left me practically alone at this time to face the opponents of Belarusian-Russian integration. You remember the heated polemics and struggle that raged in Belarus in 1994–1995 over questions of rapprochement between Belarus and Russia. That was the first time I had occasion to appeal to the people, and they decided that Belarusian-Russian integration should go ahead. [Since then] the forces that were removed from power have stepped up their activity in the struggle against the Belarusian president's domestic and foreign policy. Therefore, in order to save the present Belarusian leadership's course, which centers on the unification of the two Slav peoples, I have been forced once again to appeal to the Belarusian people.

In signing the Treaty on the Union of Belarus and Russia in April, the president of the fraternal state and I wanted to set an example to others and to take the path of rapprochement between our peoples. Esteemed friends, let us not be embarrassed and make excuses for our peoples' desire to live together. When people say to me that, by changing its attitude toward Russia, Belarus could gain points in the West, I always reply that you cannot build happiness on the betrayal of your brothers.

We were and remain a country with highly productive agriculture and superb industry, built not by Belarusians alone, but by Belarusians, Russians, and the other peoples of a once-great country. Let us find our way together out of the crisis in which we find ourselves through no fault of our own. We already have some good examples of cooperation. Together with the Gazprom Russian Joint-Stock Company, we are creating an efficient system for supplying natural gas to consumers not only in Belarus but throughout the western part of the former Soviet Union.

We must together seek an appropriate response [to NATO expansion], lest the withdrawal of nuclear weapons from Belarus's territory coincide with the siting of nuclear missiles and munitions on the territory of the new NATO members. Certain Russian politicians and officials clearly underestimate the importance of Belarus as a strategic partner. However, today Belarus fully ensures Russia's security to the west. Incidentally, it costs our state around $300 million a year to maintain the air defense system and the border and customs controls to Russia's west. For your information, in a year, according to current calculations, we owe Russia a little more than $100 million.

Russian TV channels are today the main mouthpiece of the [Belarusian] anti-presidential opposition. I know of no other instances in the world in which a state's mass media are waging information warfare against their closest ally and strategic partner. I think it is in the interests of both Russia and our bilateral relations for the situation in Belarus to be covered objectively. We are in favor of press freedom, but this freedom must not be exploited to spread disinformation and slander. The Russian Public Television channel—it acts unpardonably—appointed as its representative a person of nationalist inclinations. While NTV has gone the whole way: it appointed as its journalist not a citizen of Belarus, not a citizen of Russia, but a citizen of—where do you think?—Israel.

There is no alternative to Belarusian-Russian integration. Our peoples have made this choice. And we politicians must clearly realize that Belarus and Russia must travel the same road today, tomorrow, and forever. We must act vigorously and assertively day after day in the name of the sacred cause of unity, strengthening the [Russo-Belarusian] Community and creating the conditions for a decent life for our people.

What should we do next? We must impart dynamism to our community; otherwise we will ruin a great idea in general and be shamed before the whole world. After all, with the [signing of the integration treaty] relayed to the whole world, we covered it up, and we stopped. We must move forward!

Ukraine

Population:	50,853,000
Capital:	Kyiv (pop. 2.5 million)
Major cities:	Kharkiv (pop. 1.5 million), Odesa (pop. 1.1 million), Dnipropetrovsk (pop. 1.1 million)
Area:	603,700 sq. km.
Major ethnic groups:	Ukrainian 72.7%, Russian 22.1%, Jewish 0.9%, Belarusian 0.9%, Moldovan 0.6%, Bulgarian 0.5%, Polish 0.4%
Economy:	GDP growth: –10%
	Inflation rate: 40%
	Average monthly income: $80
	Unemployment rate: 1.5%

UKRAINE'S CONTINUING EVOLUTION

by CHRYSTYNA LAPYCHAK *and* USTINA MARKUS

Although Ukrainian statehood was further consolidated over the course of 1996, the country's leaders had a mixed record in moving Ukraine toward democracy and free-market reforms.

The adoption of a new constitution by means of a political compromise and the successful introduction of a new permanent currency, the hryvnya, were Ukraine's most obvious accomplishments of the year. There was also progress in the development of an independent judiciary with the long-delayed formation of the country's first Constitutional Court. The same can be said for the leadership's success in maintaining fiscal discipline and substantially curbing inflation by the end of the year.

While the government of Pavlo Lazarenko was more willing than that of his deposed predecessor, Yevhen Marchuk, to take some unpopular steps, it postponed some of the most painful but crucial measures to restructure the economy. Despite the adoption of the new constitution, the power struggle among the president, the prime minister, and the legislature continued and even acquired a systemic character. The battle continues over interpretation of the new basic law and the many bills that still require adoption before it can be fully implemented. The democratic principles and human- and civil-rights guarantees within the new constitution, as well as the five-year track record of resolving political differences through compromise, provide grounds for optimism. However, Ukraine still has far to go in developing a genuine European democracy. Ukrainian leaders have retained a habit of using law enforcement and the justice system against political opponents and have stepped up intimidation of critics in the media.

The year also featured a troubling rise in tensions among the powerful regional and sectoral elites in Ukraine. The rivalry between the two most influential clans, in Donetsk and Dnipropetrovsk, took a higher profile and grew bloodier—even posing a possible threat to the country's stability. The attempted assassination in July of Prime Minister Lazarenko, who comes from Dnipropetrovsk, as well as the sensational murder of a wealthy magnate and lawmaker from Donetsk in November, underscored not only the power of the competing groups but the powerlessness of the state against the rising tide of crime and corruption.

A NEW CONSTITUTION

Ukraine was the last of the former Soviet republics to adopt a new constitution after years of political wrangling. At the end of a 23–hour, all-night session on 28 June, the Ukrainian legislature adopted a compromise version of the new constitution, which in essence preserved much of the status quo that had existed since independence.

Following Kuchma's election in July 1994, the president found himself at odds with parliament over the extent of his authority, and began pressing for a constitution which would delineate the legislature's powers and create a strong executive. After almost a year of wrangling, Kuchma threatened to hold a referendum on the issue in May 1995. As opinion polls indicated that the public held more confidence in the president than in the parliament, the legislature backed down and reached a "Constitutional Agreement" in June, giving Kuchma some extraordinary powers until a new constitution could be adopted. In October 1995 a Constitutional Committee was set up to draft a new constitution, and in March it presented its draft to the parliament.

Parliament approved the document in its first reading that month, and sent it back to the committee to incorporate its amendments. The strongest opposition to the document came from communists and left-wingers who hold some 170 seats in the 450 seat legislature. They were opposed to the guarantees on the right to private property, a strong presidency, and creating a bicameral legislature.

As it was generally believed that no constitution would be able to garner a two-thirds majority in parliament (301 out of 450 votes) to be adopted, alternative adoption methods were proposed. These included passage by a simple majority and holding a popular referendum over the document. Leftist deputies' rejection of articles concerning language, national symbols, and private property led Kuchma to deliver an ultimatum on 26 June. He announced that a national referendum would be held on 25 September on the original draft approved in March, without regard for any of the changes made by parliament since then.

In an effort to avoid a face-off with the president in the polls, lawmakers speedily set to work to hammer out compromises on the most contentious provisions: the division of government powers, language and ethnic-minority rights, the status of Crimea, private property and civil rights, and state symbols and social guarantees. The parliamentary vote on 28 June approving the compromise draft canceled the referendum, and averted a potential showdown between the president and legislature. After the vote, 28 June was declared a national holiday.

The new basic law states that Ukraine is a sovereign, democratic, and unitary state that respects the rule of law. The wording was a clear victory for proponents of a unitary system, who feared that the federalism advocated by some regional clans and leftists in the east and Crimea would deepen the existing regional cleavages and encourage separatism. Although the new constitution sanctions Crimean autonomy and a Crimean regional constitution, it restricts the Crimean legislature from passing laws that contravene Ukrainian legislation.

The same political forces were successful in pressing for articles retaining Ukraine's post-Soviet flag and anthem, upholding a single citizenship, and enshrining Ukrainian as the sole state language. To accommodate the deputies who pushed for state or official status for the Russian language, the national democratic and centrist lawmakers incorporated guarantees for the free development of other ethnic languages spoken by citizens.

While the constitution provides for a strong presidency, as Kuchma had wanted, it also includes checks and balances among the three branches of power. While the president remains head of state, the prime minister runs the government. The president nominates the premier but must win the parliament's approval for the candidate. The legislature remains a unicameral body, elected for a four-year term.

A new bill aimed at boosting the role of political parties in the country's electoral system has yet to be adopted. Electoral reform in favor of greater party participation is considered a crucial step toward encouraging coalition building among Ukraine's 40 weak, mostly regionally based political parties and could help narrow the gap between the country's ruling elite and the electorate. So far, it appears the most popular version of the bill among deputies would split the elections between single-mandate districts and a party-list vote. Currently, legislators are elected only in single-mandate districts.

Although the new constitution offers some protection for freedom of expression, association, privacy, worship, and the press, it also lists many instances in which the state can limit those freedoms. It does safeguard private property rights, including the right to own land, and offers some Soviet-style social entitlements to pensions, housing, health care, and other benefits.

The new basic law also provided for the establishment of an 18–member Constitutional Court: the president, parliament, and a congress of judges each appoint six members. After much stalling, the legislature finally passed a law on the Constitutional Court in October and 16 justices were sworn in. Lawmakers must still select the final two. While the new court has yet to hand down any decisions, it is expected to play a key role in regulating the jurisdictional struggle among the president, government, and legislature. The parliament must still approve important new legislation on elections, the cabinet of ministers, local self-government, and other matters for the new constitution to be fully implemented.

In accordance with the constitution, the whole government resigned in July. President Kuchma reappointed as prime minister Lazarenko, who won easy approval in parliament. A team consisting of a mixture of old and new faces was named to the government over the ensuing months. Lazarenko had replaced Yevhen Marchuk as premier after the latter was ousted by Kuchma in May over policy differences as well as a personal rivalry. Hailing from Kuchma's native Dnipropetrovsk, Lazarenko was expected to be more loyal. He brought many other colleagues from his hometown into the government, greatly boosting the influence of the Dnipropetrovsk financial and industrial elite in government affairs. That, as well as a number of other measures that either directly or indirectly eroded the influence and position of the Donetsk regional and coal-mine barons, intensified the rivalry between the two powerful clans.

A personal rivalry also developed between Kuchma and Lazarenko as the latter garnered more supporters and pursued an independent line. Media observers speculated that it was Lazarenko's growth in prominence that spurred Kuchma to announce in September that he would seek re-election as president— even though the election isn't until the fall of 1999.

SOCIAL AND ECONOMIC POLICIES

Kuchma's announcement intensified what had already looked like a campaign by his administration to gain control of Ukraine's media. His reorganization of the Information Ministry and his appointment of Zinovii Kulyk, the loyal acting president of Ukrainian State Television and noted censor of independent programming, as information minister were a main part of the effort to control coverage. The number of incidents of censorship and intimidation against critical journalists or media outlets grew at an alarming rate this year.

The government used another occasion to weaken political opponents. In February and July, coal miners in the eastern oblasts, chiefly in Donetsk, held mass strikes protesting the government's burgeoning wage and pension arrears. Although Kyiv promised to pay its debt to miners, it came down hard on several independent strike organizations, which it blamed for organizing the "illegal" strikes for political reasons. A Donetsk regional court disbanded the Donetsk Workers' Committee in August and shut down its newspaper. Three independent miners-union leaders were arrested. Petro Kyt and Mykhaylo Skrynsky were found guilty and given prison sentences of up to three years, while the third, Mykhaylo Krylov, went on trial in November.

In Crimea, political infighting among the peninsula's own politicians weakened the strength of the separatist forces. In October, the third speaker in less than three years, Vasyl Kyselyov, was elected after Yevhen Suprunyuk was overwhelmingly voted out of office amid allegations of abuse of office. Both pro-Kyiv and pro-Russian Crimean politicians voted against Suprunyuk. In addition, despite Russian claims to the Crimean port of Sevastopol, the city's mayor, Viktor Semenov, said that Sevastopol was Ukrainian and that he recognized Ukraine's constitution as the supreme law.

The biggest economic event of the year was Kyiv's successful introduction of the hryvnya, a new permanent currency, on 2 September. Much of the macroeconomic success, however, was achieved because the government simply chose to delay some tough but badly needed measures to restructure and reform Ukraine's antiquated industry and agriculture. Although the government brought inflation to its lowest level in five years, it also accumulated a huge debt on public-sector wages and pensions. Hidden unemployment soared and living standards continued to decline, prompting mass strikes in July and February. More than half of economic activity takes place within the shadow economy, while officially recorded gross domestic product continued to fall (10 percent in the first nine months of the year). Although more state-owned enterprises were privatized last year than in all five previous years combined, many of the most lucrative companies remain barred from privatization. By November, 45 percent of industrial enterprises were privately owned and produced 36 percent of total output.

Ukraine continued to be favored by international financial institutions in receiving credits for reform projects. By the end of the year, international donors had pledged more than $5 billion in aid to Ukraine over the next five years, with $3.5 billion to be dispersed in 1997. The International Monetary Fund (IMF) released the eighth of nine tranches of an $867 million standby credit worth around $100 million in mid-December. As a result of the borrowing, Ukraine's foreign debt rose to $8 billion in September. Around $5 billion of that was owed to Russia and Turkmenistan for gas supplies and $3 billion was for IMF, World Bank, U.S., German, and Japanese credits.

Credits from the IMF enabled Ukraine to meet its payments for current gas supplies from Russia. At the same time, the Ukrainian government took a harder line against consumers who failed to pay their bills. Energy imports from Russia and Turkmenistan meant that Ukraine continued to run a trade deficit with Commonwealth of Independent States (CIS) countries. At the same time, in the first and second quarter of the year it registered a slight trade surplus with non-CIS states.

DISPUTES WITH RUSSIA

Relations with Russia remained contradictory. Kuchma and Foreign Minister Hennadii Udovenko repeatedly emphasized that Russia was a priority in Ukraine's foreign relations. But the long-delayed treaty on friendship and cooperation between the two countries remained unsigned, and several issues, particularly the status of the port at Sevastopol and the basing of the Black Sea Fleet, continued to strain relations.

In January, a dispute erupted over transit fees for Russian oil pumped through Ukraine's Druzhba pipeline to Central Europe. Russia claimed Ukraine had unilaterally raised the transit fee without warning. Ukraine's State Committee for Oil and Gas claimed that it warned Russian oil exporters a month and a half before raising the rates. Individual Russian oil exporters agreed to pay the higher fee to keep their supplies flowing west, but the Russian Fuel and Energy Ministry refused to acknowledge the legitimacy of the new rates, and several rounds of talks were held before the issue died down.

Although Russia and Ukraine remained each other's largest trading partners, the two began a trade war in September after Russia imposed a 20 percent value-added tax on several Ukrainian goods, particularly vodka. Moscow justified the move by pointing out that Kyiv had earlier imposed a similar tax on Russian imports. A 1 million ton quota on Ukrainian sugar was also imposed.

The economic differences were overshadowed by a more serious problem in Russian-Ukrainian relations: the basing of the Black Sea Fleet. After a half-hour meeting between Kuchma and Russian President Boris Yeltsin in October, Yeltsin's press secretary announced that all of the remaining issues surrounding the division of the fleet had been resolved, including the status of its main base in Sevastopol. The announcement was premature. Over the next month, it became apparent that neither side was willing to budge on the basing issue. Russian naval commanders continued to insist that Sevastopol had to be the exclusive base of the Russian Black Sea Fleet; Ukrainian leaders refused to allow that. Russia was also pressing for a 25–year lease, while Ukraine preferred a lease only long enough to allow a new base to be constructed in Russia. Under the new constitution, foreign troops may not be stationed in Ukraine, but bases may be temporarily leased.

With little progress being made over the basing issue, some deputies began calling for drafting a law on foreign troops that would evict all Russian forces from Ukraine. The Russian State Duma added to the friction when it voted in October to halt the division of the fleet. As the negotiations were stalling, a number of prominent Russian politicians, including Moscow Mayor Yurii Luzhkov and then-Security Council chief Aleksandr Lebed, claimed that Sevastopol had Russian status because it had never been handed over administratively to Ukraine. In early December, the Russian Federation Council voted overwhelmingly to give Sevastopol Russian status. When Ukrainian politicians demanded an explanation, the Russian Foreign Ministry said the vote had no legal force and the government did not support any policy laying claim to Ukrainian territory.

OTHER FOREIGN RELATIONS

Relations with Western states were on a better footing. Ukraine remained the third largest recipient of U.S. aid, receiving around $330 million over the course of the year. In February, Kuchma traveled to Washington and signed an agreement allowing Ukraine into the commercial satellite market. Kuchma, who was once head of the world's largest missile plant at Pivdenmash, had made winning admission into the potentially lucrative market one of his main goals as president.

Two events gave rise to some tension in Ukrainian-Chinese relations. In January, three Chinese nationals were deported for allegedly spying at the Pivdenmash missile plant in Dnipropetrovsk. Beijing denied the three were spies and demanded that Kyiv take action over the incident. As a result, the acting chief of Ukraine's Security Service, Andrii Khomych, and the Dnipropetrovsk head of the Security Service, Volodymyr Sobodenyuk, were dismissed. In August, relations were again strained after Taiwanese Vice President and Prime Minister Lien Chan made an unofficial visit to Ukraine. While the visit was strictly a private one, Taiwanese media depicted it as a sign of Ukrainian support for Taiwan. That led China to cancel a visit by a high-level delegation at the last minute. Nonetheless, at the UN meeting in New York in September, China and Ukraine reaffirmed their friendly ties, and Ukraine reiterated its adherence to the one-China principle.

In April, Ukraine had its status downgraded by the UN. As that reduced its fees to the organization, it had been a longtime goal for Kyiv. Toward the end of the year, Kuchma announced that membership in the European Union was one of Ukraine's long-term goals. Under the Tacis program, the EU is to provide $700 million to Ukraine between 1996 and 1999 for various economic projects.

SECURITY ISSUES

In June, the last nuclear warhead was removed from Ukraine. The 1,600 strategic warheads Ukraine had been left with when the USSR broke up had made it the world's third largest nuclear power and had been a consuming issue during the country's first two years of independence.

But by 1996, the main security issue in Eastern Europe had shifted from nuclear disarmament to NATO expansion. Kyiv's attitude toward NATO expansion was consistent throughout the year. Ukraine maintained that it was a nonaligned, neutral state and did not seek membership in the organization. Still, Ukrainian officials said, NATO should take other parties'—especially Russia's and Ukraine's—interests into account in any expansion plans. Since NATO expansion looked very probable, Ukraine said it was interested in a separate agreement with NATO. Ukrainian politicians also voiced opposition to the deployment of any nuclear weapons on the territory of new member states, pointing out that Ukraine had voluntarily disarmed itself of nuclear weapons on its territory. The United States assured Kyiv it had no intention of deploying nuclear weapons in new member states, and Ukraine was very active in participating in the NATO Partnership for Peace military exercises. Ukraine also had forces participating in six out of the 16 international peacekeeping missions.

Concern over the condition of the armed forces continued. Wages for military personnel were two months in arrears, on average, and there were numerous complaints about the low quality of recruits. Several high-ranking military officials were replaced during the year. In February, Chief of Staff Colonel-General Anatolii Lopata was dismissed over differences with the president on downsizing Ukraine's armed forces. In July, Defense Minister Valerii Shmarov, the first civilian to hold the post, stepped down and was replaced by a military officer, Lieutenant General Oleksandr Kuzmuk. In October, naval commander Volodymyr Bezkorovainy resigned, along with his first deputy and another deputy naval commander. Bezkorovainy was reportedly displeased over concessions being made to Russia regarding the Black Sea Fleet. He was made a member of the Black Sea Fleet negotiating team after his resignation, and Rear Admiral Mykhailo Yezhel was appointed as the new navy commander.

Profile: **PAVLO LAZARENKO: CAUTION IS THE KEY**

by OLEG VARFOLOMEYEV

Pavlo Lazarenko is Ukraine's sixth prime minister in five years. His greatest challenge may be to remain in office long enough to have an impact.

A prominent Ukrainian nationalist, Dmytro Korchynskii, once said that the reason there are no terrorist attacks on statesmen in Ukraine is that there are no statesmen worth the trouble. This serves as a kind of compliment to Prime Minister Pavlo Lazarenko, who survived an assassination attempt in July 1996, just three weeks after his appointment. If Lazarenko's limousine, on its way to the airport early in the morning, had not swerved just at the right moment to pass a bus, the remote-controlled bomb would certainly have killed him. As it was, the bomb, planted in the street by unknown assailants, left a crater four and a half feet deep and six feet wide.

The 43–year-old prime minister had already stepped on many toes, both in the state power structures and among the regional tycoons. As deputy prime minister, he had energetically set about restructuring the most lucrative sectors of the economy, such as the natural-gas trade. But the move that made him the most enemies was levying sin taxes on liquor and cigarettes in September 1996, after just several months as prime minister. That deprived hundreds of illegal producers and traders of a steady and strong flow of cash—90 percent of tobacco products were being smuggled into the country, and some 65 percent to 70 percent of the black market was involved in the illegal-liquor trade.

Lazarenko, who along with many top officials comes from President Leonid Kuchma's native region of Dnipropetrovsk, is regarded as a man of the president, one of the Dnipropetrovsk clan. Since his appearance in the Ukrainian government in September 1995, he accumulated plenty of political capital—and some people say that is not the only kind of capital he has amassed.

Though a tall man of impressive appearance, he seems to dislike appearing in public or drawing attention to himself. Neither an eloquent nor a skillful speaker, Lazarenko is usually terse but emotional in his interviews and speeches. Ukraine has had six prime ministers in the five years since independence; two of them were fired in the last two years. Most of them were accused of talking more than they were doing. Lazarenko seems to be just the opposite kind of statesman. Still, none of his predecessors lasted long enough to achieve very much. Lazarenko's greatest challenge as prime minister, therefore, will be to hold on to his job long enough to implement the economic reform and attract the foreign aid that Ukraine badly needs. As he is close to the president and the president has the power to dismiss him, keeping his job will depend on keeping Kuchma's goodwill.

RISE TO THE TOP

Lazarenko started out as a driver on a collective farm. At age 24, after graduating from the local agrarian institute, he worked as an agronomist. Then, in his native Dnipropetrovsk Oblast, he was appointed director of a collective farm, which he succeeded in making one of the most productive in the region. In the late 1980s, he was appointed head of the agrarian department of the Dnipropetrovsk Communist Party Central Committee.

Lazarenko was plucked off the farm and pushed into active politics in 1992, when the first Ukrainian president, Leonid Kravchuk, unexpectedly appointed him head of the state administration (essentially governor) of Dnipropetrovsk, the second most economically important region in Ukraine. To promote an agrarian to such a high position in the heavily industrialized region was a slap in the face to the powerful local "red" industrial directors. Kravchuk was probably trying to use Lazarenko to balance the influence of industry bosses.

The unexpected promotion apparently did not mar Lazarenko's relations with the Dnipropetrovsk heavy-industry "red directors." One of them, Leonid Kuchma, the former director of the large military-equipment manufacturer, Pivdenmash, and now Ukraine's president, four years later appointed Lazarenko to head his government. Lazarenko quickly came to be regarded as a sort of ambassador to Kyiv of the successful and influential Dnipropetrovsk elite. Now he is unofficially referred to as the boss of the Dnipropetrovsk clan—a strong managerial lobby that promotes its regional interests on the state level.

Ever since 1992, Lazarenko's name had been tossed about for the prime minister's post. He managed to be on good terms with both Kravchuk and Kuchma. In the election campaign of 1994, when those two men were vying for power, Lazarenko was careful not to openly support either one. As the governor of Kuchma's native Dnipropetrovsk Oblast, but owing his post largely to Kravchuk, he could not take sides. Many observers expected that, after Kuchma's victory, Lazarenko's neutrality would cost him his position. Nevertheless, he hung on. An iron-handed manager but a cautious and prudent politician, Lazarenko very soon became Kuchma's close political ally. Both are former "red directors" from the same region, cautious reformers with a common-sense approach.

In September 1995, he was appointed first deputy prime minister with special responsibility for the strategically important energy sector in Yevhen Marchuk's government. As in 1992, Lazarenko was used as a counterbalance—this time against the liberal reformist Deputy Prime Minister Viktor Pynzenyk. A prominent Lviv economist, Pynzenyk is considered the father of Ukraine's controversial monetarist reforms. Lazarenko, on the contrary, has never shown much enthusiasm for aggressive reform. A conservative, like most of the former collective-farm directors, Lazarenko advocates a slow pace of reform to give the "red directors," both industrial and agrarian, more time to adapt to the new realities. Thinking and behavior can change only gradually.

AN ENERGETIC DOER

Before his appointment as prime minister, Lazarenko already had an impressive record of achievement. In possibly the most important area of Ukraine's foreign economic policy—gas supplies (Ukraine is the world's largest gas importer)—Lazarenko as deputy prime minister conducted fruitful talks with Russia and Turkmenistan, the two principal gas suppliers. The Ukrainian debt to the two countries, accumulated in 1992–1994 when the government had no well-defined economic policies, now amounts to $4.2 billion.

"Our first steps are to go ahead with privatization, to obtain foreign investment, and to solve the wage-payment crisis," Lazarenko announced after his appointment. His first accomplishment as prime minister was ending the coal miners' strikes in Donetsk Oblast—indeed, he was on his way there when the assassination attempt occurred. In one day, Lazarenko fired the five largest mine and mine-association directors for poor management and embezzlement of state funds. Several days later, the strikes ended, and several prominent Donetsk state officials, including the governor and the head of the local security services, were fired. Ukraine's previous prime ministers had shied away from interference in

Donetsk, afraid to cross the powerful Donetsk clan. In contrast, Lazarenko, having promised to put an end to the strikes, strode in and did it. The image of a strong man, which Lazarenko had already established as Dnipropetrovsk Oblast governor and as deputy prime minister, was amplified.

Lazarenko also has a reputation of protecting his home region and personal interests. The former collective-farm director who started his career as a driver is now named among the wealthiest men in Ukraine—a charge he vehemently denies. But some say Lazarenko's activities in the energy sector were not confined to merely talking with major gas suppliers. The media accused him of using illegal methods of privatization. Worse, there were claims that he restructured the gas market too much in favor of one company—United Energy Systems of Ukraine—that is said to be controlled by the Dnipropetrovsk group. The scandal reverberated in parliament, where some deputies threatened to start proceedings to dismiss Lazarenko last September. Yet the procurator-general's office, having investigated the deal, seemingly did not find any serious breaches of law. Those who committed minor infractions were cited only in a confidential report to Kuchma, who was to personally punish those responsible. Lazarenko, the president's man, was not punished.

Another major accomplishment of Deputy Prime Minister Lazarenko was launching the third Ukrainian metro in January 1996 in his home town of Dnipropetrovsk. That earned him the Jaroslav the Wise medal from President Kuchma. Dnipropetrovsk was also graced with an international airport and one of the largest bus stations in Europe, prompting the joke: "What is good for Dnipropetrovsk is good for the country." It is true that the city of 1.2 million people desperately needed the metro, and construction had begun before Lazarenko received his first government appointment. Nevertheless, conventional wisdom ascribed the relatively quick completion of the Dnipropetrovsk metro to Lazarenko's preferential treatment.

BALANCING ACT

Lazarenko has a quality that is very rare in politicians, especially in a post-Soviet country: he is on good terms with both the left and the right. While he needed only 226 out of 450 votes in parliament to be confirmed as prime minister, he received a hefty 344. The right-wing forces, which come mainly from the west of the country, praise Lazarenko for his energy and for not ousting from his government the main reformist and virtually the only representative of the western regions in the current government, Viktor Pynzenyk. But right-wingers have other reasons to support him. They see the prime minister as a symbol of Ukrainian statehood, which might suffer if the government is unstable. The fact that Lazarenko speaks Ukrainian better than Russian is also important for nationalists. He is the first prime minister to have such a good command of Ukrainian, a fluency that is especially surprising because he comes from the predominantly Russian-speaking east.

The left-wing forces admire—or at least, used to admire—Lazarenko for his communist collective-farm past and for obeying them almost every time they voice their malcontent over the government's pro-Western or pro-reformist economic policies. Lazarenko avoided a confrontation with the leftist majority in the parliament by catering his new three-year program for the Ukrainian economy to their tastes when it came to a vote last October. Lazarenko removed from the program the points considered too reformist by the collective farms and "red directors" lobby. The program's support for domestic industry borders on protectionism, and its approach to restructuring agriculture is overcautious, leaving too many characteristics of the old collective-farm system.

Some measures recently undertaken by the Lazarenko government raise doubts as to whether Ukraine will move toward a market economy at all. Real privatization of land has been postponed, and the pace of privatization of industry has been slowed down. The government raised tariffs on imports, in particular agricultural imports. Lazarenko says his top priority is to ensure homegrown economic growth by stimulating output and protecting Ukrainian industry.

The anti-free market measures endorsed by the left could end up creating an artificial oasis for the Soviet-style industry and agricultural directors, who are neither efficient nor innovative enough to compete with foreign or private domestic firms.

On the other hand, the drastic monetary measures proposed by Lazarenko's government for next year will hardly be welcomed by the left. Parliament's leftist majority wants Lazarenko to amend the draft of the 1997 state-budget draft to offset potential shortfalls caused by the new tax legislation. Lazarenko, with Kuchma's backing, refuses to do that. The new tax legislation proposed by the government would abolish redundant taxes that have seriously hampered the revival of the Ukrainian economy. Other controversial proposals include cutting social benefits to the most vulnerable citizens—war veterans, pensioners, students. The government is trying to make the 1997 budget deficit as small as possible in order to meet International Monetary Fund requirements and preserve the relatively low inflation of 1996. Still, any attempt to cut social benefits would be very dangerous just now and could provoke serious social disturbances.

STRONG ENOUGH TO BE A THREAT

Kuchma fully understands the danger of social unrest. In December 1996, he severely reprimanded Lazarenko for his proposal to cut social services, accusing the government of inefficiency and lack of responsibility and urging that it "stop once and for all any attempts to infringe on people's basic rights." Kuchma had never used such harsh words with Lazarenko before. Just a day later, Kuchma softened, saying he had no disagreements with his prime minister on major issues. Nevertheless, his sharp criticism showed Lazarenko can no longer feel safe in his position.

Lazarenko's popularity and strength as a possible presidential candidate is continuing to grow. One mistake could cost him his post now. The media have been feeding the fire by frequently referring to the prime minister as a strong potential candidate. Lazarenko protests ever louder that he has no plans to run, but many, including powerful National Security Council Secretary Volodymyr Horbulin, doubt his sincerity. "Of all [the candidates], only the prime minister has not announced his plans for the presidency, but we shall see how much that corresponds with reality," Horbulin said a few months ago.

As early as November 1996, rumors began to spread that Kuchma was going to fire the prime minister. That was a mere four months after Lazarenko's appointment—but then, four out of five of Lazarenko's predecessors did not manage to keep the post for more than a year. Similar rumors had been heard several months before the dismissal of Lazarenko's immediate predecessor, former Ukrainian KGB head Yevhen Marchuk. And one of the main reasons Kuchma fired Marchuk was that he did not like Marchuk's growing popularity and apparent ambition; in Kuchma's view, Marchuk was reaching beyond his post. Kuchma openly accused Marchuk, whom he saw as a potentially strong rival in the 1999 presidential race, of focusing on his own political image instead of restructuring the ailing Ukrainian economy.

As Lazarenko's position grew to look slightly unstable, his disclaimers became more frequent. The cautious politician has never expressed a wish to run for president—in fact, he uses every opportunity to pledge his loyalty to Kuchma and says he will back the president's re-election bid. "I have never had far-reaching political ambitions. I have never manifested either an aspiration or a wish [to become president]," he repeats, protesting perhaps too much. Yet his practical skills and political wisdom have earned him vast support. Potentially, he would be a very strong candidate for the presidency.

Still, the dismissal of a third prime minister in two years would be too much even for Ukraine. Such a move would not add credibility to the image of the poor country with an ailing economy, struggling to overcome its communist past and get more credits and investments from abroad.

Sidebar: ASSASSINATION LIFTS LID ON UKRAINIAN CLAN POLITICS

by OLEG VARFOLOMEYEV

On 3 November, Yevhen Shcherban, a parliamentary deputy and one of the richest men in Ukraine, was murdered at Donetsk airport. Shcherban headed the successful international trading corporation Aton, was one of the leaders of the Social Market Choice faction in parliament, and was a crony of his namesake—ousted Donetsk Governor Volodymyr Shcherban. Together, the two Shcherbans made the oblast's industrial sector one of the most privatized in Ukraine. Such achievements meant Shcherban led a high-risk lifestyle in a country where central power is too weak to battle organized crime effectively.

The late Shcherban had been accused of involvement in the July attempted assassination of Prime Minister Pavlo Lazarenko—a charge he always denied. The two strongest economic interest groups in Ukraine are the rival Dnipropetrovsk and the Donetsk groups. Their economic clout makes them powerful lobbies in Ukraine's politics, and thus a political factor to be reckoned with.

The most recent case of a Donetsk boss falling out of favor with President Leonid Kuchma and losing his post was Volodymyr Shcherban. His removal as governor of Donetsk took place immediately after the assassination attempt on Lazarenko. The reason given for his dismissal was his failure to cope with the miners' strikes that paralyzed the Donbas in the first half of July, although these were in fact caused by the government's strict monetary policy, which resulted in miners not being paid for several months.

As the most influential politicians from the Donetsk group were losing their positions, the region sought allies to preserve its clout. The Donetsk group joined forces with the Social Market Choice faction in parliament, led by former Prime Minister Yevhen Marchuk. That faction consists mainly of members of the Liberal Party of Ukraine, which includes mainly Donetsk businessmen and is headed by Volodymyr Shcherban. Marchuk, who is perceived as a potentially strong rival to Kuchma in the 1999 presidential race, joined the faction after stepping down as prime minister in May 1996. Marchuk insists that the Shcherban assasination was a political killing, while the government said it was a contract killing without any political motivation.

Such an explanation is credible. Yevhen Shcherban, a "new Ukrainian" businessman, was known to have underworld connections. He was involved in the lucrative gas and metallurgy monopolies, which have had Donetsk, Dnipropetrovsk, and Moscow groups competing for shares in enterprises. The murder could be also connected to score settling between business groups in Donetsk and Mariupol. This summer, Mariupol's mayor accused Shcherban of blackmailing him. Last year another prominent Donetsk businessman, Akhat Bragin, was blown up at a Donetsk soccer stadium.

Sidebar: UKRAINE'S ECONOMIC PROGRAM—MORE MUDDLING THROUGH?

by BEN SLAY

The Ukrainian government's long-awaited three-year economic program was officially presented to parliament by Prime Minister Pavlo Lazarenko on 15

October. Coming on the heels of the major reductions in inflation recorded earlier in 1996, as well as the successful introduction of Ukraine's national currency, the hryvnya, in September, many observers saw the program as an opportunity for consolidating and deepening recent economic progress. Instead, the 134-page program was as a compromise document, likely to satisfy neither proponents nor opponents of the government's policies. While political compromises may have been sensible and unavoidable—the leftist-dominated parliament quickly approved the program by a 252–64 vote—they run the risk of compromising the program's economic integrity.

In many respects, the program was a call to stay the course and quicken the pace of market reform and structural change. Higher energy prices and tighter budget constraints were supposed to push enterprises to become more efficient and reduce energy usage by 50%, which should help Ukraine's trade balance and industrial productivity. The consolidated budget deficit in 1997 was to be held to 4% of GDP, and consumer price inflation was to drop to 24.9% from the 45%-48% forecast for 1996. On the other hand, the program placed a strong emphasis on increasing domestic production, and forecast a 1.7% increase in GDP for 1997. In light of the 56% decline in Ukraine's GDP officially recorded during 1991–1995—and another 6–6.5% drop forecast for 1996—such an emphasis is hardly surprising. Indeed, as the program's authors point out, the attainment of financial stabilization in 1996—inflation is 40 percent well below the 182% rate of 1995, not to mention the 10,000% hyperinflation of 1993—means that policy makers can turn their attention toward fostering economic recovery and raising living standards.

The tension between those two goals—further reducing inflation through fiscal austerity while simultaneously promoting economic growth—points to one of the compromises in the program: the attempt at reconciling austerity and restructuring on the one hand with social needs on the other. Wage arrears skyrocketed in 1996, and reached some $1.5 billion–$1.7 billion. The economic program promised to pay off the state budget's arrears in 1997, in monthly installments of $117 million. That will be difficult to do without increasing government spending and the government budget deficit. Likewise, the government balked at the social costs involved in shutting down the 50 coal mines it had promised the International Monetary Fund and World Bank would be closed in 1997. Instead, the program only called for shutting down nine. That will mean higher wage arrears in or budget subsidies for the coal industry, either of which would be difficult to square with maintaining fiscal austerity and reducing inflation.

A second tension apparent in the program concerns industrial policy. Although the program is meant to be in keeping with Ukraine's transition to a market economy, it views market forces and free trade with some hostility. The program contains some 40 programs to support restructuring in the large state enterprises whose lobbying strength has strongly influenced Ukrainian economic policy since 1992. Special support is apparently targeted for the aircraft, automobile, combine-harvester, and telecommunications equipment industries. Those lobbies can be expected to rally much of Ukraine's leftist-dominated parliament to their cause, and push industrial policy further towards state protection and subsidization of "key" sectors and firms. The agro-industrial complex is also slated for special treatment, both in terms of renewed subsidies and in the government's failure to aggressively privatize land.

In addition to fiscal subsidies and tax breaks, the program also calls upon the ostensibly independent National Bank of Ukraine (NBU) to provide financial support for those programs. That is reminiscent of a 1995 campaign of government-directed and NBU-financed "restructuring" of large enterprises, which helped increase inflation and partly precipitated the temporary suspension of assistance for Ukraine's stabilization program from the IMF.

In effect, the program attempts to combine the continuation of the 1995–1996 stabilization and liberalization policy regime with specific promotion of Ukraine's "best" firms—many of which are linked to the regional groupings that dominate Ukrainian politics—in an effort to stimulate economic growth. While such an attitude on the part of the former Soviet-era managers and apparatchiks making economic policy in Kyiv is understandable, it amounts to a postponement of the painful choices involved in the urgently needed restructuring of the enterprise, financial, and budgetary sectors. By not confronting those issues more directly, the program runs the risk of quickly becoming irrelevant—which is what happened to most of its predecessors.

Sidebar: TENTH ANNIVERSARY OF THE CHORNOBYL ACCIDENT

by USTINA MARKUS

The tenth anniversary of the accident at the Chornobyl nuclear power station was marked by ceremonies in Ukraine, Belarus, and other countries. Thousands gathered outside of the 30 kilometer Chornobyl exclusion zone in the town of Slavutich and held a minute of silence at 1:24 A.M. on 26 April 1996 to commemorate the exact moment the roof blew off of the no. 4 reactor spewing a cloud of radiation into the air. The explosion released 200 times more radiation into the atmosphere than the bombs dropped on Hiroshima and Nagasaki. Winds carried the radioactive cloud over Belarus contaminating close to 30 percent of Belarusian territory, 7 percent of Ukrainian territory, and 1.6 percent of Russia. In all, some 26,000 square kilometers of land were contaminated. Belarus has had to devote as much as a quarter of its annual budget to deal with the aftermath of the disaster. Ukraine has been spending around 10–15 percent.

Although Soviet authorities reported only two people killed in the explosion and thirty dying of radiation sickness afterwards, most sources concur that the real toll is much higher. Ukraine's Ambassador to Austria Mykola Makarevych has said that 4,229 people have died as a result of radiation exposure since the explosion, and 2,929 of those had taken part in the clean-up operations. Others say over 100,000 have died as a result of the radiation. In addition, as many as five million people were exposed to radioactive fallout. Even though almost a quarter million were evacuated from contaminated areas over the next four years, it is estimated that at least that many continue to live in contaminated areas. Due to housing shortages in Belarus, people have been moving into the evacuated homes. This will pose an additional burden on the country's health care system in the future if these individuals contract cancer or other diseases connected to radiation exposure.

Despite all of these problems, Kyiv has been unable to close the power plant. In 1991 it was decided that the plant would be closed by the end of 1993. That same year a fire damaged the no. 2 reactor forcing it to close. Towards the end of 1993, however, Ukraine's parliament voted against closing the station because it did not have alternatives to make up for the lost energy. Chornobyl's two working reactors provided some 7 percent of the country's electricity. The International Atomic Energy Agency reported numerous safety deficiencies at the plant in March 1994, and an endless string of accidents at the station have raised concerns over its continued operation. The last incident occurred the day before the tenth anniversary when a small radiation leak raised the level of radiation to seven times its normal rate. Just before that, a major fire broke out in five abandoned villages in the exclusion zone, and in forests close to Chornobyl in southern Belarus, raising fear over increased radiation levels.

In December 1995 President Leonid Kuchma signed an agreement with the G-7 in Ottawa over the closure of the Chornobyl plant. The deal promises Ukraine over $3 billion in aid in the form of credits and grants to help close the station and find alternative means of making up for the energy loss. At a recent summit on nuclear safety in Moscow Kuchma promised to close the oldest no. 1 reactor by the end of the year, and said the second working reactor would be shut down by the end of the decade. The closure is contingent on the promised G-7 aid materializing, however. For the moment, despite the aftermath of the 1986 accident and worrisome reports on safety, the Chornobyl station continues to function with some 5,000 employees being ferried into the plant in the middle of the exclusion zone each day.

Document: UKRAINE FREE OF NUCLEAR WEAPONS

On 1 June 1996, Ukraine announced the removal from its territory of the last of the strategic warheads it inherited from the Soviet Union. Ukraine's surrender of *the weapons to Russia was the subject of prolonged negotiations with Russia and the United States, ending in a January 1994 trilateral agreement that promised Ukraine $1 billion in compensation, mostly in the form of nuclear fuel rods. In a statement read on Ukrainian television, President Leonid Kuchma said Ukraine's action pointed the way for other countries to move toward global nuclear disarmament, and called for the establishment of a "nuclear-free Central and Eastern Europe."*

The withdrawal of strategic nuclear warheads from Ukraine was completed on 1 June 1996. In this way, the Ukrainian state demonstrated to the world its commitment to the idea of global nuclear disarmament. The people of Ukraine once had to finance an exhausting nuclear arms race during the Cold War, at the expense of their own well-being and economic development. Having proclaimed itself the owner of nuclear weapons deployed on its territory and inherited from the former USSR, Ukraine regarded these weapons not as an active military force but above all as an asset that could at least partially compensate for its losses. No nuclear threat to mankind ever emerged from independent Ukraine.

Guided by the same principle, the Ukrainian Supreme Council announced in the Declaration on State Sovereignty in 1990 that Ukraine would abide by three non nuclear principles: non deployment, non production, and non acquisition of nuclear weapons. . . . The removal of the last nuclear warhead from Ukraine is the logical conclusion of this process and convincing proof that our policy is consistent and predictable. . . .

The complete elimination of nuclear weapons deployed on Ukrainian territory provides a unique opportunity to implement the idea of a nuclear-free Central and Eastern Europe from the Black Sea to the Baltic Sea. Its creation will promote the development of an atmosphere of trust among countries in the region and will considerably reduce the danger of new lines of division emerging on the European continent. The people of Ukraine, who have experienced the destructive consequences of the accident at the Chornobyl nuclear power plant, are all too aware of the real threat of catastrophe posed by nuclear arms. That is why Ukraine is confident in its choice of a nuclear-free status and urges other countries, first of all the nuclear powers, to follow the same road and do their best to remove nuclear weapons from the face of our planet as soon as possible and forever.

SOUTHEASTERN
EUROPE

IV

Slovenia

Population:	1,990,000 (1995)
Capital:	Ljubljana (population 270,000)
Major cities:	Maribor (pop. 103,512), Celje (pop. 39,942), Kranj (pop. 36,808)
Area:	20,251 sq. km.
Major ethnic groups:	Slovenian 90%, small numbers of ethnic Serbs, Croats, Albanians, Hungarians, and Italians
Economy:	GDP growth: 3.5%
	Inflation rate: 9%
	Average monthly income: $626
	Unemployment rate: 14.4%

SLOVENIA INCHES AHEAD

by STAN MARKOTICH

Coalition squabbling dominated the domestic political scene in Slovenia, while the economy showed signs of growth and Ljubljana laid the groundwork for improved relations with Belgrade.

Slovenia entered 1996 with a governing coalition that was already somewhat rocky. The coalition consisted of the Liberal Democratic Party (LDS), with 30 of 90 legislative seats; the Christian Democratic Party (SKD), with 15 seats; and the former communists, the United List of Social Democrats (ZLSD), with 14 seats. Problems surfaced early in January, when the ZLSD voiced objections to a demand by Prime Minister Janez Drnovsek, an LDS member, that Economics Minister Maks Tajnikar, a ZLSD member, resign. ZLSD officials charged that the government had failed to do enough to support local enterprises and was derelict in providing for trade unionists, the poor, and those living on pensions.

The LDS retorted that Tajnikar was guilty of abusing his office. The affair came to a head on 29 January, when the ZLSD issued a statement that all four of its ministers would resign their seats in protest and 10 party state secretaries would tender resignations after the appointment of new ministers.

Both Drnovsek and President Milan Kucan played down the significance of the controversy, saying the remaining parties in the coalition could govern until elections were held at their scheduled time—near the end of the year. And, for several months, all appeared to be calm. But on 7 May, Radio Slovenija reported that a seemingly irreparable strain in the relations between the SKD and LDS had developed. SKD leader Lojze Peterle openly spoke about a collapse of the coalition, blaming the LDS. According to Peterle, the LDS and, specifically, Foreign Minister Zoran Thaler were responsible for a breakdown in relations with neighboring Italy.

SHIFTING TO THE RIGHT

That crisis peaked on 16 May when the legislature held a confidence vote on Thaler. Thaler lost the vote by a margin of 48 to 26 but stayed on as acting foreign minister. In the wake of that vote, Drnovsek delivered arguably his most eloquent defense of Thaler and apparently confirmed that the coalition with the SKD was dead. The next morning, however, Drnovsek told a press conference he would continue to cooperate with the SKD as a coalition partner.

But once again, political stability and calm lasted for only a few months. When Slovenes went to the polls on 10 November, they shifted overwhelmingly to the right. It was clear that no matter what last-minute fine-tuning had to be made to the ultimate seat count before the official announcement of the results on 15 November, Drnovsek's LDS would emerge the single strongest party. It won 27.05 percent of the vote—an increase of about 3 percent from its share in the 1992 elections—and 25 seats.

But making inroads were two rightist parties, Marjan Podobnik's Slovenian People's Party (SLS) and Janez Jansa's Social Democratic Party of Slovenia. Podobnik's stated goal was to form and maintain a coalition government of conservative parties under the banner "Slovenian Spring," although cooperation with Drnovsek was not ruled out. Even SKD leader Peterle said his top priority was to maintain the Slovenian Spring alliance, but that, he added, did not preclude welcoming others, presumably the LDS, into a coalition. He said: "If all three Slovenian Spring parties keep their promises the way we [intend], then a Slovenian Spring coalition will be formed, and it might also be decided to invite somebody else to join in."

In fact, Podobnik's SLS came in second, winning 19 seats, and Jansa's came in third, with 16. Coming in fourth in terms of popular vote was the SKD, winning 10 seats. Not too far behind was the ZLSD, winning roughly 9 percent of the vote and nine seats. Next came the Democratic Party of the Retired, with 4.3 percent of the vote and five seats. Another party that fared far worse was the Slovenian National Party, which fell from 10 percent of the vote in 1992 to 3.2 percent and claimed four seats. The voters of the ethnic Italian and Hungarian communities, with one representative each, re-elected their incumbents.

Wrangling over who would form Slovenia's next government continued through the end of the year. Slovenian President Milan Kucan on 18 December ended a second round of talks with party leaders aimed at finding a candidate for prime minister.

NORMALIZING RELATIONS WITH BELGRADE

On the foreign-relations and foreign-policy front, 1996 was a lively year. For a brief while, it appeared that relations with neighboring Italy could be at least set back. In March, Thaler said publicly he would seek Slovenia's direct membership in the European Union, Rome's objections notwithstanding. But by fall, bilateral relations were back on a stable course. Italian Foreign Minister Lamberto Dini said at a 3 September press conference that "Italy will give full support to Slovenia's intentions" to seek membership in NATO and the EU. Those remarks came after Slovenia's new foreign minister, Davorin Kracun, had met with Dini in Rome that same day. For his part, Kracun told the press that the parties had signed two agreements aimed at allowing citizens of each country to travel to the other without passport or visa requirements. Slovenian-Italian relations have improved steadily since May 1996, after Ljubljana dropped its objections to foreigners' owning property in the country, a move widely regarded as enabling Italian nationals—whose property was nationalized when they left Slovenia after World War II—to buy back real estate.

Slovenia in 1996 also appeared to be forging a new policy toward Belgrade. On 17 July, Kucan met with the leader of the New Democracy party, Dusan Mihailovic. New Democracy is a small party in the Federal Republic of Yugoslavia, functioning in practice as a wing of Serbian President Slobodan Milosevic's Socialist Party of Serbia. Kucan said that the normalization of relations with Belgrade was among Ljubljana's priorities, adding that "Serbs and Slovenes were never at odds." Mihailovic, almost certainly acting as Milosevic's envoy, reciprocated, saying that the normalization of bilateral relations was a priority for his party.

As far back as mid-June, Slovenia signaled it could be serious about wanting a thaw in dealings with Belgrade. At one point, Ljubljana was rumored to be considering appointing as foreign minister Miran Mejak, Slovenia's chief negotiator on succession issues relating to former Yugoslavia. That Mejak, with his interests and training in Balkan affairs, was tipped for the post may have been enough to suggest to Belgrade that Slovenia was intent on giving attention to relations with federal Yugoslavia. But the issue of succession and the division of assets remained unresolved throughout 1996.

Finally, the foreign-relations sphere demonstrated that tinges of scandal still remain in Slovenian politics. Nicholas Oman, Slovenia's honorary consul to Liberia, was dismissed from his post on 21 August, some two months after an Italian prosecutor issued an arrest warrant accusing Oman of smuggling arms to Croatia, Bosnia-Herzegovina, and Slovenia. Ljubljana offered no details on why it removed Oman from the post he had held since 1993. A spokesman said only that "a decision was made on July 25, but it remained confidential until now because the man and the country in question had to be notified first."

There were few surprises on the economic front. Unemployment dropped slightly from just over 14 percent, where it had been for at least a year, to 13.5 percent by August. At the beginning of the year, the average monthly wage was about $575: that increased to $620 by August, 3.7 percent more than the previous month, marking a steady increase compared with an average of about $374 in 1991. Inflation showed signs of slowing; average annual inflation came in at 8 percent, compared with 12.6 percent at the end of 1995 and 19.8 percent in 1994.

The year 1996 may be remembered as the year of industrial action. The usually placid country was stirred by waves of major strikes, which included medical professionals, rail workers, and even journalists. For journalists, strikes began on 18 March. Those employed at the state-funded RTV Slovenija demanded higher salaries and improved working conditions for freelancers. Their action caused a news blackout on both radio and television. Of the company's roughly 350 employees, 10 percent were freelancers. The full-time staffers demanded a 15 percent pay hike, to raise the average monthly gross salary to about $1,200. That job action, dramatic while it lasted, was short-lived, ending after just three days, when management agreed to the pay increase.

Sidebar: SLOVENIA: AN ECONOMIC SUCCESS STORY

by MICHAEL WYZAN

During the five-year tenure of Prime Minister Janez Drnovsek Slovenia made steady progress toward becoming a normal European market economy. Opposition parties criticize the government's record mainly in terms of protection of domestic farmers (People's Party) or the high unemployment rate (the United List of Social Democrats, the former communists).

Slovenia's economy is in many ways the envy of the postcommunist world. It remains an oasis of political and economic stability among the former Yugoslav republics. Consistent with its signing the Central European Free Trade Agreement (CEFTA) on 25 November 1995, Slovenia has more in common economically and politically with the Visegrad countries than with other such republics.

It has an average net monthly wage of $620, single-digit annual inflation, positive economic growth since 1993, budget deficits of less than 1 percent of gross domestic product (GDP), low public debt, foreign trade long strongly oriented toward the European Union (EU), and a manageable foreign debt even after assuming a sizable share of former Yugoslavia's liabilities.

In May 1996, three ratings agencies—Standard & Poor's, Moody's, and ICBA—all gave the country A ratings, the first post-communist country to earn that distinction. That good news came on the eve of the country's first ($325 million) Eurobond flotation in June. Slovenia was the first former Yugoslav republic to agree with the London Club of commercial banks on a settlement of its debts, issuing dollars and Deutsche-mark denominated bonds for that purpose in June. However, wrangling continues with Belgrade over this and other succession-related questions.

Slovenia already met or was close to meeting three of the five Maastricht criteria that EU members must satisfy to participate in European Monetary Union—those on public debt, budget balance, and interest rates. Only the criteria on inflation and the exchange rate mechanism remain unmet, putting the country in better shape in this regard than many EU members.

However, many Western and local observers accuse it of being "too stable." Concern about foreigners buying up the country's valuable assets have led to the adoption of complex, insider-favoring methods of privatization that have contributed to the relatively low level of foreign investment.

It is useful to compare Slovenia with Estonia, another tiny, prosperous "new" country with a stable economy. Estonia has based its privatization efforts on a model inspired by Germany's Treuhandanstalt, based on sales of assets and companies, especially to foreign interests. It experienced much larger inflows of foreign direct investment (FDI). The flows of such investment in Slovenia were

$412 million during 1993–95, compared with almost $1.2 billion in Estonia over that period. A low level of FDI is harmful, since recent evidence suggests that Slovenian firms with foreign ownership outperform those without it. Criticism is also leveled at restrictions on trading in bonds and Treasury bills by foreigners.

Moreover, an unwillingness to allow foreigners to own land has been a stumbling block in relations with Italy. An association agreement with the EU was finally initialed on 10 June, well after such agreements had been reached with all Visegrad countries, Baltic states, and Romania and Bulgaria.

The land ownership issue is important because ethnic Italians from Istria whose real estate was nationalized by the Yugoslav government after the war want its return. Ljubljana pledged recently that Italian citizens who had lived in present-day Slovenia for three years or longer would be allowed to reacquire their property as soon as the association agreement is ratified.

Slowly developing cooperation with the EU is just one of several nagging economic problems facing Slovenia. Despite wages that are by far the highest among transitional economies in dollar terms, strikes are frequent, even among such relatively well-paid professionals as doctors.

A strong tolar moving in synch with the German mark has caused a decline in competitiveness, contributing to slow growth of exports and GDP. In the early post-independence years, the country's foreign trade deficits were more than matched by positive net service earnings, leading to current account surpluses. That is no longer the case, however, as 1995 and 1996 have seen (still manageable) current account deficits.

Finally, privatization has moved slowly, with the privatization agency by September having approved privatization programs at only 666 of 1,500 enterprises slated for such treatment. And doubts abound on whether the chosen method will result in changes in the way firms are managed.

Croatia

Population:	4,800,000 (1991 census)
Capital:	Zagreb (pop. 994,000)
Major cities:	Split (pop. 207,000), Rijeka (pop. 206,000), Osijek (pop. 165,000)
Area:	56,538 sq. km.
Major ethnic groups:	90% Croatian, 3%–4% Serbian
Economy:	GDP growth: 4.4%
	Inflation rate: 3%
	Average monthly income: $397
	Unemployment rate: 15.9%

A GROUNDSWELL OF DISSATISFACTION IN CROATIA

by DARIA SITO SUCIC

Social unrest increased as Croats refocused their energies, turning away from nationalism to more earthly issues, such as living standards. Meanwhile, President Franjo Tudjman stepped up his attacks on anyone critical of his policies—although he also sought to win the approval of the international community.

If 1995 is best described as the year of great military victories—which enabled Croatia to claim state sovereignty over most of its territories after four years of fighting—1996 might be said to be a year of low-key achievements in all other areas, and particularly slow steps toward democratization.

Croatia's foreign policy was marked by efforts to prove to the democratic governments of Europe that it was one of them; none, however, was truly convinced. The country's internal situation was characterized by a growing societal polarization in which ruling-party members run the country and most of the impoverished population and an impotent opposition stand on the sidelines. The arrogant attitude of Croatian President Franjo Tudjman and his ruling Croatian Democratic Community (HDZ) toward anyone whose opinion differs—the opposition, worker unions, nongovernmental organizations, or human-rights groups—has resulted in a negative perception of the Croatian government both domestically and internationally.

RIDING ROUGHSHOD TO EUROPE

Despite the oft-repeated statement that joining "European integration" is a top priority, the Croatian ruling elite stubbornly pursued things its own way. However, as that has not exactly impressed the international community, Croatia has encountered obstacles and earned criticism on its road to Europe. In an unprecedented move, the Council of Europe postponed Croatia's entry into its membership, citing the country's poor human-rights record and shoddy treatment of the independent media. By November, Croatia was finally admitted—after several embarrassing months spent trying to convince the international organization that it would meet all the requirements for admission, while assuring the public that the country's admittance into the council was only a formality.

Croatia's bad-boy reputation also resulted from not cooperating with the Hague-based war-crimes tribunal for the former Yugoslavia and from protecting indicted war criminals. In order to be recognized as a "regional power and a factor of stabilization in the Balkans," as Tudjman put it, Croatia was pressured by the international community, particularly by the United States, to support the implementation of the Dayton peace accord in Bosnia-Herzegovina and the strengthening of the Muslim-Croat federation.

While its international relations remained in a quagmire, Croatia also faced many internal problems in the course of 1996. Eastern Slavonia, the last Serb-held region of Croatia, has yet to be reintegrated into the rest of the country, despite the government's hopes. The Zagreb municipal government remained in a deadlock that began in 1995 when the opposition won the local elections in the Croatian capital but was not allowed to rule the city. Tudjman has rejected four opposition mayoral candidates; finally he appointed his protégée Marina Matulovic-Dopulic as Zagreb's administrator. The last months of 1996 were marked by huge demonstrations against the government's grip over the independent media, indicative of the waves of social unrest. Pensioners, teachers, railway workers—all expressed a common dissatisfaction with the low quality of life in "independent, sovereign Croatia." The people finally realized that lofty words and national self-absorption would not fill their empty stomachs.

WHEN ACTIONS AND WORDS COLLIDE

The country's two most important achievements on the foreign-policy plane were its admittance to the Council of Europe in November 1996 and the signing in August of an agreement on normalizing relations with Belgrade.

Croatia first applied for membership in the council in 1992, but its application was frozen in 1993 and 1994 due to Croatia's involvement in the Croat-Muslim conflict in Bosnia-Herzegovina. In 1995, it was further delayed as a result of military operations Blitz and Storm, in which Croatia recaptured most of its territories from Serbian control. Membership was finally approved on 24 April 1996 by the council's parliamentary assembly, but it was again put on hold in July by the council's executive committee. At issue was Zagreb's failure to act on a 21–point democracy and human-rights program previously agreed upon with the council. Press freedom, resolution of the Zagreb city-council deadlock, cooperation with the tribunal in The Hague, and Tudjman's influence on the Croatian nationalists in the divided Herzegovinian city of Mostar were issues of special importance.

Foreign Minister Mate Granic tirelessly reiterated that Croatia had met all the conditions set by the council; after six more months, on 6 November, Croatia at last became the 40th member of the Council of Europe. But the problems cited by the council as reason for delaying Croatia's acceptance were far from resolved. The ruling elite's strategy was always to demonstrate a transparent act of positive will, and then to do things its own way. For example, several days before the Council of Europe's decision on Croatia's admittance, charges were dropped against two journalists for the satirical weekly *Feral Tribune* who had been accused of insulting Tudjman. But after Croatia's admittance to the council, the state prosecutor appealed the case. Even the ceremony of Croatia's acceptance into the council in Strasbourg, France, was shadowed by demonstrations against the prosecutor's appeal organized by members of the international media organization Reporters Sans Frontiers.

Another move typical of the Croatian government was the signing of a bilateral-relations agreement with the Federal Republic of Yugoslavia. An unexpected meeting between Tudjman and his Serbian counterpart, Slobodan Milosevic, on 7 August in Greece first raised questions, most of which were based on the possibility of a new deal between the two "old partners," probably once again at the expense of Bosnia. On 23 August, Foreign Minister Granic and Federal Yugoslav Foreign Minister Milan Milutinovic signed an agreement in Belgrade saying that "within 15 days of signing" the two countries would establish full diplomatic and consular relations, including the exchange of ambassadors. But by the end of the year, none of the disputed issues between the two had been resolved. Of primary concern is the border dispute; Zagreb wants Belgrade to recognize its internationally accepted borders, which include both Serb-held eastern Slavonia and the Prevlaka peninsula. Belgrade wants the latter as part of its strategic defense for its only deep-sea naval base at Kotor in Montenegro.

Croatia's relationship with the leaders of Herceg-Bosna, the Bosnian Croat para-state in neighboring Bosnia-Herzegovina, is just one more example of Croatia's strategy of "promise, but do not act." From the beginning of the year, both Tudjman and the Bosnian Croat nationalist elite were pressured by Western diplomats to abolish Herceg-Bosna and strengthen the Croat-Muslim federation. All kinds of promises were doled out to the various envoys of the international community. But the promises remained on paper only, and Herceg-Bosna continued to exist.

A POLARIZED PUBLIC

Croatia's internal-policy analysts watched one endless, boring game in the course of last year. The ruling HDZ's long-lasting game of cat and mouse against the opposition alliance became too predictable. HDZ fat cats no longer bother to eat the opposition mice anymore, since the latter posed no credible threat to the governing party.

Tudjman refused to confirm any of the four mayoral candidates proposed by the opposition-dominated Zagreb city council and eventually appointed his party comrade Matulovic-Dopulic to the post. In his elaboration of the move, Tudjman said he was determined not to let the opposition get into power because those "communists and fascists" would turn "democracy into anarchy." Tudjman was obviously determined to defend his political turf, while the opposition seemed to put up only a superficial fight for its legal rights. A new trend developed afterward in which opposition politicians would leave their parties and sign with the HDZ for a few promises and comfortable positions.

When they realized they could not beat Tudjman by legal means, some opposition leaders began to suggest that the negotiations with the ruling party seemed the only way out of the city-council deadlock. The disagreement that ensued seemed at one moment ready to split the coalition of seven opposition parties. In June, the media reported that secret negotiations had taken place between the HDZ and the main opposition party, the Croatian Social-Liberals (HSLS). Public reaction was strongly against it, catching HSLS leader Vlado Gotovac by surprise. Later, he said it was at that point that he had realized how dangerously polarized Croatian society had become. The HDZ was perceived as the negative force and the opposition as the positive force. Blending those two was immoral, according to public opinion. Thus, no resolution of the Zagreb crisis was in sight.

The year began and ended with strikes and manifestations of social unrest. A wave of strikes started in February with a one-day strike at Croatian Post and Telecommunications. And the year ended with a weeks-long strike of railway workers. Meanwhile, war veterans and invalids, as well as pensioners and teachers, held peaceful demonstrations to call the government's attention to their grievances. But the government remained deaf to their demands. In typical fashion, one HDZ official said that striking railway workers "can strike till Easter" as far as he was concerned, because "they will gain nothing anyway."

LITTLE REGARD FOR LIFE

The past year was not Croatia's best where human rights were concerned. Every few months, a new negative report on human rights in Croatia was issued either from the UN Security Council and its secretary-general, Boutros Boutros-Ghali, or from Elizabeth Rehn, the UN reporter for human rights; negative reports were also issued by other human-rights organizations. Most of those critics included the human-rights situation in former UN-protected areas in Croatia, where the remaining Serbs were reportedly intimidated and their property looted by "unidentified thugs," often wearing Croatian army uniforms. Despite its many promises to investigate human-rights violations perpetrated during military operations in 1995, the Croatian government did not close a single case. In addition, few Croatian Serbs returned to their homes, partly due to the numerous administrative obstacles set by both the Croatian and Serbian authorities. The Croatian Serb refugee situation revealed what both governments had in common: a complete absence of regard for human beings once their role as pawns in the power game was completed.

The amnesty that was so generously granted by Tudjman to 455 people at the beginning of the year turned out to be another trick for the outside world. After their release, reports followed that Serbs who had been granted amnesty were then rearrested under the excuse of being war criminals. According to the new amnesty law, rebel Serbs who participated in an occupation of parts of Croatian territory were given amnesty unless they were considered war criminals.

Adoption of the new amnesty law was one of the conditions presented by the international community for reintegration of (still) Serb-held eastern Slavonia into the Croatian legal system. Because of its poor record on treatment of the Serbian minority, the UN Security Council hesitated to hand over the administration of the region to Croatian authorities. Finally, the decision was to extend the presence of the UN Transitional Administration for eastern Slavonia for another six months after it expired in January 1997. But UN troops are to stay through the end of 1997 and observe the development of the events.

The latest events signal that Tudjman and the Croatian ruling elite have become increasingly nervous and less capable of coping with domestic and international calls for democracy. When reports surfaced that Tudjman was allegedly seriously ill, he lost his patience and started to crack down on his critics, putting continuous pressure on the independent media, sacking moderate politicians and officials who did not agree with his ideas, and harassing those involved with human-rights groups and nongovernmental organizations. Those moves seemed to have only increased criticism. The existing situation—in which Tudjman blacklists prominent Croats who are critical of his party as well as foreign news agencies reporting on Croatia—indirectly promotes isolationism, reminiscent of the communist-era lists of "internal and external" enemies.

That is certainly not the way to mobilize the nation after the fall of communism. Appeals to xenophobic nationalism seem to be out of date in Croatia today. People are more concerned with the realities of daily life; salaries are more important than alleged enemies. If Tudjman does not realize that soon, large-scale protests, as seen in Belgrade, could be the result. Demonstrations against the shutting down of independent station Radio 101 already brought some 100,000 people on the streets of Zagreb. It remains within the realm of possibility that people will decide to speak out against those who want to keep them silent, as it seems, forever.

Profile: FRANJO TUDJMAN: THE AWKWARD PATRIOT

by PATRICK MOORE

Croatian President Franjo Tudjman provokes controversy at home and abroad. But neither the fawning paeans of his admirers nor the epithets of his critics can capture the complexities of a man who has prevailed through the most volatile of times.

Tudjman is one of the most controversial and complex figures on Europe's post-communist political scene. To his supporters, he is the man who restored Croatian independent statehood for the first time since the nation was linked to Hungary in 1102. To his detractors, he is an insensitive nationalist, egotist, and autocrat who is intolerant of other points of view and brands all who disagree with him as enemies of Croatia. The Croatian president is not a man who inspires neutral or noncommittal reactions. Most articles about him in the domestic or international media tend to fit this pattern, portraying him as either the undisputed father of the nation or a fascistic tyrant, depending on the political views of the author.

A MAN OF HIS TIMES

Born into a peasant family in Zagorje in 1922, the young Tudjman rejected the extreme nationalism of the pro-Axis Ustashe group that Hitler had put into power. Like many other Croats of his generation, he joined Josip Broz Tito's Partisans, and in 1942 became a member of the Communist Party of Yugoslavia.

He has since claimed that he was attracted to the party primarily because of Tito's promise that postwar Yugoslavia would be a federal state and not the Serb-dominated, centralized one it had been for most of the interwar period.

Tudjman later claimed that he became disenchanted with the Communists within months of joining. He nonetheless stayed with the party, eventually rising to the rank of major-general in the postwar Yugoslav People's Army. He retired from the military in 1961 and devoted himself to the study of Croatian history and to Croatian nationalist political causes.

His political activities won him a prominent leadership role in the Croatian Spring movement in 1971. Tito branded the movement extreme-nationalist and crushed it, although its goals of cultural and political autonomy now seem tame compared with what emerged in Yugoslavia in the late 1980s. Tito sent Tudjman to jail for three years in 1971, having earlier forced his expulsion as a nationalist from the party.

For Tudjman and many of the Croats involved in the heady days of early 1971, the legacy of the Croatian Spring and its destruction was twofold. First, the events of 1971 eliminated any hope they still might have had for Yugoslavia as a state in which Croats could feel like Croats and be masters in their own home. Instead, such individuals came to feel like political subjects in a colony run from Belgrade with the help of Serbs from Croatia and of opportunist ethnic Croatians. Second, the events of 1971 helped to firmly establish the political credentials of those who led the movement. The political legacy of the Croatian Spring did not involve a desire for Western-style democracy; the main goal of the movement had been national autonomy.

After a second jail term in the 1980s for nationalist activities, Tudjman traveled abroad and laid the foundations for what would become the Croatian Democratic Community (HDZ), which is now the governing party. Traditionally, Croatia has been a country of emigrants, and earlier generations of economic migrants were joined abroad by many Ustashe and other anti-communists who fled the country at the end of the war. There were thus large groups of often quite prosperous Croats in North America, Australia, and Western Europe, many of whom had little love for either Yugoslavia as a multiethnic state or for the communists. It was among such people that Tudjman launched the HDZ.

On his travels, he met the Herzegovinian Gojko Susak, who ran a pizza parlor in Toronto. Susak helped Tudjman meet other Croatian businessmen, many from the poor and rugged land of Herzegovina, who provided the financial backing he needed. Tudjman never forgot his political debts to these men, and Susak—now Croatian defense minister—is widely regarded as the second most powerful man in Croatia. Critics of Tudjman would go on to say that the "Herzegovinian lobby"—as his benefactors have become known—wields a disproportionately large share of political and economic power in general.

THE DIE IS CAST

Tudjman was elected president by the Sabor, or parliament, after Croatia's first free multiparty elections in 1990. He later received a direct popular mandate in

1992, and he governs as head of state through a constitution—written especially for him—that established a very strong, French-style presidency.

His career as president has hardly been smooth sailing, however. It is debatable whether his ham-fisted dealings with the Serbian minority in 1990 actually led to their rebellion or whether the Serbs simply used that as an excuse to do what they had planned anyway. In any event, their rebellion, which began late in 1990, was remarkably well-organized and equally well-armed. But the centralist-minded president had not reassured them earlier when he denied them any real political autonomy and took away the advantages they had enjoyed for so long in some areas of employment and patronage, such as in the police and security forces.

The HDZ-dominated Sabor, moreover, approved state symbols that many Serbs associated with the Ustashe, even though those symbols were centuries old, were not carbon copies of those used by the Ustashe, and had been used to some extent even by the communist regime. Tudjman soon gained a reputation for insensitive actions and remarks, such as his statement to the effect that he was glad his wife is neither a Serb nor a Jew.

For Tudjman and his supporters, however, the important issues in his career center on the struggle for independence that began in earnest in the summer of 1991. Serbian President Slobodan Milosevic was blocking attempts at constitutional reform, such as the compromise formulas worked out by Macedonia and Bosnia and Herzegovina. The result was that Croatia and Slovenia both declared independence on the evening of 25 June 1991. The Serb-dominated Yugoslav People's Army struck first at Slovenia, but met their defeat at the hands of well-armed and well-motivated Slovenian militia units. The Serbs had more luck in Croatia, however, and not just because that country had a 12 percent Serbian minority that was in an advanced state of rebellion. In Slovenia, the arms stored in the arsenals of the Territorial Defense, a sort of citizens' militia, had been turned against the Yugoslav People's Army. But Tudjman seems to have let the Serbs take charge of the arsenals, with the result that his soldiers were poorly prepared for the conflict, especially in terms of heavy weapons.

Perhaps Tudjman's biggest political mistake came in the spring of 1993, when he followed his own mistrust of Islam and the advice of the Herzegovinians and launched a fratricidal war against the Bosnian Muslims. Tudjman was extricated from that unpopular conflict by the patient diplomacy of his friends and allies, above all by that of U.S. Ambassador Peter Galbraith. In the course of the conflict, the Croatian position was consolidated in Herzegovina at the expense of the Muslims, but in central Bosnia, where the Muslims held sway, dozens of Croatian communities dating back to the Middle Ages were driven into exile. Tudjman's launching of the war fueled rumors that he had plotted with Milosevic to split up Bosnia between Croatia and Serbia.

A MIXED RECORD

Tudjman continues to be accused of being intolerant and autocratic. Apparently frustrated by the HDZ's failure to win two-thirds of the seats in the Sabor in the fall 1995 elections, he dubbed the opposition majority on the Zagreb city council "enemies of state policy" and hamstrung their operations. He placed his son Miroslav in charge of the secret services, presumably in order to ensure those forces' personal loyalty. Tudjman's office flouted international opinion by announcing the promotion of an officer just one day after that man's indictment for war crimes by the International Criminal Tribunal for the Former Yugoslavia in The Hague. Among the public at large, the HDZ government was widely believed to be using privatization as a means to reward Tudjman's cronies. Critics both at home and abroad objected to the HDZ's virtual monopoly of the electronic media and its dominance in the print media, as well as its practice of hounding the few independent periodicals with lawsuits and fines.

Part of Tudjman's strength, however, comes from the weakness of the opposition, which has been unable to close ranks against the HDZ or produce a serious alternative to Tudjman. Unlike Milosevic, he is regarded as an honest if excessively blunt man who sincerely believes in his nationalist principles.

But enigmas remain. His political standing at home and abroad improved after the ending of the war with the Muslims at the start of 1994 and the conclusion of the Dayton peace agreement for Bosnia in late 1995. His policies in general appear to have been vindicated, moreover, by the military's successful Operation Blitz and Operation Storm in May and August of 1995 which effectively destroyed the Serbian rebels' state and sent the Serbian civilian population fleeing.

When he took a triumphal train trip through much of the captured region, however, he made a number of remarks about the Serbs who had left that led critics to charge that he was as insensitive as ever to the concerns and welfare of ethnic minorities. And he failed to turn the military victories into political capital in the snap legislative elections he called for October 1995, in which the HDZ failed to get the two-thirds majority it had hoped for. Some observers suggested that the voters had served notice on Tudjman and the HDZ that they were tired of autocratic, one-party rule and that they wanted to get down to the business of building democracy and prosperity now that the war could no longer be used as an excuse to delay reform.

Document: KRAJINA LIBERATION ARMY WARNS CROATIA

With a devastating attack on a Croatian arms factory on 26 July, the self-proclaimed Krajina Liberation Army (KOA) launched what it promised would be a campaign of terror against Croatia to reclaim the Krajina region. Croatia took back the Krajina from rebel Croatian Serbs in an August 1995 military campaign that surprised most observers with its speed and efficiency. In a fax pub-

lished by the Belgrade daily Dnevni telegraf *on 31 July 1996, a new group calling itself the KOA took responsibility for the bombing of Croatia's largest agricultural and military equipment production plant, located 250 kilometers east of Zagreb in Slavonski Brod. The blast injured 18 people and demolished the factory, which produced weapons for the Croatian army during the 1991– 1992 war against the Croatian Serbs. The group has also allegedly issued a list of targets for liquidation, mostly Serbs loyal to the Croatian government. On 13 August, the Croatian state-run daily* Vjesnik *also reported receiving a message from the KOA that said it had planted the bombs that damaged the Zagreb statue of former Mayor Vjeceslav Holjevac.* Vjesnik's *correspondent, however, questioned whether there really was such a group as the KOA. He alleged that the message was an invention of the Serbian media designed to cause panic and chaos in Croatia; in response, the Serbian independent daily* Nasa Borba *also suggested the KOA was a fabrication, but one created by the Croatian state-run media to excuse any future action taken against Croatian Serbs. The initial KOA statement, translated by BBC monitoring and printed below, was addressed to the Association of Croatian Serbs; Milan Martic, former president of the self-proclaimed Republic of Serb Krajina in Croatia; and other Krajina associations and committees.*

"Dear Sirs!

What gives you the right to speak on behalf of us Serbs from the Republic of Serb Krajina and to represent us in general? Who has authorized you to do that? We certainly have not!

We have had enough of your empty talk (you could go on like that forever), your writings, your appearances on television and your association with foreigners and the authorities here in Serbia, all of this behind our backs. None of this has brought our return to our homes any closer!

We are taking our destiny into our own hands and, from now on, be advised that the KOA will begin an all-out confrontation with the traitors among the Serb people.

Be advised that Croatians will pay for 4 and 5 August 1995 [when Croatia took control of the Krajina region] and for all the ensuing years whenever they celebrate their victory over the Republic of Serb Krajina. Wherever they gather to celebrate, they will bathe in their own blood—that we can promise, and you can convey the message to them. We shall avenge our dead, who were left throughout all parts of the Krajina only to be trodden on by wild Ustashe [Croatian fascist] hordes. On those dates, all of Croatia will be in flames! We will not be responsible for the casualties, no matter how many they may be, just as they were not responsible!

We have our weapons, ammunition, and all we need, and we are keeping that hidden in the right place. We are trained well enough, and we are courageous enough to embark on our sacred mission.

The liberation of the Krajina and the destruction of the Ustashe! We have nothing to lose except our lives, which no one cares about anyway, because they are pushing us wherever they want, even though we extend from here to the Albanian border.

We no longer give you the right to represent us, because of what you are doing in the Krajina—looking after your own interests only and not caring about the poor and hungry people. We shall bring all of our enemies before our people's tribunal—the Krajina Liberation Tribunal—we are not going to wait for [the war crimes tribunal in] The Hague.

Inform all those whom it may concern so that they do not say that they were not informed!

Freedom for the Krajina!!!"

Bosnia-Herzegovina

Population:	3,200,000
	Bosnian federation: 2,300,000
	Republika Srpska: 900,000
Capital:	Sarajevo (pop. 350,000)
Major cities:	Banja Luka (240,000), Tuzla (pop. 240,000 including refugees), Zenica (pop. 160,000), Mostar (pop. 100,000)
Area:	51,233 sq. km.
Major ethnic groups:	Muslim 43.7%, Serbian 31.4%, Croatian 17.3%, other 7.6% (1991 census)
Economy:	GDP growth: 35% (World Bank estimate)
. . . .	Inflation rate: 3%
. . . .	Average monthly income:
. . . .	Bosnian federation: $153
. . . .	Republika Srpska: $25–$35
. . . .	Unemployment rate: 50%–60%

UNITED ON PAPER BUT NOT IN DEED IN BOSNIA-HERZEGOVINA

by PATRICK MOORE

Implementation of the Dayton peace accord, or lack thereof, has shown that the road to Balkan peace continues to be long and rocky.

The Dayton peace accord was signed on 14 December 1995 in Paris, the result of months of diplomatic activity by Washington's chief envoy to the former Yugoslavia, Assistant Secretary of State Richard Holbrooke. The Dayton agreement was not only the result of that activity; it came about also because Serbian President Slobodan Milosevic decided he needed to end to the war-linked sanctions strangling the economy of the Federal Republic of Yugoslavia. The military position of the Bosnian Serbs, moreover, was rapidly collapsing under a Croat-Muslim offensive, together with NATO air strikes and a no-nonsense approach by the NATO Rapid Reaction Force in Sarajevo.

The treaty's implementation garnered mixed—often disappointed—reactions, even though the political prestige of the international community and NATO were on the line. The biggest success was that the fighting stopped, and Dayton's military provisions were generally met—in part because the fighting in the course of 1995 had worn the Serbs down and thrown them on the defensive, while the Muslims and the Croats had valuable political, military, and economic incentives to do as Washington wished.

All was not the best it could be, however, on the military front. Experts on all sides agreed that the hundreds of thousands of mines scattered throughout Bosnia-Herzegovina will probably never all be found and neutralized. Moreover, journalists often accuse NATO's Implementation Force (IFOR) of looking the other way in the face of illegal-arms caches unless the press was present to call attention to it.

Last fall, skirmishes broke out as Muslims tried to return to their homes in Serb-held territory; Dayton had given them the right to go home. That was especially the case in the area between Muslim-held Celic and Serb-controlled Koraj in northeastern Bosnia, just south of the strategic Brcko region. IFOR, the UN's International Police Task Force (IPTF), and the Serbs accused the Muslims of staging a provocation by bringing weapons into a demilitarized zone. The UN High Commissioner for Refugees finally helped to establish orderly procedures to enable refugees to return, but the Muslims charged that the Serbs were using the lists of applicants to target Muslim homes for destruction.

There were, of course, some successes in the civilian sector as well. Elections took place on 14 September for all but the local-level offices, and if the nationalist parties won, that was not the fault of the election monitors. New government structures to connect the federation with the Republika Srpska came into being.

If they were proving unworkable, it was the fault of Dayton's complexities, not the implementation of it. Some reconstruction and investment projects were launched, even though not all the money pledged was actually delivered, and even though only 2 percent of those funds found their way to the impoverished Republika Srpska. International reconstruction agencies have remarked that tens of thousands of young men were sitting around without work, the only skill that many of them knew was killing, though precious little has been done to employ or train them.

But that is just about all there is on the positive side of the Bosnian balance sheet. Most civilian provisions of Dayton were honored more in the breach than in the practice. That was because the international community and its representatives on the ground—including IFOR and the IPTF—had neither the will nor the mandate to enforce them. The result was that Bosnia-Herzegovina remained effectively divided into three states governed by the respective nationalist parties of each ethnicity: Serbs, Croats, and Muslims. A united country existed only on the pages of the Dayton agreement.

NATIONALISTS IN THE SADDLE

The Dayton agreement called for elections, but free elections could not be possible without free discussion. But the Dayton provision stressing the need to establish or develop free media and above all to ban the propagation of ethnic hatred remained largely a dead letter. While some independent periodicals and radio stations were established primarily on Muslim territory and even in the Republika Srpska, the all-important medium of television remained largely in nationalist hands. Physical violence was used by the police or by mysteriously well-organized gangs against opposition parties on all three sides.

Against that background, it came as no surprise that the Party of Democratic Action (SDA) of Alija Izetbegovic triumphed among the Muslims, easily defeating a challenge from former Prime Minister Haris Silajdzic and his new Party for Bosnia and Herzegovina (SBiH). The SDA contained a wing that took very seriously the idea of maintaining a unified, multiethnic state, but largely out of the realization that only such an entity offered the best opportunity for the long-term political and physical survival of the Muslims. The party, moreover, also had a faction of Islamic hard-liners, including some high-ranking security and military personnel with close wartime ties to Iran and the Muslim world. But Bosnian Muslim society remained largely secular and European. The hard-liners accordingly remained a minority that was mainly of interest to Serbs, Croats, and others seeking to frighten foreign audiences into thinking that there was some sort of Iran-in-the-making in the western Balkans.

Similarly, Kresimir Zubak's Croatian Democratic Community (HDZ)—which is simply a branch organization of the governing party in Croatia of the same name—won among the Croats. This was especially the case in western Herzegovina and the adjoining areas, known as the Croatian Republic (or Community) of Herceg-Bosna. That para-state was to have been abolished not only under Dayton but, according to the original Croat-Muslim peace agreement concluded in early 1994, almost two years earlier.

In any event, Croatian officials from President Franjo Tudjman on down had repeatedly signed documents promising that Herceg-Bosna would disappear. But by December 1996, it was still very much alive. It had even set up offices in a building that was supposed to have housed a unified Mostar city government of Croats, Muslims, and Serbs. The Croat-Muslim federation remained, in fact, very much one confined to paper, and nowhere were the tensions more pronounced than in sharply divided Mostar. Hopes that the elections in June would lead to a real reunification of the city proved unfounded. By the end of the year, the remaining Muslims continued to be evicted from their homes in Croat-held west Mostar, just as the few Croats left in Muslim-controlled central Bosnia faced discrimination from local officials.

The Republika Srpska similarly ended the year with the nationalists sitting firmly in the saddle. True, the governing Serbian Democratic Party (SDS) won "only" about two-thirds of the vote in the 14 September ballot despite its control of the media and the police (it was expected to win by more). But its main challenger for the Serbian vote had not been any multiethnic party, but rather a Serbian coalition—the Alliance for Peace and Progress—with links to Milosevic. Many voted for the alliance simply because they wanted closer ties to federal Yugoslavia, not because they were anti-nationalist. And within the Republika Srpska's own legislature, the SDS took 45 seats, compared with 14 for the SDA and only 10 for the alliance.

DEAD LETTERS, OPEN QUESTIONS

Since the same nationalists who fought the war thus remained in control on all three sides, the only way Dayton's civilian provisions could succeed was if IFOR and the IPTF took a tough approach in enforcing them. Unfortunately for Dayton and its concept of a multiethnic, unified Bosnia-Herzegovina, both IFOR and the IPTF interpreted their mandates very narrowly, which in practice meant doing little more than preventing any resumption of hostilities.

One key point stressed in Dayton but left unenforced was the right to freedom of movement throughout the republic. Not only did this not exist between the federation and the Republika Srpska, but it was little honored between the Croatian and Muslim areas within the federation itself.

A second and related issue was the right of refugees to return home, regardless of which nationality might now be in control there. That provision was not observed at all. Typically, refugees attempting to go home on foot or in buses would be blocked by groups of nasty crowds armed with sticks and projectiles. That was especially true of Muslims trying to go back to the Republika Srpska, but each nationality could cite similar examples at the hands of the other two. In any event, IFOR and IPTF forces would not try to teach the wrongdoers a lesson; they simply sought to prevent any clashes. The result was the consolidation—even the continuation—of "ethnic cleansing."

A third problem was the failure to arrest indicted war criminals and bring them to justice. They continued to roam and work freely, in some cases regularly passing under the noses of IFOR and IPTF patrols that just looked the other way rather than risk casualties. That was despite pleas from The Hague that the arrest and trial of such individuals was necessary for lasting peace; it would put an end to the idea that one nationality or another was guilty. That had been a key principle behind the war-crimes trials at the end of World War II, but by the end of 1996, only seven of the dozens of indicted war criminals had actually gone to The Hague. Those included none of the big fish, although former Bosnian Serb civilian leader Radovan Karadzic had been forced to leave public life in July. His military counterpart, General Ratko Mladic, was sent into retirement by Karadzic's hand-picked successor, Biljana Plavsic, in November, but that reflected a long-term civilian-military rivalry among the Bosnian Serb leadership rather than any desire to help the tribunal.

Finally, there were some key unresolved issues in 1996 that were held over for 1997. Those issues remained a potential source of instability or worse. The first involved the disarmament of the Serbs, who lagged behind schedule in reducing their weapons stockpiles. The United States and some of its friends were rapidly working to narrow the arms gap between the Republika Srpska and the federation by helping the latter, but the Serbs dragged their feet on disarming. And rumors abounded on all three sides that fighting could resume as early as the fall of 1997.

The second open question was the status of Brcko and its surrounding corridor, which was the only territorial issue not resolved at Dayton. It was left for international arbitration in December, but the deadline was postponed to February 1997 because the Serbs refused to attend the meetings. They had good reason to hamstring the talks, since any change in their present control over the once-Muslim town and its neighboring region threatened to cut communications between the eastern and western halves of the Republika Srpska. Brcko remained a high-stakes game.

The third main unresolved issue was the local elections. Those were postponed from 14 September into the new year following a dispute over what was called the P-2 option. That provision stated that voters might register to cast their ballots in any town where they claimed they would eventually live. The Bosnian Serb authorities in particular had used this to force voters into registering for strategic towns—such as Brcko or Srebrenica—over which Pale wanted to consolidate its power. The Muslims then complained of fraud and forced the Organization for Security and Cooperation in Europe to postpone the vote. The Serbs, for their part, refused to honor any new ballot without the P-2 option. By the end of 1996, the matter was no nearer to resolution than it was in September.

CHANGE FROM WITHOUT?

But if little changed inside Bosnia itself, the feeling grew by the end of the year that developments in Croatia and in Serbia might break the logjam. November and December witnessed massive social and political protests in Zagreb at a time when President Franjo Tudjman was widely believed to be dying of cancer. His responses to criticism sounded increasingly paranoid and shrill, prompting many observers to recall the collapse of other regimes in Eastern Europe in 1989. Some feared that were Tudjman to die, hard-liners might try to stage a coup and sabotage the Dayton process, but others felt that Croatia stood on the threshold of a new era of peace and democracy. In any event, there was little support in Croatia for the Herceg-Bosna crowd, who were generally regarded as a corrupt group of thugs who had gained too much power in Croatia.

And the spirit of 1989 was present in Belgrade as well. Western leaders avoided the temptation to cling to Milosevic as the guarantor of stability in Bosnia; instead, they called upon the Serbian leadership to respect the 17 November election results. But the United States and other Western countries stopped short of fully embracing the opposition parties and the demonstrators, and with good reason where Bosnia was concerned.

First, the opposition's Vuk Draskovic and Zoran Djindjic had long-standing ties to the Bosnian Serb nationalists. Draskovic once had links to the notorious paramilitaries, and Djindjic was particularly close to the SDS. He had also stated that Bosnia will eventually fragment into three ethnically based states and that the Croatian and Serbian components would gravitate toward Croatia and Serbia, respectively. Of the three main leaders of the Zajedno coalition, only Vesna Pesic was a solid democrat and a supporter of civil society. It was not clear, moreover, what those people would actually do if their coalition came to power, provided, of course that it did not disintegrate first.

Second, the demonstrations in Belgrade did not include only democrats but also nationalists, particularly but not only among the students. Those were people who were angry with Milosevic for what they regarded as the sellout of the Krajina and Bosnian Serbs in 1995. Plavsic had already praised these students and said that she would march with them if she were in Belgrade.

By December, attention was thus centered more on Serbia than on Bosnia, but with good reason: the political pressures that ultimately destroyed Josip Broz Tito's Yugoslavia in 1991 began in Serbia and then spread to the multiethnic community that had been Bosnia and Herzegovina in 1992. It was only through the establishment of democracy in Serbia that real peace in the region was possible, particularly given the failure of the international community to enforce the Dayton agreement for Bosnia that the international community itself had sponsored. For more analysis of the Dayton accord see the articles by Susan Woodward and Janusz Bugajski later in this volume (pp. 384–401).

Profile: ALIJA IZETBEGOVIC: FROM AMATEUR POLITICIAN TO MASTER MANIPULATOR

by ZLATAN CABARAVDIC

Alija Izetbegovic's career abounds with contradictions and unclarities, ambiguous political positions and half-finished business, forgotten ideas, and discarded associates, defeats, and victories. But, despite everything, Izetbegovic is the undisputed ruler of Bosnia, equally respected at home and abroad.

Izetbegovic appeared on the Bosnian political scene in 1990 as a founder and the first president of the Party of Democratic Action (SDA), whose main task was to "advocate the interests of people pertaining to the Islamic cultural circle." A former lawyer, Izetbegovic is a prolific writer, who had problems publishing his works, since his essays and treatises dealing with issues related to Islam were not well received by the communist authorities. He was twice sentenced, in 1946 and in 1983, for "counterrevolutionary activity"—that is, for his Islamic activism.

When Izetbegovic was elected president of Bosnia-Herzegovina in the first multiparty elections in 1990, many thought it was a ploy by the then-ruling communists to show the public that even a devoutly religious Muslim new to politics could become the head of a state that had been ruled exclusively by atheists for 45 years. But the ensuing chain of events clearly shows that Izetbegovic has managed to fool the communists, as well as political analysts and all those who had thought that the amateur politician would falter in the face of the first serious problem.

Quite to the contrary, Izetbegovic was a fast learner who quickly transformed himself into a professional. The first to discover this were his SDA co-founders, Adil Zulfikarpasic and Muhamed Filipovic. The two better-known and more widely recognized politicians tried to oust Izetbegovic from the post of party president on the eve of the 1990 elections, only to find themselves expelled from the party and subsequently marginalized on the larger political scene. Next in the line of contenders for primacy within the SDA and the presidency of Bosnia-Herzegovina was Fikret Abdic. Abdic, a former member of the Central Committee of the League of Communists of Yugoslavia and a political and business kingpin in the Bihac region, had come to believe that he had accumulated enough political experience, knowledge, and power for a successful showdown with Izetbegovic, whom he labeled a "pensioner pretending to be a politician." But Izetbegovic again outwitted his opponent. Instead of entering into an open conflict—as he had done with Zulfikarpasic and Filipovic—this time he opted for a behind-the-scenes approach. The public was simply informed of the fait accompli.

His treatment of the opposition is the best example of Izetbegovic's increasing political mastery. Whenever he was in need of parading a "multiethnic Bosnia" on the international scene, Izetbegovic grew closer to the so-called civic—as opposed to nationalist—opposition parties and included some of their leaders (mainly ethnic Serbs and Croats) in the state delegations. But whenever important decisions were being made, he had no time to talk to the opposition.

Although it has been obvious for quite some time that Izetbegovic controls the government, the police, the army, the judiciary, radio and television, and a good part of the print media and religious institutions, the overwhelming majority of the Bosnian public and a part of the international public perceive him as a fighter for democracy and civic freedom.

For the majority of Bosniaks—the ethnic but not necessarily practicing

Muslims of Bosnia-Herzegovina—Izetbegovic is also the "father of the nation," although his SDA vehemently opposed use of the term "Bosniak." (Until 1993, the SDA favored the term "Muslim" to describe the nationality.) But when it became obvious that the use of "Bosniak" could not be easily stopped, the SDA co-sponsored the Bosniak Assembly—a national convention that assembled almost all of the leading names from political, religious, and cultural spheres in the country. The gathering adopted a decision on "returning the historical—Bosniak—name to the nation and returning the term Muslim to its rightful place—to the sphere of religion." Izetbegovic's party passionately opposes any mention of the existence of Catholic Bosniaks, Orthodox Bosniaks, and atheist Bosniaks, despite decades of insistence by some that Bosnia is inhabited by a single nation—the Bosniaks—professing different religious creeds. For the SDA, at this moment, Bosniaks are only those citizens of Bosnia-Herzegovina whose origin is linked to the Islamic religion and culture.

One of Izetbegovic's political adversaries—Nenad Kecmanovic, the Bosnian Serb former leader of the nonnationalist Reform Party predicts that Izetbegovic will remain in power even after the planned 1998 presidential election, and sees failing health the only serious potential challenge to Izetbegovic on the political scene.

[Translated by Sava Tatic]

Federal Repulic of Yugoslavia_____

Population:	11,100,000
Capital:	Belgrade (pop. 1,087,915)
Major cities:	Nis (pop. 247,898); Novi Sad (pop. 170,029); Pristina, Kosovo (pop. 108,020); Podgorica, Montenegro (pop. 96,074)
Area:	102,350 sq. km.
Major ethnic groups:	Serbian 63%, Albanian 14%, Montenegrin 6%, Hungarian 4%, other 13%
Economy:	GDP growth: 4.3%
....	Inflation rate: 60%
....	Average monthly income: $123
....	Unemployment rate: 26.1

BACKTRACKING TOWARD DICTATOR-
SHIP IN SERBIA AND MONTENEGRO

by STAN MARKOTICH

In the Federal Republic of Yugoslavia, Serbian President Slobodan Milosevic continued his campaign to woo the international community. He contended that he has been the architect of regional peace, not of the savage bloodletting in former Yugoslavia. Near the close of 1996, Serbian President Slobodan Milosevic's true colors resurfaced. Once again, he showed himself to be no stalwart of peace and democracy, but a regional dictator, bent on centralizing all the power of his office. The issue this time was the municipal elections. At first, it seemed hardly conceivable that the government's attempt to subvert opposition wins in the 17 November municipal runoffs could form the basis for a sustained series of daily peaceful mass protests against Milosevic's dictatorship.

The trigger was the second round of local balloting; the opposition Zajedno (Together) coalition—made up of Vuk Draskovic's Serbian Renewal Movement, Zoran Djindjic's Democratic Party, and Vesna Pesic's Serbian Civic League, later joined by Vojislav Kostunica's Democratic Party of Serbia—won majorities in the republic's 12 largest municipalities, which account for about 60 percent of Serbia's total population. The local Belgrade electoral commission initially announced that Zajedno might have picked up at least 60 of the 110 seats in the Belgrade Municipal Assembly. That meant that Djindjic, Zajedno's mayoral candidate, was poised to become Belgrade's first noncommunist mayor since 1945. Official state-media reports hastened to add that those were merely preliminary returns, and as a portend of what was ahead, said the results could be contested. The Socialist Party of Serbia wasted little time in bringing legal action, which resulted in the nullification of election results and paved the way for a third round of balloting that enabled the Socialists to claim tainted victories.

Within days of the local-election runoffs, Zajedno leaders, addressing a crowd of approximately 35,000 gathered in Nis, Serbia's second largest city, said the ruling Socialists were not prepared to accept defeat and were embarking on a wave of postelection fraud. In some cases, the commission delayed the release of official results, and in some jurisdictions, yet another round of runoffs was slated to take place to fill seats that allegedly had not been decided. Zajedno called for a boycott of that round, which in some places—notably Belgrade—enabled the Socialists to send their supporters to the polls to secure a third-round victory.

Almost immediately, the demonstrations gained a momentum of their own. Later they expanded into calls for Milosevic's resignation. Zajedno leaders repeatedly said that they would not call off the peaceful protests before the opposition victories were recognized. On several days, the number of street demonstrators in Belgrade swelled to more than 250,000. The government wavered between appearing to make concessions and taking a hard line that bordered on a crackdown. Among the hardest hit were the independent media. Belgrade's independent Radio B 92 had its frequencies jammed and finally on 3 December was taken off the air, along with the student-run Radio Index and other outlets. But heavy public pressure as well as a groundswell from the international community made the government back off, and the stations were back on the air after only two days. Other media outlets, such as the daily *Blic*, founded in 1996, were pressured to conform with government accounts of the mass demonstrations.

Toward the end of the year, the Milosevic regime started organizing its own demonstrations. Those took place in smaller towns and villages and attracted only several thousand, mainly diehard communists and the elderly.

BACK AND FORTH

What emerged as a pattern for the regime in its dealings with the demonstrators was a seeming willingness to play both the reconciler and the stalwart opponent of any concessions. For example, while mass demonstrations continued across Serbia, and the independent trade union Nezavisnost led another huge rally in Belgrade, Milosevic met with students on 17 December. A student delegation that had marched to Belgrade from Serbia's second-largest city, Nis, presented Milosevic with a protest letter and samples of spoiled ballots. Milosevic pledged to investigate allegations of electoral improprieties and a state-television broadcast quoted him as saying, "Mistakes are always possible. I assure you that this state will not protect someone who has broken the law, whether that someone is a citizen or an official."

At the same time, Milosevic struck a note of defiance, telling the students he would not tolerate their alleged promoting of foreign meddling in Serbian "domestic" affairs. "We must be completely clear, however much your leaders go to embassies and send envoys and travel to world capitals, a foreign hand shall not rule Serbia," Reuters quoted him saying. Meanwhile, the Organization for Security and Cooperation in Europe (OSCE) confirmed on 17 December that it would send a delegation, headed by former Spanish Prime Minister Felipe Gonzalez, to Belgrade to investigate circumstances surrounding the disputed election results.

Milan Milutinovic, the Federal Republic of Yugoslavia's foreign minister, said on 19 December that yet another round of municipal elections in those centers where the Zajedno coalition had originally scored victories could not be ruled out, but such elections would be made contingent on a recommendation by the OSCE. "Should the OSCE delegation recommend, after making a thorough and impartial review, new elections in Serbia, we would accept that," he said. Moreover, Milutinovic also refrained from taking a hard line, heaping criticism at the demonstrators and telling them that their strategy of peaceful mass protest had outlived its usefulness. "Here in Serbia, there is an old saying that when the song is over, you stop singing," he said.

With the international focus on Serbia's municipal elections, the national elections and republican Montenegrin elections in November were almost obscured. One of the main issues was Milosevic's political future. His second term as Serbian president expires in late 1997, and he is constitutionally barred from seeking a third. To continue at the helm of Belgrade politics, he will likely seek the federal presidency for a possible seven-year term. Milosevic needs allies in the federal parliament, since it elects the president.

Yet officials' behavior just hours after the polls closed suggested they never really doubted the outcome. Only hours after voting stopped at 8 P.M., a Socialist representative told the press that Milosevic's leftist coalition had "an overwhelming lead" over Zajedno, and that all that remained uncertain was the final margin of victory. Opposition parties, however, did raise serious and substantive questions over alleged electoral improprieties. Djindjic said he was barred from monitoring polls in several districts. Others observed that throughout the campaign, the Socialists dominated most media coverage of the elections—which failed to even mention opposition-party rallies—and that the Socialists still controlled vote counting. In addition, independent and pro-opposition media encountered difficulties in reporting returns, prompting allegations of government interference.

Ultimately, however, the leftist coalition headed by Milosevic and his wife, Mirjana Markovic, and their potential supporters failed to win a two-thirds majority in the 138–seat federal parliament. A two-thirds vote would assure a candidate election to the post of federal president. *Nasa Borba* on 7 November reported that Milosevic's leftist coalition had won 64 seats and that the Democratic Socialist Party, a likely ally and Montenegro's ruling party, had won 20. Zajedno received 22 seats, the ultranationalist Serbian Radical Party, led by accused war criminal Vojislav Seselj, garnered 16. The remaining seats were parceled out among six minor parties and coalitions. Milosevic is likely to curry favor with the minor parties as a way of gaining the support of 91 deputies in a bid for the federal presidency.

DIPLOMATIC STRIDES

Well through mid-year, things looked to be going Milosevic's way. For a time, it seemed that Serbia would continue to reap gains from the Dayton peace agreement. Since Dayton, Belgrade has in fact accomplished a series of diplomatic steps, all aimed at gaining international recognition. Two stand out: following the formal conclusion of hostilities in Bosnia and Herzegovina, Milosevic was front and center in the diplomatic offensive to extend recognition to a number of former republics of Tito's Yugoslavia. The first landmark event of the year came on 8 April. Milutinovic and his Macedonian counterpart Ljubomir Frckovski met in Belgrade and signed a treaty of mutual recognition and cooperation. Initially, Milosevic himself was to fly to Macedonia to attend the 20 March proceeding for at least setting in motion the normalization process. That trip, however, was abruptly canceled with no official explanation. It is tempting to speculate that Milosevic canceled his visit to Macedonia so as not to overly antagonize Athens, which had supported federal Yugoslavia during its period of isolation during the regional wars and which was involved in a series of disputes with Macedonia, including Greece's contention that the name "Macedonia" implied territorial claims on Greece.

Nevertheless, recognizing Macedonia yielded windfalls. Well prior to the 8 April event, at least one diplomat, Michael Weninger, Austria's charge d'affaires in Belgrade, said that the European Union would be prepared to extend full diplomatic relations to Belgrade "just as soon as mutual recognition between Yugoslavia and Macedonia takes place." On 10 April, the EU issued a statement saying that Belgrade-Skopje recognition "opens the way to recognition by [EU] member states of the Federal Republic of Yugoslavia as one of the successor states of the Socialist Federal Republic of Yugoslavia." And recognition was forthcoming. On 22 April, Finland—following similar moves by France, Britain, Sweden, Denmark, Norway, the Netherlands, Portugal, Italy, and Germany—became the 10th country to recognize rump Yugoslavia as the Federal Republic of Yugoslavia. At last, it seemed that Milosevic had found the key to ending his diplomatic isolation. The other major diplomatic event of 1996 was the recognition between Zagreb and Belgrade.

Related events began unfolding when Milosevic met Croatian President Franjo Tudjman near Athens in the spa resort of Vouliagmeni on 7 August. That was the first official meeting between the two since Croatia declared independence in 1991, although the two reportedly met secretly on at least one occasion to discuss the partitioning of Bosnia. Even though that meeting has been officially denied, the parallel between it and the Greek meeting sparked speculation in the international press that at least talk of partitioning Bosnia may have been on the agenda in Greece, too. That notwithstanding, when Croatian Foreign Minister Mate Granic met with his counterpart Milutinovic on 23 August, a normalization accord was signed. Its exact text—and precisely how it would ultimately be interpreted—triggered some disputes in both nations' media.

Nevertheless, Milosevic's canceling of the local elections ended his streak of diplomatic wins. The international community responded by threatening to renew sanctions, undoubtedly reminding Milosevic that not so long ago, federal Yugoslavia had been relegated to wholesale pariah status.

MONTENEGRO'S POSITION

Throughout 1996, some apparent evidence surfaced that may have convinced some observers that even within the Yugoslav federation, Milosevic had serious opponents. Montenegro, the argument went, posed a problem for Milosevic's authoritarian central rule. Closer examination, however, threw such conclusions into question.

At several points during 1996, Montenegro did seem to be standing up to Belgrade. For example, on 21 April 1996, Montenegrin Premier Milo Djukanovic and Predrag Goranovic, the republic's foreign minister, traveled to the United States for what local media dubbed "a working visit." There, they reportedly aimed to further the republic's goals of "normalizing and intensifying relations with the United States and leading financial institutions, which is a priority of Montenegro's foreign policy." The visit may have been disapproved of: the Belgrade embassy in Washington claimed it had no knowledge of

Djukanovic's mission. And while in the United States, Djukanovic commented on an unfolding issue in Belgrade, presenting a point of view not shared by federal authorities and certainly not by Milosevic.

Meanwhile, National Bank Governor Dragoslav Avramovic was in the process of being ousted. He was not removed from his post until 15 May, but while the Montenegrins were in the United States signs were emerging that Avramovic was on his way out. Even though Avramovic had done little to challenge Milosevic's regime, he had come to be regarded as a reformer. In January 1994, he stemmed hyperinflation by introducing the "super dinar," pegged to the German mark at an exchange rate of 1:1. Also, he briefly led the Zajedno electoral list for the November 1996 elections before suddenly withdrawing. By early 1996, he had become an open advocate of Belgrade's rejoining major international financial institutions. That likely put him at odds with Milosevic, who was unwilling to make blanket concessions to the reforms needed to re-establish ties with the International Monetary Fund (IMF) and the World Bank. Probably for his unwillingness to back away from his very public and highly vocal demands for Belgrade to seek reintegration, Avramovic was sacked.

On 23 April, federal Finance Minister Jovan Zebic was named Belgrade's chief negotiator with the IMF, replacing Avramovic. Back in the United States, the Montenegrins sided with Avramovic, also endorsing his policy that the best route for rump Yugoslavia to take was that of reform and membership in the World Bank and IMF.

In reality, however, Montenegrin politicians' demands, which appear to put them at odds with Milosevic and Belgrade, are mitigated by a desire to iron out any differences amicably. Bulatovic has said he will back Milosevic in his bid to become federal president. To be sure, at times Montenegro's backing of Milosevic has been clumsy at best. One example stands out: Bulatovic's defense of accused war criminal General Ratko Mladic, former head of the Bosnian Serb army.

In a show of bravado, Mladic at one point made a high-profile public appearance in Belgrade. The occasion was the funeral of his colleague General Djordje Djukic, who had also been indicted by the Hague war-crimes tribunal but was freed because of his failing health. Djukic died in Belgrade on 18 May 1996. And Mladic was not the only accused war criminal at the funeral. Colonel Veselin Sljivancanin, one of three officers accused in the mass murder of 260 civilians in 1991 in the Croatian town of Vukovar, also attended. Some unconfirmed reports, ultimately proved false, even placed then-Bosnian Serb President Radovan Karadzic at the funeral.

Bulatovic himself, not Milosevic, publicly explained why Mladic had made such a high-profile public appearance in Belgrade and why he was not apprehended to face charges of war crimes. Bulatovic said at a 26 May press conference that war criminals were unwelcome in federal Yugoslavia. That assertion was undermined the second Bulatovic focused on Mladic, who Bulatovic said had entered Serbia because of police "inattention." The Montenegrin president said that "the policy of Yugoslavia precludes the entrance of war criminals onto the territory of the federal state. But in the meantime, we do not carry out the policies of some police state."

THE SAME OLD SONG

Early 1996 had something in common with the close of the year: Milosevic was engaged in one of his periodic campaigns of repression. In February 1996, Belgrade's only politically independent television broadcaster, Studio B, fell victim. As they had done in previous cases, the authorities argued that the station's incorporation was improper and went to court. Ultimately, most of the journalists working for the broadcaster simply resigned in protest, thereby allowing the government to replace 20 of 27 departing journalists with people loyal to the Milosevic line. Thus, it did not take the judicial process to bring Studio B to heel. Only some two weeks after launching its attack on Studio B, Belgrade turned its attention to humanitarian organizations, notably the Soros Foundation. Arguing that the foundation had been illegally constituted, Belgrade forced it to close until it was able to reconstitute itself.

The year also saw labor unrest and strikes. The case of Dragoljub Stosic was illustrative. Stosic, head of the Belgrade municipal-transit union, was released from prison on 8 November. He had been arrested on the night of 28–29 October when Belgrade police, along with paramilitaries in combat gear, broke up a transit strike. He was charged with inciting strike violence, and for several days his whereabouts and information about his well-being were kept secret.

Profile: **SLOBODAN MILOSEVIC: "A CONSUMATE POLITICIAN AND A PATHOLOGICAL LIAR"**

by STAN MARKOTICH

Mired in obscurity for the first 45 years of his life, Slobodan Milosevic has managed to ignite the bloodiest conflict Europe has experienced since World War II. As one author observed, what may be the integral and defining aspect of the Serbian leader's persona is his ability to be both "a consummate politician and a pathological liar."[1]

His parents were Montenegrins, but Milosevic was born in Serbia proper, in the town of Pozarevac, on 29 August 1941. He graduated from the University of Belgrade with a law degree in 1964 and four years later took his first executive position at the state-run company Technogas. In 1973, he became the company's general director. Between 1978 and 1983, he worked as head of the Bank of Belgrade. He married his high-school girlfriend, Mirjana Markovic, who teaches sociology at the University of Belgrade and heads her own communist political organization, the Yugoslav United Left. In 1996 Milosevic began promoting his wife's political fortunes, a signal that she may play an important political role alongside him in the near future.

Milosevic did not turn his back on banking to involve himself in politics full time until 1984, when he became chairman of the Belgrade City League of Communists of Yugoslavia (SKJ), which he had joined in 1959. His political star rose quickly, thanks largely to his mentor and, at the time, close personal friend, Ivan Stambolic, who became president of the Serbian republic in 1986. With his own promotion, Stambolic paved the way for Milosevic to become chairman of the Central Committee of the Serbian party at the same time.

Milosevic's rise to absolute power in Serbia began in 1987 and took approximately two years. He won the hearts and minds of vast numbers of Serbs across the former Yugoslavia through tough and demagogic speeches that were widely publicized by the bulk of the Serbian media, which he had brought under his control. He played upon popular perceptions and fears that the Serbs had been reduced to second-class status within Yugoslavia and especially that the ethnic Albanian majority in Serbia's province of Kosovo had become too numerous and politically powerful. He never spelled out precisely how he intended to deal with the Albanians, but the aggressive vocabulary and tone of his speeches clearly implied that he was ready to use force.

In taking power, he did indeed resort to some violence in what his propagandists called the "anti-bureaucratic revolution." This involved bussing large and well-orchestrated crowds around Serbia to stage "meetings" designed to intimidate Milosevic's political enemies or drive them from office. The tactic worked, and by 1989 Milosevic was master of Serbia. One of his major speeches came on 28 June of that year, the Serbian national holiday of Vidovdan, the 600th anniversary of the Battle of Kosovo. He delivered a speech in the predominantly ethnic Albanian province in which he extolled the virtues of Serbian nationalism. Although the speech was relatively restrained compared with some he had made previously, it marked the start of his campaign to promote the idea of joining all Serbs in one state.

A MASTER PLAN

In 1991, the other republics, beginning with Slovenia, began to break away, chafing under Milosevic's unabashed promotion of Serbian nationalism and growing totalitarian tendencies. Their departure allowed him to pursue his actual agenda: reuniting the Serb-populated areas outside of Serbia in an enlarged, ethnically pure Serbian state, or greater Serbia. Likely motivating Milosevic was his awareness that he could not emerge the uncontested leader in a multiethnic Yugoslavia as existed prior to 1991 but could within an attenuated state. Only Montenegro did not break away, opting to remain with Serbia in the present Yugoslav federation following a 1992 referendum. Failing to hijack Yugoslavia for his own power purposes, Milosevic chose to destroy it instead.

Following Yugoslavia's collapse, Milosevic threw himself into the effort to create a unified and strongly centralized Serbian state, with lands in Bosnia and Croatia becoming the most hotly contested battlegrounds in Europe since the end of World War II. The first few years of his regime were marked by support for local warlords—now accused or indicted war criminals, such as Milan Babic and Milan Martic in the Serb-held parts of Croatia and Bosnian Serb civilian leader

Radovan Karadzic and his military counterpart, General Ratko Mladic. While Milosevic did not formally integrate parts of Serb-populated Bosnia and Croatia under his jurisdiction, he has used no such restraint on the domestic front. Beginning in September 1990, Milosevic oversaw the centralization of what was to become the rump Yugoslav state, beginning with the introduction and implementation of a new Serbian constitution that effectively revoked autonomy for the provinces of Kosovo and Vojvodina. After the imposition of international sanctions against his regime in May 1992, Milosevic began backtracking in an attempt to overhaul his image, promoting an image as an advocate of regional peace and ethnic harmony. Lies to be sure, but repeated often enough through the state-controlled media to have found an audience.

Milosevic brooks no opposition within Serbia to his grip on power. He has cracked down on the free media, leaving only a few sources of truly independent expression, such as the daily *Nasa Borba* and the weekly *Vreme*. He rules without regard to basic civil rights, engaging the services of a police force and governing through repression, notably in Kosovo. At the same time, he insists that his regime is moderate and respectful of democratic norms, and that it is he and his government that are weak and victimized by the dark forces of political conspiracy.

Milosevic increased the pressure on Bosnian Serb leaders to broker a peace. On 4 August 1994 Milosevic announced that he would be closing the border with Bosnia-Herzegovina following the Bosnian Serb leaders' refusal to accept an international peace plan granting them 49 percent of Bosnian territory in Bosnian Serb hands. His "blockade" of the Bosnian Serbs was internationally acknowledged to be as tight as a sieve, but he claimed it was for real, and on 5 October 1995 the international community partially lifted sanctions against Belgrade for the first time. Since then, Milosevic's policies have won him more and more acceptance, ending his country's standing as an international pariah. From at least August 1995, he was recognized by the international community as the Bosnian Serbs' de facto peace negotiator, by the end of that year even putting his name to the Dayton peace accord, obligating himself and his erstwhile clients across the Drina to ending the war in Bosnia. His image has been further softened since then, following such developments as his 8 April 1996 normalization of relations with Macedonia. That move paved the way for a number of countries, beginning with those of the European Union, to announce the re-establishment of diplomatic ties with Belgrade. In effect, Milosevic succeeded in redefining himself from the most loathsome leader in the Balkans to a figure who appears to be the key to securing regional peace.

It is worth noting that although Milosevic has never used the term "greater Serbia" to describe his aims, nor has he expressly condemned the policy of building a greater Serbia. He may yet intend, perhaps through non-military means, to bring the Bosnian Serbs' Republika Srpska into some sort of de facto political arrangement with rump Yugoslavia.

[1]J.F. Brown, *Hopes and Shadows: Eastern Europe After Communism* (Durham, North Carolina: Duke University Press, 1994), p. 239.

Profile: ZORAN DJINDJIC: THE POLITICIAN OF "REASON"

by STAN MARKOTICH

At last, Zoran Djindjic, leader of the Democratic Party (DS), is making himself known on the international stage. For at least the past six years, Djindjic has been among the handful of major opposition leaders in the Federal Republic of Yugoslavia. Internationally, he has been upstaged by the flamboyant and charismatic leader of the opposition Serbian Renewal Movement (SPO), Vuk Draskovic. Draskovic, known for his inspiring speeches and outgoing personality, has stood in sharp contrast, almost as alter ego, to the generally pensive, clean-cut, and low-key Djindjic.

While Draskovic emphasized fiery rhetoric and emotional appeals to the public sense of morality and longing to remedy the totalitarianism of the regime of Serbian President Slobodan Milosevic, Djindjic's brand of politics has emphasized reason, rationality, and compromise.

At times, Djindjic's willingness to compromise has even led him to the brink of advocating reaching an accord with Milosevic. But time and developments in 1996 suggest that Djindjic may be growing and learning and understanding that compromise with Serbia's dictator is an impossibility.

Djindjic's early years were prosaic enough. He was born on 1 August 1952 in Travnik in Bosnia. He earned his first degree from the school of philosophy in Belgrade and went on to finish doctoral work at the University of Konstanz in Germany. During his student days in socialist Yugoslavia in 1974, Djindjic showed the first hint of his political inclinations. Along with student leaders from Zagreb and Ljubljana, he attempted to set up autonomous student organizations. That move garnered him a year in prison.

In 1989 Djindjic became one of the revivers of the DS. Today's DS traces its roots back to roughly the turn of this century, when a group within Serbia's ruling Radical Party split off and established the Independent Radical Party. In 1919 that organization merged with political groups in Croatia and Slovenia to form the Democratic Party, which was banned by Josip Broz Tito in the wake of World War II.

It was not until 1989, when a group of intellectuals, including Djindjic, sought to breathe new life into the DS. Its constituent congress finally took place in Belgrade on 3 February 1990. Since its founding, intraparty quarreling has led to fragmentation, and what once was simply the Democratic Party has fragmented into the DS proper, the Democratic party of Serbia, the Liberal Party, and the Democratic Center. With Djindjic's growing prominence, it is tempting to speculate whether or not Djindjic can be a catalyst that reunites the various "democratic" parties. Djindjic, always one of the most influential and high-profile leaders within the party, became its president in 1994.

For his part, Djindjic professes an addiction to politics. In a profile published in Belgrade's independent *Nasa Borba* on 23–24 November 1996 he remarks: "It [politics] just hooked me. I never thought of myself as a political leader. But politics is like a drug. After a certain dose is taken, the boundaries are just removed, and it just keeps you under a spell."

In the years after 1990, Djindjic was keen to portray himself as the candidate of cooperation, and articulated a willingness to work and compromise with any political players. While on several occasions flirting with other opposition coalitions aimed at ousting the ruling Socialists, Djindjic has tended, until recently, to stay clear. His words following Serbia's December 1993 parliamentary elections were indicative. Following those elections, the DS emerged with 29 of 250 parliamentary seats. At the time, speculation in the independent media suggested Djindjic's campaign received favorable coverage from the state-run media because of his reluctance to openly attack the ruling Socialists. And during campaigning, Djindjic attempted to stress that he could reach a modus vivendi with Milosevic, saying: "After the elections anything is possible. . . . Let every party spell out its conditions for cooperation with other parties. Let that be done by the SPS [Socialist Party of Serbia], the SRS [Serbian Radical Party led by accused war criminal Vojislav Seselj], the DSS, the Democratic Party. . . . We can even form a government of all parties, if the base is that wide" [*Nasa Borba*, 29 October 1993].

But by 1996, Djindjic had arrived at the conclusion that the Socialists were anathema. What got him in hot water was his open and repeated criticism of the ruling SPS, alleging that even Serbia's Premier Mirko Marjanovic was deeply embroiled in corruption. Belgrade prosecutor Svetozar Vujacic filed criminal charges against Djindjic in November. According to Vujacic, Djindjic had, while addressing a crowd of about 6,000 during an election rally in Vranje on 10 October, slurred Milosevic, calling him a "sick man." Vujacic charged Djindjic with insulting the president and defaming Serbia's reputation. Earlier, on 20 September, Djindjic received a four-month suspended sentence after being found guilty of libeling Serbian Premier Mirko Marjanovic in an advertisement placed in *Nedeljni Telegraf,* in which Djindjic alleged government officials' complicity in misappropriating resources, specifically grain stocks.

By the time of the 3 November elections, Djindjic was ready to cooperate fully with other opposition leaders in the Zajedno [Together] coalition. Following the 17 November runoff municipal elections, Zajedno won majorities in Serbia's 12 largest municipalities, claiming at least 60 of 110 seats in that local assembly, and Djindjic—Zajedno's mayoralty candidate—was poised to become the city's first noncommunist mayor since 1945. The authorities' nullification of those returns triggered a wave of mass protests across Serbia, the largest on the continent since the collapse of the Iron Curtain in 1989. It was Djindjic's key role in those protests that has secured him international attention.

Document: A PLEA TO SUPPORT A DEMOCRATIC SERBIA

In a letter to Western foreign ministers, Serbian Renewal Movement Chairman Vuk Draskovic reproached Western powers for appearing to give Serbian President Slobodan Milosevic a free hand to intensify domestic repression since the Dayton peace accord was signed. Published in the independent Belgrade daily Nasa Borba *on 26 March, the letter provoked a hail of condemnation from Serbia's state-run media.*

Serbian President Slobodan Milosevic has increased the campaign of terror against the democratic opposition particularly after Dayton and Paris. He has banned the last independent electronic media. He is preventing privatization in the economy, and he is forcefully nationalizing the existing private property. He has expanded the system of police repression, drafted members of the democratic opposition for military exercises, [and] forced thousands of people to join his party. . . .

He has abolished television coverage of parliamentary proceedings and banned the state television and press from reporting on the activities of the democratic opposition. He has ordered the Supreme Court to ban the only independent television station . . . and committed a scandalous act by proclaiming the privately owned shares of Studio B to be state-owned.

The country is shrouded in information darkness. The citizens are given only the views of Milosevic's procommunist party and those of his wife's openly communist party. After Dayton and Paris, a marital system of authority has been introduced in Serbia. The army, the police, all the media, the banks, companies, the Mafia, everything is in the hands of Milosevic and his wife. This suggests to the citizens that in Dayton and Paris, Milosevic got support from the United States, Russia, Great Britain, France, Germany, the European Union, and NATO to do whatever he pleases in Serbia.

Expelled from parliament and without access to the media, the democratic opposition (without the fascist parties that Milosevic formed during the war) has started to organize mass rallies throughout Serbia, demanding Milosevic's departure and urgent and fundamental European reforms in Serbia. We organized one such meeting on 9 March in Belgrade. Milosevic ordered the police to ban the rally, and when he heard about the democratic opposition's tens of thousands of supporters, he barred us from setting up the stage and loudspeakers. That a head of state should concern himself with this!

Following Milosevic's orders, state television shot scenes of the half-empty city square three hours before the rally began and broadcast these to the viewers that evening, completely ignoring the fact that tens of thousands of citizens were calling for Milosevic's resignation, that they were calling for reconciliation and cooperation among the republics of the former Yugoslavia, for free media, privatization, cooperation with the EU, and Serbia's integration into the family of European and world democracies.

Milosevic's regime is the only one in Europe that rules by lies and naked force. However, this regime steps back when faced with force. For example, Milosevic recently banned the activities of the Soros Foundation, but as soon as he got a letter [from U.S. Secretary of State Warren Christopher] he reconsidered. I am glad that Mr. Christopher sent the letter; but I am not glad that the governments of the great democratic states do not show equal decisiveness when it comes to the defense of the independent media.

Of course, the struggle for democracy in Serbia cannot be fought by foreign governments. The democratic forces in Serbia have more supporters than Milosevic and his wife, but this minority rules exclusively, thanks to the fact that all the media, police, and money are in its hands. Free media and fair elections under international control would ensure more than a two-thirds-majority victory for the pro-European democratic forces in Serbia. . . . I hope, esteemed ministers, that you too believe that there can be no lasting peace and reconciliation on the territory of the former Yugoslavia without the victory of democratic and anti-war forces, primarily in Serbia, Croatia, and Bosnia-Herzegovina.

I believe that the international community is wasting valuable time if it expects that lasting peace can be ensured by those who started the war and conducted it, and if it believes that dictators can turn into democrats. The Al Capones of the Balkans can never turn into Mahatma Ghandis. In the name of a democratic Serbia, the one that is struggling in complete media darkness, that is lacking both money and equipment and is exposed to police repression, I ask your governments for support.

Document: **CAMPAIGN OF VIOLENCE IN KOSOVO**

The self-proclaimed Liberation Army of Kosovo (UCK) launched a campaign of violent attacks in 1996. In "Communiqué No. 22," published on 10 August by the Swiss Albanian-language weekly Bota Sot, *the UCK claimed responsibility for recent bomb attacks on police stations in Podujevo and Pristina, cities in the mainly ethnic-Albanian-Serbian province of Kosovo. Nobody was hurt, but in addition to the police buildings, a municipal building and a Red Cross warehouse were damaged by one of the blasts. The UCK first appeared in February 1996 when members allegedly fire-bombed the homes of ethnic-Serbian refugees from Serbia and Bosnia who had settled in Kosovo. Since then, armed with grenades and submachine guns, they are reported to have conducted various attacks, typically arbitrary—and sometimes fatal—shootings of policemen and people they mistakenly believed to be policemen. The parallel ethnic-Albanian shadow state has sharply denied the existence of the UCK and blamed the aggression on agents provocateurs. The Serbian police force, however, has followed each attack by stepping up its pres-*

ence and by raiding Albanian homes. The August bombing also apparently prompted an unexpected parade through Kosovo by indicted felon and accused war criminal Zeljko Raznatovic (alias Arkan) and his private army, the Tigers. The visit by Arkan, who is believed to have led some of the Bosnian war's worst ethnic cleansing, was clearly intended to intimidate the local Albanian population.

On 2 August, in Operational Zone No. 1, our guerrilla units launched four armed attacks against the occupying Serbian police posts. Our attacks were intended to destroy the Serbian police targets and inflict heavy material losses.

The target of the attacks was chosen on the basis of a decision made by the UCK leaders. The Albanian people of Kosovo will not be cheated by defeatists and rabbits who are overwhelmed with fear and panic. They know quite well that their best sons are leading the actions, and they will not lay down their arms until the occupied territories have been liberated.

Through this communiqué, we would like to state clearly to the current Serbian political leadership that they must withdraw from our territories as soon as possible, or our attacks to liberate the country will be fierce and merciless.

The decision-making centers should be aware that we are not terrorists, as the Serbs are trying to call us, but warriors of liberty. In view of the fact that the international decision-making centers have so far ignored the demands of our people, we are obliged to use force to liberate our territories.

Macedonia

Population:	2,075,196 (1994 census)
Capital:	Skopje (pop. 450,000)
Major cities:	Bitola (pop. 80,000), Kumanovo (pop. 70,000), Prilep (pop. 70,000)
Area:	25,713 sq. km.
Major ethnic groups:	Macedonian 67%, Albanian 23%, Turkish 4%, Romani 2%, Serbian 2%, other 2%
Economy:	GDP growth: 1.6%
	Inflation rate: 0%
	Average monthly income: $222
	Unemployment rate: 39.8%

MOVING TOWARD FIRMER GROUND IN MACEDONIA

by STEFAN KRAUSE

Despite the breakup of the ruling coalition and the strengthening of the nationalist opposition in the first post-independence local elections, Macedonia enjoyed relative political stability. Internationally, mutual-recognition and free-trade accords with the Federal Republic of Yugoslavia contributed to further normalization between Macedonia and its neighbors.

On both the domestic and international fronts, Macedonia saw an eventful year. Two major political events—the breakup of the ruling coalition and the first post-independence local elections—highlighted domestic political news. But problems persisted as the nationalist opposition made inroads and as differences between the government and ethnic Albanian parties remained unresolved. Macedonia's international position was further strengthened in 1996. Relations with Greece were relatively stable, although the name issue remained unresolved. More importantly, Skopje managed to gain diplomatic recognition from Belgrade, and the two countries also signed a free-trade agreement.

In early February, a crisis between the two biggest parties in the ruling coalition, the Social-Democratic Union of Macedonia (SDSM) and the Liberal Party (LP), resulted in the coalition's breakup despite President Kiro Gligorov's pledges for unity. The conflict centered around privatization policy and monetary politics. But the Liberals also called the government corrupt and accused the Social Democrats of trying to concentrate all political power in their hands. Liberal Party leaders were in turn accused of profiting from the sale of the country's most lucrative enterprises. The Liberals—who, in sheer numbers, are far weaker than the Social Democrats—were the richest party and were pushing for more political power and influence. The struggle over privatization apparently originated in mid-1995, but 1996 saw the conflict come to a head.

EXCEEDING THE LIMITS

The first victim of the crisis was Saso Ordanoski, director and editor-in-chief of the state-run Macedonian Television, who, although not an SDSM member, had been nominated to that post by the Social Democrats. Ordanoski was dismissed on 4 February by Macedonian Radio and Television Director-General Melpomeni Korneti, a Liberal, after he predicted that there would be no Liberals in the next government. He accused them of having exceeded "the limits of political decency" after an attempt on Gligorov's life on 3 October 1995 that left him incapacitated for several months. At that time, Stojan Andov, president of the parliament and LP chairman, was acting president, and he was quite frank about his own ambitions for the presidency if Gligorov could not resume his duties. As a result of that crisis, Korneti would also lose her job in late June.

Although Gligorov on 6 February said a reconstructed government excluding one of the member parties in the Alliance for Macedonia—which ran as a coalition in the 1994 parliamentary elections—"is not a platform I represent [or] the will of our voters," the Social Democrats, as the biggest party, decided to reject the participation of LP ministers in any future government. Consequently, Prime Minister Branko Crvenkovski on 10 February proposed a new government excluding the Liberals. In an extensive government reshuffle, the four LP ministers were dropped. Most notably, former Interior Minister Ljubomir Frckovski replaced Stevo Crvenkovski, a Liberal, as foreign minister. Of the 20 new government members, 13 are Social Democrats, five belong to the ethnic Albanian Party of Democratic Prosperity (PPD), and two belong to the small Socialist Party. Gligorov again expressed skepticism, saying that the new government "no longer represents the political formation that brought me to the head of the country and for which the electorate voted." Nevertheless, the parliament on 23 February approved the new government by 83 of 120 votes. The same day, Andov resigned as president of the parliament. He was replaced by the Social Democrat Tito Petkovski on 6 March.

Following the government crisis, the nationalist opposition—composed mainly of the Internal Macedonian Revolutionary Organization-Democratic Party for Macedonian National Unity (VMRO-DPMNE) and the Democratic Party (DP)—organized a petition drive aimed at dissolving parliament and calling early elections. The Liberals at the same time called for parliament's dissolution by 15 September at the latest. Both initiatives failed. The LP motion was rejected by the ruling majority in the parliament on 3 April. And though it gathered about 162,000 signatures, the petition drive failed even earlier. The parliament on 28 March passed a law on citizens' petition drives that invalidated that particular one, despite the Liberals' protests.

ELECTION FERVOR

On 17 November and 1 December, Macedonians went to the polls to elect city council members and mayors in the first local elections since the country gained independence in 1991. The Social Democrats emerged as the strongest party, getting slightly more than one-quarter of the 1,903 council seats at stake nationwide. The nationalist-opposition parties as a whole received slightly less than the Social Democrats, while Socialists, Liberals, and ethnic Albanian parties each won between 100 and 160 seats. The remainder went to smaller parties and independent candidates. The SDSM won 52 of the 124 mayoralties, followed by 15 VMRO-DPMNE and 13 DP candidates. PPD candidates won 12 races, and another one was won by a candidate supported by the PPD and the ethnic Albanian Democratic People's Party (PDP). The Party of Democratic Prosperity of the Albanians (PPDSH) won four mayoralties, and another three in a coalition with the PDP. The Socialists won seven races, the Turkish Democratic Party two, and the Serbian Democratic Party and the Party for the Full Emancipation of the Roma one each.

While the SDSM remained the strongest party nationwide, the nationalist opposition interpreted the poll as a victory and repeated its call for early parliamentary elections. The Skopje race was won by the DP candidate, which further boosted the opposition's spirits. Having boycotted the second round of the 1994 elections, it saw a chance to regain parliamentary representation through an early vote. The chances of an early vote remain slim. Still, it seems unlikely that the nationalists could win a majority in the parliament under the present electoral law with its two-round majority system. The elections also underscored the solid support the ethnic Albanian parties enjoy in the country's western districts, where ethnic Albanians are in the majority.

The atmosphere remained tense between the government and ethnic Albanians throughout 1996. Friction centered around the independent Albanian-language university in Tetovo, which the government continued to regard as illegal. In July, police clashes occurred during demonstrations against the jailing of the Tetovo university dean, Fadil Sulejmani, and several other Albanian activists. And in the fall, some 1,000 ethnic Albanian schoolchildren were affected by a mysterious illness and complained of abdominal pains, headache, weakness, and breathing problems. Although all the children recovered after two or three days, many were hospitalized, and the outbreak caused considerable unease. Ethnic Albanians claimed the children might have been poisoned, while ethnic Macedonians accused the Albanians of trying to create tensions ahead of the local elections. A World Health Organization team found no proof of poisoning or infection but attributed the illness to psychological reasons.

BELGRADE ACCORD

Macedonia's position on the international front improved significantly in 1996. On 8 April, Macedonia and the Federal Republic of Yugoslavia signed a mutual-recognition accord, the first mutual agreement between Belgrade and a former Yugoslav republic. In September, the two signed a trade agreement abolishing most tariffs. For Macedonia, those agreements signaled a major breakthrough. Most notably, they will help ward off possible political pressure from Macedonia's northern border. Besides, it means normalization with Greece's main ally. Bilateral relations with Greece developed relatively well in 1996, although there was no breakthrough on the issue of Macedonia's name despite several rounds of talks. But as stipulated in a September 1995 interim accord, liaison offices opened in January and visa fees were reduced in February. Bilateral economic relations also picked up during 1996. Macedonia and the European Union in June 1996 concluded a cooperation agreement, which went into effect on 1 January. In another positive development, in September, German President Roman Herzog was the first head of state of an EU member country to visit Macedonia. Relations with Albania worsened, however, mostly because of the Tetovo university crisis.

Throughout 1996, a UN contingent of around 1,100 troops remained in Macedonia. In February, the UN Preventive Deployment Force became independent from other UN missions in the former Yugoslavia. In November, its mandate was extended by another six months, but its strength was to be reduced by 300 over the following months. Because of Russian reservations, that extension might have been the last.

In the realm of economics, preliminary data suggest that the Macedonian economy picked up during 1996. Inflation remained the lowest in the region at around 3 percent, while gross domestic product was expected to grow by 1.5 percent to 2 percent. But high unemployment remained a big problem, and foreign trade went down, especially exports. The country's agricultural sector suffered from an epidemic of hoof-and-mouth disease that forced the killing of several thousand animals and virtually halted meat exports. Still, Macedonia was accepted to the EU's aid program in February, and both state and private banks got loans from the International Monetary Fund, the World Bank, and the European Bank for Reconstruction and Development in 1996.

Albania

Population:	3,249,136
Capital:	Tirana (pop. 270,000–300,000)
Major cities:	Durres (pop.130,000), Elbasan (pop. 100,000), Shkoder (pop. 81,000–100,000)
Area:	28,750 sq. km.
Major ethnic groups:	Albanian 95%, Greek 3%, other 2%
Economy:	GDP growth: 8.5%
	Inflation rate: 17.4%
	Average monthly income: $60
	Unemployment rate: 12.1%

ALBANIA'S DEMOCRATS CONSOLIDATE POWER

by FABIAN SCHMIDT

Presidential and local elections dominated domestic politics in 1996. Despite international observers' charges of election fraud, cooperation with the West steadily improved.

The 1996 national parliamentary and local elections pushed the Democratic Party, in control of parliament since 1992, to a zenith of power consolidation. Yet political conflict continued to grow during the year, with the opposition accusing President Sali Berisha and his Democratic Party of establishing authoritarian rule through election fraud and of extending their control over the legislative, executive, and judicial branches of the government, as well as the media.

Early in the year, the Democrats and the opposition waged bitter rhetorical fights in preparation for the May national parliamentary elections. The opposition accused the Democrats of introducing legislation aimed at reducing the opposition's chances at the ballot box. Legislative changes included a genocide law and a related verification law, which banned former high-ranking communist officials and collaborators of the secret police, Sigurimi, from running for public office. The opposition charged that applying the law during the campaign was not judicious and that people accused as "spies" were not allowed to see documents allegedly confirming the charges against them. The electoral law was also modified in favor of direct representation, reducing chances for smaller parties. In the 1992 elections, 40 of the 140 seats were chosen by proportional representation; in 1996, the number was reduced to only 25.

More important, the manner in which the elections were conducted contributed heavily to the final election outcome and the resulting political polarization. Numerous irregularities, including intimidation and violence against the opposition both during the election campaign and on voting day, resulted in a boycott of the runoff election by most opposition parties. (See following article.)

ELECTION FRAUD

Socialist Party leader Fatos Nano remained in prison throughout the year. He had been arrested in 1993 on embezzlement charges, but the Socialists consider Nano a political prisoner, a position also supported by the human-rights group Amnesty International. That group also called for the release of seven other people who were arrested and sentenced after founding a communist party in the spring. Berisha, who grants amnesty to prisoners of his choosing every New Year's Day, reduced Nano's term by six months and released two of the seven communists.

In the May election the Democrats won control of the legislature by the two-thirds majority necessary for constitutional changes. This paved the way for future adoption of a new constitution, which Berisha failed to pass by popular referendum in 1994. The Democrats came out of the 26 May balloting with 122 seats, just over 87 percent of the parliament, even though it won only 55.5 percent of the vote.

The Socialists, who garnered 20.4 percent of the vote and 10 parliamentary seats, continued their parliamentary boycott until the end of the year. The only other parties represented in the legislature were the right-wing Republicans; the ethnic Greek Unity for Human Rights Party; and the National Front, Balli Kombetar; each gained three seats or less. But the election controversy resulted in a split of Balli Kombetar. Abas Ermenji, who led the party when it was a nationalist partisan movement during World War II, left Albania for a second time and returned to his communist-era exile in Paris in protest against the party's recognition of the election results.

The dispute over the parliamentary elections had a profound effect on the local elections of 20 October. The Socialists and various other opposition parties threatened to boycott the vote, while the United States, the Council of Europe, and the Organization of Security and Cooperation in Europe (OSCE) put pressure on the Democrats to reform the electoral process. After months, a round table between the Democrats and the opposition finally paved the way for all parties to participate in the local polling. The parties agreed on a package of legislative reforms designed to ensure a free and fair vote and balanced media coverage.

Although all parties agreed to participate in the October voting, one critical issue remained unresolved. The opposition had demanded that the OSCE's Office for Democratic Institutions and Human Rights (ODIHR) be allowed to monitor the balloting. But just days before the vote, the Albanian Foreign Ministry denied accreditation to all ODIHR monitors. Subsequently, the OSCE withdrew completely. The Council of Europe, which coordinated monitoring instead, called the voting essentially free and fair. The Democrats won an overwhelming majority in those elections as well, winning mayoralties in 58 of 64 town halls and in 268 of 309 communities.

On election day, the opposition and the Democrats began charging each other with election irregularities, but, unlike during the parliamentary balloting, the Socialists did not boycott the seats they had won, apparently fearing they might otherwise lose all influence at the local level. Nonetheless, they concluded that the local elections, too, were a farce, arguing that the international monitors covered only a few polling stations and did not have the expertise of the ODIHR monitors. They also continued to demand new national parliamentary elections. It is, however, unlikely the Democrats will give in to that demand, even though it was also supported by the Council of Europe, the European Union, and the U.S. State Department.

After the local elections, the Democrats faced an internal split when 1990 student leader and legislator Azem Hajdari broke with the party line and had himself elected leader of the Union of Independent Trade Unions in November. While the courts did not recognize Hajdari's election, he managed to gather popular support and staged a protest in December involving workers and students. He charged the government with corruption, authoritarianism, and control of the media.

LOOKING WESTWARD

Despite disputes caused by election irregularities, cooperation has steadily increased between Albania and the West. Albania took a leading role in the region by holding joint exercises in the framework of NATO's Partnership for Peace program. The cooperation throughout the year included a conference of Balkan and Mediterranean defense ministers in March, the opening of a U.S. military-training base in the Martanesh Mountains, and a series of maneuvers there (involving troops from neighboring Greece and Macedonia as well as Slovenia, Romania, Bulgaria, Turkey, Italy, and Germany). The first 40–strong Albanian peacekeeping contingent participated in the German Implementation Force contingent. The United States gave Albania a $100 million military aid package, and Greece and Italy have both pledged to support full Albanian NATO membership.

Relations with Greece have improved considerably, and Greek Foreign Minister Teodoros Pangalos pledged to support the increase of EU assistance for Albania. In June, the National Bank of Greece opened a branch in Tirana. Albania will receive EU grants amounting to 212 million ecu by the year 2000 for various infrastructure projects, and Italy has expressed support for an Albanian-EU association. The largest projects, also partly supported by the World Bank, include upgrading the country's road system and electric-power and water networks. In 1996, the German company Siemens started upgrading the only international passenger airport in Rinas.

Tirana's first stock exchange opened on 2 May, the result of continuing privatization. Later, one of the largest foreign investors, the German company Preussag, bought 80 percent of the shares in the Albanian chromium-mining industry. The year also saw continued oil exploration in cooperation with various international companies.

The economy continued to grow; the official growth-rate estimate for the year was 8.5 percent. A value-added tax took the place of the turnover tax, and price controls and subsidies on bread, fuel, and electricity were lifted, giving the economy a boost. The state, however, suffered from a severe budget deficit of 23.9 billion lek (around $240 million) by October. That deficit, largely due to smuggling and tax evasion, is the equivalent of 10 percent of gross domestic product. Inflation increased from 7 percent in 1995 to an estimated 17.4 percent in 1996. International Monetary Fund experts expressed doubts about the country's apparently continuing economic progress. They warned that pyramid schemes, pledging big returns on small investments, are shaking consumer spending and distorting currency markets. Such investment companies, offering monthly interest rates between 8 percent and 50 percent, have existed in Albania for three years but have mushroomed since early 1996. The system is likely to implode, robbing ordinary people of their savings and paralyzing the economy. Also, emigrants sent their foreign wages home to buy lek and to invest. That contributed to a dizzying rally by the lek against Western currencies, with the dollar falling below 100 lek in November. The lek has not traded that high since late 1995. In November, the first pyramid scheme collapsed, and its founder disappeared with $13 million. A second scheme collapsed in December.

Other crime—particularly domestic terrorism—was on the increase. Incidents included a bomb attack on a supermarket in Tirana on 26 February and a series of assassinations of justice officials and police. Shortly before the local elections, police arrested a number of people in connection with the attacks, alleging that they were part of a left-wing group named Revenge of Justice. Those arrested included the sons of high-ranking communist-era officials and Klement Kolaneci, the son-in-law of the late dictator Enver Hoxha. The investigations results were not made public, and Kolaneci denied any guilt.

The February bombing was used as a pretext by the authorities to crack down on the independent and opposition media, which throughout the year suffered severe interference from authorities. The drafting of a long-awaited law providing for private television and radio was further delayed.

Sidebar: ALBANIAN ELECTIONS: OPPOSITION CLAIMS FRAUD

by FABIAN SCHMIDT

Albanian's third poststalinist parliamentary elections on 26 May 1996 were overshadowed by allegations of the opposition that the ruling Democratic Party (PD) used a vast number of illegal means to ensure its victory, including intimidation, violence and fraud. With the PD having won complete control over the parliament, the opposition feared that the party and the president would not only strengthen the presidency but also deepen their control over the police, the secret police and the judiciary even more than they had already.

Massive irregularities started in the last weeks before the elections. All over the country opposition politicians were intimidated by what they claimed were both police and secret service (SHIK) agents. Thus, when party leaders attempted to travel to other cities from Tirana, their cars were frequently stopped at roadblocks. In various cases it was reported that PD supporters smashed car windows, beat up and severely injured opposition supporters. Also, individual cases of arrest and severe beating in detention were reported. While the PD held its rallies in the open and on central places such as Skanderbeg Square in Tirana, opposition rallies were banned from the center of towns to remote places or into closed buildings.

Just days before the elections, the Socialists held a rally in the Sports Palace in Durres. While going there, people were blocked outside the city and badly beaten by PD supporters. Police, according to international monitors, did not attempt to arrest the culprits. When the meeting was about to begin, the electricity in the building was shut off and it ended in the dark. According to the PS daily *Zeri i Popullit* only between early May and election day, more than 200 Socialist supporters or members had been "threatened, beaten, or detained" by police and PD supporters.

Further arrests and beatings were reported throughout polling day itself. According to Socialist leader Luan Hajdaraga over 20 people were arrested only in the electoral district No. 47 of Tirana, where he was running for parliament. But the violence did not affect only the Socialists. At a press conference of the Democratic Alliance and the Social Democrats one hour later, a witness from Lezha, north of Tirana, noted that there was no single polling station left in the city in which the electoral commissions continued to work regularly.

The government had another interpretation. On the day before the elections, deputy Interior Minister Agim Shehu charged the Socialists with having built up a parallel paramilitary force and with having tried to forge balloting documents. He added that three people, including former transition government prime minister Ylli Bufi, had been arrested.

The major opposition parties decided to withdraw from the electoral commissions in the middle of election day and not to sign the return forms of the ballots, which all electoral commission members are supposed to sign. Unconfirmed reports on election day said that some commission members were arrested and forced to sign the return forms. But according to later media reports, the reports were only signed by the opposition in some 40 percent of the electoral districts.

International monitors confirmed the irregularities. A group of two British and nine Norwegian OSCE monitors issued a statement on 28 May, saying that "the elections did not meet international standards for free and fair elections and they did not conform with the requirements of the election law." The monitors charged the government with failing to guarantee freedom from intimidation and multi-party representation in the election commissions. They also said that ballot casts were altered and invalidated resulting in "extremely high" numbers of invalid votes, up to 50 percent. The group concluded that "the will of the Albanian people was not expressed in a free manner in the elections."

The official OSCE statement published in Vienna on 29 May also said the elections fell short of legal standards and government cooperation with monitors was insufficient. The OSCE said that "the observers noted with regret that in many instances the implementation of the law failed to meet its own criteria," adding that decisions of the polling station commissions were not made by majority vote, but by the arbitrary decisions of the government appointed chairman and secretary.

Bulgaria

Population:	8,487,317 (1992 census)
Capital:	Sofia (pop. 1,190,126)
Major cities:	Plovdiv (pop. 377,637), Varna (pop. 297,090),
	Burgas (pop. 188,367)
Area:	110,994 sq. km.
Major ethnic groups:	Bulgarian 85.7%, Turkish 9.4%, Romani 3.7%
Economy:	GDP growth: –10.0%
....	Inflation rate: 311%
....	Average monthly income: $50–$60
....	Unemployment rate: 12.5%

BULGARIA SURVIVES A DIRE YEAR

by STEFAN KRAUSE

Despite several personnel reshuffles, Prime Minister Zhan Videnov's government was impotent against a torrent of economic and political downturns, prompting his resignation in late December.

1996 was catastrophic for Bulgaria, the worst year since reforms began. The economy crashed after a year of apparent stabilization. The national currency's value fell to new lows, inflation soared, and, by the end of 1996, a large majority of the population was living below the poverty line. As the government proved unable to deal with the economic crisis, trust in the ruling Bulgarian Socialist Party (BSP) all but vanished. In late December, general discontent and mounting opposition within the party prompted Zhan Videnov to resign as prime minister and BSP chairman. Members of the opposition, meanwhile, seemed to find more and more common ground. In the single most notable political event of the year, the major opposition parties fielded a common presidential candidate who, in a fall election, crushed the BSP candidate.

On the domestic political scene, the government apparently failed to resolve the ongoing and worsening economic crisis. That, in turn, led to a crisis within the BSP, with leading party members calling for the resignation of Videnov from both of his posts and for the formation of a new government. Some groups within the BSP, mainly the reform-oriented Alliance for Social Democracy, even warned that the party would split if it were not thoroughly reformed. Videnov finally resigned on 21 December, at the opening of an extraordinary BSP congress.

In a second major domestic development, and in contrast to the fights within the BSP, the opposition mastered the first steps toward unity. Contacts were institutionalized, and the presidential election proved that that was wise. Although the newfound unity must still prove its viability, the opposition took the initiative and managed to portray itself as a credible alternative to the present Socialist-led majority in the parliament.

During 1996, Videnov twice reshuffled his government. The first time was in January, when then-Agriculture Minister Vasil Chichibaba resigned due to his failure in dealing with the grain crisis that hit Bulgaria in fall 1995 and lasted through 1996. The second reshuffling occurred in June, when Chichibaba's successor, Svetoslav Shivarov, also resigned. That time, Videnov, under party pressure, had to agree to a major government reorganization. The ministers of agriculture, industry, and culture were replaced, and an Energy Ministry was set up. The post of interior minister had already gone from Lyubomir Nachev to Nikolay Dobrev in May. But none of those changes resolved the country's political or economic problems.

Within the BSP, reactions to Videnov's attempts to resolve the crisis by replacing cabinet members were lukewarm at best. Former BSP Chairman Aleksandar Lilov, who remained an influential BSP power broker behind the scenes, summed up the dilemma. In June, he said the BSP had to form a strong government immediately, with or without Videnov. The public's reaction to the government's failure to resolve problems was even more negative. The government changes could not reverse the waning of public trust in the BSP and its government. In 1996, Bulgarians became increasingly frustrated and disillusioned with politics in general and with the government and the BSP in particular. Protesters repeatedly took to the streets, and in November the Confederation of Independent Trade Unions in Bulgaria staged a relatively unsuccessful one-day national strike. Frustration with the government was also one of the reasons that about 1 million people turned out last spring in Sofia alone to greet former Tsar Simeon, who in late May arrived for his first visit to Bulgaria after 50 years in exile. Simeon's visit met with huge interest both in Bulgaria and abroad, but after he returned to Madrid in June he rarely commented on Bulgarian affairs. His visit was an important but isolated event in 1996; it definitely did not signal a return to the monarchic idea in Bulgaria.

Despite its problems and growing pressure, the government survived two votes of no confidence called by the opposition in January and June. But it did so mainly because party discipline still worked within the BSP and because it was supported by deputies of the Bulgarian Business Bloc (BBB). Before the second vote, in June, many BSP legislators made it clear that their trust in the government was nearly gone, although they did not go as far as to vote with the opposition.

OPPOSITION UNITES

While the BSP's internal problems remained unresolved, leading to increased fragmentation within the party, the once-divided opposition embarked on the road to unity. In the spring, the major opposition formations—the Union of Democratic Forces (SDS), the People's Union, and the mainly ethnic-Turkish Movement for Rights and Freedom—agreed to present a common candidate for the presidential election. To that end, they held a U.S.-style primary on 1 June in which the SDS's Petar Stoyanov soundly defeated the incumbent president, Zhelyu Zhelev, with around two-thirds of the vote. The opposition then signed a formal cooperation agreement and institutionalized an umbrella organization called the United Democratic Forces (ODS). The 27 October/3 November presidential election was convincingly won by Stoyanov, who in the second round crushed the BSP candidate, Culture Minister Ivan Marazov, 60 percent to 40 percent, coming out on top in almost every electoral district in the country. The original BSP choice for the presidency, Foreign Minister Georgi Pirinski, was barred from running for president by the Constitutional Court and the Supreme Court on grounds of not being a "Bulgarian citizen by birth" as required by the constitution. Interestingly, populist BBB leader Georges Ganchev scored a surprisingly strong 22 percent in the first round, and in both rounds voter turnout was relatively low, at around 62 percent. Those two facts further underscored the public's general mistrust of politics.

After the presidential vote the opposition continued to cooperate with the clearly stated aim of bringing about early parliamentary elections in 1997 and driving the Socialists from power. At the same time, however, SDS Chairman Ivan Kostov stirred up controversy when he proposed in November to turn the SDS into a single party rather than an alliance of the 15 political parties and movements that currently make up the union. The idea was rejected by many SDS member organizations and leaders alike, but no decision was made in 1996. Still, Kostov's position within the SDS remained unchallenged, and his politics of cooperation among the elements of the opposition and his slogan of "reasonable change" gained ground.

While the opposition was going strong after the presidential election, the BSP went through yet another crisis. On 5 November, 19 leading party members representing all intraparty groups issued a call for a new government, and, during a 20–hour BSP plenary meeting on 13 November, Videnov barely survived an internal confidence vote. The delegates called an extraordinary BSP congress for late December. During the plenary meeting, several leading BSP politicians—including Deputy Chairman Yanaki Stoilov—resigned. And on 14 November, Georgi Pirinski resigned as foreign minister in protest of the party's continuing support for Videnov.

At the beginning of the BSP congress on 21 December, Videnov, surprisingly, announced his resignation as BSP leader and premier, citing lack of trust within the party and society as a whole. On 24 December, he was succeeded as BSP leader by Georgi Parvanov, one of Videnov's deputies within the BSP. Parvanov won by a large margin, defeating the outspoken reformers Pirinski and Stoilov. Although some see Parvanov as another Videnov (he had been Videnov's close confidant in recent years), others say he embodies the compromise between rival factions within the BSP. While a split of the party was averted for the time being, the congress failed to resolve programmatic issues that are the primary reason for most intraparty problems. On 28 December, the parliament virtually unanimously approved the resignation of Videnov's government.

In October 1996, Bulgaria was shaken by the first open act of political terrorism since 1989. Leading BSP politician Andrey Lukanov, a former prime minister, was shot dead outside his home in Sofia. The perpetrator remained unknown as of the end of the year, but it is commonly speculated that Lukanov was killed for both political and economic reasons—he was a leading reformer within the BSP and a wealthy businessman with close contacts to (sometimes shady) business conglomerates. It was probably that combination and the behind-the-scenes influence he exercised that cost him his life.

The media also reflected the government's woes. In early June, the BSP majority in the parliament dismissed Bulgarian National Television head Ivan Granitski, ostensibly for professional reasons but, in fact, because the Socialists blamed him for not reporting favorably on Videnov's government. The media, however, did manage to escape some of the government's moves to increase control. Later in the year, the Constitutional Court invalidated large parts of the Socialist-sponsored electronic-media law because it limited freedom of expression and opened the door to government interference in the media.

ECONOMIC CATASTROPHE

The economy—even more than politics—left deep wounds in Bulgaria in 1996. While many problems were structural and defied short-term resolution, the government managed to aggravate existing problems.

The national currency, the lev, took a nose dive in 1996. At the beginning of the year, the lev was exchanged at around 71 leva to the U.S. dollar; by the end of December, it had sunk to 495 leva to the dollar. The lev's value declined steadily over the course of the year, plunging heavily in May and November–December, when it lost most of its value. Interest rates shot up while salaries fell, despite several adjustments of the minimum wage. In January, the average salary was around $120, but it dropped considerably during the year. By September, the official average wage was around $80, up from $67 the previous month. Unofficial figures suggested that by December it had dropped to a mere $28, the lowest in the region. Unemployment rose from about 10 percent to 12.5 percent. Year-end inflation was estimated at 311 percent, while gross domestic product fell by between 8 percent and 10 percent. Both imports and exports fell in 1996, but Bulgaria still had a trade surplus.

Bulgaria also had considerable trouble with foreign lenders. The government did secure one new standby loan from the International Monetary Fund (IMF) in the summer, on the condition that it would speed up economic reform, close down 64 money-losing state enterprises (cutting another 70 off from state bank loans), and begin bankruptcy proceedings against 13 state and private banks and restrict the activity of another seven. Bulgaria received the first installment of that loan but consequently failed to pass an IMF review and did not get the second disbursement in the fall. By the end of the year, it seemed very likely that Bulgaria would adopt an IMF-proposed currency board in order to guarantee strict budgetary discipline and restore trust in the lev. Talk had it that Bulgaria might be forced to default on foreign-debt payments for the second time since 1990, but ultimately that did not happen.

During spring 1996, Bulgaria's mass privatization program was finally launched; vouchers were sold at a nominal price to every Bulgarian over 18. Privatization funds sprang up in the summer and fall, but at the end of the year the course and success of the program were far from certain.

UNEVENTFUL FOREIGN RELATIONS

In foreign affairs, 1996 was much of a continuation of the previous year. Relations with neighboring countries remained relatively good. Greece and Bulgaria agreed to open three new border crossings, in addition to the two currently operating. While all relevant political forces reaffirmed their commitment to closer ties with the European Union and ultimately full EU membership, the issue of NATO membership remained unresolved. The opposition and Zhelev urged the government to clarify its position on the Atlantic alliance and apply for full membership, but the BSP and the Videnov government failed to do so. Anti-Western sentiments and consideration for Russia's position on NATO enlargement kept the government from finding clear words on the issue.

It was probably also out of consideration for Russia that the government demurred before it issued a formal note of protest against a controversial statement by Russian President Boris Yeltsin. In late March, after the signing of a regional integration agreement by Russia, Belarus, Kazakstan, and Kyrgyzstan, Yeltsin said, "the community is open to other states perhaps, for example, Bulgaria." The opposition and Zhelev, however, immediately rejected the idea and called on the government to clarify whether it was engaged in backstage dealings with Moscow and to reject the idea of what the opposition called "USSR 2." Although the government rejected Yeltsin's statement, it waited a week before issuing any formal statement, apparently to avoid straining relations with Moscow.

Profile: PETAR STOYANOV: A "NEW FACE"

by MARIA KOINOVA

Petar Stoyanov, a 44–year-old lawyer and deputy chairman of the opposition Union of Democratic Forces (SDS), won Bulgaria's presidential election runoff on 3 November. Virtually unknown to the general public when the campaign began, the "new face" of the SDS managed to unite an opposition that had been fragmented for several years, and to defeat the incumbent president, Zhelyu Zhelev, in a U.S.-style primary aimed at selecting a single opposition presidential candidate.

As the triumphant candidate, Stoyanov's embodied the SDS's new way of thinking. Although he was deputy justice minister in 1991–1992, he was not linked with the confrontational style that the SDS projected under its former leader, Filip Dimitrov. Indeed, Stoyanov's "outstretched hand" policy helped overcome the SDS's strong internal divisions and its intolerance toward other opposition parties, thus supporting the reform process started by SDS Chairman Ivan Kostov two years earlier.

With a reputation for tact and welcoming open discussion and dialogue, Stoyanov best suited the SDS's profile of a candidate who might have a real chance of leading the party back into power. Stoyanov was chosen as the SDS's presidential candidate at the party's national conference in March with 77 percent of the vote. He emerged victorious in the 1 June primary election with 66 percent of the vote.

In contrast to the strident campaigning that has dominated the Bulgarian political landscape, Stoyanov avoided overblown or illusory promises and instead stressed the need for "reasonable change." At the very top of his agenda is Bulgarian membership in NATO and the European Union. On the domestic front, in mid-October, Stoyanov—concerned about the deepening economic crisis—put forward the idea of a National Salvation Council of experts and respected public figures to advise the government on economic issues. Stoyanov made a concerted effort to address youth concerns, and portrayed himself as a guitar-playing member of a generation that came of age with the Beatles.

Stoyanov won favorable attention internationally after winning the nomination, being the first Bulgarian official received by German Chancellor Helmut Kohl since his visit to Bulgaria in 1993. Equally important, Poland's socialist president Aleksander Kwasniewski said his "fingers [were] crossed" for Stoyanov after the two met in Warsaw in early October.

In the presidential election, Stoyanov was supported by the SDS, the People's Union, the ethnic Turkish Movement for Rights and Freedom, and the Bulgarian Social Democratic Party. His support was boosted by people blaming the Socialists for leading the country into severe economic crisis.

Some analysts predicted that with Stoyanov as president, the "war between the institutions"—between the president and the legislature—will go on. Some others, however, claim there is hope for traditionally divided Bulgaria to ultimately have a president for all, since Stoyanov managed to gradually unite his union's members, the other opposition parties, and finally politically nonaligned voters in the second round. At his 3 November press conference, Stoyanov declared, "After I and [vice president-elect] Todor Kavaldzhiev received a definitive vote from the nation, the only party that remains for us is called Bulgaria."

Romania

Population:	22,680,951 (November 1996)
Capital:	Bucharest (pop. 2,066,723)
Major cities:	Constanta (pop. 348,985), Iasi (pop. 337,643), Timisoara (pop. 325,359)
Area:	237,500 sq. km.
Major ethnic groups:	Romanian 89.4%, Hungarian 7.1%, Romani 1.8% (according to 1991 census—although Roma are generally estimated at 7% to 8% of the population)
Economy:	GDP growth: 4.1%
	Inflation rate: 57%
	Average monthly income: $145
	Unemployment rate: 6.3%

RADICAL POLITICAL CHANGE IN ROMANIA

by MICHAEL SHAFIR *and* DAN IONESCU

The year 1996 will undoubtedly figure in future histories of Romania as a year of radical political departure. The Party of Social Democracy in Romania (PDSR), which has ruled the country alone or in coalition with other formations since 1990, was voted out of power and President Ion Iliescu was replaced by Emil Constantinescu, who ran against him as the candidate of the main opposition alliance, the Democratic Convention of Romania (CDR). In fact, 1996 has a significance that runs well beyond the country's post-communist political era. For the victory of the opposition in the elections held on 3 November marked the first time since 1937 that a government in Romania was changed at the polling stations. Furthermore, Constantinescu's election as president on 17 November was the first time the country's head of state was changed in a democratic process rather than by death, execution, or coup d'etat.

NEW POLITICAL MAP

The demise of the PDSR had been in the offing for some time, as public-opinion polls had been predicting for more than half a year. The main reasons for the change were the country's deteriorating economic performance combined with recurrent corruption scandals in which PDSR officials or their protégés were involved in one way or another. The party had been ruling alone since September, when it broke with its last coalition partner, the Party of Romanian National Unity (PUNR). Earlier, in March, the PDSR had formally ended its coalition alliance with the Socialist Labor Party (PSM). The extreme-nationalist Greater Romania Party (PRM) had already been forced out of the coalition in 1995; in view of that legacy, nothing but bad memories survived of the so-called red-quadrangle coalition that had ruled Romania most of the time since the 1992 elections. On the face of it, the PUNR had been forced to leave the coalition because of its adamant opposition to the signing of the basic treaty with Hungary. But in fact (and this also applies to the PDSR's decision to break with the PSM earlier in the year), the ruling party hoped that by replacing prefects in counties where the PUNR or the PSM was in charge, it would manage to better control the electoral process.

The opposition CDR, however, was well aware of such intentions and very suspicious of the PDSR's potential manipulation of the electoral outcome. It therefore intensified controls and reached agreement with other opposition formations for joint supervision of the electoral process on the eve of the ballot. The parliamentary elections produced a new electoral map in which the CDR had primacy. With 122 seats in the Chamber of Deputies and 53 seats in the Senate, the CDR emerged as the strongest political formation. Even before the presidential runoff of 17 November was over, the CDR agreed on a coalition government with the Social Democratic Union (USD) headed by former Prime Minister Petre Roman in exchange for Roman's support of Constantinescu in the runoff. Roman, who came in third in the first presidential contest held on 3 November, eventually became chairman of the Senate, but the new governing coalition would have been weak had it not been joined by the Hungarian Democratic Federation of Romania (UDMR). With the ethnic Hungarians' presence in the government, on the other hand, the coalition can count on a strong (more than 60 percent) majority in parliament.

The UDMR's joining of the ruling coalition is in itself revolutionary, seen against the background of the interethnic conflicts that have plagued Romania throughout its modern history. Viewed from that angle, the presence of Gyorgy Tokay, a moderate UDMR lawyer, at the head of the Department for National Minorities bodes well for the future. The new government is headed by Victor Ciorbea and includes 27 ministers. Ciorbea had been elected mayor of Bucharest, at the head of the CDR list, in June. He is a member of the main force in the CDR alliance, the National Peasant Party Christian Democratic. In the short time since his election as mayor, Ciorbea had impressed observers with his no-nonsense policy of anti-corruption measures and a clear intention to implement electoral promises.

Whether or not the new government will indeed be able to implement the promises remains to be seen, for those promises included many populist measures that are hardly compatible with the country's urgent need for economic austerity. Soon after taking office, Ciorbea presented parliament with a short-term (six-month) program that attempted to respond to some of the promises (such as raising the minimum allocation to families with children) but combined them with some expected cuts in public spending. Yet, under pressure from the International Monetary Fund (IMF), in December Ciorbea said the measures aimed at improving living standards would have to be postponed, and furthermore, he announced a doubling of energy prices, a move likely to trigger a huge increase in the cost of living. Without such measures, as the IMF made clear, the legacy of the former government would have left the country on the brink of collapse and would have certainly forestalled a much-needed standby loan from the IMF. In stark contrast to the Vacaroiu government, from the start the CDR-USD-UDMR coalition promised to encourage foreign investment, speed up privatization, and take drastic measures against corruption, among other things by setting up a special anti-corruption department within the premier's office.

With only 91 seats in the Chamber of Deputies and 41 in the Senate, the PDSR was the clear loser of the elections. It had tried to avoid that outcome by twice cosmetically reshuffling the government of former Prime Minister Nicolae

Vacaroiu in January and in September, but the local elections of June clearly showed that the PDSR was out of grace with the electorate and that the main sentiment dominating public opinion was "enough was enough." True, the PDSR had a plurality among elected mayors and among local councilors. But in the larger and urban settlements, the CDR came out on top and, more important, it obtained most of the seats in the elections for county councilors, where the electoral system used was similar to that of the November parliamentary elections.

Those parliamentary elections demonstrated that the PDSR had lost the part of the electorate that had been critical for its previous victories: the workers and the emerging entrepreneurial strata. That also explains why Iliescu, who had won against Constantinescu in 1992, lost in 1996 by a margin of nine percentage points—45.5 to 54.4.

Other losers in the 1996 contests are the PSM, the PUNR, the Party of Civic Alliance (PAC), the Liberal Party '93, and the Democratic Agrarian Party of Romania. The latter party had somehow managed to squeeze into the Senate, but not into the Chamber of Deputies, in 1992. In 1996, although running in alliance with two other formations, it failed to clear the 3 percent electoral hurdle. The PSM likewise scored less than three percentage points and will no longer be represented in parliament, where, in fact, the left wing of the political spectrum is no longer represented. One can expect that the PDSR will now attempt to fill that gap, perhaps attracting parties left out of the legislature, such as the PSM and even the PRM. The PRM, which is headed by Senator Corneliu Vadim Tudor, had been throwing punches at the PDSR and at Iliescu (who is now Tudor's peer, a senator) and a renewed alliance between them will prove difficult, though not impossible. Tudor had lost his parliamentary immunity in the previous legislature for having insulted Iliescu, but that immunity was automatically restored to him with his re-election. His PRM did slightly better than in 1992 and now has 19 deputies and eight senators.

The PRM's gain was, to no little extent, the PUNR's loss, for it was from that segment of the electorate that Tudor's formation apparently drew its increased support. The PUNR, on the other hand, had been discredited by both intraparty fighting and by its chairman's crusade against the treaty with Hungary. The credibility of that crusade had to suffer in view of the fact that Gheorghe Funar's furious attacks were almost carbon copies of the attacks by the opposition in Hungary itself. The PUNR is now represented in the legislature by only 18 deputies and seven senators, having lost almost half of its previous electoral support. Still, it did better than the PAC and the Liberal Party '93, which had joined forces in the center-right National Liberal Alliance. Due to the polarization of the electorate around the CDR or the PDSR on the eve of the elections, however, the alliance failed to enlist the minimum 3 percent needed for representation in parliament.

ECONOMIC MALAISE

At least some of the sweeping political changes in 1996 are rooted in Romania's post-communist economic and social malaise. Despite a series of positive developments, Romania's economy continued to be in bad shape, while efforts to reform it and to attract more foreign investment were mostly unsuccessful. The year started with a serious crisis in the energy sector, caused by a prolonged cold spell combined with a lack of the hard currency needed for importing additional fuel and energy. Acute energy shortages forced factories to send thousands of workers home, sparking a wave of labor protests. The CDR eventually presented a nonbinding resolution to parliament accusing the government of "disastrous" energy policies. On 26 February, the motion passed in the Chamber of Deputies but failed to garner enough support for adoption in the Senate. Even so, the vote marked a turning point in Romania's post-communist parliamentary proceedings and was perceived as a serious warning to the government. The debate contributed to speeding up the completion of Romania's first nuclear reactor at the Cernavoda power plant, which was officially inaugurated on 17 April. The project, started in the late 1970s with Canadian assistance, has been described as Romania's biggest industrial investment ever. It is expected to cover 8 percent to 10 percent of the country's electricity needs.

Another major reason for growing popular discontent was the evolution of prices for staples and energy. In view of the upcoming local, general, and presidential elections, Vacaroiu's cabinet first tried to keep prices for basic products artificially low. But a sharp devaluation of the leu in May–June forced the government to massively increase prices for gasoline, electricity, natural gas, and bread on 2 July—only two weeks after the local elections. In autumn and winter, the national currency registered a further sharp devaluation, with the official exchange rate passing the 3,600 lei to the dollar threshold in mid-December (compared with about 2,600 to the dollar at the start of 1996). The difference between the rates of exchange at exchange bureaus and on the interbank market reached a record high of nearly 30 percentage points. The continuous devaluation of the leu was accompanied by a crisis in the banking system that forced the National Bank in March to tighten controls over currency markets. In July, two of Romania's largest private banks went bankrupt.

Inflation was another key problem in Romania's economy in 1996. Official forecasts of an annual inflation rate of up to 20 percent proved thoroughly unrealistic. In November, the National Statistical Board said the rate was 45 percent, while some experts put the true figure at some 70 percent. International financial organizations expressed concern over Romania's inability to hold back inflation and meet other performance criteria required for new loans. According to Ciorbea, the estimated budget deficit for 1996 was five to six times higher than the 2.2 percent of gross domestic product originally agreed with the IMF—a figure that had later been adjusted to 3 percent. Under the circumstances, the IMF and the World Bank suspended their credit programs to Romania, a move that affected Romania's credibility on financial markets and discouraged foreign investment (since 1989, slightly over $2 billion has been invested in Romania, compared with $13 billion in neighboring Hungary, whose population is half the size of Romania's). The slow pace of privatization and industrial restructuring contributed to the negative developments. A mass-privatization scheme was completed on 31 March, three months behind schedule. But the process of putting big state-owned enterprises into private hands has continued to stall.

The accession to power of the reform-minded opposition had a beneficial effect on Romania's image abroad. IMF representatives praised the economic program presented by Ciorbea's cabinet to parliament on 11 December and announced that negotiations over a new credit arrangement would start in January, conditional on the implementation of austerity measures which, indeed, have already been implemented. The government's plan provides for speeding up reforms in order to ultimately ensure an annual growth rate of between 4.5 percent and 6 percent. According to National Bank Governor Mugur Isarescu, Romania needs some $1.5 billion of foreign financial help in 1997 to cope with its ambitious reform goals.

FOREIGN POLICY PRIORITIES

Integration into European and Euro-Atlantic structures was proclaimed a top priority by Romania's new coalition government. On 11 December, Ciorbea told parliament: "If we miss the opportunity of integrating into the European Union and NATO, we will have wasted a huge chance." One day earlier, his foreign minister, Adrian Severin of the USD, insisted that Romania's relations with the West must have priority over those with the East. Such a resolute pro-Western orientation, shared by many former communist countries in Eastern and Central Europe, is nothing new in Romania. The previous left-wing administration had encouraged a similar policy, especially after 1993–1994; but its ability to persuade the West of its commitment was limited. Bucharest has shown a keen interest in joining NATO, rooted in its apprehension that the alliance's eastward expansion might create a new dividing line on the continent through preferential treatment extended to a particular country or group of countries (neighboring Hungary in the first place). In 1996, Romania was one of the most active participants in the Partnership for Peace program (it had been the first former communist country to sign up for it, in January 1994). It also contributed to the IFOR peacekeeping forces in Bosnia. Romania's chance to be admitted to the alliance in the near future grew palpably after the victory of the democratic opposition in the November elections.

The awareness that NATO and the EU are not prepared to let in potential troublemakers from the former communist bloc that have failed to solve their disputes is the main reason behind Romania's efforts to improve relations with some of its neighbors. The most unproblematic decision was to sign a basic treaty with the current Yugoslav Federation, with which Romania has traditionally been on friendly terms. That took place on 17 May in Belgrade, during an official visit by Iliescu. But the true diplomatic event of the year was the signing on 16 September in Timisoara of a basic treaty with Hungary after more than five years of tough negotiations. The event came one year after Iliescu had launched an initiative for a "historic reconciliation" between the two countries. But the very day the new cabinet was sworn in (12 December), Severin stated that his country's relations with Hungary should be based on a future-oriented partnership rather than on Iliescu's reconciliation proposal, which dealt primarily with past conflicts. Severin also paid his first visit as foreign minister in December to Budapest, where the sides agreed, among other things, to open consulates in Cluj and Debrecen. That decision had a symbolic value, since the consulates had been closed by Ceausescu in the 1980s as part of his anti-Hungarian policies. Attempts to sign basic treaties with Moldova, Ukraine, and Russia were less successful. The main stumbling block was Romania's insistence that those documents include a formal denunciation of the 1939 Molotov-Ribbentrop secret pact, which had resulted in Greater Romania's losing Bessarabia and Northern Bukovina to the Soviet Union. The three former Soviet republics see such a clause as expressing thinly veiled territorial claims on Romania's part. Moldova's president-elect, Petru Lucinschi, in late December paid an unofficial visit to Romania. While he agreed with Constantinescu on a series of steps aimed at improving economic cooperation, the treaty issue remained as problematic as it had been before the visit.

Interview: "THE PEOPLE ARE READY FOR CHANGE"

Just a few months after replacing a former communist as president, Emil Constantinescu was filled with optimism and a steady sense of the magnitude of his task. He told Colin Woodard in an interview in Bucharest on 22 January 1997 that he intends to guide Romania through a severe and painful economic-reform process and lead it away from the distrust left over from years of corruption and secret-police machinations.

NEW DIRECTION

"The popular mentality has changed a great deal in the past seven years," Constantinescu said. "People are ready for real change and reform and are prepared to bear the costs. They're ready to accept private ownership of land, foreign ownership of businesses, and the need to make fundamental changes to our economic system. Profound economic reform is the only way Romania can emerge from its economic crisis.

"Our biggest problems are not undoing communism but beating the problems created over the past seven years," he said, referring to the long tenure of Ion Iliescu and his political allies, who seized power during the 1989 revolt against Nicolae Ceausescu. "We're working to establish the rule of law in this country. People are even more interested in justice being done than they are about the standard of living or day-to-day economic problems."

"I feel confident that people will understand that their prosperity implies a real reform of society, that the fulfilling of this goal means a lot of difficulties," the president said when asked about the social implications of the austerity package introduced by Prime Minister Ciorbea. "[But] the ones ruling the country nowadays will not ignore them and will constantly act according to the principle that our role is to serve the citizen and not the other way around."

INVESTIGATING 1989

While the economic reforms may not have popular support, the president's anti-corruption campaign does. In public speeches, he has promised to investigate Romania's mysterious 1989 revolution and reveal the truth. "My expectations are the same as everyone interested in finding the truth about the events in December 1989," he said. "Who were the terrorists? What was the role played by the army and the Securitate [secret police]? Did foreign secret services intervene in Romania? These are the main questions that need to be answered. I am aware that the entire truth cannot be found out now, seven years after the events. However, part of the truth can and must be known and made public." [Rogue ex-Securitate members] still exist," Constantinescu admitted. "But the extent of popular support during the elections made them afraid to take action." "We [in the government] have the support of the people and we cannot be blackmailed or bought [by the Securitate]," he said. "There is no chance for their backstage games. They have nowhere to go."

THE DISAPPOINTING WEST

Constantinescu said his biggest surprise on taking office was not the presence of the Securitate but the attitude of the West toward the Balkans. He expressed disappointment with the West's post-Cold War policy in Eastern Europe. Western governments, he said, have actually provided support to authoritarian governments in the interests of stability.

"After 200 years of successful democracy, I'm afraid even the United States seems most unconfident in the strength of popular democracy," he said. "The West is always inclined to support stability abroad, and the most convenient form of stability is often authoritarian or dictatorial." The president's remarks came while popular demonstrations were challenging less-than-democratic regimes in Bulgaria, Serbia, and Albania as the West watched passively.

"The neo-communist regimes in Eastern Europe are often very convenient for the Western world. It provided them protection against organized crime and unwanted immigration and even gave them a basis for feeling superior," he said. "But by supporting them, the West betrayed those fighting for democratic change."

"The West is interested in what happens here—in the true human story of the trial and transition from communism. They ask us, 'How are you?' in the American way, to which the only appropriate answer is 'fine.' Neither the U.S. administration nor the university liberals are interested in the real answers about what is happening here. All fighters of communism feel—and have a right to feel—betrayed. But today our illusions have ended. We understand clearly that we cannot talk for real with the West, except in terms of profit and mutual interest. The rest, as Hamlet said, is silence."

Profile: VICTOR CIORBEA: ROMANIA'S NEW PRIME MINISTER

by MICHAEL SHAFIR

Victor Ciorbea (pronounced Chorbea), was nominated by the leadership of the National Peasant Party Christian Democratic (PNTCD) on 19 November to be Romania's new premier. Ciorbea's name surfaced as a possible option in the wake of the parliamentary elections of 3 November, which altered Romania's political map, with the Democratic Convention of Romania (CDR) emerging as the country's largest political force.

At 42, the new premier is even younger than his former competitors. What is more, in the short time that had passed since his election as mayor of Bucharest in the June 1992 local elections, he proved to be a good and efficient manager. The city's face had been rapidly changing since Ciorbea took over the mayor-alty, though only a fool could have expected wonders in view of the Ceausescu-era legacy of urban deterioration and the inefficiency—some even claim corruption—of Ciorbea's predecessor, who was also a member of the CDR. What is more, Ciorbea promptly started implementing what he had promised during his electoral campaign, and that was really novel for Romania, histori-cally speaking. A large post box hung outside the mayor's office for citizens to deposit their complaints and suggestions; and Ciorbea made good his promise to have free-travel on public transportation for poorer pensioners and students. He was known to have a 20–hour workday, much of it dedicated to eradicating corruption and lifting up the city's orientalized face. It became more difficult to get things "moved" in Bucharest with the help of kickbacks to city employees.

In other words, Ciorbea was implementing his "Contract with Bucharest," modeled on the 1992 US Republican Party campaign platform. By appointing him, the PNTCD clearly wished to signal its intention to genuinely start im-plementing the nationwide parallel "Contract with Romania," with which the CDR had won the parliamentary elections.

The key question is whether Ciorbea can achieve this program in light of the country's harsh economic realities. He should be aided in this regard by his background as a union leader. After 1989, Ciorbea became a prominent figure in the country's reborn trade-union movement. He was chairman of the teachers' trade union and eventually became chairman of one of the country's largest umbrella trade-union organization, Fratia. He will undoubtedly need all the ne-gotiating skills he acquired in that position, but this time at the other end of the negotiating table, to persuade Romanian workers to accept the likely austerity measures.

A lawyer by training, Ciorbea worked for a few years as a military prosecutor under the former regime. That may sound worse than was actually the case, for junior-level military prosecutors were more involved with disciplinary cases than with pursuing "communist justice." In 1981 he joined the Romanian Communist Party, but was just one of the nearly 4 million rank-and-file members for whom party membership has been described as the equivalent of having a drivers' license: career-wise, nobody could move without it. Eventually, he became a member of the staff of the Bucharest Law School and is reputed to have been a lecturer admired by students. His past under Ceausescu should reassure those worried that the CDR intends to launch a witch hunt against former members of the Communist Party and those who had positions suspected of linkage with the former repressive apparat.

Sidebar: THE ROMANIAN-HUNGARIAN BASIC TREATY: END OR BEGINNING?

by DAN IONESCU

The signing on 16 September of a basic treaty between Romania and Hungary marked the end of five years of tough negotiations—a diplomatic purgatory that the outside world learned to watch with almost a pinch of hopelessness. Claude Karnoouh, a French political analyst, described the breakthrough in the treaty talks as "a divine surprise," in light of the traditional rivalry between the two countries over what is now the Romanian province of Transylvania, a territory that belonged for centuries to the Hungarian Kingdom and later to the Austro-Hungarian Empire. Transylvania is still home to a large ethnic Hungarian minority that presses for more rights, including some form of autonomy.

At closer look, however, the signing appeared neither unexpected nor divine. It was in the air for quite some time, despite doubts on both sides about some of the treaty's provisions, including a direct reference to the controversial Recommendation No. 1201 of the Council of Europe that allows collective minority rights and territorial autonomy. Romania never concealed its reservations about those two concepts, which it saw as opening the door to possible secession with all the nefarious effects experienced by former Yugoslavia and other East-European regions.

The reasons behind the long-delayed agreement are quite mundane: both countries badly needed the treaty to show the West that they are ripe for joining European and Euro-Atlantic structures—NATO and the European Union in the first place. The West, for its part, made no secret of the fact that it was not prepared to accept potential trouble-makers from the former communist bloc unless they could bring proof of their determination to solve generations-old conflicts and get along with each other.

Once the treaty was signed, the question arose of how to prevent it from becoming just another scrap of paper, as the previous Romanian-Hungarian treaty, signed in 1972 by former communist leaders Nicolae Ceausescu and Janos Kadar unfortunately proved. No easy task, indeed, if one thinks of the opposition the treaty has met in both countries, with nationalist circles accusing their respective governments of betraying national interests. In Romania, the chauvinistic Party of Romanian National Unity (PUNR) and the Greater Romania Party were among the most vociferous critics of the new treaty. The latter found a renegade Hungarian in the person of its vice-president and deputy in parliament, Iuliu-Ioan Furo, to sound the alarm against any "transaction with the national territory, which is sacred, inalienable, and indivisible." And PUNR deputy chairman Ioan Gavra spoke of a "dangerous precedent" that turns Romania into "a testing ground for ethnic anomalies" in Europe. He further depicted the treaty as a "victory of both Hungary and the Hungarian Democratic Federation of Romania," the main political organization of the Magyar minority. Such language may appeal to many in a country where the discriminatory treatment of the Romanian majority population in Transylvania during the Austro-Hungarian "dualism" and the Hortyist atrocities in north-west Transylvania in 1940–1944 are still remembered.

On the other side, political leaders of the Hungarian minority in Romania expressed dismay over what they perceive as the treaty's failure to safeguard the rights of the 1.5 million-strong community. In particular, they were disappointed by the relegation of Recommendation 1201 to the annex of the treaty and by its obvious dilution through an additional interpretation.

On 12 September, Reformed Bishop Laszlo Tokes made a last-minute attempt to convince Hungarian Premier Gyula Horn to postpone the treaty's signing until after the presidential and general elections in Romania, scheduled for 3 November. Behind this request was certainly the idea that Romania's incumbent President Ion Iliescu would try to make political capital by posing again as the architect of the Romanian-Hungarian reconciliation, as he did in the past. Tokes, whose opposition to Ceausescu's dictatorship sparked an uprising in Timisoara in December 1989 that led to the collapse of the communist regime, also urged Horn to change the venue of the ceremony. Timisoara, he had suggested earlier, has to remain a symbol of anti-communist resistance, and the presence at the ceremony of Iliescu—a former senior communist official—was "undesirable." But symbols apart, the treaty, which still had to be ratified by the two countries' parliaments, appears as a new beginning on the convoluted road to reconciliation. On the condition that both sides seek—and find—the mixture of good faith and good will that is required for a true happy end of the story.

Moldova

Population:	4,300,000
Capital:	Chisinau (pop. 754,000)
Major cities:	Tiraspol (capital of the self-proclaimed "Dniester Republic," pop. 185,000), Balti (pop. 158,000)
Area:	33,700 sq. km.
Major ethnic groups:	Moldovan 65%, Ukrainian 14%, Russian 13%, Gagauz 3.5%
Economy:	GDP growth: –8%
	Inflation rate: 15.1%
	Average monthly income: $42.30 (1995)
	Unemployment rate: 1.5%

MOLDOVA SLIDES BACK AND TO THE LEFT

by DAN IONESCU

The republic of Moldova in 1996 continued through a series of major political realignments that began in the summer of 1995, when former President Mircea Snegur left the ruling Agrarian Democratic Party (PDAM) to form his own presidential party, known as the Party of Revival and Conciliation in Moldova (PRCM). In addition, 1996 was a presidential-election year—a fact that brought political passions to paroxysms. Moldova offered the rare example of a presidential race in which no less than three power branches were directly involved: the presidential, the executive, and the legislative.

Snegur, Andrei Sangheli, and Petru Lucinschi, who until December 1995 were president, prime minister, and parliament speaker, respectively, entered one after the other into a presidential contest that became increasingly personal. Their battle inevitably led to a polarization not only of the administration, but also of the media and society at large. Snegur repeatedly threatened to dismiss Sangheli's cabinet for incompetence, particularly for its inability to solve serious social issues such as the huge arrears in pensions and salary payments to state employees. However, his constitutional powers eventually proved insufficient to sack a single minister. In mid-March, he tried to fire Defense Minister Pavel Creanga for allegedly condoning corruption in his department, but the Constitutional Court overturned his decision in early April. The tug-of-war over Creanga's post continued unsuccessfully until September.

Snegur's frustration surfaced in his oft-repeated pledge that, if he were re-elected president in November, he would fight for changing Moldova into a presidential republic in which he would enjoy broad prerogatives and would be in direct control of the government. Less than two weeks before the election, he reiterated earlier threats to dissolve the parliament and to call for a referendum to oust the PDAM from power. The parliament, on the other hand, did its utmost to block all his legislative initiatives. On 9 February, it rejected Snegur's constitutional proposal to rename the official language Romanian instead of Moldovan. (That issue had been a key political one in 1995, leading to mass demonstrations in Chisinau and a split in the ruling party.) In March, the parliament considered Snegur's impeachment over the Creanga case, and in May, it rejected his plea to reshuffle the cabinet.

Snegur gradually succeeded in winning the support of right-wing forces. They finally joined a pro-Snegur "civic movement" that was set up on 7 August and included, besides the PRCM, 16 other parties and associations, among them the Christian Democratic Popular Front (FPCD), the most influential organization advocating a union with neighboring Romania. Both Snegur and the FPCD subsequently tried to depict their alliance as a pragmatic one, with the latter suggesting that Snegur was the "lesser evil" compared to the overtly pro-Russian Sangheli and Lucinschi. No less than 16 hopefuls initially announced their intention to participate in the presidential race. Seven of those, however, proved unable to collect the 20,000 signatures required to enter the race. Among them, the best known were Ilie Ilascu, a political prisoner from the Dniester region, and film director Emil Loteanu. Ilascu, who had been sentenced to death by the Dniester secessionists on charges of terrorism following the spring–summer 1992 warlike conflict in eastern Moldova, is still being held in a Dniester jail. In September, he quit the FPCD, sharply attacking the party's decision to back Snegur, whom he described as "unfriendly to our national ideals" (read: reunification with Romania). Behind Ilascu's move, some analysts saw Lucinschi's efforts to split the unionist camp and the right in general.

ELECTORAL FEVER

Political confrontation culminated in the weeks preceding the two rounds of the presidential election on 17 November and 1 December. On 8 November, the national television channel aired an illegally recorded telephone conversation between Nicolae Andronic, Snegur's campaign chief, and Alexandru Burian, Moldova's ambassador to Germany. The two were discussing how to ensure a maximum of publicity for Burian's revelations of alleged financial irregularities at the Foreign Ministry and Moldova's embassies abroad. Although the scandal, considered by many a Moldovan "Watergate," considerably marred the election campaign, Lucinschi and his team prevented it from being debated in parliament before the election. Amid growing tension, the first round of the election failed to bring final clarification, since no candidate could garner more than 50 percent of the votes. Snegur ranked first, with almost 39 percent of the votes, followed by Lucinschi with about 28 percent; Vladimir Voronin, the leader of the Communist Party of Moldova, with more than 10 percent; Sangheli with 9.5 percent; and Valeriu Matei, the chairman of the moderately pro-Romanian Party of Democratic Forces, with nearly 9 percent. Four more candidates received between 0.43 percent and 2.13 percent. The biggest surprise in the first round was Voronin's performance, which signaled the communists' rather spectacular comeback to public favor.

The 1 December runoff resulted in a further radicalization of the electorate, splitting it into center-right and left-wing camps. Matei urged his supporters to vote for Snegur. But that could not counterbalance the leftist coalition that took shape around Lucinschi, despite his claims of running as an independent social democrat with no party affiliation. The coalition included the Party of Social Progress (a pro-Lucinschi organization created in late spring 1995); the PDAM, which had supported Sangheli in the first round; Voronin's communists; most of the socialists; as well as the Pro-Moldova and Unitate/Edinstvo movements, which cultivate nostalgia for the Soviet past. Lucinschi eventually won with 54 percent of the votes—a comfortable 8 percent margin over Snegur. His triumph triggered a chain reaction at the top. On 2 December, Sangheli's cabinet resigned en masse in order to pave the way for a government that could cooperate more closely with the new president; the following day, parliament accepted the resignation.

RUSSIA AND THE DNIESTER FACTOR

The 56–year-old Lucinschi was to officially take office on 15 January 1997. His political career includes a stint as Central Committee secretary of the defunct Communist Party of the Soviet Union, the only ethnic Moldovan to ever hold such a high position in the party's hierarchy. Though that happened in the last years of Mikhail Gorbachev's rule, under the auspicious star of reform, his earlier career with the party was in no way different from that of other ambitious apparatchiks in the former Soviet Union.

Immediately after his victory was announced, Lucinschi made a series of statements that amounted to an overt display of pro-Russian feeling. He was quoted in Trud, for instance, as saying he had "close personal contacts with the Russian leadership" and that he intended "to use them for the benefit of our country." And he repeatedly advocated the restoration of closer ties with the former Soviet republics, now members of the Commonwealth of Independent States.

Lucinschi's victory could bring deep changes in the policy of cautious rapprochement with the West conducted under Snegur. Russia's role in the region may grow, especially since it keeps a military presence in Moldova's breakaway Dniester region and continues to be Moldova's main source of energy and fuel. In late October, Lucinschi headed a parliamentary delegation to Moscow, where he met with Russian Premier Viktor Chernomyrdin, the new Security Council Secretary Ivan Rybkin, and the chairmen of the Russian parliament's two chambers. The talks focused on the delayed ratification of the Moldovan-Russian basic treaty and the bilateral agreement of 21 October 1994 on the withdrawal of the Russian troops from the Dniester region, as well as on ways to solve the Dniester issue. At the end of the visit, Lucinschi stated that "relations with the Russian Federation are a top priority for Moldova" and pledged to "improve them considerably" if elected president. But on 13 November, the Russian State Duma adopted a second resolution within one year demanding that the government declare the Dniester region a zone of special strategic interest for Russia. Lucinschi reacted promptly, speaking of the "brutal" interference in Moldova's affairs and a "premeditated act plotted by certain extremist forces in Moscow and Tiraspol." However, his tough stance was largely interpreted as a defense against widespread accusations of playing into Moscow's hand.

Analysts give Lucinschi a better chance to solve the protracted conflict between Moldova and the Dniester separatists than to his predecessor. Negotiations between the two sides over a special status for the Dniester region within the Moldovan state are currently deadlocked, after failed attempts in May and July, to sign a memorandum on normalizing bilateral ties. Those attempts were made in accordance with a joint declaration on the Dniester issue signed on 19 January in Moscow by the presidents of Moldova, Russia, and Ukraine. But Snegur later started playing for time, for fear that the matter might be turned into an election issue. Now that the presidential race is over, the cards are being shuffled again. Valerii Litskai, who functions as the equivalent of a foreign minister in the government of the self-declared "Dniester republic," stated on 3 December that Lucinschi's election would "have a positive influence" on bilateral talks. The price the new Moldovan president may pay for the conflict's settlement could be the de facto recognition of Moldova's territorial amputation for the sake of a symbolic unification.

RUSSIA

V

Domestic Affairs

Foreign Policy

The Economy

Social Issues

Domestic Affairs

Population:	147,700,000
Capital:	Moscow (1994 pop. 8,793,000)
Major cities:	St. Petersburg (pop. 4,883,000), Nizhnii Novgorod
	(pop. 1,425,000), Novosibirsk (pop. 1,418,000)
Area:	17,075,400 sq. km.
Major ethnic groups:	Russian 81.5%, Tatar 3.8%, Ukrainian 3%, Chuvash
	1.2%, Bashkir 0.9%, Belarusian 0.8%, other 8.8%
Economy:	GDP growth: -6%
. . . .	Inflation rate: 22%
. . . .	Average monthly income: $150
. . . .	Unemployment rate: 9.3%

RUSSIA ELECTS A FRAGILE POLITICAL STABILITY

by LAURA BELIN *and* ROBERT W. ORTTUNG

Russia's fledgling democracy remained closely tied to the personalized rule of Boris Yeltsin, whose poor health in the second half of the year left the country's future uncertain. Russia continued to be polarized between a hard core of Communist supporters who reject the reforms and a broad mass of voters who reject communism yet still feel relatively powerless to influence their rulers.

Although 1996 began amid widespread skepticism that President Boris Yeltsin would allow any elections to take place, the presidential election was held on time in June, and 48 Russian regions elected their leaders in the autumn. The fact that the elections took place seemed to confirm that the norms of democratic procedure have taken root in Russia. The voting, however, tended to reaffirm the status quo and did little to resolve the country's acute social and economic problems. Yeltsin's poor health, and the increasingly open power struggle among his lieutenants, destabilized the political scene during the second half of the year.

Yeltsin began the year with poor prospects for re-election following the strong anti-government showing in the December 1995 State Duma elections. In the parliamentary elections, the Communist Party of the Russian Federation (KPRF) and allied left-wing groups won more than twice as many votes and three times as many Duma seats as the pro-government Our Home Is Russia bloc. The botched hostage crisis at the Dagestani village of Pervomaiskoe in January brought Yeltsin's popularity ratings down into the single digits. To improve his image, Yeltsin made the largest shake-up in three years among his ministers and in the administration. His most important sacrifice, on 16 January, was First Deputy Prime Minister Anatolii Chubais, the last of the reformers left from acting Yegor Gaidar's 1992 government and the key coordinator of Russian economic policy. Yeltsin blamed Chubais for the poor performance of Our Home Is Russia in the December elections. He also fired, among others, Foreign Minister Andrei Kozyrev, Deputy Prime Minister Sergei Shakhrai, and liberal Presidential Chief of Staff Sergei Filatov.

Convinced that Yeltsin had no chance of victory, some former backers, including Gaidar, tried to persuade the president to give up his re-election plans. Nevertheless, on 15 February, Yeltsin made a carefully stage-managed visit to his hometown of Yekaterinburg to announce that he would seek to retain his position as "father of the nation." The very day Yeltsin was "going to the people," the KPRF opened its fourth conference, where party leader Gennadii Zyuganov was nominated for president.

YELTSIN'S EFFECTIVE CAMPAIGN

Although plagued by some initial blunders and vicious infighting among cliques of his closest advisers, Yeltsin mounted an effective campaign. He replaced Oleg Poptsov, the chairman of state-run Russian Television (Channel 2), with the loyal Eduard Sagalaev. After lagging several weeks behind Zyuganov in the process of collecting the 1 million signatures needed to register, Yeltsin removed First Deputy Prime Minister Oleg Soskovets from the helm of his campaign team on 23 March and gave the job to Chubais. Members of the liberal intelligentsia, who had been fiercely critical of Yeltsin over the Chechen war, rallied to his cause as they realized there was a real chance that Zyuganov would win the presidential race. Chubais put together a team of "image makers" to rescue the Yeltsin campaign and drew upon the help of a group of leading bankers and media kingpins, including Boris Berezovskii of LogoVAZ and Russian Public Television, the Channel 1 broadcaster; Vladimir Potanin of Oneximbank; and Igor Malashenko, president of the leading private network, NTV. Yeltsin's daughter, Tatyana Dyachenko, provided the group with crucial access to the president. Although the Yeltsin campaign officially reported spending 14.4 billion rubles (about $2.9 million), it was rumored to have spent more than $100 million, much of it on print and electronic media.

Apparently fully recovered from his two bouts of heart trouble in 1995, Yeltsin traveled around the country, visiting more than 20 regions and promising to deliver more money and federal support everywhere he went. To neutralize the electoral handicap of the ongoing fighting in Chechnya, Nationalities Minister Vyacheslav Mikhailov signed an agreement in Nazran on 10 June—less than a week before the election—under which Moscow pledged to withdraw Russian troops from the republic by the end of August.

Meanwhile, Zyuganov's campaign started strong, with support above 20 percent in February, while other candidates were stuck in the single digits. The Duma election had cemented the KPRF's position as the dominant opposition party, but Zyuganov realized that he would have to broaden his electoral base if he was to attract more than 50 percent of the votes and win the presidency. Zyuganov distanced himself from communist ideology, but instead of turning to social democracy—as did the reformed communists in Eastern Europe—he chose to embrace the rhetoric of patriotism. His election platform did not mention Marxism-Leninism or the class struggle. Instead, it promised to rebuild a strong Russian state and reverse the national "humiliations" that had accompanied the transition to market economy and democracy. Zyuganov persuaded some prominent figures in Russia's "patriotic" camp—including former Vice President Aleksandr Rutskoi and Duma Deputy Speaker Sergei Baburin—to join his coalition. Officially, Zyuganov did not run for president as the Communist Party nominee but as the candidate of Russia's "popular-patriotic forces." Zyuganov also tried to keep the support of the more hard-line elements of the Communist camp, such as Workers' Russia leader Viktor Anpilov.

The pro-Yeltsin media sought to frame the election as a referendum on whether the country should return to communism, equating Zyuganov with the darkest features of the Soviet past. As Gaidar later put it, Yeltsin won because he ran both as president and as the candidate of the opposition—the anti-Communist opposition. The Yeltsin message received a boost on 15 March when the Communist-dominated Duma passed a resolution denouncing the December 1991 Belavezha accords, which dissolved the Soviet Union.

Whether the elections would actually take place remained the subject of intense speculation throughout the spring. Some thought Yeltsin would use the Duma's 15 March vote as an excuse to dissolve the parliament. On 27 April, *Izvestiya* published a letter from 13 leading bankers and entrepreneurs—including Berezovskii and MOST Group Chairman Vladimir Gusinskii—calling on Yeltsin and Zyuganov to reach a political compromise to avoid a civil war. Some viewed the "letter of the 13" as a trial balloon for canceling the election. The following week, Presidential Security Service chief Aleksandr Korzhakov, Yeltsin's close confidant, explicitly called for postponing the elections in a 5 May interview with the British newspaper *The Observer*.

LEBED AS KINGMAKER

In the first round of voting on 16 June, Yeltsin narrowly led Zyuganov, 35.28 percent to 32.03 percent. Retired Lieutenant-General Aleksandr Lebed finished third, with 14.52 percent, putting him in the position of kingmaker. He had campaigned as an honest general, tough on crime and corruption, who would draw upon his experience in Moldova to end the war in Chechnya. His election platform, called "An Ideology of Common Sense," also promised to support economic liberalization, protect Russians living in the "near abroad," and implement military reform. Despite his appeal to Russian patriotism, Lebed showed no interest in forming an alliance with the communist-patriots. On the contrary: Lebed struck a secret deal with Yeltsin's campaign team—possibly as early as March—in which he was offered financial support and massive media exposure during the final weeks of the campaign. Yeltsin's team correctly guessed that Lebed would be able to draw protest votes away from Zyuganov and hoped Lebed could channel them to their candidate in the second round. On 18 June, Yeltsin made Lebed chairman of the Security Council and his national-security adviser. In return, Lebed called on his voters to back Yeltsin.

On the same day he appointed Lebed, Yeltsin fired the unpopular defense minister, Pavel Grachev. Grachev was blamed for the army's humiliation in Chechnya and was seen as responsible for rampant corruption among senior officers. Events then took an unexpected turn. On the night of 19–20 June, two Yeltsin campaign workers with close ties to Chubais were caught carrying $500,000 in cash out of a government building. They were detained and questioned for several hours by members of Korzhakov's Presidential Security Service. Tipped off by Chubais, television networks broadcast updates on the unfolding scandal through the night, portraying the arrests as an attempted coup by Korzhakov. The following morning, Chubais persuaded the president to sack Korzhakov, Soskovets, and Federal Security Service Director Mikhail Barsukov. Chubais told reporters that the money had been planted on his associates in a sinister plot to derail the second round of the presidential election. Media commentaries portrayed the ouster of the hard-liners as a victory for democracy, saying little about the $500,000.

About 70 percent of the electorate had turned out on 16 June, and, in the days before the runoff, the Yeltsin campaign team grew concerned that a low turnout (below 60 percent) could hand victory to Zyuganov, whose supporters were considered more disciplined than the president's. To ensure that Yeltsin would not lose the votes of the comparatively affluent—the "dacha vote"—the president moved the election from the traditional Sunday to Wednesday, 3 July. Although Yeltsin suffered a serious recurrence of heart trouble and disappeared from public view after 26 June, the media studiously ignored his medical problems. News reports kept up an anti-Communist drumbeat, savaging a Zyuganov proposal for a coalition government, while the airwaves were saturated with Yeltsin commercials suggesting that a Communist victory would mean civil war, famine, and repression. In the end, Yeltsin took 53.83 percent (40,203,948 votes) to Zyuganov's 40.30 percent (30,102,288).

THE AILING PRESIDENT

Yeltsin's illness significantly impaired his ability to function at the beginning of his second term. He avoided public appearances, and most journalists colluded with officials in trying to disguise the seriousness of his condition. Television footage of Yeltsin at the brief inauguration ceremony on 9 August, however, showed that Yeltsin was obviously unwell. Finally, on 5 September, he publicly admitted that he needed heart surgery and said the operation would take place by the end of the month. It later transpired that Yeltsin's health was worse than the Kremlin was willing to admit and that he needed time to regain his strength before surgery. After undergoing a successful quintuple-bypass operation on 5 November, Yeltsin finally returned to the Kremlin on 23 December. (Little more than two weeks later, he checked into the hospital again with pneumonia.)

In mid-July, at the height of the concern about his health, Yeltsin shocked the political community by appointing Anatolii Chubais as his chief of staff in place of Nikolai Yegorov, the Korzhakov ally who had held the job since the January reshuffle. Chubais's return to high-level politics was unexpected because he was still widely reviled for spearheading a privatization program that has been perceived as giving away state property to well-connected insiders. Yeltsin had promised shortly before the second round of the election that he would not offer Chubais a high post.

Chubais quickly sought to consolidate control over the fractious administration. The key to his power was a decree issued in mid-August that required all presidential decrees to first go through the office of the chief of staff—in effect, giving Chubais the power to pre-approve presidential decisions. Given the lack of legislation defining key areas of political and economic life in Russia, having such control over decree power made Chubais arguably the most powerful man in the country during Yeltsin's extended "vacation."

In Yeltsin's absence, Prime Minister Viktor Chernomyrdin also assumed more authority. The constitution gives the Duma the right to approve or reject the prime minister after presidential elections, but in practice the Duma had little choice but to confirm Chernomyrdin in August. The Communist-dominated Duma did not want to be accused of plunging the country into political confusion by refusing to reappoint the prime minister. (Had the lower house voted down the proposed prime minister three times in a row, the president could have exercised his constitutional right to disband the Duma.) In any case, Zyuganov had a good working relationship with Chernomyrdin, and one leading Zyuganov ally in the upper house of parliament, Aman Tuleev, was appointed to the government as minister for cooperation with the Commonwealth of Independent States.

Chernomyrdin and Chubais had worked together in the cabinet for years, and they appeared to settle on an informal power-sharing agreement while Yeltsin was away. The third major figure in the Kremlin camp after the election was the newcomer Lebed, who was a destabilizing element in the system. In July, he managed to get his favored candidate, Colonel-General Igor Rodionov, appointed defense minister. But Lebed soon found himself marginalized within the presidential administration, while Chubais used his influence with the media to start a campaign to undermine Lebed's authority.

LEBED'S CHECHNYA COUP

Fighting flared up in Chechnya in early August, when the separatists successfully recaptured the republic's capital, Grozny. Lebed blamed Interior Minister

Anatolii Kulikov for the debacle and threatened to quit if Yeltsin did not fire Kulikov. Lebed was named presidential representative for Chechnya on 10 August and within three weeks had negotiated the Khasavyurt accords, pledging the withdrawal of Russian forces in return for a five-year moratorium on defining the republic's status. Most of the political establishment reacted with suspicion to the deal. Kulikov denounced it as "treason," while Moscow Mayor Yurii Luzhkov branded it "a bomb under the constitution." However, Yeltsin cautiously supported the plan, and Lebed's popularity soared. In September, as Yeltsin's poor health became a matter of public record, Lebed appeared the strongest contender should an early presidential election be necessary.

The attacks on Lebed by politicians and journalists intensified in the middle of October. On the 13th, Lebed endorsed Korzhakov's bid to capture the Duma seat Lebed once held. Korzhakov was threatening to reveal compromising information about various Kremlin luminaries, especially Chubais. Two days later, Lebed received a standing ovation from generals of paratroop divisions when he denounced the planned cuts in the airborne forces that had been announced by Defense Minister Rodionov (who had fallen out with Lebed after being appointed).

The next day, Kulikov accused the Security Council secretary of plotting a military coup. Few people took the coup allegations seriously, but the media gave them wide exposure. Yeltsin fired Lebed on 17 October on national television, chiding him for being too ambitious and not cooperating with his cabinet colleagues.

Lebed was replaced as Security Council secretary by Yeltsin loyalist Ivan Rybkin. Shortly thereafter, businessman and Chubais associate Boris Berezovskii was appointed as Rybkin's deputy in charge of relations with Chechnya. The appointment provoked a storm of criticism. Berezovskii made his money through the car dealership LogoVAZ. He was widely perceived to have mafia connections and had been the target of a car bomb in 1994. *Komsomolskaya pravda* leaked the story that Berezovskii had obtained Israeli citizenship and was therefore unfit for a high state office. Duma Speaker Gennadii Seleznev, a Communist, demanded Chubais's resignation over the scandal, but the unpopular chief of staff weathered the storm, and he and Berezovskii remained in office.

The attacks on Chubais continued in November. *Moskovskii komsomolets* published a transcript of a conversation allegedly held on 22 June between Chubais and two others on the Yeltsin campaign. The transcript indicated that the $500,000 found on Chubais's associates in June was not planted by Korzhakov's men, and it directly implicated Chubais in illegal campaign financing, lies, and obstruction of justice. Procurator-General Yurii Skuratov announced an investigation, but no results had been announced at year's end. Despite the mounting pressure, Yeltsin did not remove Chubais, although in December he brought Sergei Shakhrai back into the administration as deputy chief of staff. The move was viewed as providing a counterweight to Chubais, who does not get along with Shakhrai.

The parliament mainly stood on the sidelines during Yeltsin's protracted absence and the upheavals in the Kremlin. The Duma passed many nonbinding resolutions and held numerous hearings in 1996, but it did not pass important measures such as the list of exploration sites covered by the Law on Production Sharing. It did finally pass a land code (setting rules for land ownership), but that was rejected by the Federation Council. Deputies also shied away from confrontation with the government, calculating that passing a vote of no confidence was not worth the risk of dissolution by Yeltsin. The KPRF (with 147 seats) and the allied Popular Power (37 seats) and Agrarian (37 seats) factions held a working majority in the 450–seat Duma. The 65 deputies from the pro-government Our Home Is Russia faction were usually backed by Russian Regions (which held 42 seats) and occasionally by the Liberal Democratic Party (with 51 seats). Grigorii Yavlinskii's Yabloko faction (46 seats) has been a consistent critic of the government, but Yavlinskii, who finished fourth in the first round of the presidential race, has refused to ally with pro- or anti-government parties.

MIXED RESULTS IN REGIONAL ELECTIONS

Against the backdrop of uncertainty surrounding Yeltsin's health and bitter rivalries in Moscow, 45 oblasts and krais held gubernatorial elections between September and December, forcing governors appointed by Yeltsin to face the voters. (Three of Russia's ethnic republics also elected their top executives in December.) Elections for leaders of oblasts and krais had first been proposed in late 1991, but Yeltsin resisted giving up the power to name governors. Yeltsin had only allowed elections to be held in a handful of regions in 1995, mostly where the administration felt confident of victory. The rest were postponed until after the 1996 presidential election, probably because governors—who owed their jobs to Yeltsin—would presumably work on his behalf during the campaign.

The gubernatorial elections produced a mixed result, allowing both the Communists and the "party of power" to claim victory. Incumbents lost their bid for re-election in 24 regions, but only about two-thirds of the new governors had been nominated by the KPRF. Many of the rest were backed by the Reforms-New Course movement of Yeltsin ally Vladimir Shumeiko and generally supported Yeltsin's political agenda. Furthermore, even the most staunch opposition candidates pragmatically pledged to work with the federal authorities soon after being elected. For instance, shortly after his election in Kursk Oblast, Aleksandr Rutskoi—the nationalist and defender of the White House in October 1993—had a friendly meeting with Chubais, whom he had vilified in the past.

Still, given the acute social and economic problems that regional governors face, one can expect their relations with Moscow to be full of conflict and tension in the future. The new, popularly elected governors cannot be removed by presidential decree, and they will thus owe less allegiance to the Kremlin than their predecessors did. Moscow's trump card is the continuing dependence of the regions and republics on subsidies and special favors from the center. Only 10 of the 89 federation subjects are net donors to the federal budget.

The elections were important because the governors exercise considerable power in their regions and also because they automatically take up seats in the

Federation Council—the upper house of parliament. The Yeltsin camp relied on loyalists in the Federation Council to block legislative initiatives from the Communist-dominated lower house. Despite the Communist gains in the gubernatorial elections, there was little chance that parliament would mount a serious challenge to the Yeltsin administration—for example, by trying to pass constitutional amendments to limit presidential powers.

PROSPECTS FOR DEMOCRACY

That the regional elections were actually held and that losing incumbents for the most part stepped down gracefully augurs well for Russia's democratic development. But the overall condition of constitutional legality in Russia appeared less robust. Disturbing cases in 1966 raised questions about respect for constitutional liberties in Yeltsin's Russia. Moscow Mayor Yurii Luzhkov, a strong Yeltsin ally, restored the Soviet-era residency registration requirements in March, making it nearly impossible for outsiders to move to the capital, even though the Russian constitution guarantees the right to choose one's place of residence and freedom of movement.

In February, the Federal Security Service (FSB) arrested Aleksandr Nikitin, a former nuclear-submarine commander. He was accused of revealing state secrets in a report he wrote on nuclear waste for the Norwegian environmental group Bellona. Nikitin claimed that all his information had come from published sources. Amnesty International declared Nikitin a prisoner of conscience in August, but he continued to be held without bail until December, pending treason charges. Even when Nikitin was finally released from pretrial detention, the charges against him were not dropped, and he was told not to leave St. Petersburg.

Meanwhile, a criminal case was quietly reopened in April against Valeriya Novodvorskaya, a former Soviet dissident. She was charged with inciting ethnic hatred toward Russians on the basis of two newspaper articles and one television interview dating from 1993 and 1994. The media mostly ridiculed the case against Novodvorskaya; commentators regarded the articles in question as political satire. Novodvorskaya's defenders also argued that the FSB director for Moscow, 20–year KGB veteran Anatolii Trofimov, was pursuing a political vendetta against the noisy former dissident. Although a similar case against her was eventually dropped for lack of evidence in 1995, Novodvorskaya was barred from leaving Moscow through the summer, and trial proceedings began in September.

Five years into independence, Russia's fledgling democracy is still closely tied to the personalized rule of Boris Yeltsin. It is hard to predict whether the political system will work in a stable fashion once Yeltsin leaves the scene. The country remains polarized between a hard core of Communist supporters who reject the reform trajectory followed since 1991 and a broad mass of voters who reject attempts by the Communists to return to power. Although the presidential election proved that Russia has more anti-Communists than Communists, a vast number of voters are still worried by crime and corruption, feel relatively powerless to influence their rulers, and anxiously await an economic upturn.

Profile: VIKTOR CHERNOMYRDIN: A DISCREET AUTHORITY

by PETER RUTLAND

Viktor Chernomyrdin has served as Russian Prime Minister since 1992. He was undoubtedly the second most powerful man in Russia during that time. Despite the powerful position he holds, Chernomyrdin remains an enigmatic figure, both to Russians and to outside observers. He has been careful to avoid political controversy, and stayed in the shadows through the tumultuous events of recent years—the August 1991 coup, the storming of parliament in 1993, the launching of the Chechen war in 1994. Uniquely in Russia's fractious political climate, Chernomyrdin has been able to stay on good terms with politicians on all sides of the political spectrum, from liberals to communists.

Chernomyrdin sees himself as a manager rather than a politician, and proudly describes himself as simply an "industrialist" *(proizvodstvennik)*. He avoids taking a stand on political issues, and prefers back-room compromise to grandstanding in the media. He is less than charismatic as a public speaker, and has never won a freely contested election to public office. In 1990 he ran for a seat in the Congress of People's Deputies in his home town of Orenburg, but lost to the well-known historian Dmitrii Volkogonov. Chernomyrdin has never shown any interest in running for the post of president, although now he is widely seen as Yeltsin's most likely successor.

As the former head of the Gazprom monopoly, Chernomyrdin is credited with keeping Russia's oil and gas industries going through the chaos of post-communist transition, and that is the key to his success. He has tried to damp down political infighting between the rival clans struggling for power in the free-for-all that passes for politics in democratic Russia. His goal was to preserve the government bureaucracy as a functioning entity. One could hardly say that he has been successful in this endeavor, but the apparatus would have fallen apart even more quickly if Chernomyrdin had not been around. His detractors accuse him of becoming extremely wealthy by tapping off the profits from oil and gas exports. But none of those charges has ever been substantiated, and anyway, corruption long since ceased to be a disqualification for holding public office in Russia.

The 58-year-old Chernomyrdin is a quintessential product of the Soviet system. Born in Orenburg, he started working as a fitter in the Orsk oil refinery in 1955. He returned to the plant after a three-year stint in the army, joined the Communist Party, and in 1962 enrolled in the polytechnic in Kuibyshev (now called Samara), where he was an average student. Upon graduation in 1967, he started to work for the Orsk Communist Party, monitoring heavy industry in the city. In 1973 he was appointed director of the Orenburg Gas Works, and in 1978 he was promoted to the industrial department of the Communist Party Central Committee in Moscow.

In 1982 he was appointed deputy minister for oil and gas in the Soviet government, where he presided over the massive expansion of the Tyumen natural-gas fields in Western Siberia. At that point he got to know Boris Yeltsin, who headed the party committee in nearby Sverdlovsk. The Brezhnev leadership opted for the so-called "big gas" policy, and poured huge investments into developing the Tyumen fields and the pipeline infrastructure to carry the gas to Eastern Europe and farther west. In the 1970s, West Germany and Italy signed 20–year contracts with the USSR to cover about one-third of their gas needs: the Western Europeans grew to know Chernomyrdin as a reliable partner.

Chernomyrdin became Minister for Oil and Gas Industry in 1985, under the reformist Mikhail Gorbachev. Chernomyrdin sided with the cautious Prime Minister Nikolai Ryzhkov (now an opposition leader) in blocking more ambitious economic-reform plans, such as Grigorii Yavlinskii's "500 days." Under perestroika, the Soviet economy started to fall apart, and in 1989 Chernomyrdin turned most of his ministry's assets over to a new "state concern," Gazprom. That was the first semi-independent company of its type; Chernomyrdin was chairman of its board.

In January 1992, the Russian government of Yegor Gaidar launched the radical economic reforms known as "shock therapy." Russia's oil and gas leaders were able to block the liberalization of energy prices, however, and in May 1992 Chernomyrdin entered the government as deputy prime minister. Gazprom managed to survive the post-1992 economic reforms as a coherent entity, in contrast to the oil industry, which was broken up into a dozen competing firms during the privatization process. In December 1992, opposition from the parliament forced Gaidar from office, and Yeltsin chose Chernomyrdin to replace him as prime minister.

Chernomyrdin supported Yeltsin in his clashes with the parliament in 1993, but avoided being drawn into the controversy and declined to run for election to the new Duma in December 1993. Chernomyrdin invited Gaidar back into the government in September of that year, but Gaidar quit early in 1994, arguing that the government was not committed to economic reform. In fact, to everybody's surprise, in the course of 1994 Chernomyrdin proceeded to implement precisely the sort of strict monetary and fiscal policy that had eluded the initial 1992 Gaidar government. Chernomyrdin's stabilization program was maintained through 1995 and 1996, bringing inflation down to 130 percent in 1995 and less than 30 percent in 1996. The costs fell most heavily on the defense industry, the farmers, and public-sector employees in general. By mid-1995, the strains of the program were putting great pressure on the coalition of interest groups that made up the Yeltsin administration. Chernomyrdin stayed the course, supported by the sole remaining liberal in the government, Anatolii Chubais (who was fired in January 1996).

Chernomyrdin's political profile started to rise in 1995. In June 1995, he stepped in to sort out the horrific hostage-taking in Budennovsk, which left 150 hostages dead. He negotiated directly with the leader of the guerrillas, Shamil Basaev, and managed to secure the release of the remaining 1,500 hostages. The talks were aired live on Russian television. In April 1995 Chernomyrdin sponsored the formation of a new political movement, Our Home Is Russia, which ran candidates in the December 1995 Duma elections. However, the pro-government party fared poorly, finishing in third place with 10.1 percent of the vote.

Chernomyrdin's political power base is still the network of friends, allies, and clients in the oil and gas industries. Most regions and enterprises are heavily in debt for their energy supplies; they do not have to be told where there interests lie as winter approaches. In 1996, the government became heavily dependent on the drip-feed of financial aid from the International Monetary Fund under the Extended Fund Facility approved in March, which was bringing them $340 million per month. Despite that, Gazprom has been able to fight off efforts to increase its taxes and deregulate the industry.

Chernomyrdin is said to be fond of the phrase "We hoped for the best, but got the usual." It could also serve him as a fitting political epitaph.

Document: GENNADII ZYUGANOV IN HIS OWN WORDS

The nationalist ideas that Gennadii Zyuganov voiced on the campaign trail were outlined in two of his recent books: Za gorizontom [Beyond the Horizon] *(Orel: Veshnie Vody, 1995) and* Rossiya i sovremennyi mir [Russia and the Contemporary World] *(Moscow: Informpechat, 1995). Excerpts from the books follow.*

ON STALIN AND GEOPOLITICS:

[Stalin] understood the vital necessity for new realities to correspond with a centuries-old Russian tradition. This understanding led to the Soviet Union's sharp change in government ideology from 1944 to 1953. At the foundation of this new policy lay the struggle to create an effective and contemporary ideology of patriotism. . . [T]he first task was to reinstate several pages of authentic Russian history and decisively end the persecution of the church.

The USSR won the most terrible and bloody war in the history of mankind. In complete accordance with its interests, it extended its sphere of influence toward the sea and ocean and, from that time on, blocked any attempt to directly threaten its borders. In record time, it overcame the postwar destruction and established its autonomy and a self-sufficient economic system capable of ensuring sustained growth of living standards through the skillful use of the country's colossal natural resources. If [Stalin's] ideological perestroika could have kept its momentum, there is no doubt that within 10 to 15 years the USSR would have completely overcome the negative spiritual consequences of the revolutionary storms and have achieved very constructive results. The creation of our own nuclear weapon precluded any possibility of strong interference in our internal affairs.

Such prospects brought the West—the traditional citadel of an "oceanic geopolitical strategy"—close to panic. They had their reasons. The USSR—continuing Russia's geopolitical tradition—formed a powerful alternative center of world influence, embodying justice and sovereignty of the people. . . .

During this time, the West tried to use anti-communist rhetoric about a "free world" and hypocritical concern about "human rights" as an ideological screen to hide its pursuit of its centuries-old geopolitical interests, which require the weakening and, if possible, annihilation of Russia. This hypocrisy has become especially obvious now. With the overt violation of the rights of millions of Russians and Russian speakers who have found themselves as second-class people in the new ethnic governments of the [Commonwealth of Independent States], the "civilized" West is not only refraining from calling for judgment but is silently approving.

Capitalism organically does not fit with the flesh and blood, the way of life, the habits and psychology of our society. It already led once to a civil war, and today it is not taking root—and will not take root—in Russian soil.

ON THE CONSPIRACY TO DESTROY THE SOVIET UNION

The period from the beginning of the Cold War . . . through the dramatic final act of 1991 can be divided into three stages—three sequential steps in the development of geopolitical sabotage against the USSR.

The first began immediately after Stalin's death. . . . Even before his body had cooled in the mausoleum, his successors had sharply changed his ideological course. . . .The economic situation inside the USSR became progressively worse: the ideological, religious, and cultural vacuum created an unprecedented opportunity for infiltrating society with foreign values, destructive ideologies, and selfishly parasitic stereotypes of social consciousness.

It was in these conditions that generational turnover in the upper echelons of the Kremlin allowed Russia's opponents to begin the second stage of the dismantlement of the USSR: creating an ideological basis for its breakup. The period was 1985 to 1990, largely under Gorbachev's "perestroika." . . . The fundamental components of the ideological war against the union were an open Russophobia within part of society; a supercharge of anti-patriotic hysteria, cunningly stuck in the same package with frenzied anti-communism; and deafening propaganda about the "delights" of liberal-democratic ideology.

The third and final stage of global geopolitical sabotage lasted two years (1990 and 1991) and focused on ensuring the disintegration of a united Soviet government. . . . The plan was the following:

(1) Disorient society through forced economic and political changes and wide-scale cultivation of the "democratic" spirit and cause it to lose its intuitive, healthy conservatism and instinct for self preservation.

(2) After crushing society's self-protection mechanisms, ensure the breakup

of a united government against the background of an operatic "coup."

(3) On the wave of this shocking cataclysm: assume key positions in all the leading areas of public life.

(4) Ensure Russia's economic, political, and military dependence on foreign (Western) influence to the greatest degree possible.

(5) Most importantly—by taking advantage of the worsening chaos, economic crisis, and shocked state of society launch the mechanisms for internal Russian disintegration, based on national separatism, regional conflicts, and civil war among Moscow clans.

Document: OPEN LETTER FROM SERGEI KOVALEV TO PRESIDENT BORIS YELTSIN

Human rights activist Sergei Kovalev resigned as head of Russia's Presidential Commission on Human Rights on 23 January 1996. In an open letter to Boris Yeltsin, published in Izvestiya *on 24 January and excerpted below, Kovalev accused Yeltsin of abandoning the course of democratic reform. In March 1995, the parliament stripped Kovalev of the post of human rights commissioner for his outspoken opposition to the government's policy in Chechnya, and he was subsequently ignored by Yeltsin.*

Recently, while continuing to assure the public of your unwavering commitment to democratic ideals, you have begun, slowly at first but then more rapidly, to change your style of leadership. At the moment, your administration is trying to turn the country in a direction that is utterly opposed to the one chosen in August 1991. . . .

I am not going to recall all your numerous mistakes and miscalculations—you will find plenty of people willing to do that. It is not a matter of specific failures but of the reasons for them: the wrong choice of priorities and criteria in state policy.

Since the end of 1993, if not before, you have been consistently making the wrong decisions, not ones that would strengthen the rule of law in a democracy but ones that revive the dumb and inhumane power of a state machine that is beyond the law and the people. Your enemies assert that you did this to strengthen your personal power. Even if they are wrong, it does not change anything.

In the tragic days of the fall of 1993, I—though not without serious reservations—chose to support you, and I do not shirk responsibility for that support. I thought the use of force at that time was an unavoidable necessity in the face of a looming civil war. I was aware then that the October developments could create a situation in which the administration would regard violence as a convenient and habitual instrument for settling political problems. But I hoped that, having overcome the crisis of legitimacy and created a basic legal foundation in Russia, the president and the government would do their best to secure the peaceful and free development of Russia. . . . I believed you would choose the latter path, but I was wrong.

The 1993 constitution gives the president vast powers but also immense responsibilities—namely, to guarantee the rights and freedoms of the country's citizens, to ensure their security, and to protect law and order. How have you used your powers? How have you dealt with your responsibilities? You suspended judicial reform, which should have made justice truly independent of the other branches of power. You began openly to preach the principle of letting the innocent suffer to punish the guilty.

You publicly declared a fight against organized crime in the country. . . . What was the result? The criminals are still at large, while law-abiding citizens are forced to endure bureaucratic as well as criminal outrages. You stated that your aim was the preservation and strengthening of the territorial integrity of the [Russian] Federation. What was the result? The shameful and senseless civil war that has been raging for over a year in the North Caucasus.

Under the guise of strengthening Russia's defense capability, you checked all attempts at military reform that could give Russia effective and modern armed forces. What was the result? Military spending is increasing, the number of generals has reached an indecent level, [yet] soldiers and officers are poorly fed and clothed. And the traditions of humiliation, lawlessness, and corruption are as strong as before. . . .

You talk of an open policy and glasnost while signing secret decrees concerning vital state interests, creating closed institutions, and keeping secret an increasing amount of information about the work of the power structures and the situation in the country. The mechanism for presidential decision making has become almost as closed as the decision-making process was during the Politburo era. You are increasingly reliant upon the secret services and their system of closed information in your work. Are you really not convinced that this information is biased and inaccurate?

Your personnel policy is becoming clearer every day. At first, there were many competent and unselfish people around you. But you favored those whose only virtue was their personal loyalty to you. Gradually that Soviet Communist Party principle became your main guide in the selection of personnel. The people with the most successful careers were those who . . . pursued their own interests, sometimes criminally. Take a look at the faces of your present colleagues and you will understand why the country no longer trusts them and, consequently, you.

Still, you and all your high-ranking officials care little about public opinion. Instead of open and honest explanations in moments of crisis, you and your appointees feed us such utter and blatant lies that we are dumbfounded. The fragile understanding between the public and the authorities has been broken again. Just over a year after October 1993, you began the war in Chechnya. . . . [which] revealed yet another appalling quality of your regime: complete indifference to human life. . . .

I do not want to lay the entire blame on you. The totalitarian system, which received a serious, but not fatal blow, is protecting itself in characteristic ways: triggering a crisis, corrupting the population, and replacing human values. Your guilt is in the fact that you did not oppose this trend but facilitated it. . . . You are restoring the old Bolshevik mire, only the communist phraseology is replaced for the time being by anti-communist rhetoric. . . .

You swore you would build a state by the people for the people but instead erected a bureaucratic pyramid over them and against them. You rejected democratic values and principles, while constantly talking about democracy. . . . If democracy is to survive in Russia (and I believe it. will), it will live not thanks to you but in spite of you. . . .

Currently, you are presenting yourself as the only alternative to [Communist Party leader Gennadii] Zyuganov and [Liberal Democratic Party of Russia leader [Vladimir] Zhirinovsky. But in vain. The similarities between you are greater than the differences. If we have to choose among you . . . many would grudgingly vote for those who present the lesser threat to their pockets and lives. I hate both the communists and the nationalists. But I will not vote for you, either. Nor would I advise other decent people to do so.

Document: "RUSSIA CLOSE TO ITS DEATH BED"

Aleksandr Solzhenitsyn, widely considered to be Russia's greatest living writer, leveled an angry polemic against the post-Soviet government of President Boris Yeltsin in the 25 November edition of the Moscow-based weekly Obshchaya gazeta. *The article was simultaneously published by the French daily* Le Monde.

How does Europe currently perceive Russia? Usually, Western observers focus their attention on events of momentary significance—the Duma elections, the presidential election, replacements of top officials, Lebed's dismissal, the president's heart operation—while ignoring more important characteristics of the situation in Russia and the process going on there.

As far as I can see, there is a strong belief in the West that during recent years a democracy of some kind has been established in Russia (although the governmental system is dangerously weak). As for Russia's economy, there is a belief that the most vital market reforms have been accomplished and have thus opened the way to a free market.

Both beliefs are fallacies. The current so-called Russian democracy is a mask for a completely different form of government. Glasnost—in other words, the right of free expression in the press—is not democracy, it is a means toward democracy. (And besides, to a significant degree in Russia today, glasnost is an illusion, as newspapers that attempt to discuss issues of vital importance face a fence of taboos erected by their financial supporters.) Unquestionably, democracy implies that power rests with the people, that the people are the genuine masters of their lives, that they can influence their historical destiny. Nothing resembling democracy currently exists in Russia.

In October 1993, the "Soviets of People's Deputies" were abolished throughout the country. (During Communist Party rule, the soviets played the role of ersatz local self-governments.) Since then, for almost four years, the presidential apparatus, the government, the State Duma, and the leaders of political parties, along with a majority of regional governors, have been preventing the establishment of local self-governments by blocking any possibility of financial support for them.

On the lowest level, in towns, rural districts, and raions, there is no self-government whatsoever; everything is decided by local officials belonging to the governmental vertical axis. On the regional level, there are regional legislative assemblies, but since their salaries are paid by regional executive bodies, they are entirely under the command of the governors. There is no legal way for people to attain self-rule. It can only be achieved by a public struggle. The only real power is a vertical axis leading from the president and the government. (Until recently, governors were appointed by the president; now, some of them are elected, though far from all.) That structure is duplicated by a second axis of appointed presidential representatives (spies) to each region.

According to the 1993 constitution, which was rushed through the approval procedure and lacked proper legality, the powers of the State Duma are severely limited by presidential power. Besides, since the electoral system is not managed well, a lot of Duma members were elected by mere chance, and were not even personally elected. In the current (1995) Duma as well in the previous (1993) one, many deputies are not equal to the position.

Under the existing governmental system, the presidential elections held every four years are of the greatest importance to the country's future. But in 1996, the election was not—and could not have been—responsible and balanced. When making their choice, people were burdened by the sense of an approaching "communist storm cloud"—how could that communist win? Yeltsin's party emphasized that danger to make the point that he was the country's only possible savior. (As for the communists, they were afraid of winning, since they had no solution to the crisis.)

In its efforts to win the election, Yeltsin's party modeled its campaign on the worst examples, using expensive campaign trappings paid for, no doubt, with public funds. At the same time, there were no pre-election discussions or election speeches. Nobody reviewed the errors, mistakes, and misrule of the presidency over the previous five years. Nobody discussed the nominees' programs, which were presented in a cunning way—about 10 days before election day. Both programs consisted of 100 to 120 pages of vague texts. Moreover, the electorate was not able to obtain them, read them, examine them, ask questions, or hear answers. All the national television channels were running an insistent and tendentious campaign of support for the acting head of the state, and there was no way to protest.

(Having been repeatedly invited by NTV, the so-called independent television channel, I gave them a 10–minute interview. I mentioned that both competing sides were guilty of severe crimes against the people's interests—the Communists during the 70 years of their rule, the other side during the 5 years of its rule. I appealed to the electorate to vote against both sides, which could result in the election's postponement and the nomination of new candidates. But NTV could not allow me to break the taboos. They cut my interview. The edited version consisted of two fragmentary minutes, which made the words incoherent and nonsensical.)

That explains how the president came to power the second time, avoiding any responsibility for all the misrule of his previous five-year term of power. He is free to continue doing the same for the next four years, or to make the suppression even tougher.

In such circumstances, the central power system is as uncontrollable, immune from punishment, and lacking in public responsibility as was the Communist regime. As much as we wish to, we cannot call the current ruling system a democracy. All the authorities' important motives, decisions, intentions, and actions, all of their personnel appointments, are veiled in total darkness. Merely their final results are made open to the public. In the event of a dismissal, such vague formulas as "at his own request" or "he will move to another appointment" (without specification) are commonly used. And never, even when a person has obviously done something wrong, is the real cause of dismissal indicated. After a short while, without any explanation, the same person might be appointed to a more important position. The moral imperative of those who hold power is, "We neither betray our people nor reveal their guilt."

Thus, a stable and tight oligarchy of 150 to 200 people, including the most cunning representatives of the top and middle strata of the former-communist ruling structure, along with nouveaux riches who amassed their recent fortunes through banditry, has been established. Oligarchy aptly describes the system that currently rules Russia. This system is not a tree growing from the roots of the Russian state; it is a forcibly jabbed-in dry stick, or these days, even a rod of iron. The members of this oligarchy are bound together by their lust for power and selfish ends. Lofty aims to serve the people and the Motherland are far removed from their intentions.

During the 10–year period of hasty reforms (the mid-1980s to the mid-1990s), our leaders have not taken a single skillful step. Even worse, during this 10–year period, our ruling clique has not displayed higher moral standards than the former communists. During this period, Russia has been tortured with crimes. National property worth billions and billions was plundered, without a single significant denunciation or open trial. Whatever the people in power do—any serious wrongdoing or real crime, ruining the whole country or millions of its inhabitants, or leading to the deaths of thousands of people—they will not be punished, as the ability of the judiciary system and investigating bodies to act is restricted.

Since the Constitutional Court is just a trinket and the State Duma's oversight is very weak (and many of its members are also only concerned with their well-being), dozens of "councils" (starting with the famous "Security Council") and "commissions" are being cultivated around the president. Even though the constitution makes no provision for their existence, those bodies duplicate the powers of the government and its ministries, creating a chaotic and irresponsible multipower system. Not so long ago, we thought that a more senseless and ponderous bureaucracy than the communist apparatus could not possibly exist. Over the last 10 years, the bureaucracy has probably doubled, nay, trebled—and all at the expense of the people. That has resulted in a state power system that is too weak to rule the country effectively but is very tenacious in maintaining the advantages it seized.

As for the people, they are deprived of their legal self-governments and any guarantees or protection of their rights. And thousands and thousands of the most gifted and inventive individuals cannot make proper use of their creativity, because wherever they turn they hit their heads against a brick wall of bureaucracy. What sort of democracy is it in which the government slumbers sweetly while all around the country the people en masse have not been paid the money they legally earned for the past six months?

Recently, people in various places came up with the idea of "rescue committees." Those committees, self-elected local bodies, are supposed to duplicate governmental functions to protect against the erosion of people's lives. In other countries, a similar situation would be enough to create a social outburst. In Russia—after 70 years of stifling conditions, of selective annihilation of all active, protesting individuals, and then 10 years of being plunged into poverty, causing a loss of a million Russians lives a year—there is no energy for such an outburst. But it will come.

The West is more familiar with the economic situation in Russia, though the knowledge there about the so-called "economic reforms"—first during Gorbachev's time, in 1987–1990, then during Yeltsin's, in 1992–1995—is not always adequate. When Gorbachev loudly announced his slogan of "perestroika," he had in mind a gradual transition enabling party cadres to adapt to new economic circumstances; he was also concerned with preserving the assets that used to belong to the Communist Party. He took no measures to stimulate the emergence of small and medium-sized private enterprises. Nevertheless, he destroyed and threw into disarray the former communist economy's whole system of vertical and horizontal connections, which, albeit poorly, was still functioning.

Thus he paved the way to economic chaos in Russia. That was followed by Gaidar's "reform" and Chubais's "privatization."

I put the word "reform" in quotation marks, because real reform is a balanced, integral system of many constructive measures that are supposed to lead to a certain established goal. After 1992, no program of this type was ever published in Russia. Naturally. The reason is clear: the government simply did not have such a program. The "reform" as a whole, giddy and poorly planned as it was, consisted of two separate moves. Nobody thought of coordinating the two, not to speak of the country's economic benefits.

The first of those two moves was Gaidar's "price liberalization" of 1992. At that time, there was no climate for competition in Russia, which had inherited from communism monopolistic producers in every branch of the economy. As a result, "price liberalization" opened the way to an endless growth of prices, and at the same time, a reduction in the volume of output and a cutback in investment. Before long, this "reform" began to quickly destroy the production system. For a huge portion of the population, it made consumer goods and many kinds of food inaccessible.

The second move was a raging storm of privatization. "The world has never seen such a pace," as Chubais expressed it. Just to fool the population and mask the program's further goals, the first step was "voucher privatization." That meant that the state provided each citizen with a kind of bond that was supposed to certify his "share" of the national wealth accumulated under the communist regime. In practice, the total value of the vouchers amounted to a small fraction of 1 percent of the national wealth. But while distributing that small slice, the government managed to swindle the population.

The second step was an unprecedented bargain sale, an almost free distribution. A number of state-owned enterprises—some of them huge—were parceled out among private individuals (sometimes for a price equal to .01 percent of the real value). The majority of those people had no managerial experience and were just trying to get easy money. The Mayor of Moscow, [Yurii] Luzhkov, called Chubais's privatization "the most terrible catastrophe in world history." It was an exceptional case—the state allowed the national wealth to be given to dubious people without making any significant profit.

That is the major cause of the financial weakness of the Russian state at the present time—and in the long term. There are also two additional causes. First, throughout the country there are opportunities (basically official privileges) for individuals to steal on a large scale without any oversight. Every year at least $25 billion, acquired illegally or fraudulently, has disappeared abroad, transferred to the personal accounts of profiteers. Second, there is the incompetent interference of the International Monetary Fund (IMF) into the Russian economic chaos with its definitive recommendations, which the Russian authorities follow obediently and thoughtlessly. For example, the lifting of export taxes on energy—in return they were promised that a part of their losses would be covered by an IMF loan! The process as a whole appears to be like a Titanic pump irreversibly sucking away Russia's natural resources, wealth, and brains.

In addition to the economic chaos, the country suffers from mafia activity, which no one has ever tried to stop. Plundering the country, the mafia is accumulating tremendous wealth. The property gap between the rich and the impoverished majority has reached a scale never seen either in the West or in pre-revolutionary Russia.

More than that. The bandits who acquired their wealth so easily (such an effortless gain is unprecedented in Western history) are looking for effective ways to fuse with state power. And they have found them. There are a lot of examples, even on the highest level. As for the medium level, the corruption there is hard to decipher and exceeds far beyond the Western notion of it. The fusion of this strong, new criminal capital with state power will block the development of a free-market economy and competition in Russia. That process still has not started—and, under these circumstances, will not start. The closed, oligarchic state power system is supplemented with the dictates of big capital.

The Chechnya slaughter very clearly exposed the current situation in Russia. No doubt, the war in Chechnya is tightly bound up with and clearly reveals the vices of the current power in Russia. In the fall of 1991, when [Dzhokhar] Dudaev declared Chechnya's independence, the central government first hurried to decree a state of emergency, and then, after three days, canceled it—and for the next three years did absolutely nothing. It was unbelievable: a part of the country with its own strong army and a lot of arms, both heavy and light (all those arms had been left thoughtlessly by the central government), declared its independence. That led to the mass-scale plundering of the non-Chechen population (which numbered about half a million). People were kicked out of their apartments, sometimes thrown from the windows of multistory buildings, driven out of Chechnya, murdered. Women were kidnapped and raped. The central authorities did not do anything to protect victims—for the whole three years!

Neither blindness nor hard-heartedness on the part of the central authorities can explain that. It can be explained by the fact that powerful and influential persons were interested in a secret deal with Dudaev. According to that deal, they shared the profits from the oil coming from Tyumen to the Grozny oil refinery; after it arrived a huge part of the oil usually disappeared.

Did the deal go wrong? It's hard to say, but in December 1994, after three years of avoiding any action, all of a sudden military action was taken. And again, it was very typical of the present authorities: after starting the war, they acted in the manner of dim-witted generals—inflicting huge losses, not so much on the enemy, but mostly on inexperienced Russian draftees and the mixed Chechen-Russian civilian populations of Grozny and other places. With infinite casualties and destruction, the federal troops had captured the greater part of Chechnya by summer 1995. Then there was the terrorist act in Budennovsk. That brought a new riddle. The Moscow authorities capitulated—not just to the terrorists, but also to the Chechen fighters. They stopped carrying out the war, and the Chechen fighters were able to recapture all the lost territories without engaging in battle.

The Russian side launched two new comedies, while simultaneously continuing military actions and exchanging fire: the comedy of "electing" [Doku] Zavgaev's functionaries as a legal authority and the comedy of Chechen "reconstruction"—right in the middle of the war theater and continued fighting. Stupidity? No, it was a well-calculated move: the millions invested were going into private accounts. As for houses that were not built, they were written off as destroyed in the war.

Our government, inert in its thoughts and actions, was in a blind alley, totally incapable of extracting itself from the war. Then a new person appeared, completely alien to the present oligarchy and its vices. It was General [Aleksandr] Lebed. He had the courage and energy to admit that the Russian authorities had already lost this military campaign—and brought an end to the war in Chechnya. (As a token of gratitude, he was dismissed.) But did they let Chechnya go? No. The ruling clique of Russian power is still stubbornly attached to its old idea of keeping Chechnya nominally part of Russia. For the sake of that idea, they are ready to sacrifice their protégé Zavgaev and company, to give Chechnya any possible privileges, to let it live at Russia's expense. But that's impossible; it's too late now. No doubt, devastated Chechnya will first accept reparations from devastated Russia—and then will inevitably secede. The Chechens were fighting to secede.

The whole destructive course of events in Russia over the past 10 years stems from the fact that the regime chose to borrow stupidly from foreign models, totally neglecting the original creativity, mentality, and all of the multisecular spiritual and social traditions of its people.

[Translated by Natasha Zanegina and Dora Slaba. 1996 Editions Fayard. Reprinted with permission.]

Foreign Policy _____

FOREIGN POLICY: STRUGGLING TO SURVIVE IN THE FORMER EMPIRE'S SHADOW

by SCOTT PARRISH

Despite continued Western worries that Russia might return to the imperialist policies of its Soviet past, Russia's foreign policy remained that of a retrenching state, pedaling hard in an often futile attempt to stop the erosion of its international position. Russian commentators often compare the current period to the early 1920s, when the young Soviet state—its economic and military power shattered by World War I and the subsequent civil war—relied on diplomacy to give the country breathing space.

The January 1996 replacement of the liberal Andrei Kozyrev as foreign minister by the former head of the Foreign Intelligence Service, Yevgennii Primakov, seemed to signal a hardening of Russia's stance. With Russia's economy collapsing and the armed forces in disarray, Primakov has had to rely almost entirely on political means to defend Russian interests. Moscow's strategy for minimizing the negative consequences of Russia's weakness has combined a holding action against NATO expansion in the West, a push for closer ties with China, and growing links with "pariah" states such as Iran and Iraq. Russia also continued to pressure its Commonwealth of Independent States (CIS) neighbors to accelerate political, military, and economic integration, but it has had only mixed success. Overall, Primakov's strategy has delivered meager results, as, with a few exceptions, Russia found itself weaker and more isolated on a range of international issues at the end of 1996 than it had been at the beginning of the year.

The Defense Ministry faces an even more difficult task: reforming the disintegrating and demoralized post-Soviet Russian military that in 1996 could neither defeat Chechen insurgents nor pay most of its own personnel on time. Defense Minister Igor Rodionov, who replaced Pavel Grachev in July, has set military reform as his top priority. While a new Defense Council was established that same month to coordinate defense policy, Rodionov has admitted that budgetary constraints may postpone reform into the next century.

TO DEAL OR NOT TO DEAL WITH NATO?

Russia continued a rearguard action against NATO expansion during 1996, as Russian politicians across the political spectrum remained adamantly opposed to the alliance's growth. President Boris Yeltsin and Primakov added a new twist by suggesting that Moscow could accept a "French variant" for new NATO members— Eastern European countries would join NATO's political but not its military structures. The proposal was rejected by NATO and Eastern European officials, who argued that it would consign the new members to second-class status within the alliance. Moscow also tried to promote the idea of a strengthened Organization for Security and Cooperation in Europe (OSCE) as the core of a new European security architecture instead of NATO expansion. Moscow also warned that NATO expansion could torpedo arms-control agreements such as START II and the Conventional Forces in Europe (CFE) treaty, trigger changes in Russian military doctrine, and lead Moscow to reorient its foreign policy toward China and the Far East. Many liberal commentators in Moscow felt a sense of betrayal, arguing that the Soviet Union had unilaterally withdrawn from Eastern Europe and Russia was now being "rewarded" with NATO expansion, which would isolate it from European institutions. As 1996 drew to a close, some still hoped that NATO and Moscow would find a mutually acceptable formula, along the lines of a NATO-Moscow charter, which could address some of Russia's concerns. But no such compromise was yet in sight. (See Scott Parrish, "Bargaining over NATO Enlargement," pp. 198–204, and Peter Rutland, "Yavlinskii on NATO Expansion," pp. 205–6.)

CHILLIER RELATIONS WITH WASHINGTON

Although Yeltsin and Clinton continued to pay lip service to Russian-American partnership, 1996 produced few concrete achievements to back up the rhetoric. The bilateral climate was chillier than a year earlier, as both presidents concentrated on being re-elected. While talk of a new cold war remains exaggerated, deep divides persist between Moscow and Washington on NATO expansion, arms control, and relations with such countries as Iran, Iraq, and Cuba.

The U.S. Senate did finally ratify the 1993 START II agreement in January, but the Russian Federal Assembly is still considering it with skepticism. Leaders in both houses of the Russian parliament called for substantial amendments and linked the treaty's ratification to resolution of the NATO dispute. U.S. Secretary of Defense William Perry got a cold welcome in Moscow when he addressed the State Duma in October to urge ratification. Talks aimed at defining the technical parameters of missile defense systems permitted under the 1972 Anti-Ballistic Missile (ABM) treaty, which Russian diplomats say must be completed before START II can be ratified, acrimoniously collapsed in October.

On the positive side of the arms-control ledger, the United States helped engineer changes to the 1990 CFE treaty in June, addressing Russian concerns about force limits on its northern and southern borders. In December, the 30 CFE signatories agreed to open talks on revising the Cold War-era treaty to address the new security challenges facing Europe, a longtime Russian demand. In September, despite Indian objections, Clinton and Primakov joined more than 70 other countries in signing the Comprehensive Nuclear Test Ban treaty, which will outlaw all nuclear tests once it enters into force.

A wide range of agreements promoting scientific and economic cooperation were signed at the January and June meetings of the bilateral commission led by U.S. Vice President Al Gore and Russian Prime Minister Viktor Chernomyrdin. But despite the relief in Washington at Yeltsin's re-election, the year ended on a sour note, with a spate of espionage scandals involving Russian moles inside the Federal Bureau of Investigation and the Central Intelligence Agency. Clinton's December appointment of Czech-born Madeleine Albright as secretary of state drew a negative reaction from many Moscow commentators, who saw her as an ardent supporter of NATO expansion and generally unsympathetic to Russian concerns.

WARMER TIES IN THE EAST

Warming ties with China must be counted as Russia's foreign-policy triumph of 1996. Yeltsin's April visit to Beijing was easily his most visible foreign trip of the year and included the signing of a border confidence-building agreement with his Chinese, Kazakstani, and Kyrgyz counterparts. Yeltsin pledged to finish demarcating the Russo-Chinese border in accordance with the 1991 Soviet-Chinese border treaty. In a thinly veiled attack on the United States, Beijing and Moscow also jointly denounced attempts by unnamed third powers to create a "unipolar" international system. China publicly declared its opposition to NATO expansion, while Russia expressed its support for Beijing's "one China" policy on Taiwan. Political and military ties with China are now closer than they have been since the 1950s, but many Russians are still suspicious of the Chinese—as shown in a December speech by Defense Minister Rodionov, which listed China as a potential military threat.

A continuing drive to build better ties with India, China's traditional rival, also prevents Russia from forging a true alliance with Beijing. Like China, India is one of the biggest purchasers of Russian weapons. In December, India agreed to purchase 40 advanced SU-30 fighters in a deal worth $1.8 billion. Russia and India are also united in their opposition to the Pakistan-backed Taliban movement that now controls most of Afghanistan.

Moscow made some progress in thawing its relations with Japan. Early in the year, Primakov raised hackles in Tokyo when he suggested postponing resolution of the Kuril Islands dispute until "the next generation." But when he visited Japan in November, he brought proposals for the joint development of the islands, which the Japanese—in a departure from previous policy—agreed to study. At the same time, Tokyo released a $500 million loan package that had been frozen since 1991. At the end of the year, both countries said they were close to signing an agreement regulating fishing in waters near the Kurils, a locale of repeated incidents.

Russia continued to play the role of patron for such "rogue" states as Yugoslavia, Iraq, and Iran, although it gained little benefit from doing so. While participating in the NATO-led Implementation Force in Bosnia, for example, Russia gave rhetorical support to Serbia, and Moscow prevented the OSCE summit in December from condemning Serbian President Slobodan Milosevic's cancellation of opposition victories in local elections. Russia played a major role in the United Nations' decision to partially lift the UN embargo on Iraq. Moscow also pushed for closer ties with Iran, cemented by their common antagonism toward the Taliban in Afghanistan. In December, for example, Primakov vowed to continue civilian nuclear cooperation with Tehran despite American objections.

DRAMA OVER SUBSTANCE IN THE CIS

Amid talk of a Russian drive to re-establish the Soviet empire, or at least a sphere of dominant influence in the former Soviet Union, Moscow made only modest progress in advancing CIS integration. (For the debate over Moscow's role in the "near abroad," see "Will the Union be Reborn?") The fears raised by the Duma's March resolution denouncing the 1991 Belavezha accords—which created the CIS—proved unjustified. The Duma resolution—like the Russia-Belarus-Kazakstan-Kyrgyzstan integration treaty signed later that month and the April Russo-Belarusian community agreement—turned out to be little more than a maneuver in the Russian presidential-election campaign.

Only insignificant progress has been made toward reaching the lofty goals of those agreements, even in the case of Belarus, whose president, Alyaksandr Lukashenka, is an ardent advocate of union with Russia. Although the two countries are supposed to have a customs union, Russian officials were actually advocating tighter controls on the frontier with Belarus in December, pointing to Minsk's lax customs policies. Russia supported Lukashenka in his showdown with the Belarusian parliament during the fall, at the cost of considerable international embarrassment. Moscow found itself standing alone at his side at the December OSCE summit. The potential value of Belarus as a transit route for Russian oil and gas exports appears to motivate this policy, but it may backfire if Lukashenka falls from power.

The integration agreements also showed the limits of Russian influence, as the other members of the CIS, except the Tajiks, showed no interest in such grandiose schemes. Uzbek President Islam Karimov explicitly rejected them. There was also no sign that Russia would be able to promote CIS military integration to counterbalance NATO expansion. A November CIS meeting of defense ministers rebuffed Russian efforts to nominate a Russian general as head of the CIS military-cooperation staff, since the post had been held by a Russian since 1992.

An even bigger setback was the deterioration in relations with Ukraine, Russia's most important CIS neighbor. The long-anticipated bilateral friendship treaty remains unsigned, and the year saw no conclusion to the festering dispute over the division and basing of the Black Sea Fleet. Trade disputes over vodka and oil-pipeline fees soured economic relations, and the Russian parliament passed provocative resolutions in November and December claiming the Crimean port of Sevastopol as Russian territory.

Relations with the Baltic states remained frosty. Lithuania, Latvia, and Estonia want to settle their border disputes with Russia in order to boost their chances for EU and NATO admission. The border treaties languish unsigned, however, and Russia has now explicitly linked them to "respect for the human rights of Russian speakers."

In the Caucasus, Russian efforts to push for resolution of the Nagorno-Karabakh and Abkhaz conflicts delivered no results. The only real foreign-policy success for Russia in that region was securing increased participation of Russian companies in several Caspian region oil consortia. In the struggle for control of Caspian shelf oil resources, Moscow also maneuvered to obtain the support of Iran, Kazakstan, and Turkmenistan for its position on the legal status of the Caspian Sea. The Russians want to treat the sea as a lake, allowing Russia to share in huge offshore oil and gas reserves, which would belong to Azerbaijan if the sea were legally regarded as an ocean and divided into national sectors, as Baku desires.

MILITARY IN CRISIS

While the Foreign Ministry could at least celebrate a few successes amid a generally bleak outlook, the same cannot be said of the military. Defeat in Chechnya, financial crisis, and stalled reform made 1996 a year of almost relentless bad news. The only potential bright spot was the June sacking of Defense Minister Grachev and his replacement by Rodionov, the longtime head of the General Staff Academy. Grachev was widely regarded not only as incompetent but also as corrupt. Following his removal, six senior generals were also dismissed amid accusations of corruption.

Rodionov inherited a tough job. The Russian military remains divided among more than 20 overlapping and often competing federal agencies, with large paramilitary forces such as the 264,000–strong Internal Troops and the approximately 300,000–man Border Guards outside the control of the Defense Ministry. Although the armed forces under the Defense Ministry have an authorized strength of 1.7 million personnel, their actual size has fallen to 1.2 million. Conscription has failed to fill the shortfall, as existing legislation grants exemptions to over 70 percent of draft-age men, while draft evasion is rampant among the rest. As a result of downsizing and budget problems—including wage arrears of up to five months in 1996—about 150,000 officers have left the armed forces since 1992. The younger and better-qualified officers were the first to leave. The poor showing of the military in Chechnya, exemplified by the rebel seizure of Grozny in August, showed that the Russian military had learned almost nothing since the conflict began 21 months earlier.

Budget cuts have not been matched by reductions in the number of units, meaning most units are severely undermanned. Lack of funds means inadequate training in all services. The military cannot afford to buy food or pay salaries, let alone purchase new weapons. The ground forces, for example, purchased 2,000 tanks annually in the mid-1980s, but now they buy almost none. The air force did not buy a single combat aircraft in 1996. The navy did launch a new missile cruiser, the Peter the Great, although it had taken 10 years to complete. Reflecting the belief that Russia can remain a great power only if it maintains its nuclear deterrent, the keel was also laid in December for a new ballistic-missile submarine, the Yurii Dolgorukii—the first built since the collapse of the USSR—while the Strategic Rocket Forces continued to test the new SS-25 Topol M intercontinental ballistic missile.

Taken together, those personnel, training, and equipment problems have undermined the Russian military's ability to conduct sustained offensive military operations. Western experts have estimated it could take a decade or more to rebuild an effective military force.

Rodionov was unable to deal with those problems, even the question of pay arrears. His reputation was injured by a November scandal stemming from his attempt to fire the commander of the ground forces, General Vladimir Semenov. He continues to preach the necessity of serious military reform, which would downsize and professionalize the army. But an overall reform plan has yet to be approved, and a new military doctrine for such a streamlined force is still missing. Rodionov—who became a civilian in December while remaining defense minister—has argued that reform will actually require increasing the military budget in the short run. But the 1997 draft budget allocates only 104.3 trillion rubles ($18.9 billion) to the military, while the Defense Ministry had contended that 160 trillion was the absolute minimum needed to survive.

Former Security Council Secretary Aleksandr Lebed has suggested that the situation was so dire that the military might mutiny. But no sign of open unrest has yet appeared. The military has become disoriented and has not developed a capacity to function as an independent political actor in the post-Soviet era.

BARGAINING OVER NATO ENLARGEMENT

by SCOTT PARRISH

Throughout 1996 Russia and NATO were groping toward a compromise in which Russia would enter into a "special partnership" with NATO while acquiescing in a limited eastward expansion of the alliance. But Moscow held out for terms that NATO was so far unwilling to deliver.

For most of 1996, the issue of NATO enlargement cast a long shadow over Russia's relationship with the West. Despite repeated meetings between Russian officials and their NATO counterparts, only marginal progress was made toward bridging the gap that divided Moscow from the leading countries of the alliance on the topic. Government officials and commentators on both sides have spent much time repeating the same tired arguments for and against expansion, with little discernible result.

Although some influential voices in the West, especially in the United States, began to publicly voice doubts about the wisdom of enlarging NATO, both the U.S. and German governments seemed firmly committed to the expansion project. U.S. President Bill Clinton even set a date: he announced on 22 October 1996 that Washington wants the first new Eastern European members admitted in 1999. Meanwhile, Russia's political elite remained resolutely opposed to enlargement. The State Duma on 25 October unanimously passed a resolution warning that NATO expansion could trigger an international crisis on the scale of that which followed NATO's 1979 decision to deploy new intermediate-range nuclear missiles in Europe.

While the rhetorical war continued, both sides showed some new flexibility, hinting that a compromise on the thorny issue might emerge. Under such a deal, Moscow would acquiesce to limited NATO enlargement and receive certain guarantees and a formally codified special relationship with the alliance in return. Russian Foreign Minister Yevgenii Primakov, appointed in January 1996, had for months been floating trial balloons suggesting a diplomatic bargain along those lines. Initially, he received little positive response from his Western and Eastern European interlocutors. In September, however, American proposals for a formal Russia-NATO pact and a special Russia-NATO partnership that offered Moscow a status just short of membership appeared to lay the basis for a compromise deal, and held out some hope that an unpredictable confrontation over NATO expansion can be avoided.

PRIMAKOV LOOKS TO BARGAIN

Since becoming foreign minister, Primakov was unrelenting in his opposition to NATO enlargement. Still, he proved much more tactically flexible than his predecessor, Andrei Kozyrev, whose position as the whipping boy of the nationalist opposition robbed him of any real maneuvering room on the symbolically loaded issue. The veteran Primakov, with much better-established credentials as a defender of Russian national interests was able to make suggestions that would have provoked howls of criticism had they been voiced by Kozyrev. The cornerstone of Primakov's policy was the evident realization that Russia lacks the clout to entirely block NATO enlargement. The foreign minister focused instead on influencing the terms and scope of expansion, limiting its military and political consequences for Moscow. Primakov strove to look like a reasonable bargaining partner, saying that Moscow cannot "veto" the expansion of NATO but insisting that Russia has the right to object and that other countries should carefully consider Moscow's point of view and work toward a "political resolution" of the dispute.

Already at a March meeting with Hungarian Foreign Minister Lazlo Kovacs, whose country is widely regarded as likely to be among the first invited to join NATO, Primakov expressed the hope that the expansion issue could be resolved by "taking into account the concerns of all sides." He suggested that the basis of a compromise could be an agreement with NATO on "nonmovement of NATO's military structure to our borders," hinting that Moscow might not object to a limited form of NATO membership for some of the East European countries. Kovacs, however, reiterated that Hungary wants to become a full member of the alliance.

President Boris Yeltsin lent his support to the proposed compromise during his visit to Norway on 25 March, when he suggested that Eastern European countries should follow the "French model" and join only NATO's political structures, not its military organization. Unfortunately for Primakov, those feelers generated no enthusiasm among either NATO officials or Eastern European leaders. In a series of meetings in March and April, the proposed "French model" was rejected not only by Budapest, but also by Czech and Slovak leaders, NATO Secretary-General Javier Solana, U.S. Secretary of State Warren Christopher, and Polish President Aleksander Kwasniewski. They argued that accepting Moscow's proposal would consign Eastern European states to an unacceptable "second class" of NATO membership. Instead, Christopher and Solana insisted that NATO enlargement would move forward, reiterating that the move was not directed against Russia.

Yeltsin pushed for a similar compromise at the Moscow G-7 nuclear-safety summit in mid-April. He proposed a nuclear-free zone in Central Europe, saying all nuclear powers should pledge to deploy nuclear weapons only on their own soil, following Russia's example. By effectively precluding the deployment of American tactical nuclear weapons in Europe, the proposed zone would have addressed Russian worries that NATO might deploy nuclear weapons on the territory of the new Eastern European members. According to a report on Russian Public Television (ORT), Yeltsin harangued his guests with the proposal for 45 minutes during a pre-summit dinner. But the proposal was rejected by the other nuclear powers at the summit. Yeltsin's subsequent clumsy attempt at a post-summit press conference to claim that Clinton had promised not to "accelerate" expansion backfired when Clinton said Moscow's and Washington's differences on the issue were "well known" and remained unchanged.

With the failure of those compromise offers, Russian spokesmen adopted a more coercive tack, renewing threats about the possible negative consequences of NATO enlargement. On 29 April, Duma Speaker Gennadii Seleznev repeated earlier warnings that if NATO expanded, the Duma would not ratify the START II nuclear-arms-control agreement. He argued that since the treaty had been signed in 1993, when NATO enlargement was not an issue, its provisions would have to be reconsidered if the alliance accepted new members. In mid-May, while visiting Minsk, then-Defense Minister Pavel Grachev said that Russia and Belarus might form a "powerful" joint military group if NATO accepted new members without considering Russian objections. Later that month, Yeltsin's foreign policy aide, Dmitrii Ryurikov, publicly vented his frustration that Russia's earlier compromise proposals had been snubbed. He blamed NATO's intransigence for the continued deadlock on the issue, saying that the alliance had "no serious thoughts" about substantive cooperation with Moscow.

HINTS AT COMPROMISE

Amid such renewed threats, however, Primakov continued to hold out the possibility of a compromise. In a 2 June interview with Russian Television, Primakov expressed surprise at the failure of the West to respond to Russian suggestions. While terming the extension of NATO military infrastructure into areas near Russian borders unacceptable, he said that "everything else may be subject to compromise." He added, however, the now-ritual warning that Russia would reconsider arms-control treaties and its military doctrine if the alliance took on new members "without any search for a formula acceptable to us."

Two days later, Primakov met in Berlin with his counterparts from NATO's 16 member states. The Russian government had specifically requested the meeting in the "16 + 1" format to discuss the expansion issue. With the first round of the Russian presidential election less than two weeks away and all Western leaders supporting the re-election of Yeltsin, Moscow may have calculated that the time was right to use the fear of an anti-NATO backlash in Russia to leverage some concessions from the alliance. That calculation may have been somewhat accurate, as at the session NATO took some steps toward Primakov's position, partially breaking the deadlock that had persisted since the beginning of the year.

Some Western news agencies misleadingly reported that Primakov had softened his stance at the meeting. In fact, he merely reiterated his long-standing proposals that Eastern European countries join only the political, not the military, structures of NATO. Primakov said Moscow could not accept the expansion of the NATO military "infrastructure," which he defined as including NATO's unified command and communications structures as well as the sharing of military facilities and intelligence data. More interesting was NATO's position. Primakov's interlocutors reportedly assured him that NATO was not planning to conduct large-scale maneuvers on the territory of new members or to construct military bases near Russia's borders. Primakov said the "frank" session showed that NATO was now willing to discuss the expansion issue "in dialogue with Russia." Foreign Ministry spokesman Grigorii Karasin later argued that NATO had become more responsive because of Yeltsin's firm opposition to NATO expansion.

Yet the Berlin meeting still left the two sides far apart. NATO officials were quick to say, for example, that while they wanted to develop a partnership with Russia in parallel with expansion, there would be no "co-decision-making" on the expansion issue. And German Defense Minister Volker Ruhe, a leading proponent of NATO expansion, explained that while the alliance had no plans for deployment of troops or nuclear weapons in new Eastern European member states, they would be "militarily integrated" and assume the same rights and obligations as other NATO members. So although the alliance would meet

Russia halfway on many of its concrete concerns, it was not willing to formally codify a compromise deal.

A NATO-RUSSIA CHARTER?

Many believed that Yeltsin's re-election on 3 July would clear the way for some resolution of the NATO dispute. It turned out, however, that Russian opposition was not motivated simply by electoral calculations; Yeltsin's stance changed little after the election. On 24 July, Solana declared that in the wake of Yeltsin's victory, NATO wanted to signal to Moscow its readiness to deepen cooperation. He proposed that Russia and NATO should begin working on a "political framework document" that would define their relationship and that they should move forward with concrete joint projects.

Russian officials did not respond immediately to that proposal, but a commentary in the official government newspaper, *Rossiiskaya gazeta*, urged that Moscow explore it closely. It argued that since Russia could not hope to block enlargement, it should make the best possible deal. Meanwhile, in a letter to Clinton, Yeltsin made clear the limits of Moscow's willingness to compromise, declaring any extension of NATO to the Baltic states "unacceptable." But a Russian presidential spokesman angrily denied reports that Yeltsin had agreed to accept NATO membership for Poland, the Czech Republic, and Hungary in return for a promise that the Baltic states would never be admitted to the alliance.

After early September, attention in the NATO-Russia dialogue largely focused on the development of Solana's earlier proposal that NATO and Russia conclude an agreement outlining their relationship. The idea received explicit backing from Secretary of State Christopher in a speech he delivered in Stuttgart, Germany, on 6 September, when he said Russia and NATO should conclude a "formal charter" creating "standing arrangements for consultation and joint action." Yeltsin and Primakov have endorsed the idea of a charter that would formalize a "special relationship" between Russia and the alliance. But many hurdles remain.

First was the question of timing. Yeltsin insisted the charter be concluded before NATO accepts new members, presumably so that Moscow could use the agreement to influence the terms of NATO enlargement. Western officials demurred, saying the agreement should be hammered out "in parallel" with enlargement. Solana declared that the proposed NATO-Russia pact had "no relationship" to enlargement and said that the two processes would not move "in sequence," but would rather "converge." He said he hoped the charter would be signed by mid-1997, when a NATO summit was scheduled to name the first Eastern European candidates for membership.

While the two sides supported such an agreement in principle, they were still far apart on the details. Primakov insisted that the charter be "maximally concrete" and not merely "declarative." He suggested that to satisfy Russia, the agreement would have to outline joint obligations and responsibilities, detail mechanisms for joint political decision making, and effectively subordinate NATO to the Organization for Security and Cooperation in Europe (OSCE), of which Moscow is a full member. In the same article, Primakov, with an eye on the upcoming December Lisbon OSCE summit, suggested that the OSCE should be the core of any new European security system, although he admitted that NATO would play an important role. Judging from Primakov's public statements, he wanted a charter granting Moscow levers to prevent NATO from deploying nuclear weapons or troops in new member states and to block expansion from moving beyond the most likely first wave—Poland, the Czech Republic, and Hungary.

However, NATO would not accept those terms. Making the OSCE the centerpiece of a new European security architecture, long advocated by Moscow, had been rejected consistently by Western leaders. On joint decision making, U.S. Defense Secretary William Perry said in September that he envisioned a NATO-Russia partnership granting Russia a voice in NATO decisions, but not a vote on them. Primakov wanted a NATO pledge not to deploy nuclear weapons, but the most that officials like Perry and Solana offered were statements that the alliance did not plan such deployment; Perry categorically ruled out any guarantees of nondeployment. And while Moscow clearly hoped to limit expansion geographically, Clinton declared that NATO's doors will remain open even after it accepts the first wave of new members. To further complicate matters, East Europeans publicly expressed fears that the proposed charter could be a new "Munich" or "Yalta"—a cynical great-power deal at their expense.

Ironically, on some of the issues that have generated the most rhetorical heat, NATO and Russia were not as far apart as public statements suggest. For example, the alliance is not likely to base nuclear weapons on the territory of new members. NATO has only a small number of air-delivered tactical nuclear weapons left in Europe. Dual-use, nuclear-capable missiles were eliminated by the 1987 Intermediate Nuclear Forces (INF) treaty, and many other systems, such as nuclear artillery shells and land mines, have been withdrawn. Permanent basing of NATO troops in new member states also seems highly unlikely, as NATO has dispensed with the "forward-deployment" strategy of the Cold War. Besides, NATO's leading members are cutting military budgets and are unlikely to look favorably on new foreign deployments.

The practical results of NATO expansion, then, will probably look very much like what Primakov has said Russia could accept. But deadlock persisted through 1996, since the alliance was unwilling to formally codify that arrangement, and Moscow insisted on formal guarantees. Luckily, however, there was considerably more time to hammer out a compromise than commonly assumed. NATO, with its 16 members, can be a cumbersome organization. Clinton set 1999 as a target date for admitting the first group of new members, but negotiation and ratification of accession agreements with new members could easily take until the early years of the 21st century.

In the meantime, however attractive the abstract idea of a charter, the Russian elite seems as solid as ever in its opposition to NATO enlargement. The Duma not only passed the 25 October resolution denouncing expansion but also gave Perry a cold welcome when he visited Moscow the previous week to lobby for the ratification of the START II arms control agreement. Duma deputies were reportedly especially annoyed by what they termed Perry's "stubborn unwillingness to discuss the military-political implications of NATO expansion." They warned that if NATO fails to address Russian concerns about expansion, the Duma will certainly not ratify START II. Primakov insisted that Russia would not plunge itself into international isolation if the alliance expands. But there can be no certainty that Primakov's views will prevail if NATO and Russia should fail to find a mutually acceptable resolution to the issue—especially considering Yeltsin's poor health.

Even if a compromise charter is hammered out, however, other troublesome problems are likely to appear soon. There is the issue of the Kaliningrad Oblast enclave, for example, which houses up to 200,000 Russian troops and will border directly on NATO if Poland joins the alliance. Then there is the question of how far east NATO will ultimately expand. Moscow may swallow a limited enlargement, but it has signaled vehement opposition to Baltic or Ukrainian NATO membership. While Kyiv denies that it hopes to join the alliance, the Baltic states are fervent applicants, and Clinton has promised that NATO expansion will not end with the "first wave" of new members. A charter leaving that issue unresolved will not resolve the enlargement dispute but merely postpone its next round.

YAVLINSKII ON NATO EXPANSION: YALTA OR VERSAILLES?

by PETER RUTLAND

Speaking to the Bohemiae Foundation in Prague on 13 January 1997, Yabloko leader Grigorii Yavlinskii made a sophisticated case against NATO expansion. He argued that Russia's long-term strategic interest lies in partnership with the West, and that the NATO enlargement is a distraction from the long-term convergence of interests between Russia and the West.

Yavlinskii argued that national interests are not really at stake in NATO expansion—neither the national interest of countries like the Czech Republic, nor those of Russia itself. Rather, Yavlinskii said "I am looking at this as a psychological event . . . or even for some countries a psychiatric issue." In the case of Central Europe, it has to do with healing the wounds to the national psyche left by Western "betrayal" at Yalta and Munich. For Russia, NATO is also a psychological issue—but one of rejection, rather than acceptance. NATO expansion would represent "the final stage of defeat for Russian foreign policy," and would be equivalent to the rejection that Germany experienced after the 1919 Treaty of Versailles.

Yavlinskii followed up this point by arguing that bringing NATO closer to Russia's borders would tilt the balance in Russia's domestic politics away from the democrats and friends of the West. He conceded that foreign policy had not been a decisive issue to date in internal political debates in Russia, but he said that this could change very quickly—particularly given the capacity of Russia's mass media to manipulate public opinion on such a topic. He noted that military reform in Russia was currently stymied because the Defense Ministry was dominated by generals who were trained to fight a war with the West. NATO expansion would given them another excuse to cling to power for a few more years. Yavlinskii said "there are some people we have to take out and replace" with generals who can deal with "the real threats that face Russia—from the south and possibly the south-east." In response to questions Yavlinskii sharply disavowed the hard-line policy positions over Chechnya and Sevastopol espoused by his fellow Yabloko leader, Vladimir Lukin, who is also chairman of the State Duma Foreign Affairs Committee

Yavlinskii also hinted that baser motives were at work behind the NATO debate. He suggested that NATO officials have a vested interest in finding new tasks for their bureaucracy to perform; and he argued that the debate provided a convenient rationale for delaying the more significant—and more expensive—question of when the Central European countries can enter the European Union. On several occasions he cited countries like Sweden and Finland to rebut arguments that being part of Europe necessarily requires membership in the NATO military alliance.

Yavlinskii clearly thought NATO expansion was a bad idea, but he was careful not to directly state his opposition to the move. He did not want to be accused of trying to exercise a "veto" over the security interests of other countries. He joked that "I would not object to NATO expansion, but I could not say that it is something I have been looking forward to all my life."

Yavlinskii stated that "there is not a military threat in Europe any more," and suggested that the real challenges lie in the proliferation of nuclear and chemical weapons, the spread of terrorism, and ecological catastrophes like Chornobyl. Not only is NATO "unable to deal with these real threats," but also the ongoing debate over new NATO members interferes with a joint search for solutions to them.

Several of the Czech speakers challenged Yavlinskii's views. For example, Michal Lobkowitz, a parliamentary deputy, noted the positive role NATO had played in the former Yugoslavia. Yavlinskii countered by pointing to NATO's inability to avert the growing tension between Greece and Turkey, and by suggesting that if civil war spread through parts of the former Soviet Union it would be extremely unlikely that NATO would get involved on the same scale as in Bosnia. Lobkowitz also talked of NATO expansion as needed in order "to destroy the Iron Curtain which in a sense persists"—which seemed to vindicate Yavlinskii's psychological interpretation.

Document: "WILL THE UNION BE REBORN?"

Nezavisimaya gazeta on 23 May 1996 published a proposal by the Council on Foreign and Defense Policy to "reintegrate" most former Soviet states over the long term by bolstering Russia's natural economic dominance in the region. While some Western commentators saw the document, excerpted here, as a call to arms, others suggested that it represents serious thinking about creating an "enlightened" Russian sphere of influence.

RUSSIA'S INTERESTS

Russia (the Russian Federation) has not yet taken final shape as a state, and has not fully found its identity. Rapid social changes and acute political struggle have impeded the hammering out of a consensus on Russia's national interests, including relations with the former Soviet republics.

Russia's interests regarding the former Soviet republics can be divided into (1) vitally important—those the state must be ready to use all means, including force, to protect, (2) important, and (3) less important.

Vitally important interests include:
* Providing freedom, increasing well-being for Russian citizens, and the territorial integrity and independence of Russia.

- Preventing the dominance, especially military-political, of other powers on the territory of the former USSR.
- Preventing the formation of coalitions hostile to Russia, including those in response to Russian actions in the former USSR.
- Unimpeded access to resources that have strategic value, including former USSR transport arteries and ports, naturally, on a fair commercial basis.
- Preventing local wars and large-scale military conflicts in bordering states.
- Preventing large-scale and forcible violations of human and minority rights—first and foremost of [ethnic] Russians—in the former Soviet republics.
- Establishing the closest possible political, economic, and military-political union with Belarus, Kazakstan, and Kyrgyzstan.

Important interests include:

- Maintaining access to the raw materials, labor, and markets of the former Soviet states, especially to Caspian region oil; and creating, for this purpose, the necessary political, economic, and legal conditions.
- Joint use of neighboring states' borders, territories, and parts of their military infrastructure (air defense and early-warning systems, etc.) to prevent military threats to Russia, and its further internal destabilization as a result of the influx and transit of criminals, drugs, weapons, smuggling of raw materials, nuclear materials, and "dual use" technologies.
- Using the political, economic, military, and other potentials of the former Soviet republics to strengthen both Russia and the other states in case of their forming a close alliance in their international political positions.
- Preventing their use as political buffers and counter-balances to Russia.
- Providing basic civil and other rights for all national minorities, first of all for ethnic Russians.
- Preventing the exacerbation of Russian and bordering states' populations' feeling of "division" in case "real" borders are established. [The text notes Konstantin Zatulin's argument to the contrary: that feelings of Russian national division are grounds for unification, and thus it is not necessary for Russia to try and prevent these feelings from being sharpened if borders between countries of the former USSR are tightened.]
- Preserving and strengthening the Russian language and Russian culture in bordering states.
- The continuation of economic reforms in key—from Russia's point of view—CIS states: Belarus, Kazakstan, and Ukraine.
- Strengthening the Russian national currency on the territory of the former USSR.
- Strengthening Russia's position as economic and technological leader in the CIS.
- Strengthening Russia's positions in bilateral dialogue with these states.

- Strengthening cooperation in the military-political sphere. However, Russia is not interested in the creation of a rigid and expensive defense union, which in addition would be perceived as a threat by other bordering states.
- Preserving and developing multilateral cooperation and mechanisms of regulating transport, law enforcement, and economic, financial, ecological, and other activities in the CIS framework.

Less important interests include:

- Fostering democratic development in bordering states.
- Strengthening multilateral CIS structures.
- Restoring some industrial links destroyed by the collapse of the USSR.
- Strengthening mechanisms and procedures for coordinating the foreign-policy activities of Russia and the other states of the former USSR.

The Economy

ANOTHER LOST YEAR FOR THE RUSSIAN ECONOMY

by PETER RUTLAND

There were some positive trends in the Russian economy in 1996, such as dramatically reduced inflation, but output fell even faster than in 1995. There was little sign of economic restructuring, while financial elites apparently increased their influence over the political system.

Most international observers believe that 1996 was the year the Russian economy finally stabilized. Inflation was conquered, falling from 131 percent in 1995 to 22 percent in 1996. In March, the International Monetary Fund (IMF) agreed to release a $10.1 billion loan, and in November, Russia successfully launched $1 billion in Eurobonds on international markets.

Those achievements were not accompanied by any substantial structural reform, however, and output fell for the seventh straight year. Gross domestic product dropped 6 percent in 1996, steeper than the 4 percent fall in 1995. The one bright spot was that Russian exports continued to rise, generating a substantial trade surplus.

While Russia's industry stagnated, there was an increasing sense that control over economic affairs was concentrated in the hands of a small financial-political oligarchy. Bankers sharply increased their political visibility in 1996 and are thought to have put hundreds of millions of dollars into funding President Boris Yeltsin's slick re-election campaign.

POLICY STALEMATE

Economic policy in 1996 was deadlocked because of the presidential election and because the government of Prime Minister Viktor Chernomyrdin was split between rival factions. The "industrialists" wanted state subsidies and a protectionist trade policy, while the "financialists" wanted more liberalization.

The "industrialists" received a boost in January, when Yeltsin sacked First

Deputy Prime Minister Anatolii Chubais, blaming him for wage and tax arrears (the latter had already reached 30 trillion rubles, or $6.5 billion). Chubais was replaced by Vladimir Kadannikov, the former head of the AvtoVAZ auto dinosaur, and an ally of the chief "industrialist," First Deputy Prime Minister Oleg Soskovets. Kadannikov was balanced by the promotion of Chubais associate Aleksandr Kazakov to head the State Property Committee.

In February, Kadannikov and Soskovets pushed for a hike in import tariffs but were deflected by the IMF. In order to finance the deficit without inflationary money creation, Russia needed the new IMF loan, to be doled out in $340 million monthly installments, and had to sell a large volume of government securities (GKOs), for which the cooperation of the international banking community was essential.

Chubais resurfaced to run Yeltsin's campaign, and in June he was able to engineer the dismissal of Soskovets. Chubais was appointed presidential chief of staff, and in August, Kadannikov was replaced with Chubais ally Vladimir Potanin, the 34-year-old head of Oneksimbank. Aleksei Bolshakov, an industrialist known to Chubais from his Leningrad days, took over Soskovets's slot. Finance Minister Vladimir Panskov was replaced by former presidential adviser Aleksandr Livshits, but the centrist ministers for economics (Yevgenii Yasin) and foreign economic relations (Oleg Davydov) remained in place. In August, Chubais had Yeltsin issue decrees canceling his pre-election promises, which would have cost the government some 50 trillion rubles ($9.4 billion).

Tax revenues in June were only 60 percent of the expected level, and the government was forced to withhold planned spending in order to keep the budget deficit within the limits agreed on with the IMF. In August, for example, the Defense Ministry received not a single kopeck. Arrears in wages and pensions caused considerable social distress. The 1997 draft budget followed IMF guidelines but included no substantial new ideas for improving tax collection. It was initially rejected by the Duma in September, but conditionally accepted in December. Russia's rulers have always relied on vodka as a source of revenue: in December the government announced that a state monopoly on alcohol would be reintroduced.

FISCAL AND MONETARY POLICY

The IMF was sufficiently confident in Russia's financial stabilization to approve a $10.1 billion, three-year Extended Fund Facility loan in March, subject to monthly monitoring. Russia agreed to keep the deficit below 3.85 percent of GDP and inflation below 1.9 percent a month and to abolish export duties, reduce import tariffs, and cut tax privileges.

The deficit was covered by securities (61 percent) and foreign loans (39 percent) and not through printing money. Cash emission was 40 percent below the 1995 level. The monetary squeeze combined with investor uncertainty to keep interest rates obstinately high. The Central Bank's refinance rate rose from 160 percent in January to 212 percent on 14 June, falling to 48 percent by December.

Critics complained that the ruble money supply had fallen below 15 percent of GDP and was too low to allow economic recovery. The ruble was increasingly supplemented by U.S. dollars and by barter transactions. The net inflow of dollars over 1996 probably exceeded $10 billion. A wide variety of money surrogates entered circulation. Many factories paid wages with goods or coupons, as did municipalities paying social benefits. Russian banks issued 20 trillion rubles' worth of bills of exchange (vekselya) in the first half of the year and companies another 7 trillion. The government allowed firms to pay taxes with "treasury tax exemptions," which rose to 30 percent of tax payments in June. The Central Bank maintained a degree of independence but in May and June was forced to buy 3 trillion rubles' worth of state platinum reserves and hand over 5 trillion rubles from its 1994 profits.

Economic recession and tax evasion caused tax arrears to rise to 59 trillion rubles by June. Directors were waiting for the presidential election: they assumed that if Zyuganov won, they would be bailed out. Federal tax receipts fell to 13 percent of GDP in the third quarter (rising to 14 percent in the fourth). Worries over falling tax revenues led the IMF to delay its monthly loan payments for July and October.

On 18 August, presidential decrees were issued requiring all firms to have a single bank account and imposing taxes on transfers into private accounts, although that was later rescinded after a storm of protest. In October, Yeltsin created a Temporary Extraordinary Commission for Tax and Budget Discipline under Chubais: its initials mimicked those of Lenin's secret police, the "Cheka." One of its first acts was to place tax inspectors inside every distillery. Federal tax receipts rose from 8.1 trillion rubles in September to 14.6 trillion in October, 20.1 trillion in November, and 25 trillion in December. At the end of the year, the deficit was 3.5 percent of GDP using Finance Ministry definitions (or 7.7 percent, if one includes payments on treasury bills, or GKOs). Revenue was 80 percent of the target level, meaning spending had also been cut by 20 percent.

The Central Bank tightened its control over commercial banks, phasing in higher reserve requirements. There were 2,295 banks in January, of which some 200 closed during the year. In May, Unikombank (Russia's 12th largest commercial bank) was temporarily placed into receivership, and in July, Tveruniversalbank (the 17th largest) collapsed. In previous years, banks had profited from speculation in foreign currency, privatization vouchers, shares, debt, and then tax waivers. In 1996 they probably made most of their money from buying government securities, whose interest rates rose to 150 percent, falling to 40 percent by year's end.

By mid-December, the stock of outstanding government bonds had risen to 233 trillion rubles ($42 billion). Since February, foreigners had been allowed to buy GKOs through Russian banks (subject to a limit of a 19 percent return); they bought roughly $3.5 billion worth over the year. Critics charged that the government was only able to meet IMF stabilization targets by running up domestic and international debts, sowing problems for the future.

INDUSTRIAL DOLDRUMS

Industrial output fell by 6 percent in 1996, and the decline accelerated during the summer. Optimists argued that the figures are deceptive, since much output goes unreported to avoid taxes. They pointed out that electricity production, which is accurately measured and is an indicator of overall activity, fell by just 0.7 percent in the first 10 months of 1996. The recorded annual fall was sharpest in light industry (27 percent), agricultural machinery (42 percent), and the defense industry (40 percent). Increased output was reported for some export commodities, such as natural gas (1 percent) and raw aluminum (5 percent). Investment fell 17 percent.

Federal subsidies for agriculture stood at 11 trillion rubles, which covered a mere 8 percent of total farm costs. Total food output was down 6 percent, despite a good grain harvest of 68 million metric tons, up 6 percent from 1995. Food imports stood at $13.5 billion, about 35 percent of consumption. In March, Yeltsin passed a decree easing restrictions on land ownership, in the absence of a new land code from the Duma. It is unlikely to be implemented any more effectively than the similar decree issued by Yeltsin in October 1993.

By year's end, interfirm debts topped 490 trillion rubles, or 25 percent of GDP (compared with 15 percent in 1995) and federal tax arrears another 61 trillion. Barter is increasingly common, accounting for perhaps 80 percent of payments to energy producers. Most firms have learned not to ship goods unless their clients pay cash up front. But the producers of natural gas, electricity, and coal—Gazprom, EES Rossii (Unified Energy System), and Rosugol—were forbidden from shutting off supplies to delinquent customers. In return, they were allowed to keep their monopoly status and were not broken up into competing firms, as the oil industry had been.

In April, in response to IMF pressure, Yeltsin abolished Gazprom's tax-exempt stabilization fund but took other steps, such as lowering the gas excise duty, to compensate the firm. In September, Chairman Rem Vyakhirev noted that Gazprom had paid 15 trillion rubles in taxes and owed another 15 trillion rubles but was in turn owed 48 trillion by its customers. He warned that if Gazprom were squeezed, it would start cutting off debtor cities.

The coal industry, with its 800,000 politically mobilized miners, was the second largest recipient of state subsidies after the farm sector, receiving 10 trillion rubles. In July and December, the World Bank disbursed a $525 million loan to help restructure the industry.

The Russian Space Agency had a desperate year and was only able to survive thanks to Western funding, which accounted for 60 percent of its income. From September to December, Russia was unable to launch new satellites to maintain its military-surveillance capacity. In October, the head of Chelyabinsk-70, a leading nuclear-research center in Snezinsk, shot himself in despair over his inability to pay his staff their salaries, and in December, a faulty $300 million Mars probe plunged back into the Pacific.

While Russian aerospace plants lay idle, in September Aeroflot signed a letter of intent with Boeing to lease 10 of the American manufacturer's mid-sized 737 airplanes. Aeroflot will also use an $850 million American loan to finance construction of new Ilyushin 96 airliners equipped with Pratt and Whitney engines—much to the annoyance of the Perm Motors plant. U.S. producers have more advanced technology and easier access to credit than their Russian rivals.

There was little progress on the privatization front. Although some 70 percent of Russian firms are now private, insider owners continue to dominate, and the expected shake-out of money-losing plants failed to materialize. The banks that had acquired blocks of shares under the controversial loans-for-shares auctions of late 1995 found it difficult to establish their ownership rights, as shown by Oneksimbank's long political and legal struggle to replace the director of Norilsk Nickel. In the course of 1996, most of the banks opted to sell off their share blocks. The state raised only 1.9 trillion rubles from privatization in 1996, less than the 2.8 trillion raised in 1995, and below the target of 12 trillion. In March, Gazprom and the oil firm YUKOS began selling off 8 percent of their shares for cash, as did EES in December.

There were still very few examples of major firms being pushed into bankruptcy. Seven leading firms that had paid less than 20 percent of their taxes were warned in October and issued bankruptcy papers at the beginning of December. The most notable victim was the auto giant AvtoVAZ, which was forced to agree to sell 51 percent of its shares because of tax debts. The Tatarstan truck giant KamAZ was initially on the list, but it was taken off a week later after some blunt lobbying by President Mintimer Shaimiev.

On paper, Russia had 15,000 joint stock companies with 40 million shareholders, the world's largest on both counts. The Credit Suisse First Boston index of leading Russian shares surged from a year low of 525 points in March to nearly 1,500 in July, but trading volume was low. The Duma passed a new law on the securities market in March, requiring quarterly reports and the disclosure of major transactions, and an August presidential decree further strengthened shareholder rights. There was no progress in rationalizing the tax code, however, and only two-thirds of the new civil code was passed into law.

CAVEAT INVESTOR

Direct foreign investment in 1996 was estimated at about the same level as in 1995, a mere $1.5 billion. Corruption, taxation, red tape, and legal uncertainty are still major barriers. Only a handful of new manufacturing projects were begun in 1996—such as a $140 million Snickers candy-bar plant. An auto-assembly plant was inaugurated by General Motors in Tatarstan, and South Korea's KIA Motors announced plans for another in Kaliningrad. But in February, IBM announced it would stop assembling personal computers in Zelenograd, blaming the removal of tax breaks on imported equipment the previous year.

The energy sector urgently needs an injection of foreign capital and technology: oil production had fallen by 40 percent since 1987, and it dropped another 2 percent in 1996. However, the Duma refused to pass the list of approved oil and gas sites without which the 1995 law on production sharing cannot go into effect.

Gazprom began work in October on its own $3.5 billion, 1150–kilometer Yamal pipeline, which is to carry gas across Belarus and Poland.

The government made no progress with the privatization of the telecommunications company Svyazinvest, which had been canceled at the last minute in December 1995. In February 1996, De Beers provisionally agreed to renew its contract as the primary seller of Russia's $1.2 billion-a-year diamond exports, but Russian firms began selling stones independently of De Beers, while the government publicly questioned whether the deal was in Russia's national interest. De Beers let the arrangement lapse as of 1 January 1997.

Russia made some progress in its own foreign ventures. In December, it persuaded the Caspian Sea Consortium, formed to build a $1.5 billion pipeline to export Kazak oil through Novorossiisk, to increase Russia's share to a 44 percent stake while reducing Kazakstan's stake to 21 percent and Chevron's to 15 percent. In October, Russia persuaded Turkmenistan and Kazakstan to accept its view of the Caspian Sea as a "lake" whose resources should be jointly exploited, while widening the coastal strip to 75 kilometers. Azerbaijan wants the Caspian to be treated as an international sea, divided into national zones.

FOREIGN-TRADE BOOM

Exports in 1996 rose 8.3 percent to $86.5 billion and imports were little changed at $46.6 billion, giving Russia a trade surplus of $40 billion. From that should be subtracted the estimated $8 billion of goods brought in by individual "shuttle" traders. Oil and gas accounted for 45 percent of exports. Russia's arms exporters probably earned $3 billion, and they signed deals for fighter sales to China and India. Imports were mainly machinery, meat, sugar, and alcohol. The year saw a modest revival of trade with the Commonwealth of Independent States (CIS). CIS countries took 20 percent of exports and provided 30 percent of imports: a rise of 12.5 percent and 8.3 percent, respectively.

As part of the IMF agreement, export duties were lifted from all goods save oil in April, and from oil in July, although the revenue loss was compensated for by an increase in oil excise duties (paid also by domestic consumers). Import tariffs were rearranged in May, although the average tariff stayed at between 14 percent and 15 percent. There was a brief "chicken war" with the United States in the spring. The United States sold Russia $600 million of chicken parts in 1995, causing Russia to hike the import tariff to 98 percent. After U.S. President Bill Clinton complained, the tariff was cut to 30 percent. In September, the government announced that quotas on alcohol imports would be introduced from 1 January 1997, stimulating protests from the European Union and Ukraine.

In 1996, the ruble held its value against the dollar in real terms, easing from 4,630 on 31 December 1995 to 5,550 on 23 December 1996—a 20 percent nominal depreciation, roughly equal to the domestic-inflation rate. The Central Bank kept the ruble within the "corridor" introduced in July 1995, and in July 1996 it switched to an inclined corridor (akin to a crawling peg) with parameters announced six months in advance. In May, Russia announced its intention to conform to Article 8 of the IMF Charter, meaning current-account convertibility

Table 1. Russia's Economic Performance		
	First 9 months of 1996 (in trillions of rubles)	Change over first 9 months of 1995* (in percentages)
Gross domestic product	1,609	−6
Industrial output	926	−5
Agricultural output	242	−8
Retail turnover	547	−3
Services	145	−7
Real disposable income	NA	−0.8

*Based on constant (inflation-adjusted) prices.

Source: *Ekonomika Rossii Yanvar–Sentyabr 1996 g.* [Russia's Economy January–September 1996] (Moscow: Goskomstat, 1996).

for the ruble. Official reserves declined slightly to around $16 billion by November, while capital outflow amounted to about $12 billion over the year. Russian individuals and firms now hold a total of $40 billion to $50 billion abroad.

In addition to the $10.1 billion IMF loan, in 1996 the World Bank approved eight loans totaling $1.8 billion for enterprise restructuring and social infrastructure. In October, Russian state bonds received an improved ranking from international rating agencies. The same month, Gazprom shares were quoted on the London Stock Exchange, and Western investors were offered $429 million worth of shares in the firm. In November, Vimpel-Communications, a mobile-phone company, became the first Russian company to be listed on the New York Stock Exchange.

Russia's foreign debt amounted to around $130 billion dollars at the end of 1996, equal to about 35 percent of GDP. The value of its debt on the secondary international market doubled during the year, partly because of the November 1995 rescheduling agreement with the London Club of commercial lenders. Preliminary agreement was reached with the Paris Club of official creditors in April, postponing payment for 25 years.

Despite those signs of international recognition, when Chernomyrdin attended the Group of Seven meeting in Lyons in June, he only took part in the political discussions, and Russia was not allowed to join the club. Similarly, at the World Trade Organization meeting in Singapore in December, Russia was told its application for membership would not be accepted in the immediate future.

At the close of 1996, Russia's economic performance was as paradoxical as ever. Viktor Chernomyrdin said that 1997 "will be a breakthrough year" and predicted GDP growth of 2 percent, while *Finansovye izvestiya* commentator Yevgenii Vasilchuk said Russia is "moving rapidly toward complete intellectual and industrial degradation, financial disorder, the formation of a criminal elite, and regional disintegration from the federal center."

Social Issues

A SOCIETY UNDER STRAIN

by PENNY MORVANT *and* PETER RUTLAND

The costs of economic transition continued to be carried by Russia's workers and pensioners. Although living standards stabilized for most of the population, chronic wage arrears prompted strikes by workers in several sectors.

Despite the continuing economic recession, the "social explosion" predicted by some oppositionists failed to materialize in Russia in 1996. Poverty and crime were more acute problems than in Soviet times, but Russia's social fabric was still, if barely, intact. The costs of ongoing deprivation were borne at household level: families survived by pooling their resources and seeking additional sources of income. The food grown on private plots was an important means of sustenance even for urban, professional families.

Living standards, as reflected in official statistics, remained fairly stable in 1996, in contrast to the deterioration in 1995. The average monthly wage from January through September was 773,000 rubles (about $150). Adjusting for purchasing-power parity and unreported income, Russia comes out with a per capita income of about $5,000 a year, roughly on a par with Brazil, Turkey, or Iran. Real disposable income fell just 0.8 percent from January to September as compared with the same period in 1995. The government thus seems to have been correct when it argued that conquering inflation would be beneficial to the poor.

The share of people living below the poverty line declined, from 25 percent in January to 20 percent in September. (That figure had peaked at 34 percent in January 1995.) Income differentials also declined somewhat, with the income of the richest 10 percent of the population exceeding that of the poorest decile 12:9 times, down from a ratio of 13:4 in the first nine months of 1995. But all these figures must be taken with a grain of salt: there was massive underreporting of income by both rich and poor (although the rich obviously have more to conceal). Employers also tended to understate salaries in order to reduce their tax and social-security payments. On the other hand, reported income may be exaggerated, since statistics usually record the wages and pensions to which people were entitled and do not allow for payments arrears.

Cuts in government spending and mounting interfirm debts meant that many people were not actually receiving the sums they were due. One group hit hard by payment arrears was Russia's 37 million pensioners. On paper, they should have been better off than in 1995. As part of his pre-election spending spree, Boris Yeltsin issued a decree in April doubling the cost-of-living compensation payments for pensioners. In 1995, the average pension was 3 percent below the subsistence minimum, while from January to September 1996 the average pension was 11 percent above the poverty line. Still, those receiving only the minimum pension were left with incomes far below subsistence level.

However, by summer, many pensioners found they had to wait two to three months for their money. By November, the state pension fund, formally independent of the federal budget, was owed about 50 trillion rubles in payroll deductions, and 68 of the 89 regions needed subsidies to meet pension commitments. The delays caused angry protests, with retirees picketing government buildings and blocking roads and railways. The arrears also prompted regional leaders—many of whom were running for re-election in the autumn—to dream up schemes to distribute food and fuel on credit to pensioners. In December, Sverdlovsk Governor Eduard Rossel even began circulating a quasi-currency—the "Urals franc"—to pay benefits.

LATE WAGES, GROWING DISCONTENT

Arrears in wage payments were also a growing problem. Lyudmilla Alekseeva, chairwoman of the Moscow Helsinki Group, said that "the main mass and disgraceful violation of human rights is the delay in the payment of wages and pensions, which violates the basic human right to life, health, and a normal family." At the start of his re-election campaign, Yeltsin pledged to eliminate wage arrears in the budget sector. Although the state's debt declined in the spring, arrears soon rose again, reaching 46.6 trillion rubles by the end of November, of which 8.6 trillion was owed by state organizations. The average worker had to wait one month to be paid; some waited up to five months. In a survey carried out by VCIOM in the autumn, only 30 percent of respondents said that they were paid on time and in full, down from 45 percent in 1995. Thirty-one percent had their wages delayed, while 39 percent of workers were not paid at all (compared with 38 percent and 17 percent in 1995).

Because of widespread hidden unemployment, open unemployment numbers rose less quickly than expected, given the drop in output. Companies typically preferred to keep workers formally on the books, even if there was no work for them or money to pay them. At any one time, up to one-third of workers were on short time or on temporary leave. At the end of September, 6.7 million people, or 9.2 percent of the work force, were unemployed, according to International Labor Organization methodology (that is, using household-survey data). That was up slightly from 8.5 percent in 1995. Because the benefits were paltry, only 2.5 million unemployed Russians, or 3.4 percent of the work force, formally registered with the Federal Employment Service.

The number of strikes increased in response to the wage-arrears problem, particularly in education, health care, and the coal industry. In the first nine months of the year, about 356,000 people were involved in strikes at 3,767 enterprises and organizations. The stoppages resulted in the loss of some 1.88 million worker-days, up from 1.36 million days lost during 1995. The fact that workers often resorted to hunger strikes—as did 13 supervisors at the Leningrad nuclear-power plant in November, for example—illustrates their feeling of powerlessness. With both employers and the government pleading insolvency, the workers did not know where to turn. On 2 September, workers at the Aviastar plant in Ulyanovsk, who had been furloughed over the summer, staged street protests to demand to be allowed to go back to work—even though they had not been paid for five months.

The problem of wage arrears prompted the usually lethargic Federation of Independent Trade Unions to stage a day of action on 5 November, which attracted a higher turnout than similar protests in previous years. Workers remained suspicious of the union, the successor to the Soviet-era official unions, but new, grassroots labor organizations also made little headway. The exception was the Kuzbass coal basin in Kemerovo Oblast, which spearheaded a weeklong nationwide coal-mining strike in December. In some Kuzbass towns, "People's Salvation Committees" had been formed, which operated in parallel to the local government, like the soviets of 1917. But the workers' movement remained fragmented.

Apart from the Kuzbass, the most serious social unrest occurred in the far-eastern region of Primore. The local power company was insolvent, due to a variety of factors, including corrupt middlemen, Governor Yevgenii Nazdratenko's decision to hold down electricity prices, and the failure of the federal government to meet its financial commitments to major energy customers, such as defense enterprises. Many factories and residents found their electricity switched off on 1 July, and on 11 July local coal miners went on strike protesting five-month wage arrears. Several weeks of protests and hunger strikes followed, involving power, transport, and health-care workers. Eventually, Moscow allocated emergency funds to bail out the region, but the basic problems were not solved, and there were fears that the "Primorskii syndrome" would spread to other regions of Russia as winter set in.

Numerous public organizations—considered essential for a healthy civil society—have sprung up in Russia, but they have had only a limited impact on policymaking. One of the clearest achievements of the informal sector was a successful campaign by environmentalists in Kostroma Oblast to hold a local referendum on the construction of a nuclear-power station in the region. On 8 December, Kostroma voters rejected by 87 percent to 10 percent a proposal to complete the plant.

Criminal networks were arguably the most active informal groups. Even though the overall number of recorded crimes declined slightly, the apparent pervasiveness of organized crime caused growing concern about the "criminalization" of Russian society. In the first 10 months of the year, 450 contract killings were reported. In November, organized crime claimed its first American

Table 1. Russians Select Major Events of 1996	
In a December VCIOM poll, 1,600 Russian adults were asked to name the most significant issues of the year. Each respondent was allowed to pick three.	
Wage and pension arrears	42%
Peace in Chechnya	39%
Presidential election	26%
Lebed's stint in the Security Council	18%
Terrorist bombs in Moscow and Kaspiisk	13%
Yeltsin's heart trouble	12%
Hostage seizure in Pervomaiskoe	12%
Nationwide coalminers' strike	11%
Gubernatorial elections	9%
Escape of captive pilots from Kandahar	8%
Olympic Games in Atlanta	6%
Rebel seizure of Grozny in August	6%
Firing of Grachev, Korzhakov et al.	5%
Establishment of emergency tax commission	4%
Belarus crisis	4%
Spitsbergen air crash	4%
Re-election of Bill Clinton	4%
Appointment of Anatolii Chubais	3%
Michael Jackson concert in Moscow	2%
US issuance of new $100 dollar bill	2%
Airing of Dynasty on televsion	2%
Taliban seizure of Kabul	2%
Source: Segodnya, 31 December 1996.	

victim—Paul Tatum, manager of the luxury Radisson-Slavyanskaya Hotel. On 11 June, just before the first round of the presidential election, a bomb in a Moscow metro car killed four people. There were two more bombs in Moscow trolleybuses in mid-July; police had no leads on the perpetrators. In a mob-related hit, a bomb killed 13 mourners at the grave of a veterans-organization leader on 10 November. An unrelated bombing six days later, presumably a spillover from the conflict in Chechnya, killed 64 people in a police apartment block in Kaspiisk, Dagestan. Russia agreed to end the death penalty when it joined the Council of Europe in February, but the moratorium was not introduced until August, and by then 53 executions had taken place in 1996.

Many Russian officials expressed alarm at Russia's declining population. The crude death rate fell slightly: after peaking at 15.8 per 1,000 in 1994, it eased to 14.4 per 1,000 in 1996. However, the birthrate fell to 9 per 1,000, down from 13.4 in 1990, the result of low living standards and the uncertainties engendered by rapid socioeconomic change. The natural decline in the population was partly offset by net in-migration, mainly from the countries of the Commonwealth of Independent States: 460,000 people immigrated, while 215,000 left the country (mainly for the West). Between January and October, the total population dropped by 430,000, to 147.5 million.

NOT EVERY DAY A HOLIDAY FOR RUSSIAN WOMEN

by PENNY MORVANT

"The future of Russia is in your warm, caring hands," President Boris Yeltsin told women at a Kremlin reception two days before International Women's Day. Women were complimented and feted at a series of events in the lead-up to Women's Day on 8 March, a major holiday when men traditionally shower the fair sex with flowers and candy. The rest of the year, though, the position of women is not so auspicious.

On 4 March, representatives of more than fifty women's groups appealed to the State Duma to enact legislation that would improve their situation. In their appeal they noted high unemployment among women, discrimination against women in the workplace, low pay levels, the underrepresentation of women in decision-making positions, and high maternal mortality. A poll conducted among some 9,000 employed city-dwellers in Russia, and released on the eve of International Women's Day found that women account for 87% of respondents with a personal income of less than 100,000 rubles ($21) a month, but that only 32% of women polled earn more than 1.5 million. The higher the income bracket, the lower the proportion of women.

But although women tend to be the first to be laid off from old state firms and now make up 62% of the country's officially registered unemployed, they appear to be in a better position in new businesses, where, according to *Izvestiya*, they are often seen as more reliable employees than men. An Academy of Sciences' survey of 200 private firms found that women were either in charge or in senior management positions in about a quarter of them.

In the political sphere, the position of women is far from ideal. In an interview with RFE/RL in December, 1995, Irina Khakamada, one of Russia's best-known women politicians, said women in politics are subject to discrimination and have to be "stronger and cleverer" than men to succeed. There is still only one woman minister—Social Security Minister Lyudmila Bezklepina—and the number of women represented in the parliament has fallen since the Duma elections. While about 60 of the 450 deputies in the old Duma were women, now there are only 46 owing to the failure of Women of Russia to clear the 5% barrier. But women remain active in grass-roots political and public organizations. One example is the Committee of Soldiers' Mothers, which has taken an active part in protests against both the Chechen war and the practice of "hazing" in the military. The Committee was nominated for the Nobel Peace Prize in recognition of its efforts.

In his 6 March address, Yeltsin noted the triple burden of employment, housework, and childcare that falls on many women, stressing the importance of the last responsibility and vowing to give extra weight to social programs aimed at improving the lot of children. Russia's leaders would clearly like more women to devote all of their energies to the home, hoping that as a result birthrates will rise and juvenile delinquency fall. But although many women might be happy to give up work, especially the underpaid menial variety, financial constraints mean that few are in a position to do so. The fall in living standards since the introduction of economic reforms means that many families need the income of both partners to make ends meet. The large number of single mothers in Russia also have little choice but to work, as state benefits are low. Thus most women continue to bear the twin responsibilities of work both in and outside the home.

RUSSIA'S JUDICIAL SYSTEM: THE POOR RELATION

by PENNY MORVANT

On 30 August Moscow Judge Olga Lavrenteva was killed in her office by a street vendor she had fined $7 the previous day. Her murder sent shock waves through the judiciary, highlighting not only the issue of security for judges but also the many other problems facing the Russian judicial system.

Russia has come a long way since the days of "telephone justice," when court rulings were dictated by communist party officials, but the independence of the third branch of power is threatened by chronic underfunding and its subordinate position in relation to the executive and the legislature.

In June, the Presidium of the Council of Judges of the Russian Federation adopted a resolution on the "crisis situation" in the country's courts, noting that in some places hearings had all but stopped while pre-trial detention centers were already badly overcrowded. According to Justice Minister Valentin Kovalev, the money allocated to the judicial system from the budget (1.9 trillion) is sufficient to cover only one-third of its needs.

There were numerous reports in the regional press detailing the problems faced by local courts in meeting their wage bills, paying for communal services and security, buying equipment, and carrying out building repairs. Court clerks in Chelyabinsk threatened to take strike action in mid-October if their wages were not raised and paid regularly. *Izvestiya* on 9 July cited the case of one regional court that is able to function only because a neighboring law firm pays its electricity and gas bills and allows the judges to use its telephone. Such circumstances make judicial workers more susceptible to corruption as well as impeding the efficiency of the justice system.

The number of criminal cases increased by about two-thirds since 1992 but the number of judges has fallen because of the low pay and increased risks. Moreover, as is the case in other public funded sectors, such as the police, it was often the most qualified and experienced personnel who leave. A new spate of resignations among judges and members of the procuracy was reportedly triggered in August when austerity measures introduced by presidential decree on the 18th suspended earlier laws which promised to hire more staff for procurator's offices and to increase social benefits to judges and court officers.

Delays in hearing cases, in addition to the limited use of bail, exacerbated the appalling conditions in remand prisons, long notorious for their severe overcrowding and high rates of disease, including tuberculosis. In a recent report on crime and prisons in the former Soviet Union, Valerii Abramkin, a prominent human rights activist and former political prisoner, described the situation as "absolutely disastrous, much, much worse than it was 10 years ago or even one year ago." The overburdening of the judiciary also means that mistakes are more likely to be made in the examination of cases. At a press conference on the continued use of the death penalty, human rights activists claimed that errors are made in as much as 30 percent of the cases.

Poor funding and a lack of political will have also hampered judicial reforms. The situation with regard to trial by jury is a case in point. Jury trials were reintroduced in Russia in 1993 in five regions and later extended to four more. The experiment has been praised by legal experts and the right to a jury trial is inscribed in the constitution, but plans to introduce jury trials in other areas have stalled because of financial constraints and the failure to push through necessary legislation. The fact that juries have acquitted more defendants than other courts has also made them unpopular with law enforcement agencies.

As yet, there is also no law on the introduction of bailiffs, without which it is difficult to enforce court rulings. The lack of an efficient mechanism to implement court decisions, along with the public's low regard for law enforcement agencies, aggravates the tendency of citizens to seek their own justice, settling scores outside the legal system.

Perhaps most worrying of all, the financial and legislative constraints upon the judiciary means that it is not fully independent of the other branches of power. As a group of senior judges from Siberia noted in an open letter to the president, government, and parliament, the fact that the heads of courts are forced to turn to local governors for help in paying their debts does little to promote the principle of the independence of the judiciary from the executive—a vital element in any democratic system.

DEATH IN A MOSCOW CEMETERY

by PENNY MORVANT

Thirteen people were killed and several others seriously injured in an explosion at the Kotlyakovskoe cemetery in Moscow on 10 November. The victims were Afghan veterans and their relatives gathered for a memorial service in honor of Mikhail Likhodei, who headed the Russian Fund for Invalids of the War in Afghanistan (RFIVA) before he was killed exactly two years before. Other members of the fund, which was granted lucrative foreign trade privileges at the beginning of 1994, have also been attacked in the past. The bloody history of the fund is a good illustration of the extent to which organized crime has become intertwined with business—and even charitable—activities in Russia, when large sums of money are involved.

The RFIVA, which was set up in 1991 to help soldiers wounded during the Afghan war, has been plagued by conflicts. According to *Segodnya* on 11 November, rival factions have fought for control of the fund and hence over the commercial activities in which it is involved. At the fund's second conference in August 1992, Valerii Radchikov, a paratroop colonel who lost both legs in Afghanistan, was elected RFIVA chairman. A year later he was ousted, accused of concentrating too heavily on commercial activities, and replaced by Likhodei. Radchikov, however, continued to operate in the name of the fund from his base in its Moscow branch. Likhodei turned to the Justice Ministry in an attempt to put a stop to Radchikov's activities, and in September 1993 a criminal case was launched against Radchikov. Later that month, an attempt was made on the lives of Likhodei and Sergei Trakhirov, his deputy.

In 1994, a new conflict arose when the RFIVA was granted tax breaks under a December 1993 presidential decree on state support for organizations assisting invalids. The most important benefit the decree gave the fund was exemptions on the payment of duties on goods imported into Russia. It is estimated that imported goods, mainly alcohol and tobacco, to the tune of $800 million were involved. In the struggle to profit from those new opportunities, Radchikov was quicker off the mark than Likhodei, managing to secure the right to trade in the name of the RFIVA. After several months, Likhodei regained control, but he had little opportunity to celebrate his victory. On 10 November 1994, he was killed when a bomb exploded in the elevator in his apartment block.

The legal battle between the rival factions over control of the fund continued in 1995. And on 29 October, the next bloody incident occurred. Radchikov was badly injured and his legal adviser killed in a shooting attack in Moscow. Police speculated that Radchikov was targeted because he knew too much about the fund's business dealings, although he himself no longer played a key role in its financial affairs.

Among the victims of the explosion at the Kotlyakovskoe cemetery on 10 November was the RFIVA's current chairman Trakhirov and several other leading members of the fund. The explosives, equivalent to about 2.5 to 3 kilograms of TNT, went off as Trakhirov was preparing to address the 150 or so mourners gathered near Likhodei's grave.

Although most of the tax breaks from which the fund benefited have been abolished, the "Afghan business" has remained profitable. Rumors abound concerning responsibility for the recent tragedy, but there can be little doubt that it is linked to the fund's commercial dealings. The chairman of the Russian Union of Veteran of Afghanistan, Frants Klintsevich, was quoted as saying that criminal scores were being settled within the fund and that a "third force" was setting Afghan veterans against each other in the hope of profiting from the disputes.

Another charitable fund that benefited from trade privileges worth millions of dollars, the National Sports Fund, has also been riven by internal conflicts, and its former head, Boris Fedorov, barely survived an assassination attempt this summer. Other charities concerned with invalids are also thought to have fallen under the control of criminal groups, interested in the money-making possibilities they offer. Wherever there is money, it appears, criminal groups will vie for influence, often leaving a trail of bodies in their wake.

TRANSCAUCASUS
& CENTRAL ASIA

VI

Georgia

Azerbaijan

Armenia

Kazakstan

Uzbekistan

Tajikistan

Kyrgyzstan

Turkmenistan

Georgia

Population: 5,000,000
Capital: .... Tbilisi (pop. 1,066,000)
Major cities: .... Kutaisi (pop. 194,000), Rustavi (pop. 129,000),
                          Batumi (pop. 123,000)
Area: .... 70,000 sq. km.
Major ethnic groups: ...... Georgian, Armenian, Russian, Azerbaijani,
                          Ossetian, Greek, Abkhaz (percentage breakdown
                          unavailable)
Economy: .... GDP growth: 11.0%
.... Inflation rate: 13.0%
.... Average monthly income: $34
.... Unemployment rate: 3.2%

GEORGIA STABILIZES

by ELIZABETH FULLER

The Georgian economy continued to improve and politics continued to stabilize throughout the year. The status of the breakaway regions of Abkhazia and South Ossetia, however, remained as unclear as ever.

The parliamentary and presidential elections in November 1995 marked a turning point in Georgia's post-Soviet history and ushered in a new phase of political and economic stability. Throughout 1996, the new parliament functioned cohesively and productively to enact key legislation underpinning the foundations of a civil society and of economic reform. During the spring session alone, more than 50 laws were passed, including one further regulating the privatization of land and one creating a Constitutional Court.

Following his triumphant election as president with nearly 75 percent of the vote, Eduard Shevardnadze, the former Soviet foreign minister who had returned to his native Georgia in March 1992, moved quickly to restore order. He had his rival, Dzhaba Ioseliani, arrested and Ioseliani's paramilitary force, Mkhedrioni, disbanded for engaging in black-marketeering and alleged drug trafficking. In 1996 there were none of the violent terrorist incidents or political assassinations that were a regular occurrence from 1993 through mid-1995. Crime abated, partly as a result of the increased powers bestowed on the police and the creation of a new National Security Council subordinate to Shevardnadze.

Most opposition parties were no longer represented in parliament. The only point on which they agree, and can exert some influence, is their shared opposition to the stationing of Russian troops in Georgia. A split within the National Democratic Party—the largest opposition party in parliament—and rumored tensions between parliament Speaker Zurab Zhvania and Minister of State Niko Lekishivili had no effect on domestic politics.

Several former prominent political figures went on trial in 1996. In October, former Defense Minister Tengiz Kitovani, once viewed as a potential threat to Shevardnadze, was sentenced to eight years' imprisonment for attempting in January 1995 to organize a march on the secessionist region of Abkhazia. (One of his co-defendants, Russian national Valerii Fisyun, died in prison soon after being sentenced.) In November, Loti Kobalia, commander of the military units loyal to former President Zviad Gamsakhurdia, and three of his subordinates were sentenced to death on charges of treason and murder. Supporters of the late Gamsakhurdia staged a demonstration in Tbilisi to protest the sentences. Another opposition political figure, Constitutional Monarchist Party Chairman Temur Zhorzholiani, was sentenced to four years' imprisonment on charges of unauthorized possession of drugs and a firearm.

Others, however, were not so justly accused. Tengiz Sigua, who had served as prime minister first under Gamsakhurdia and then in 1992–1993 under Shevardnadze, and former Deputy Prime Minister Avtandil Margiani were subjected to repeated accusations of corruption and financial irregularities, but both men responded by publishing in the opposition press official documentation that substantiated their proclaimed innocence.

NO PROGRESS ON BREAKAWAY REGIONS

Relations with Russia continued to dominate foreign policy and to affect domestic politics. In particular, Georgia was vexed by Moscow's perceived failure to comply with the 1995 bilateral agreement permitting Russia to maintain four military bases in Georgia in return for assistance in re-establishing Tbilisi's control over the breakaway regions of Abkhazia and South Ossetia. The Georgian government had ceded control over Abkhazia in September 1993, after 13 months of fighting in which the Abkhaz received crucial logistical support from hard-line elements within the Russian military. UN-mediated negotiations aimed at formalizing Abkhazia's future status within a unitary Georgian state are deadlocked because the Georgian government is prepared to offer only maximum autonomy within a federation, whereas the Abkhaz will accept nothing less than a confederation.

The Commonwealth of Independent States summit in Moscow in January 1996 imposed an economic blockade on Abkhazia at Shevardnadze's urging. The mandate of the CIS peacekeepers deployed in Abkhazia was extended in January, March, and again in late July, but Shevardnadze's request that they be given police powers to protect ethnic Georgians wishing to return to their homes in Abkhazia was rejected. A meeting in late December among Georgian, Abkhaz, and Russian representatives to negotiate terms for the return to Abkhazia of the ethnic Georgian refugees failed to reach agreement, as Abkhaz Foreign Minister Konstantin Ozgan linked repatriation to the lifting of the economic sanctions imposed on Abkhazia in January.

In August, 14 opposition parties no longer represented in parliament formed a committee to agitate for the withdrawal from Georgia of all Russian military personnel. Bilateral relations with Russia cooled further in October, after the Georgian parliament condemned as illegal the Abkhaz leadership's decision to hold parliamentary elections on 23 November and voted to form a state commission to reassess Georgia's entire policy toward Russia, including the issue of Russian military bases. UN objections that elections should not be held in Abkhazia prior to the return of Georgian refugees to their homes in the region failed to persuade the Abkhaz leadership to postpone the poll. The estimated 200,000 Georgians constrained to flee from their homes in Abkhazia during the fighting condemned the vote almost unanimously in a simultaneous referendum organized by the Georgian authorities.

Shevardnadze and Lyudwig Chibirov, the parliament chairman of the self-declared Republic of South Ossetia (where a peacekeeping force from the Organization for Security and Cooperation in Europe has been deployed since mid-1992) signed an agreement in Moscow in May abjuring the use of force and economic sanctions. At a second meeting in the North Ossetiya capital,

Vladikavkaz, in late August, the two also reaffirmed their commitment to finding a peaceful solution to the issue of South Ossetia's future status within Georgia. In November, Chibirov was elected South Ossetian president in an election that was not recognized as valid by either Georgia or the international community. As in the case of Abkhazia, there was minimal progress toward resolving the issue of South Ossetia's status regarding Tbilisi; the region remains almost totally dependent on financial support from Moscow. A bloc composed of Shevardnadze's Union of Citizens of Georgia and the All-Georgian Union of Revival headed by parliament chairman Aslan Abashidze won the majority of seats in parliamentary elections in the autonomous republic of Adzharia, bordering Turkey, in September.

Georgia's relations with its southern neighbor, Armenia, were clouded by demands for greater autonomy on the part of the predominantly ethnic Armenian population of the south Georgian raions of Akhalkalaki and Akhaltsikhe, which Armenia's President Levon Ter-Petrossyan toured during an official visit to Georgia in June.

Economic activity in Georgia was mostly positive. During the early months of the year, the Georgian parliament reluctantly amended first the annual budget and then laws on land ownership and taxation, thereby meeting conditions set by the International Monetary Fund for a $246 million loan to support ongoing economic reform in 1996–1998. The World Bank allocated a $20 million loan in February to reform the transport sector and a further $14 million in April to restructure the health service. In March, Shevardnadze and Azerbaijan's President Heidar Aliev signed an agreement on construction of a major pipeline to export Azerbaijani oil via Georgia.

The economic upswing begun in 1995 continued. During the first half of the year, gross domestic product grew by 8 percent and industrial output by 10 percent; inflation fell to an annual rate of about 30 percent, and the lari maintained its value against the U.S. dollar. Up to 20 percent of the work force was unemployed, however, and widespread poverty led to increases in infant mortality and tuberculosis.

Sidebar: FORMER GEORGIAN DEFENSE MINISTER SENTENCED

by ELIZABETH FULLER

On 8 October, a Tbilisi district court finally passed sentence on Georgian warlord and former defense minister Tengiz Kitovani and two aides implicated with him in an apparently heroic but futile attempt to restore Georgian control over the breakaway Black Sea region of Abkhazia by military conquest. In January 1995, some 350 members of Kitovani's self-styled National Front for the Liberation of Abkhazia were intercepted by Georgian police on their way west from Tbilisi to the Georgian-Abkhaz border. Following an 11–month investigation and a nine-month trial, the 58–year-old Kitovani was sentenced to eight years' imprisonment on charges of organizing an illegal armed formation and illegal possession of arms. Former deputy Georgian Prime Minister Irakli Surguladze was sentenced to 21 months' imprisonment but released, given that he had been in custody since January 1995. A second Kitovani aide, Valerii Fisyun, received a six-year sentence.

Kitovani's trial was more than merely the epitaph to a romantic and unrealistic crusade: it also marked a further milestone in the systematic attempt by Georgian President Eduard Shevardnadze to neutralize any individual who could conceivably pose a challenge to him. A sculptor by profession, Kitovani had been appointed commander of Georgia's embryonic National Guard in the summer of 1991 by the country's newly elected president, Zviad Gamsakhurdia—his friend since childhood. Within months, however, Kitovani had aligned himself with a group of senior government officials and members of the intelligentsia who were alarmed at Gamsakhurdia's irrational and dictatorial leadership style, and called for his resignation. In December 1991, Kitovani joined forces with Dzhaba Ioseliani, head of the informal Mkhedrioni paramilitary. The two private armies (with backing from the Russian military garrison in Georgia, according to some reports) launched an attack on the central parliament building in Tbilisi where Gamsakhurdia was ensconced, and after 10 days of heavy fighting forced him to flee the country. In order to overcome the crisis of legitimacy precipitated by the ouster of Georgia's legally elected president and the simultaneous collapse of the USSR, Ioseliani and Kitovani persuaded former Soviet Foreign Minister Eduard Shevardnadze (who from 1972 to 1985 had been Georgian Communist Party first secretary) to return to Tbilisi and head a new national leadership.

Observers have speculated that the two warlords had intended to install Shevardnadze as a figurehead and run affairs in Georgia themselves, lining their Swiss bank accounts in the process with the proceeds from black market trading in gasoline and other commodities (including, in Ioseliani's case, narcotics). Shevardnadze himself admitted in subsequent interviews that he had greatly underestimated the problems that faced him on his return. He also hinted that it was Kitovani (by then minister of defense) who, in August 1992, precipitated the fighting in Abkhazia that culminated in Georgia's loss of jurisdiction over the region 13 months later. In May 1993, Kitovani was fired as minister of defense amid rumors that he was preparing a putsch against Shevardnadze. After spending some time in Russia, Kitovani returned to Tbilisi in the summer of 1994. Together with Tengiz Sigua (who had served as prime minister first under Gamsakhurdia and then under Shevardnadze) and Boris Kakubava, leader of the 200,000 ethnic Georgians forced to flee Abkhazia during the fighting in 1992, Kitovani founded the National Front for the Liberation of Abkhazia in the autumn of 1994.

When Kitovani's abortive crusade was halted in January 1995, Georgian security officials claimed that the real aim of the operation had been to gather a small army in western Georgia with the aim of marching on Tbilisi and ousting Shevardnadze. Kitovani himself insisted that his trial, which was described by one Russian journalist as "a tragi-farce with elements of the absurd," was politically motivated. One Georgian observer commented that "whatever the length of the sentence, as long as Shevardnadze is in power Kitovani will remain in prison."

With Kitovani's co-warlord Dzhaba Ioseliani currently in jail under investigation on charges of murder and high treason, the most prominent member of the 1992 Georgian leadership still at liberty is Tengiz Sigua. Sigua was, however, subjected to harsh criticism in fall 1996 for alleged illicit financial deals involving millions of dollars from the state budget, but has published (in *Shansi,* the newspaper of the opposition Republican Party) official documentation refuting those charges.

Meanwhile, with Kitovani safely under lock and key, Shevardnadze could turn his attention to the problem that the former was hoping to solve: Abkhazia. Ironically, Shevardnadze came under increasing pressure from the radical chairman of the Abkhaz parliament in exile, Tamaz Nadareishvili, to embark on precisely the course of action for which Kitovani was sentenced—a military campaign to restore Tbilisi's control over Abkhazia.

Azerbaijan

Population:	7,529,000
Capital:	Baku (pop. 1,550,000)
Major cities:	Genje (pop. 232,000), Sumgait (pop. 190,000)
Area:	86,600 sq. km.
Major ethnic groups:	Azeri 90%, Russian 5%
Economy:	GDP growth: 1%
	Inflation rate: 7%
	Average monthly income: $19
	Unemployment rate: 1.1%

AZERBAIJANI LEADERSHIP BROOKS NO OPPOSITION

by ELIZABETH FULLER

Politically motivated trials, executions, and firings dominated a year in which the ruling party of Heidar Aliev continued to render the opposition practically invisible, while the Karabakh conflict remained at an impasse.

President Heidar Aliev's autocratic and authoritarian rule showed no signs of weakening in 1996. A former first secretary of the Communist Party of Azerbaijan, Aliev returned to the forefront of Azerbaijani politics in June 1993 following the peaceful ouster of Abulfaz Elchibey, and he was elected president in October of that year. Since then, he has used the state apparatus to marginalize political opponents. The overwhelming majority of deputies to the new Milli Majlis (People's Assembly) elected in November 1995 are loyal Aliev supporters.

Several former government ministers and high-ranking military officers went on trial in 1996 on charges of attempting either to overthrow or assassinate the aging president. Former National Security Minister Nariman Imranov and Deputy Defense Minister Alikram Gummetov were sentenced to death in February, and former Agriculture Minister Muzamil Abdullaev in March, for their role in an alleged coup attempt in October 1994. Twenty-one people, including three former army generals, went on trial in October on charges of planning to assassinate Aliev in August 1995, and Rasim Agaev, press secretary to former President Ayaz Mutalibov, was arrested for treason in that connection in November.

Several groups of members of the OPON special police force, which was formally abolished in March 1995 in the wake of an alleged insurrection by its chief, Deputy Interior Minister Rovshan Djavadov, were also brought to trial. In March 1996, 26 former OPON officers were sentenced—and 23 more in April—to up to 15 years in prison; a group of 37 more went on trial in October, and 19 more former OPON personnel were arrested in December.

In late April, the Russian authorities extradited to Baku former Defense Minister Rahim Gaziev, who had been arrested on charges of treason in late 1993 but escaped from detention in 1994 and fled to Moscow. Gaziev was sentenced to death in absentia in February 1996. Former President Ayaz Mutalibov was also apprehended in April by Russian security officials in Moscow, where he has lived since his ouster in May 1992, but he was released after one month in detention.

In late November, political journalist and commentator Rasim Agaev, former press spokesman for Mutalibov, was detained by police in Baku and charged with treason. That move was interpreted by Azerbaijani analysts as possibly presaging a witch hunt against the intelligentsia and the independent media, given that Agaev has been characterized by *Rossiiskaya gazeta* as "one of the most law-abiding individuals imaginable."

By contrast, two former leading members of the opposition Azerbaijan Popular Front were treated with comparative leniency. Former Foreign Minister Tofik Gasymov, who was arrested in September 1995 and charged with involvement in the Djavadov "coup attempt" of that March, was released in February on grounds of failing health. Gasymov's trial, scheduled for May, was postponed indefinitely, but Turkish national Kenan Gurel and former Mutalibov aide Adil Gadjiev, who were brought to trial in the same case, were sentenced in September to 15 and 14 years' imprisonment, respectively. Former Popular Front deputy chairman Arif Pashaev was given amnesty in June after receiving a five-year sentence.

POLITICAL OPPRESSION

International human-rights organizations expressed concern at the growing number of apparently politically motivated trials and at reports that prisoners have been subjected to torture and ill-treatment during investigation: for example, three of the 37 OPON members whose trial began in October were found on examination to be suffering from fractured ribs, and others alleged they had been subjected to electric shocks. Interior Minister Ramil Usubov, a close associate of Aliev, has denied such reports. A representative from the International Committee of the Red Cross who traveled to Baku in December warned, however, that the track record of the Azerbaijani authorities, specifically the refusal to allow Red Cross representatives access to prisoners, could adversely affect the country's chances of being granted membership in the Council of Europe, for which Azerbaijan formally applied in July.

Azerbaijan's splintered political opposition had been rendered virtually irrelevant by the November 1995 parliamentary elections, in which representatives from the three most influential opposition parties won only six seats in the new 125–member Milli Majlis. (The remaining seats were shared by Aliev's Yeni Azerbaycan party and nominally independent candidates.) Three more opposition candidates won mandates in repeat elections in February. Proposed tactical alliances between several of the smaller opposition parties not represented in the Milli Majlis and a failed attempt in February by the parliamentary opposition to force a vote of no confidence in the government had no impact on policy. Delegates to a People's Convention held in April to assess the political aftereffects of the March 1995 so-called Djavadov insurrection castigated the opposition as a threat to the country's sovereignty, thereby exacerbating the climate of oppression.

At a government meeting in July, broadcast live on state television, Aliev blamed Prime Minister Fuad Kuliev for the "serious" state of the economy, after which Kuliev submitted his resignation "on grounds of ill health." Several other ministers and senior officials with responsibility for economic affairs, privatization, and transport were either fired or cautioned for inefficiency. Artur Rasi-

Zade, named acting prime minister, was confirmed in that post in November and is said to enjoy both Aliev's confidence and a reputation for intelligence, efficiency, and resourcefulness. Parliament speaker Rasul Guliev resigned in September shortly after his criticism of the government's economic policy (published in a Russian journal) incurred harsh censure from parliament deputies. Elderly academic Murtuz Alesqerov, who was chosen as his successor in October, has taken steps to curb adverse coverage by the opposition press of the parliament's proceedings, personally revoking the accreditation of a journalist with the Azerbaijan Popular Front newspaper *Azadlyg*.

The ongoing economic decline showed signs of subsiding: in August, the gross domestic product grew 1 percent in 1996, compared with drops of 30 percent in 1992–1994 and 17 percent in 1995. Prime Minister Rasi-Zade pointed in October to a fall in consumer prices and a reduction in inflation as evidence of incipient stabilization. In late summer, International Monetary Fund officials expressed cautious approval of Azerbaijan's monetary policy but made disbursement of a further $300 million loan contingent on raising domestic oil prices. Privatization of small state-owned enterprises began in June but is proceeding only sluggishly. Meanwhile, two major oil deals were signed: in June, Western, Russian, Iranian, and Turkish oil companies formed a consortium to exploit the large Shah-Deniz offshore Caspian oil field, and in December, a consortium of U.S., Saudi Arabian, and Japanese companies signed a $2 billion contract with Azerbaijan's state oil company to develop two further offshore deposits.

FOREIGN POLICY STATUS QUO

Despite several rounds of negotiations mediated by Russia and the Organization for Security and Cooperation in Europe (OSCE) Minsk Group, no progress was made toward a settlement of the Karabakh conflict. Karabakh Armenian forces continue to control seven raions of Azerbaijan that border on the self-proclaimed Republic of Nagorno-Karabakh and account for some 9 percent of the country's total territory, according to *Nezavisimaya gazeta* on 12 March. The election in November of a president of Nagorno-Karabakh (Robert Kocharyan) was condemned as potentially destabilizing by the Azerbaijani leadership and the international community. Intensive behind-the-scenes diplomacy on the part of the United States within the framework of the Minsk Group failed to persuade the leaderships of Armenia and Azerbaijan to agree to a declaration on principles for a settlement of the Karabakh conflict, to be signed at the OSCE summit in Lisbon in early December. At the summit itself, Aliev threatened to veto the proposed draft final document to be adopted by all participants unless it was amended to include an affirmation that signatories recognize Azerbaijan's territorial integrity. Armenian President Levon Ter-Petrossyan, for his part, objected to that proposed addition. The deadlock was resolved by the adoption of the disputed passage as a separate "chairman's" document.

The Lezgins—an ethnic minority whose traditional homeland straddles the

Russian-Azerbaijani frontier—continued to agitate for an independent state. (Estimates of the total number of Lezgins vary from half a million to 1 million, divided more or less equally between Dagestan and Azerbaijan.) In October, Lezgin activists demanded a share of the tariffs from the export to the Russian Federation of Azerbaijan's Caspian oil (the Baku-Tikhoretsk-Novorossiisk pipeline runs through territories claimed by the Lezgins as their historic homeland) and threatened violence if their demands were not met. Two Lezgins were sentenced to death in May for setting off a bomb in the Baku metro in 1994 that killed 14 people.

In late summer, following a meeting between Aliev and Russian Prime Minister Viktor Chernomyrdin, the Russian government finally agreed to open the frontier with Azerbaijan, which had been closed in December 1994 when Russian troops invaded Chechnya. The move did little, however, to improve the strained relations between the two countries.

Relations with Iran likewise remained acrimonious. Visiting Baku in early March, Iranian Foreign Minister Ali Akbar Velayati was subjected to criticism by his Azerbaijani counterpart Hasan Hasanov, who accused Tehran of openly siding with Armenia in the Karabakh conflict; Velayati countered by reproaching the Azerbaijani leadership for pursuing ties with Israel. In April and May, five leading members of the pro-Iranian Islamic Party of Azerbaijan were arrested; the head of Azerbaijan's security service subsequently hinted that they would be tried on charges of espionage. When Hasanov traveled to Tehran in late August, he was told by Iranian deputy parliament speaker Ali Akbar Nateq Nuri that an improvement in bilateral relations was contingent on Baku cracking down on adverse Azerbaijani media coverage of developments in Iran, specifically reprisals against ethnic Azeris in provinces bordering on Azerbaijan. Political differences did not, however, preclude Iranian participation in the Shah-Deniz consortium or the signing of bilateral agreements on economic cooperation and strengthening border controls to counter illicit trafficking in drugs and arms.

In early April, Mesut Yilmaz (who was then Turkish prime minister) visited Baku to sign an agreement on more intensive economic cooperation; he failed, however, to persuade Aliev to pressure the consortium of Western companies engaged in exploiting three major Caspian oil fields to make a firm commitment to export the oil through a projected pipeline from Baku to the Turkish terminal at Ceyhan in the eastern Mediterranean. Piqued, the Turkish leadership subsequently withdrew its offer to finance major reconstruction of an existing pipeline from Baku to Georgia's Black Sea port of Batumi. As in the case of Iran, however, tensions in one sphere of bilateral relations did not impinge on cooperation in another: for example, during a visit to Ankara in June, Defense Minister Safar Abiev and Turkish Chief of Staff General Ismail Karadayi signed a bilateral agreement on military cooperation. Two high-level Turkish military delegations traveled to Baku during the latter half of the year.

Sidebar: AZERBAIJAN'S PARLIAMENT ELECTS NEW SPEAKER

by ELIZABETH FULLER

On 16 October, Azerbaijan's Milli Mejlis (parliament) voted by an overwhelming majority to elect Murtuz Nadjaf ogly Alesqerov, the 68–year-old rector of Baku State University, as its new speaker. Alesqerov replaced 48–year-old Rasul Guliev, a multimillionaire and former director of one of Baku's two major oil refineries, who was characterized by one local political observer as the "most rational and pragmatic representative of the party of power."

Long considered a favorite of septuagenarian president Heidar Aliev, and thus a bitter rival of Foreign Minister Hasan Hasanov (both men have been viewed as possible successors to Aliev), Guliev resigned as parliament speaker in September, ostensibly for health reasons. His departure from the political scene had been widely anticipated for months in light of rumors of an estrangement between him and the president, but it was in all likelihood precipitated by an interview he had given in August to the Russian journal *Novoe vremya* criticizing government policy. Specifically, Guliev had deplored the inability of Azerbaijan's leadership to systematically implement economic reform. He argued that stubborn resistance by the bureaucracy had led to the virtual collapse of the economy and to the impoverishment of much of the population and pointed out that if change did not come from above, there was an increasing danger of revolution from below. The Milli Mejlis faction from Aliev's Yeni Azerbaycan (New Azerbaijan) party issued a statement on 9 September accusing Guliev of "attempting to destabilize the situation in the country, damaging Azerbaijan's international image, and facilitating the sale of state property to criminals." Guliev resigned two days later.

Murtuz Alesqerov is a longtime Aliev associate. A lawyer by training, he was a member of the commission that drafted the new Azerbaijani constitution adopted by a nationwide referendum in November 1995. Like the president, he was born in the exclave of Nakhichevan. After graduating in 1950 from Baku State University, he embarked on postgraduate studies in Moscow and taught for decades at the Institute for State and Law. (Aliev, it will be recalled, served in Moscow as first deputy chairman of the USSR Council of Ministers from 1982 to 1987.) Alesqerov returned to Baku at some point in the late 1980s and was for a time a member of the board of the unofficial Azerbaijan Popular Front, but left that organization in 1991. As of 1992, he and a group of like-minded colleagues began planning the return to mainstream Azerbaijani politics of Heidar Aliev, who had returned from Moscow to Nakhichevan in 1990 and was subsequently elected chairman of the local Soviet. Murtuzov was also one of the founding members of the Yeni Azerbaycan party, which Aliev created in early 1992 as his personal power base, and which currently holds a clear majority in the Milli Mejlis.

While Murtuzov is clearly a loyal Aliev ally, there are grounds to suspect that his election may have been the result of a compromise between the parliament and the president. The Milli Mejlis had failed at its first attempt—on 30 September—to agree on one candidate from a field of five that also included Mahmud Mamedkuliev, Aliev's son-in-law and Azerbaijan's Ambassador in London; Ramiz Mekhtiev, head of Aliev's presidential staff and a former Communist Party Central Committee secretary for ideology; Minister of Health Ali Insanov; and Nakhichevan parliament speaker Vagif Talybov. (All four, like Alesqerov, are members of Yeni Azerbaycan.) By mid-October, several other names had been added to that list, including the head of the Yeni Azerbaycan faction in the Milli Mejlis, Ali Nagiev (who apparently withdrew: it was he who ultimately proposed Alesqerov's candidacy). Local agencies report that consultations on 15 October between Aliev and Milli Mejlis deputies on the relative merits of the various candidates lasted five hours, and had unfolded "in a stormy atmosphere"—a formulation that implies a degree of dissent between the Milli Mejlis and the increasingly authoritarian and unpredictable president.

Document: STANDING UP TO RUSSIA

One of the founders of the Popular Front of Azerbaijan, Hikmet Hadjy-zadeh was also deputy prime minister and ambassador to Russia under the Elchibey government in 1992 and 1993. He wrote this article for Transition *journal in March 1997, when he was the chief analyst for the Musavat Party.*

Transcaucasian governments have not been particularly stable or democratic in recent years. Georgia is struggling with two regions that want to secede, Armenia's most recent election was widely condemned as rigged, and Azerbaijan's authoritarian leadership has been loath to allow the democratic opposition much room to maneuver. Many Western analysts have apparently come to the conclusion that the peoples of the Transcaucasus are simply not ready for democracy.

In their coverage both of the 1993 coup that overthrew the democratically elected government of Abulfaz Elchibey in Azerbaijan and of falsification in the November 1995 parliamentary elections, numerous Western publications quoted Azerbaijanis as saying that their nation has been given freedom but does not know what to do with it. It seems foreign journalists and editors are all too ready to offer that as the explanation for all the country's problems.

Of course we are not as ready to accept democracy as would have been desirable. But to what extent is our failure to establish a stable democracy determined by our unreadiness? Are there not other reasons? Why do scholars and observers pay so little attention to the induced instability in our countries—and, most especially, to the role of Russia?

It is well known that tension imposed on a country from outside often results in the growth of separatism, ethnic nationalism, and paternalism. Democracy cannot successfully develop in the permanent state of emergency in which we have found ourselves. Our situation is perhaps determined by our location—we are too far from God and too near to Russia.

A POLICY OF EXPANSION

Russia's view is basically this: Western countries have, at present, lost their ability to maintain an active foreign policy and are preoccupied with domestic affairs. So there will not be any particularly fervent resistance to Russian expansion in the CIS. However, the argument goes, Russia should not overestimate its ability to maintain political and economic stability in CIS countries. The mistakes of the Soviet Union mustn't be repeated. As it would be extremely expensive to form a federal state (not to mention that such a move would set Western countries against Russia), it seems more pragmatic to keep the formal independence of CIS countries in exchange for unlimited access to their resources, their markets, and their stocks and services. . . .

Could Russia accept a new reality—the independence of its former vassal states—and leave the Caucasus alone? Never! The lust for empire that was so quickly restored to Russian politicians dictates quite a different policy. "If we leave the Caucasus," they think, "others will come—Turks, Americans. And no matter who comes, the Transcaucasian republics will be lost to us." It does not enter their minds that the colonialist concept of spheres of influence has no place anymore. We are now on the threshold of the 21st century, the century of democracy, with the disappearance of borders and unification efforts all over the world, and such ambitions should be history.

Yet even Yeltsin's 1996 re-election brought no change in policy on the Transcaucasus. With the nationalist forces strong in the Duma, the president and his revamped team are required to maintain a pro-imperial attitude. Troublesome countries such as Azerbaijan and Georgia are threatened with dismemberment.

Russia exploited the problem of the ethnic Armenian enclave of Nagorno-Karabakh, located in Azerbaijan, to sow local dissension and reap its own gains. After achieving victory over Azerbaijan in alliance with Russia, Armenia fell under Russia's military, political, and economic domination. It is impossible for Armenia to continue its military operations on Azerbaijani territory without Russian support.

Armenia's borders are guarded by the Russian army. According to an agreement negotiated in Russia's interest, Russia may keep military bases on Armenian territory for 25 years. From those bases, military operations are being carried out against Azerbaijan, a country that has persisted in objecting to the Russian style of regional integration.

Russia has also maintained its interests in Georgia—to the utmost. Because of Russian support for Abkhaz separatists, the Georgian government was forced to join the CIS, to sign the agreement on the collective security of the commonwealth, and to allow three Russian military bases on Georgian territory. Some 300,000 refugees from Sukhumi, an area ravaged by Russian bombers during the Abkhaz conflict, still cannot return home. Georgia has lost control over its region of South Ossetia, which is now guarded by the Russian army. Civil war between the supporters of former President Gamsakhurdia and the current president, Eduard Shevardnadze—a war that was stirred up by Russia—has rendered the country lifeless. About a million people have left Georgia as economic emigrants. One can hardly speak about democracy in such a situation.

Russia has another interest in Georgia: Russian policymakers think it will be difficult to secure Armenia's cooperation unless Georgia is totally dependent on Russia, because Russia has no border with Armenia. Russia can reach Armenia only through Georgia or Azerbaijan.

Azerbaijan, for its part, has long been a thorn in Russia's side. It was the first CIS republic to gain the withdrawal of the Russian army and border guards from its territory. That occurred, of course, during the democratic government of Elchibey, which reoriented the country toward the West.

Of course, Russia took vengeance on Azerbaijani democrats for pursuing an independent policy. In June 1993, Elchibey's government fell, toppled by rebels backed by Russia. Just afterward, Russia helped Armenia occupy four regions on the territory of Azerbaijan, beyond the borders of Nagorno-Karabakh. The war caused former Communist Party leader Heidar Aliev, who had taken over the country, to declare a state of emergency. Azerbaijan was then tricked into joining the CIS by Grachev, who assured Aliev that Russia would immediately help Azerbaijan push Armenian troops out of the occupied lands. But in October, a month after Azerbaijan had joined the CIS, Russia instead helped Armenia occupy two more regions in Azerbaijan.

Russia has hinted that it might annex some Azerbaijani land for the Lezgins, a minority living in an area that straddles the Russian-Azerbaijani border. Such threats have several aims. Moscow wants Baku's consent to station Russian troops on Azerbaijan's borders and to allow Russian military bases on Azerbaijani territory. It wants Azerbaijan to recognize it as the only negotiator in the Karabakh conflict and to allow Russian "peacekeeping troops" to settle there. Perhaps most of all, Russia wants to take an active role in the extraction of Azerbaijan's oil. Russia has even suggested that the oil under the Caspian Sea shelf near Azerbaijan is the common property of all Caspian countries. (In the USSR, the Caspian basin and its shelf had been divided among the republics as an internal reservoir.) Russia also wants to ensure that all oil extracted from Azerbaijan, Kazakstan, and Turkmenistan is piped through Russian territory; otherwise, Russians think, they will lose leverage over those countries.

Furthermore, Azerbaijan is of great strategic value for Russia. A glance at a map shows that in the territory of the former USSR all the railways from Russia to Iran and to the oil-bearing fields of the Persian Gulf cut straight through Azerbaijan.

There is, of course, a philosophical reason for Russian opposition to true Azerbaijani independence. An independent, democratic Azerbaijan would be an attractive example for Turkmenistan, Uzbekistan, Kazakstan, and Tajikistan—all Central Asian countries trying to resist Russian influence—to follow.

So far, Russia has been unable to force Azerbaijan to agree to its demands. But how long can Azerbaijan stand against its huge and powerful neighbor without any support from the West? If Armenia goes on occupying district after district of Azerbaijani territory, Aliev will have no choice but to accept "Russian-style integration." It is already becoming increasingly difficult for democrats in the country to suggest any alternatives.

AZERBAIJAN IS CORNERED

Russia has other opportunities, besides the Karabakh crisis, to exert influence over Azerbaijan. About 40 percent of Azerbaijan's trade is with Russia. The recent closing of Russia's border as a result of the Chechnya conflict plunged the Azerbaijani economy into a desperate state. In addition, there are some 300,000 ethnic Russians in Azerbaijan. Russia cites the need to protect that minority as grounds for interference, even though their cultural rights were already guaranteed by an Elchibey decree on the rights of ethnic minorities.

Russia also takes an active part in shoring up the separatist aspirations of the Lezgins, in the north of the republic, and the Talish, who live in the south. Lately, Russia and Armenia have been trying to raise the question of the status of the Kurdish people in Azerbaijan. Armenian propaganda alleges that most regions in Azerbaijan occupied by Armenia contain pockets of Kurds who favor Armenian rule.

The representatives of the former communist nomenklatura in Azerbaijan are also, predictably, pro-Russian. That well-connected force—associated with financial, commercial, and industrial groups—is headed by former President Ayaz Mutalibov (who now lives in Russia) and is Russia's main hope for restoring its control.

Former Soviet agents are part of the nomenklatura. Elchibey's National Security Ministry estimated that about 100,000 people were linked with the KGB and other Soviet secret services in Azerbaijan. A great number of supporters of Russia belong to the supreme officer's corps of the Azerbaijani army.

Iranian secret services are also intensifying their efforts in Azerbaijan. When the democrats were in power (briefly), about 100 Iranian agents and Azerbaijani collaborators were arrested. Fundamentalist Iran, even more than Russian imperialists, does not want to see an open society near it, considering that about 20 million ethnic Azerbaijani Turks live in Iran. Clearly, the aims of Russia and Iran are similar.

The military coup d'etat instigated by Russia in the summer of 1993 was a terrible blow to democracy in Azerbaijan. In Freedom House reports on human rights, Azerbaijan dropped a category from a "partly free country" in 1993 to a "not free country" in 1994 and 1995. Still, in spite of the severe censorship and the mass arrests of democrats, it has proved impossible to turn back society to the Stalinist era. As the result of an unceasing three-year political struggle, the democratic community has gained government recognition for opposition political parties and partial freedom for the mass media. Best of all, the present government has had to continue along the foreign-policy path, forged by the democrats, toward independence and integration with the democratic world community.

Obviously, without the support of the world democratic community, Azerbaijan won't stand long against Russia and Iran. The loss of Azerbaijan for the West means the loss of prospects for a successful struggle against Russian expansion to the south and against Iranian fundamentalism; the loss of a base from which to support democratic processes in Central Asian countries; and, naturally, the loss of access to markets in those countries.

Armenia

Population:	3,754,300
Capital:	Yerevan (pop. 1,200,200)
Major cities:	Gyumri (pop. 207,000), Vanadzor (pop.146,000)
Area:	29,800 sq. km.
Major ethnic groups:	Armenian 93.3%, Kurdish 1.7%, Russian 1.5% (est.), other 3.5%
Economy:	GDP growth: 4%
	Inflation rate: 6%
	Average monthly income: $23
	Unemployment rate: 9.7%

A CRISIS OF LEGITIMACY IN ARMENIA
by EMIL DANIELYAN

Nobody could have predicted that in 1996, President Levon Ter-Petrossyan and his Armenian Pan-National Movement (HHSh) would face the strongest challenge yet to their more than six-year rule. Having virtually unlimited power given him by the new constitution as well as the overwhelming support of a weak parliament, Ter-Petrossyan seemed to have little reason to worry about his political future. The Dashnak party, a well-organized and reportedly the strongest opposition force, had been banned, and the opposition as a whole was weak and fragmented after its crushing defeat in the July 1995 parliamentary elections, which had been described by international observers as "free but not fair." So the presidential election scheduled for 22 September was considered by most commentators to be a mere formality that would legitimize a second five-year term for Ter-Petrossyan.

Speaking at the seventh congress of the HHSh in December 1995, Ter-Petrossyan announced that the new class of private owners was going to be his social base. Apparently having realized that the popularity of the HHSh was waning, Ter-Petrossyan called for the creation of a new, powerful right-wing party that would resemble "the British Conservative Party or the Republican Party in the United States." The new party, according to Ter-Petrossyan, would be set up on the basis of the Hanrapetutyun (Republic) bloc, which includes the HHSh and five other small parties and holds a majority of seats in parliament. It was to protect the interests of entrepreneurs and affluent farmers. The creation of the Union of Industrialists and Entrepreneurs in April and the Agrarian-Peasant Union in June were the first steps toward the realization of Ter-Petrossyan's aspirations. Yet both organizations seem to have failed to attract a large following, and some observers suggested they were nothing but old Soviet-style nomenklatura formations. Indeed, the Union of Industrialists and Entrepreneurs was mainly composed of directors of state-owned enterprises, while the Agrarian-Peasant Union simply brought together local government officials dealing with agriculture.

ELECTION DEBACLE

The beginning of the presidential-election campaign was rather calm, as most observers and media harbored no doubts about Ter-Petrossyan's victory. Following the initial failure by the main opposition parties to put forward a single candidate, the outcome of the election seemed a foregone conclusion. In light of Ter-Petrossyan's good chances for re-election, it was widely believed that—in contrast to the July 1995 parliamentary elections and referendum, which were marred by serious irregularities—the authorities would do everything to ensure that the vote was free and fair in order to boost Armenia's tarnished image in the West. The registration of candidates went smoothly, with almost no complaints from opposition parties.

The turning point in the campaign was the 10 September announcement by the five opposition parties that they were uniting behind one candidate, Vazgen Manukyan, leader of the National Democratic Union and former prime minister. The three other opposition candidates, Paruyr Hayrikyan, Aram Sarkisyan, and Lenser Aghalovyan, withdrew from the race. The newly formed National Accord Bloc, joined by the Dashnak party, declared the establishment of democracy in Armenia as its main goal and warned against the "impending HHSh dictatorship." Manukyan pledged that, if elected, he would form a coalition government and hold new parliamentary elections. The National Accord platform also called for the adoption of a new constitution. The number of candidates had decreased to four, but it was clear the ballot was going to be a two-horse race between Ter-Petrossyan and Manukyan, the two former comrades-in-arms. It was after 10 September that the government's propaganda machine (state-run television, in particular) started to work at full capacity. Just two days before the election, Ter-Petrossyan warned the voters in a televised address that if Manukyan came to power, the war in Nagorno-Karabakh might resume and Armenia would face other disastrous consequences.

Following the announcement of the official vote results that gave Ter-Petrossyan 51.8 percent of the vote and Manukyan 41.3 percent, supporters of Manukyan took to the streets and accused the authorities of falsifying the election. The protests culminated in clashes with security forces on 25 September as some protesters burst into the parliament building and took parliament speaker Babken Ararktsyan and his deputy Ara Sahakyan hostage. In response, Ter-Petrossyan ordered troops into the streets of Yerevan and arrested more than 50 opposition activists (as many as 250, according to some estimates), including six deputies who had been stripped of their immunity. He sealed the headquarters of Manukyan's National Democratic Union and of another constituent party in the National Accord Bloc.

Two major international election-observer groups, the OSCE's Warsaw Office for Democratic Institutions and Human Rights and the U.S.-based International Foundation for Election Systems, questioned the validity of the official figures, noting the discrepancy between the number of ballots cast and the number of registered voters and citing numerous other irregularities. The election was also condemned by the European Parliament, which called for a new round of voting in those electoral districts where the "serious violations" took place.

Meanwhile, the opposition on 24 October filed a formal appeal with the Constitutional Court, asking that it annul the election results. Manukyan's campaign officials submitted a document of more than 500 pages, containing, they said, evidence of election rigging. But the opposition leaders said that they did not expect the court—half of whose members had been appointed by Ter-Petrossyan and the other half by the HHSh-controlled parliament—to rule in their favor and that the move was merely an effort to demonstrate their adherence to law. Hence, the court's decision on 22 November to reject the opposition's appeal did not come as a surprise.

NEW GOVERNMENT, OLD PROBLEMS

On 4 November, Prime Minister Hrant Bagratyan announced his resignation, following Ter-Petrossyan's post-election promise of a "serious reshuffle" and statements by some HHSh leaders who blamed him for Ter-Petrossyan's poorer-than-expected performance in the election. A staunch supporter of radical economic reform and tight monetary policies, the 38–year-old Bagratyan had been credited by the West for Armenia's good macroeconomic indicators. Despite the blockade of trade routes by Azerbaijan and Turkey and the conflict over Nagorno-Karabakh, since late 1994 Bagratyan's government had managed to achieve slow but steady economic growth (the first in the Commonwealth of Independent States) and to curb inflation. It was during his tenure that Armenia became one of the biggest per-capita recipients of loans from the world's leading financial organizations. Speaking at his last news conference, Bagratyan said his main achievement as premier was an "ideological revolution" in a society that now sees no alternative to a market economy.

The privatization process continued throughout 1996. Although hundreds of state enterprises have been privatized—often at ridiculously low prices—few of them became efficient and competitive businesses. The privatization did not result in an influx of capital to the economy, nor did it bring substantial incomes to the state budget. Bagratyan's privatization program had consequently been criticized by the opposition and a group of leading enterprise directors headed by Ter-Petrossyan's older brother. But Bagratyan's cabinet was repeatedly praised by international financial organizations. In September, the International Monetary Fund approved a second $25 million tranche of a $148 million loan for economic stabilization. In October, the World Bank decided to allocate some $200 million in credits for Armenia.

For the majority of Armenians, however, macroeconomic stabilization has failed to bring any tangible benefits, and that is perhaps the reason the opposition, which bitterly criticized the government's socioeconomic policies, did so well in the 22 September vote. Bagratyan's resignation was seen by many observers as an attempt by Ter-Petrossyan to appease the opposition and its sizable electorate.

Armen Sarkisyan, the 43–year-old newly appointed prime minister, was a new figure in Armenian domestic politics. A physicist by training, Sarkisyan had been Armenia's ambassador to Britain since 1992. The fact that Ter-Petrossyan chose a diplomat rather than a trained economist to head the new government suggested that, in light of the country's gradual economic recovery, his priority is to promote internal dialogue and reconciliation.

The government of the newly appointed Prime Minister Sarkisyan got a vote of confidence from the parliament on 29 November. Sarkisyan said a "qualitative improvement" of reforms would be his government's top priority, ITAR-TASS reported. Many interpreted the change of government as an attempt by Ter-Petrossyan to appease the opposition and its sizable electorate. Yet the change was probably not sweeping enough to satisfy the opposition. Even though the controversial interior minister, Vano Siradeghyan, was replaced and his ministry merged with the National Security Ministry, he was immediately appointed mayor of Yerevan. Defense Minister Vazgen Sarkisyan and National Security Minister Serzh Sarkisyan retained their posts. Thus, the three men considered by the opposition to be the main organizers of the alleged vote rigging remained in power and will undoubtedly have a strong influence on Armenia's internal political life. In fact, they were said to have more power than Bagratyan.

It was clear that the new government would not resolve the problem of Ter-Petrossyan's legitimacy. With an opposition that is supported by a considerable part of the population, is not represented in state bodies, and believes it was robbed of electoral victory, the Armenian president may have to rely ever more heavily on the power ministries to uphold stability.

LOOKING AHEAD

The year ended with growing speculation about a possible legalization of the Dashnak party. Some observers (including pro-government ones) feel that such a move would promote a dialogue between the authorities and the opposition. In that regard, the 10 December verdict by Armenia's Supreme Court, which sentenced to death three members of the Dashnak party on charges of forming a clandestine terrorist group called Dro but which found no connection between Dro and the Dashnak party (a purported connection was the main justification for the party's suspension in December 1994), could give a green light to the return of the Dashnaks to legal activities.

Besides some unsuccessful attempts to normalize relations with Turkey, 1996 did not bring about any remarkable developments in Armenia's foreign relations. In early December, Turkey announced that it would not reopen its border with Armenia unless the latter recognized Azerbaijan's sovereignty over Nagorno-Karabakh. Given the current paralysis of the negotiations over Nagorno-Karabakh, any improvement of Armenia's relationship with Turkey seems unlikely.

Sidebar: TRANSCAUCASUS: BREAKAWAY REGIONS SEEK LEGITIMACY THROUGH ELECTIONS

by ELIZABETH FULLER

One of the components of the long-term diplomatic poker game engaged in by the leaderships of unrecognized states seeking to substantiate their claim on legitimacy—and thus, by extension, their albeit tenuous chances of eventual international recognition—is the holding of parliamentary and presidential elections. While those elections are invariably condemned as devoid of legitimacy both by the larger state whose territorial integrity is threatened by the secessionist aspirations of the territorial formation in question, and by the international community, the harshness of the criticism they incur varies according to whether the elections are perceived as potentially stabilizing or destabilizing. The presidential elections in Georgia's secessionist province of South Ossetiya on 10 November and in the self-proclaimed Republic of Nagorno-Karabakh on 24 November serve to illustrate that argument, as do the parliamentary elections in Abkhazia on 23 November.

Nagorno-Karabakh, the population of which is overwhelmingly ethnic Armenian, unilaterally proclaimed its independence from Azerbaijan in September 1991, but to date has not been formally recognized as an independent state, even by the Republic of Armenia. Following an impressive string of military successes, however, the armed forces of the self-proclaimed Republic of Nagorno-Karabakh succeeded in 1993–1994 in establishing control over virtually the entire territory of the enclave, as well as a land corridor linking it with Armenia to the west and a buffer zone to the south and east. In May 1994, then-Russian Defense Minister Pavel Grachev mediated a cease-fire agreement in Karabakh that remains in force to this day. Ongoing efforts by the Organization for Security and Cooperation (OSCE) to mediate a political solution are, however, deadlocked: the Azerbaijani leadership insists that the Karabakh Armenian forces withdraw from all occupied territory, in return for which they are prepared to offer "broad autonomy" within the confines of the Azerbaijan Republic—a status the Karabakh Armenians reject. The latter, for their part, insist that any political settlement must include international security guarantees for the Armenian population of the Republic of Nagorno-Karabakh (RNK).

In December 1994, the RNK parliament voted to create the office of president, to which it proceeded to elect the chairman of the State Defense Committee (the acting government of the enclave), Robert Kocharyan. In late August 1996, the RNK parliament scheduled a new presidential election for 24 November, given that Kocharyan's term was due to expire after two years. Azerbaijan's Central Electoral Commission denounced the planned presidential poll on 23 October (after a delay of almost two months) on the grounds that "legitimate bodies of power may be created on the territory of Nagorno-Karabakh only after the liberation of all Azeri territories, the return home of displaced persons of Azeri nationality and the restoration of the ethnic makeup of the region." Azerbaijani Foreign Minister Hasan Hasanov likewise denounced the planned election as "political play-acting" and a gesture of defiance, given that "one-third" of the enclave's former population has been forcibly displaced and currently reside elsewhere in Azerbaijan. (In fact, prior to 1988, Azeris made up approximately 25 percent of the total population of Nagorno-Karabakh.) Azerbaijan's parliament, the OSCE, and the European Union all appealed to the enclave's leadership to cancel the election, arguing that they could jeopardize the chances that Azerbaijan and Armenia would sign a "statement of principles" reiterating their commitment to seeking a solution to the Karabakh impasse at the Lisbon OSCE heads of state summit scheduled for early December. (The OSCE was anxious to expedite the signing of that document as proof that at least some progress has been made towards a settlement of the conflict.) Those criticisms of the proposed elections were rejected as illogical by Jirair Liparitian, senior advisor to Armenian President Levon Ter-Petrossyan. Liparitian pointed out that both Azerbaijan and other OSCE member states had signed the original Conference on Security and Cooperation in Europe document outlining the framework for mediating a settlement of the conflict, which stated inter alia that "elected representatives" of Nagorno-Karabakh should participate in the final stages of negotiating process (the so-called "Minsk conference").

Such protests notwithstanding, four candidates announced their intention to run for the RNK presidency: Kocharyan, former RNK parliament speaker Boris Arushanyan, Karabakh Communist Party leader Hrant Melkumyan, and the head of the Karabakh government Control Commission, Albert Ghazaryan. (Ghazaryan was ultimately denied registration as he failed to collect the minimum required number of signatures in his support from each of the enclave's six districts.) Like Kocharyan, both Arushanyan and Melkumyan pledged to achieve the RNK's formal recognition by the international community as an independent state. Arushanyan, however, advocated a more forceful approach, arguing that Kocharyan had been too cautious in his dealings with the Azerbaijani leadership, while Melkumyan insisted that enlisting Russian support was the key to resolving the deadlock over the enclave's status.

In the event, Kocharyan—the candidate with the most moderate approach to achieving de jure independence—was elected president with over 85 percent of the vote. (Voter turnout was estimated at 77.6 percent.) In contrast with the disputed September presidential election in Armenia, international observers registered no violations of voting procedure. The poll sparked protest demonstrations elsewhere in Azerbaijan among Azeris who had been forced to flee from their homes during the fighting in 1993–1994.

Robert Kocharyan's triumph in the presidential elections in the unrecognized Republic of Nagorno-Karabakh bears a marked similarity to that of Ludwig Chibirov, the former educator who was nominated chairman of the Supreme Soviet of the unrecognized Republic of South Ossetiya in the spring of 1994, and then elected president on 10 November, 1996. The South Ossetiyan oblast soviet had declared the region's independence from Georgia in 1990, a move that precipitated brutal reprisals by informal Georgian paramilitaries. Since mid-1992, a tripartite peacekeeping force under the auspices of the OSCE has prevented any further outbreak of hostilities. In May, 1996, Chibirov and Georgian President Eduard Shevardnadze signed a memorandum on confidence building whereby both sides abjured the use of force. As in the case of Nagorno-Karabakh, however, talks on resolving the issue of South Ossetiya's future status vis-á-vis the central Georgian government in Tbilisi were deadlocked. Like Kocharyan, Chibirov defeated several rival candidates who espoused a more radical position than he did on the issue of possible independence from Georgia and/or unification with the Republic of North Ossetiya within the Russian Federation.

The most obvious explanation of why the South Ossetiyan presidential poll did not generate the same degree of controversy and international condemnation as did that in Karabakh is the overriding desire of the international community (in the first instance the United States) to coerce the conflict parties in Nagorno-Karabakh to arrive at a political solution that would guarantee long-term regional stability, which is seen as a crucial precondition to the exploitation by Western consortiums of Azerbaijan's offshore Caspian oil. One obstacle to such an agreement is Robert Kocharyan, who has been described as self-assured, inflexible, and obdurate. Chibirov, by contrast, is said by a senior European diplomat who conducted talks with him to be meek, inexperienced, lacking in self-confidence, and subject to pressure both from Moscow, which provides most of the region's budget, and from North Ossetiya's President Akhsarbek Galazov.

Georgian criticism of the South Ossetiyan presidential poll denied its legality and deplored the fact that ethnic Georgians who had fled the region were deprived of the chance to vote. The same arguments were adduced in the case of the parliamentary elections held in Abkhazia on 23 November. The region achieved de facto independence from Georgia in autumn 1993. As in the case of Nagorno-Karabakh and South Ossetiya, negotiations on Abkhazia's status within Georgia were deadlocked. Moreover, the separatist leadership in Sukhumi headed by Vladislav Ardzinba stubbornly opposes the repatriation of some 250,000 ethnic Georgians displaced during the final weeks of the conflict. The status of the Abkhaz parliamentary elections was further complicated by the fact that there are two rival bodies claiming to be the region's legitimate parliament: one in Sukhumi, whose delegates are mainly ethnic Abkhaz, and a "parliament in exile" in Tbilisi composed of ethnic Georgians. The chairman of the latter organ, Tamaz Nadareishvili, has for months pressured the Georgian leadership to use military force if necessary to reassert Georgian control over Abkhazia.

Criticism of the planned elections by the Georgian leadership and the Russian Foreign Ministry and appeals by the UN Security Council and the European Union to postpone the poll until after the repatriation of the ethnic Georgian to their homes failed to sway the Abkhaz leadership. As a countermove, albeit one with no legal weight, the Georgian authorities organized a plebiscite among those Georgians who had fled Abkhazia, of whom 99 percent reportedly voted "no" to the question, "Do you support the decision of the separatist leadership of Abkhazia to hold elections to the Abkhazian parliament before Georgia's territorial integrity is restored and all refugees return to their homes in Abkhazia?"

The debate over the legality of holding elections in those three unrecognized Transcaucasus entities is a consequence, first, of the arbitrary territorial divisions that created autonomous formations within the constituent republics of the USSR, and second, of the contradiction between the right of nations to self-determination and the OSCE ruling that the territorial integrity of member states (which include all the successor states to the USSR) is sacrosanct. International organizations such as the UN and the OSCE are apparently either unwilling or unable to devise any innovative solution to that contradiction for fear of setting a precedent. The question of political status is, furthermore, complicated by the fact that, as the German Caucasus scholar Uwe Halbach points out, the very concept of "autonomy" has been totally devalued in the eyes of the political elites of these unrecognized post-Soviet states as a result of its abuse by the Soviet leadership to denote virtual subservience to the "parent" republic. The choice of options is therefore perceived as being limited to continued subservience—or total independence. In those conditions, once negotiations on resolving the status issue are deadlocked, as they are in Nagorno-Karabakh, Abkhazia, and South Ossetiya, elections may be seen by the leaderships of the unrecognized states as the most effective means of exerting pressure on the larger state from which they hope to wrest independence, and of demonstrating to the international community their single-minded commitment to doing so. Or, to misquote Kris Kristofferson, "Elections is just another word for nothing left to lose."

Kazakstan

Population:	17,300,000
Capital:	Almaty (pop. 1,200,000). The capital is scheduled to move to Akmola in 2000.
Major cities:	Karaganda (pop. 613,000), Shymkent (401,000), Akmola (pop. 280,000)
Area:	2,717,300 sq. km.
Major ethnic groups:	Kazak 43%, Russian 36%, Ukrainian 5.2%, German 3%, Uzbek 2%, Tatar 2%
Economy:	GDP growth: 0.5%
	Inflation rate: 29%
	Average monthly income: $91
	Unemployment rate: 4.1%

OPPOSITION FINDS A VOICE IN KAZAKSTAN

by BHAVNA DAVE

President Nursultan Nazarbayev's grip on power remained firm in 1996, but he faced an increasingly assertive opposition and a restive constituency of pensioners and workers who were no longer appeased by promises and slogans.

A newly elected and ever more pliant parliament, a new constitution practically enshrining a presidential dictatorship, an apathetic populace, and an opposition in total disarray left President Nursultan Nazarbayev in a formidable position in 1996. During the year, Nazarbayev ruled with an increasingly authoritarian hand, manifested by a clampdown on independent media, the opposition, and all forms of public dissent. But the year ended with a mounting expression of unrest and disillusionment with the government's reform rhetoric on the part of workers, pensioners, and intelligentsia. The end of the year also saw a promising coalescence of various opposition forces into a new citizens' movement, Azamat, which draws membership and support from across the country's ethnic spectrum.

Impressive macroeconomic achievements—considerable foreign investment (almost $2 billion), advances in privatization, and a lowering of the annual inflation rate to under 4 percent—have done little to improve the living standards of common citizens. One of the biggest problems faced by the leadership is the raising of funds to clear the arrears in wages and pensions. The government owes more than $500 million in unpaid wages and another $300 million in pensions. Pensioners staged protests in numerous parts of the country, mainly Ust-Kamenogorsk, Pavlodar, and Almaty. Grievances over unpaid wages have resulted in strikes by miners and workers throughout Kazakstan.

The government's bid to partially alleviate the problem of pension arrears by raising the retirement age by three years—from 55 to 58 for women and from 60 to 63 for men—sparked a new controversy in June. The government claims that such a measure was necessary because there are currently 1.8 pensioners for each working person. The lower house, the Oliy Majilis, initially refused to pass the pension bill by claiming that the new legislation was too harsh on the elderly. That unexpected defiance on the part of an institution endowed with mere rubber-stamp functions evoked fears of yet another dismissal of the country's legislative body by the president, as occurred in March 1995. The Majilis eventually passed the law, following a compromise with the government. The pension age will be raised by six months every year and the law will come into full effect by 2001.

AN ORGANIZED OPPOSITION

The disintegration of the social-welfare structure and a progressive impoverishment of the population have created a ripe social climate for the assertion of an organized opposition. The Independent Trade Unions Confederation of Kazakstan has shown a considerable level of organization and unity in fighting for the rights of workers and pensioners in place of the official trade unions. The confederation organized rallies in Almaty in the last quarter of the year demanding an improvement in the standard of living and a solution to the problem of unpaid wages. Despite the government's refusal to grant permission for holding a public rally, a coalition of opposition forces—headed by Azamat and supported by the Communist Party of Kazakstan, the Socialist Party, and the Independent Trade Unions Confederation—organized an impressive rally (by Kazakstani standards) on 8 December in Almaty in which about 3,500 people protested the worsening of living conditions and the breakdown of the social-welfare network. The government's reluctance to enforce the country's stringent laws on public meetings and take action against the protesters—some of whom even burned effigies of Nazarbayev, calling him a traitor to the nation—was surprising.

What is remarkable is that, despite strict laws regulating the activities of public associations and political parties, a movement such as Azamat—comprising leading public figures and intellectuals across a wide social and ethnic spectrum—has been able to organize itself as a new nationwide opposition.

Azamat held its inaugural congress in Almaty in April with about 400 delegates, declaring that the movement's primary goal is to "form a government of honest and competent people, based on people's trust." A strong force behind the movement is Murat Auezov, an esteemed public figure who has stayed clear of nomenklatura politics. A sinologist by training, Auezov completed a two-year term as Kazakstan's ambassador to China in mid-1995. Upon his return home, Auezov stepped into a void created by the political demise of Olzhas Suleimenov, a renowned Kazak writer, whose party, the People's Congress, was emerging as a prominent opposition force against Nazarbayev. (Amid charges of corruption and financial wrongdoing, Suleimenov was appointed Kazakstan's ambassador to Italy in late 1995.) In addition to his distinguished lineage—his father Mukhtar was one of the most highly acclaimed Kazak poets and intellectuals of the early Soviet period—Auezov has a cosmopolitan image that especially appeals to the urban middle class and intelligentsia, who are weary of nationalist politics.

In contrast to the numerous opposition parties and movements of the past few years, organized largely along ethnic lines, Azamat has committed itself to creating an alliance of civic forces in the country. (Opposition parties such as Azat, Zheltoksan, and Alash are almost exclusively Kazak in their composition, while Lad and similar organizations speak exclusively for Slavic ethnic groups.) The membership of Azamat is drawn across the various ethnic groups. Besides Auezov, the other co-chairmen of Azamat are Petr Svoik—the leader of the Socialist Party—and Turegeldy Sharmanov, a member of the Kazakstani and Russian Academies of Medical Sciences.

THE EMERGING KAZAK MAJORITY

The emigration of the non-Kazak population slowed to about 250,000 in 1996, compared with 480,000 in 1994. Aided by the arrival of about 60,000 Kazaks, mainly from Mongolia, the ethnic Kazak share of the population increased to about 45 percent, and it is likely to reach majority level by the year 2000.

The government has continued to accord protection to Kazak—the state language—although Russian remains the de facto lingua franca and the dominant language of administration. In December, the parliament approved new legislation to aid the imposition of Kazak as the state language in the Kazak-dominated administration. Kazaks who do not have sufficient command of the state language are required to be proficient in it by January 2001, whereas the same deadline for non-Kazaks is January 2006. The new law authorizes the executive to draw up a list of posts in the state sector for which Kazak proficiency is required. Television and radio stations—irrespective of their form of ownership—must allocate at least half of their airtime for Kazak-language programs.

Marat Ospanov, the speaker of the Majilis, has said that such a measure was inevitable given the continuing subordination of the state language to Russian. Critics such as Aman Tuleev, Russia's minister for cooperation with the Commonwealth of Independent States (CIS)—himself half Kazak, half Tatar—have urged the Kazakstani government to repeal the new law in order to arrest the exodus of the non-Kazak population from Kazakstan. However, the 10–year time frame given to Russian speakers to learn Kazak gives them more breathing space than the legislation initially enacted in 1992. (The previous law had required all Kazak-dominated regions to switch to Kazak as the official language of administration within a year, ethnically mixed regions to make the switch within two years, and Russian-dominated regions to conduct official proceedings in Kazak within three to four years.)

RESTRICTIONS ON INDEPENDENT MEDIA

The highlight in the government's battle with the independent media was the temporary suspension of the Moscow-based Russian daily *Komsomolskaya pravda* for publishing an article by Aleksandr Solzhenitsyn. Kazakstani officials saw Solzhenitsyn's support for a "greater Russia" as incendiary and threatening to the territorial integrity of their country. *Komsomolskaya pravda* resumed circulation within Kazakstan only after its editors issued a public statement disassociating themselves from Solzhenitsyn's views.

The government found it easier to impose restrictions on local independent radio and television stations. Seven radio stations (notably Radio M and Totem) and two television stations were shut down because they were allegedly broadcasting on frequencies that interfered with air-traffic control. Critics saw the move as an obvious attempt to penalize the nongovernment stations—which broadcast mainly in Russian—for airing the views of the opposition.

The December clampdown on independent stations coincided with the latter's diligent coverage of anti-government rallies and opposition activism of the previous two months. In response to a complaint letter to Nazarbayev from representatives of more than 80 independent television and radio stations, the government announced that frequencies would be allocated by a competitive tender to be held early in 1997. Independent radio and television stations justifiably feared that such a tender would work against them, as they do not have the resources and the clout of the state-supported companies that broadcast in Kazak.

Document: KAZAKSTAN'S CURIOUS CHOICE OF CAPITAL

Many have tried to find the reason for Kazak President Nursultan Nazarbayev's 1994 decision to move his country's capital from Almaty to Akmola, especially since Almaty is the only large, modern city in the country and Kazakstan has little spare money to spend on unnecessary projects. With the first stage of the transfer due to begin in 1997, a somewhat sarcastic commentary in the September 27–October 3 issue of Moscow's Delovoi mir, *discussed the pros and cons of the planned transfer.*

"A mediocre oblast center has become a destination of a peculiar pilgrimage. To this place come representatives of the diplomatic corps, visits from various foreign delegations are planned, and foreign investors have been invited. All this hullabaloo began in mid-1994, when Nursultan Nazarbayev disclosed his intentions to transfer the capital of the republic from Almaty to Akmola. (At that time, the idea received judicial strength in the form of a presidential decree.)

However, the planned move was not met with great enthusiasm: the economic crisis had created more pressing problems. Discussion of the idea, strangely, centered on something other than the move itself—the name of the city, which in Kazak means "White Grave." You might agree that is not the best choice of names for a capital. Suddenly, proponents of the national language and jingoists became convinced that the translation was not exact, that "Akmola" means "White Cupola," "White Mausoleum," "Blessed Foreteller, Forecaster, Oracle," or even "White Abundance"—referring to the various dairy products with which the region is blessed. Similar attempts produced nothing but nonsense. And then, to end the arguments once and for all, it was proposed that the city be renamed Ak-Ordoy, meaning "White Capital."

And why doesn't the republic's current administration like Almaty? There are several reasons. Further development is hindered by the lack of open territory. Earthquakes have leveled the city to its foundations twice, and that threat hangs over the city today. Almaty is positioned in the southeastern corner of the state in a transportational dead end that seriously complicates administrative ties from the center to the regions. Besides, the city is beset by a host of ecological problems, the solutions to which demand billions of investments.

Other arguments exist that they prefer not to talk about, because they touch on complicated interclan relations. Almaty is the traditional stronghold of the so-called older Juz—the southern Kazak clans—whose representatives have headed politics in Kazakstan for decades. The clans' influence is strong, and they frequently resist decisions by the head of state. Obviously, that influence will weaken after the capital is transferred. Also, in the northern oblasts, [Russians and other Russian-speaking Europeans] make up the majority. There is a strong inclination toward Russia, and there are constant discussions about unifying the region with Russia. The likely motive for moving the capital is a desire to shift a mass of ethnic Kazaks from the south to the north, changing the ethnic balance in the border regions.

But compared with Almaty, Akmola is in many ways no gift—although it is located in the geographical center of the state, has open tracts of land for further development, and has a developed transportation infrastructure. The city lies in a not-so-attractive swampy area with a harsh continental climate. The summers are unimaginably hot, and the winters are fiercely cold. In December of last year, a snowstorm claimed the lives of 64 people and caused 300 million tenge [$4.5 million] in damages.

Currently, Akmola is a typical provincial city with about 280,000 residents. Of 55 city industries, 39 are completely or partially shut down. The two thermo-electric power stations in the oblast center are barely able to meet the region's demand. A significant part of the city's houses are made of clay and straw or adobe, and the people who live in them don't even think about centralized heating. Water supplies are also not good—the level of the Ishim River is low; during the summer in many places it dries up. The city desperately needs a drainage system; after a bit of rain the streets become impassably muddy.

When a government commission came to study the city's ability to house central institutions, its limitations were immediately obvious. Just in the first stage of the transfer in 1997 and 1998, the government plans to move 28 ministries and government agencies to Akmola. It follows that services and housing will have to be built for the newcomers.

All of the proposals [for Akmola's development]—those turned down and those accepted—are basically similar. Most envision governmental buildings on the bank of the Ishim or on an artificial island, including the presidential palace, office towers for the higher administrative organs, a business center, and behind them the smaller buildings of the diplomatic corps and officials.

Already the first assessment of the approved project shows that it is not possible to do. Just the presidential palace on an artificial island in the middle of the Ishim and a 40–story administrative building demand a colossal investment of money that the republic does not have. Even the essentials for developing the city, such as a new thermoelectric plant or a canal connecting the Ishim and Irtysh rivers, remain dreams on paper.

Uzbekistan

Population:	22,200,000
Capital:	Tashkent (pop. 2,200,000)
Major cities:	Samarkand (pop. 388,000), Namangan (pop. 291,000), Andijan (pop. 288,000)
Area:	447,000 sq. km.
Major ethnic groups:	Uzbek 74.5%, Russian 6.5%, Tajik 4.8%, Kazakh 4.1%
Economy:	GDP growth: 2%
....	Inflation rate: 55%
....	Average monthly income: $51
....	Unemployment rate: 0.4%

HOLDING THE COURSE IN UZBEKISTAN

by ROGER D. KANGAS

If official pronouncements were to be believed, Uzbekistan became an open society in 1996. The reality, however, was more of the same: a muzzled press and mere lip service paid to human rights.

Uzbekistan actively promoted itself as a changed state in 1996. Whether discussing human rights or staging a historic meeting with the U.S. president, President Islam Karimov tried to show that he was not an authoritarian, but simply a strong leader who cared about the future of his country. The campaign seemed to have borne fruit, for the West—the United States, in particular— began to praise the country's progress and invest more in its economy. Changes in rhetoric did not necessarily translate into changes in policy, however, as the government continued to control the political process, opposition groups, and the media.

With elections not slated until December 1999, national politics in Uzbekistan was limited to cabinet reshuffling and the periodic firings of regional governors. Ismail Jurabekov, the powerful first deputy prime minister, was given the portfolio of minister for extraordinary affairs on 4 March. But in October, another deputy prime minister was given special responsibility for agriculture and water resources, a task previously under Jurabekov's control. That appointment raised speculation that, in spite of his March appointment, Jurabekov's star was fading in the top circles of power. Of course, in a strong presidential system like Uzbekistan's, the No. 2 person is an obvious political target. He was not the only one, either: two other deputy prime ministers were removed from their posts.

The appointment of Tahir Rakhimov as minister of foreign trade on 17 July highlighted Karimov's continued preference for technicians in high offices and his desire to emphasize foreign trade. Rakhimov, like other members of the presidential apparatus, rose through the ranks due to his knowledge of economics and trade, rather than any ideological background. The position had been left vacant since the promotion of Utkir Sultanov to prime minister in December 1995.

The trend of removing regional governors on grounds of mismanagement and nonfulfillment of harvest quotas continued in 1996. Ghulomqodir Khasanov of Syrdarya and Alisher Toshkenboev of Jizzak were both sacked in late October. But the inability to fulfill harvest quotas is probably due more to a general systemic failure, much like in the Soviet era, than to specific instances of mismanagement. Nationwide, only 72 percent of the grain and 80 percent of the cotton quotas were filled, frustrating the government's goal of self-sufficiency in food production and thwarting the chance to increase the sale of cotton on the international market for hard currency.

While playing political musical chairs, the president was also proclaiming his desire to change the way the system operated. Following his historic July trip to Italy and the United States, President Karimov called for a greater focus on opposition parties, a free media, and a more careful observance of human rights. Those topics had been the theme of his meetings with European Union officials in Florence and his much-sought-after first meeting with U.S. President Bill Clinton in Washington. In November, the Uzbek government passed a law on political parties that set out stricter guidelines than the current law. Parties may not accept donations from foreign, religious, or anonymous sources, nor may they have as members military personnel, foreigners, or stateless people. Whether the provisions are more than strategic rhetoric, however, remains to be seen. The government still controls the registration process for political parties and may use the new rules to prohibit opposition groups from becoming real, legal forces.

TALK ABOUT HUMAN RIGHTS

Karimov also said all the right things with respect to human rights. In years past, the West has been sharply critical of Karimov's heavy-handed treatment of opposition figures in his country. To prove his generosity in 1996, Karimov gave amnesty to many prisoners, including several well-known political prisoners. He also permitted a conference on human rights, sponsored by the Organization for Security and Cooperation in Europe, to take place in Tashkent in September. Among the participants was famed Uzbek dissident Abdumanob Pulat, who resides in exile in the United States. Not only did Pulat speak to the media, but he also attended a congress of the still-unregistered Human Rights Society of Uzbekistan, of which he is a founding member. The fanfare surrounding Pulat's visit was in sharp contrast to his 1992 arrest and beating at the hands of the government.

At the same time, however, the government still refused to release information on political dissidents who have been missing since 1992. Nor did it allow opposition groups to register as legal entities. The international organization Human Rights Watch/Helsinki, which has monitored Uzbekistan's record, wrote in May that "basic civil liberties remain suspended" in Uzbekistan and that Islamic groups are often singled out for particularly harsh treatment. The group also criticized the 9 November detention and beating of Hasan Mirsaidov, the son of Uzbek dissident Shukhrullo Mirsaidov, as well as the detention and poor treatment of a Human Rights Watch observer in Tashkent earlier in the year.

The government's justification for those actions is that it is simply trying to prevent the emergence of extremist groups and instability in Uzbekistan. To an extent, that explanation has been accepted by many foreign nations, including the United States, Germany, and Great Britain. Indeed, the belief that Uzbekistan is somehow an island of stability in the tumultuous former Soviet Union has fostered Western investment in the country. Deals with American energy companies topped $400 million, and the British tobacco company BAT, the South Korean firm Daewoo, and the German company Mercedes-Benz were not far behind.

One possible obstacle to the investment trend, however, may be the currency crisis that plagued Uzbekistan in the last four months of the year. During that time, the value of the sum dropped from 35 to over 55 against the U.S. dollar, while the black-market rate topped 110 to the dollar at year's end. The government has already increased restrictions on hard-currency acquisition in an effort to stem the tide, and officials speculated that by early 1997, the system should stabilize. Hopes of having a convertible currency by the end of 1997 appear dim.

STILL A LEADER

Foreign-policy concerns in 1996 were much the same as in previous years. Besides Karimov's meeting with Clinton and the commitment to being a close ally of the United States, Uzbekistan also spent a good deal of time clarifying its position within the Commonwealth of Independent States (CIS) and among the Central Asian states. Following the April declarations of Kyrgyzstan and Kazakstan to further integrate with Russia and Belarus, Karimov adamantly objected to any effort to revive the USSR or to force CIS member states to follow Russian-led agendas. Uzbek leaders also said that further economic integration would not be in the country's interests.

The ongoing crises in Tajikistan and Afghanistan also played dominant roles in Uzbekistan's foreign policy. Tashkent was host to a number of regional-security conferences, leadership summits, and CIS meetings, all of which were efforts to sort out the difficulties in Tajikistan and bring the sides together. The fact that Karimov is willing to talk to both sides suggests that, for him, peace is more important than victory for one side or the other. Brokering a resolution to the Tajik crisis could help Uzbekistan demonstrate its leadership role in the region. Such a role would prove a counter to any Russian encroachments in the area.

The Taliban advances in the fall of 1996, which culminated in the capture of the Afghan capital Kabul, were cause for concern, as Uzbekistan shares a 156–kilometer border with Afghanistan. Uzbek military units are now stationed along that border. Alone among the Central Asian states, Uzbekistan has no Russian troops guarding its border, both because it has the most developed military of that region and because it does not want foreign troops based on its territory.

MEDIA CAMPAIGNS

Uzbekistan's media continue to be state-controlled and void of any real editorial independence. *Narodnoe slovo*, one of the state newspapers, explained in October that in order for the media to be "fully expressive," it must be "guided by the state." Such justification for censorship and distribution control contrasts with the government's praise for the independent media developing in the country. There are two independent television stations in Samarkand and a number of independent print publications, mostly on business or social issues. Those, however, are private only with respect to financing, as they are subject to state censorship and circulation restrictions. There is no visible sign of the media's addressing politically sensitive subjects. And while it is still possible to watch Russian television, print media from that country are limited to a few publications almost exclusively available in Tashkent. In a brighter development, Radio Liberty and the BBC were given permission to open offices in Uzbekistan and broadcast on medium-wave (AM) frequencies.

The year also saw two seemingly contradictory cultural focuses: on modernization and on the need to resurrect Uzbekistan's ancient past. Large-scale urban development accelerated. The mayor of Tashkent, Kozim Tulyaganov, unveiled a drastic proposal to modernize the capital: the old city of Tashkent is being torn down and replaced with three- and four-story apartment buildings that will not only offer access to running water and telephone lines but also ease the housing shortage. The project, which is already well underway, provoked protests from residents who wanted to keep their traditional Uzbek dwellings, as well as from UNESCO representatives who were dismayed over the rapid destruction of a historic part of Uzbekistan.

At the same time, 1996 was championed as the 660th anniversary of the birth of Timur (Tamerlane). Throughout the year, conferences, celebrations, and speeches were held commemorating the 15th-century Central Asian leader. The celebrations were orchestrated to draw parallels between the Timurid dynasty's founder and the current president. Discussions focused on the need for regional stability, strong leadership, and cultural enlightenment. Thus, while some aspects of the past are being replaced, those parts that the government deems of value are being venerated.

Document: UZBEK PRESIDENT CONDEMNS CIS INTEGRATION ACCORDS

Prior to 1996, Uzbekistan's President Islam Karimov generally supported closer integration within the Commonwealth of Independent States, while insisting that the full equality and complete self-reliance of all states be preserved. On the heels of integration agreements between Russia and Belarus and among Russia, Belarus, Kazakstan, and Kyrgyzstan, the Uzbek president seemed convinced that integration was following the wrong path. In an address to the Tashkent diplomatic corps on 12 April, published the next day in the Tashkent newspaper Narodnoe slovo, *Karimov panned the accords, warning that Central Asian states could be locking themselves into a position of economic backwardness and dependence on Russia.*

Enough time has passed since the noisy Russian State Duma resolution [to annul the abolition of the Soviet Union] and the signing of the agreement of the four—Russia, Kazakstan, Kyrgyzstan, and Belarus—and the agreement of the two-Russia and Belarus. . . . Each state and its leaders have the right to take part in and sign any documents and interstate agreements on the basis of their own interests. However, in this case . . . we are insistently invited to sign these agreements to create these so-called communities or unions of integrated states. Sometimes they make the decision on our behalf as to whether it would be profitable for Uzbekistan or not. . . .

Instead of finding mechanisms to implement CIS decisions within the CIS framework, developing bilateral relations between states, and making them specific in content, we seem to give in to nostalgia for old times. . . . They think for some reason that any interstate association must have supra state structures: parliamentary, legislative, executive—a coordinating or higher council, an executive or administrative committee with a full phalanx of officials, unified military-political structures, etc.

It is no coincidence . . . that a clear trend has emerged of replacing growing problems of economic and social integration with military-political questions, with talk about forming unified commands, joint defense of borders, etc. . . . This is a deliberate attempt to mislead people as to the true reasons for the crisis that has shaken the whole post-Soviet area.

It is clear to all thinking people that the main reason for the economic crisis of the post-Soviet states is the collapse of the exhausted ideology of the totalitarian, administrative-command, centralized-order system, and the movement to the new market relations and free economy by which the whole world lives today. . . . They cannot adapt to the new conditions, they cannot find markets for their output, and they do not have the funds to maintain or develop their production.

For example, the textile enterprises of Russia's Ivanovo region, which were traditionally linked to raw materials from Uzbekistan, are now standing idle because they do not have the funds to buy cotton fiber. . . . The cotton fiber supplied in 1995 from Uzbekistan to the Ivanovo textile industry was mainly re-exported beyond Russia's borders; that is, to put it simply, certain circles in Russia made a lot of money off of this operation. . . .

What role would Uzbekistan and the other republics of Central Asia be allocated [in the CIS they envision]? Above all, this would be the role of a raw-materials supplier, basically of labor-intensive crops like cotton, with which [Central Asia] effectively supplied not only the Soviet Union, but the entire socialist camp. . . .

In the European Union, the majority of countries have roughly equal, sufficiently high economic potential. There are no states that could be said to have obvious advantages in terms of their development. There is no need to emphasize that in the CIS, Russia is a superpower, which in terms of its scale and potential dominates and surpasses all the other states of the CIS several times over.

Bearing in mind our technical and economic backwardness, and our obviously obsolete and uncompetitive technology and basic assets, any attempt to lock us within the borders of the former USSR in various unions is nothing less than a policy of condemning oneself to vegetate in the backyard of the world economy for the sake of ideological stereotypes from the past. The future generation would not forgive us for that. . . . Uzbekistan cannot join these agreements.

Sidebar: SETTING PARAMETERS FOR AN OPEN MEDIA IN UZBEKISTAN

by ROGER D. KANGAS

On 29 October, a consortium led by the Uzbek Central Bank announced that it would begin publishing a periodical entitled *Bozor, pul wa kredit* [Market, Money, and Credit], which will "familiarize" economists, entrepreneurs, and financiers with the finer points of capitalism. The week before, the organization Kamolot was able to successfully register a newspaper, also called *Kamolot,* designed to reach a younger audience. Both publications were considered by the Uzbek media to be independent of government control and outside the usual censorship. Indeed, official sources point to such developments as proof that Uzbekistan has been listening to previous criticism of its heavy-handed treatment of the media and of human-rights issues and is now changing.

Some outside observers have also noted the rise of independent media in Uzbekistan. For example, there are reports that there are two independent television stations in Samarkand, and that several more "independent" stations are in the works. Whether it is print media or television, the central theme in each of these ventures is business or cultural development rather than politics per se.

While those are efforts that should be recognized and applauded, by themselves they do not translate into a free media. The government maintained the right to censor and restrict media coverage of news in the country. The fact that political news reporting was noticeably absent from the new media projects— save the existing news coverage from the state-run papers and television stations—was indicative of the parameters set by the government.

Perhaps most telling was a 9 October report in *Narodnoe slovo* that outlined the government's position: namely, that in order for the media to be fully expressive, it must be "guided" by the state. The report noted that there are currently 515 publications in Uzbekistan, of which 67 are republic-wide newspapers, 88 are magazines, and the rest are regional and city papers. The government goes on to highlight the fact that there are publications written in every major national language—from Uzbek and Russian to Korean and Karakalpak. And yet, all are subjected to the scrutiny of the government's censors. The content tends to be apolitical and not critical of government policies. The business publications, in particular, are prone to be advocates for the government policies of privatization and regulation of foreign investment. In addition, they almost always paint an optimistic picture of the future of Uzbekistan, and given the current monetary crisis in the country, that is no small feat. It seems that after several years of that, most writers practice self-censorship, much like their predecessors in the Soviet Republic of Uzbekistan did.

Political discourse remains at the level of announcing President Islam

Karimov's foreign trips and reprints of presidential decrees. There is little chance for alternative views to be heard. The Foreign Ministry, in fact, remains critical of those who disagree with the government and only calls on opposition figures to return to Uzbekistan and help establish a civil society. Indeed, Foreign Minister Abdulaziz Komilov remarked in a 25 September interview in *Narodnoe slovo* that any naysayers should remain outside of Uzbekistan, chastising them for not wanting to "help their homeland through hard times" and not "sharing with their own people the difficulties that have arisen along the path toward democracy and a worthy life." The caveat in any of those returns is that the political discussion must be "constructive." During a late 1996 visit to Uzbekistan, the exiled opposition figure Abdumanob Pulat was able to voice his opinions in several radio interviews, although he acknowledged that the conversation had to be carefully laid out.

Like the issues of human rights and the status of opposition groups, the subject of a free media remains sensitive for Uzbek officials. Uzbek spokesmen claim that times have changed and that criticisms leveled against Uzbekistan during the first several years of statehood are no longer valid. "Mistakes of the past" have been rectified and there is a new political climate in the country. As for the media, they say, that translates into a more active, diverse, and free media. Some examples suggest there is merit to that proposition. After all, new publications are springing up in record numbers. However, such efforts would be more credible if truly independent papers, such as *Erk* and *Mustaqil haftalik* [Independent Weekly], currently banned in the country, would be allowed to circulate freely. To date, the infrequent issues of those and other "underground" papers circulate only after being smuggled in from abroad.

Tajikistan

Population:	6,000,000
Capital:	Dushanbe (pop. 600,000)
Major cities:	Khojent (Leninabad) (pop. 180,000), Kulyab (pop. 70,000), Kurgan-Tyube (pop. 45,000)
Area:	143,100 sq. km.
Major ethnic groups:	Tajik 64.9%, Uzbek 25%, Russian 3%, other 7.1%
Economy:	GDP growth: –17%
	Inflation rate: 41%
	Average monthly income: $5
	Unemployment rate: 2.4%

A YEAR OF VIOLENCE IN TAJIKISTAN
by BRUCE PANNIER

1996 was a year of renewed fighting in Tajikistan between government and opposition forces. With the rebels making steady advances toward the capital throughout the year and Russia and other Central Asian countries unwilling to get more deeply involved, the Tajik government finally agreed in December on a new cease-fire and to work with the opposition to plan elections.

The upsurge in fighting and breakdown in peace talks toward the end of 1995 presaged a difficult year for Tajikistan in 1996. Central Asian participants in the Commonwealth of Independent States (CIS) heads-of-state summit in January warned Tajik President Imomali Rakhmonov that further support for the embattled Tajik government was contingent on its demonstrating greater willingness to compromise with the opposition. Shortly afterward, two "mutinies" broke out, led by people whom the government had previously considered allies.

Ibodullo Baimatov, the former mayor of the western Tajik city of Tursun Zade, returned from self-imposed exile in Uzbekistan and took the town by force. At the same time, the commander of the army's First Brigade in Kurgan-Tyube, Mahmud Khudaberdiyev, mobilized his unit and marched toward the capital. Within a week, Baimatov's and Khudaberdiyev's forces were within 20 kilometers of Dushanbe and making demands for changes in government personnel. Prime Minister Jamshed Karimov was removed, as were First Deputy Prime Minister Makhmad Said Ubadollayev and several others. Satisfied with the changes, both groups returned to their home bases.

The Tajik opposition took advantage of the government's predicament to attack in central Tajikistan, capturing regional centers and sections of a strategic highway while inflicting heavy casualties on government forces, mostly ill-trained young conscripts. By May, opposition forces controlled the strategic town of Tavil-Dara and over the next few months advanced to take Komsomolabad, Tajikabad, Garm, and many smaller towns and villages as well.

Also in May, demonstrations were held in the northern Tajik cities of Khojent, Ura-Tyube, and several others. At first demanding only better living conditions, the demonstrations gradually took on an anti-Kulyabi character. During the Soviet era, the Kulyabis (from the southern city of Kulyab) were allied with northerners from the Leninabad region in running the country. Under Rakhmonov, who is from the southern city of Dangara, the occupation of upper-level positions around the republic by Kulyabis has come to be seen as nepotism by the remainder of the country, including the northerners. In Khojent, the Kulyabis were replaced in early May.

Meanwhile, a former presidential candidate and ambassador to Russia, Abdumalik Abdullajonov, announced the creation of the National Revival

Movement, headed by him and two former prime ministers, Abdujalil Samadov and the recently deposed Jamshed Karimov. All three groups come from the populous Leninabad region.

Toward the end of May, torrential rains caused widespread damage: floods destroyed houses, roads, and communications systems and spread cholera and typhus through the country's canals.

A TROUBLED BORDER

The summer was filled with reports of attempted incursions across the border with Afghanistan by drug runners and elements of the Tajik opposition. The Russian border guards and CIS peacekeeping forces (also led by Russian troops) once again faced near-daily attacks by small groups trying to reach the scene of fighting in central Tajikistan. Confiscated drugs, mostly opium, were counted in the hundreds of kilograms by summer's end.

The action along the Afghan-Tajik border led the Russian command into negotiations with Afghan border guards in an attempt to create a 25–kilometer buffer zone on the Afghan side of the border. For a brief time in late August and early September, Russian-CIS forces guarding the border were spectators to the Afghan border guards' operations against armed groups in northern Afghanistan, and there was a noticeable reduction in the frequency of attempted border crossings. All that changed in late September, when the Taliban movement took control of the Afghan capital, Kabul. The government of Burhanuddin Rabbani having fled to safe havens in the north, all deals with Afghan border guards were off.

The Taliban movement's success in Kabul briefly focused renewed attention on the Tajik conflict. Central Asian states and Russia expressed concern that Islamic fundamentalists would encroach on CIS territory and that parts of Uzbekistan and Tajikistan might come under Taliban influence. But a meeting of four Central Asian presidents (Rakhmonov, Kazakstan's Nursultan Nazarbayev, Kyrgyzstan's Askar Akayev, and Uzbekistan's Islam Karimov) with Russian Prime Minister Viktor Chernomyrdin in Almaty on 4 October failed to produce a common strategy in the face of the threat from the south. The five leaders agreed only that the Rabbani government was still the legitimate government of Afghanistan and that the problems in that country were purely an internal affair, worth keeping an eye on but not requiring open interference. No additional support was pledged for shoring up the porous Tajik-Afghan border.

By October, defending the border was a secondary issue. After numerous crossings, the opposition had moved the bulk of its fighters into central Tajikistan and, aware of increased Russian attention to Tajikistan, was avoiding conflict with Russian-CIS forces as much as possible. Instead, the opposition consolidated its positions around Tavil-Dara and pressed the offensive. Battles raged along the main highway running eastward from the capital, Dushanbe, usually to the detriment of government forces. In early November, the eastward highway's strategic fork was hotly contested and became impassable to all but combatants. By that time, waves of fleeing refugees had largely depopulated central Tajikistan.

In late October, the National Revival Movement was courted by both the Tajik government and the opposition. There were reports, subsequently confirmed, that Abdullajonov was meeting with United Tajik Opposition leader Said Abdullo Nuri, while Abdujalil Samadov and Jamshed Karimov were in Dushanbe, where they were offered positions by Rakhmonov. Nuri began to insist that any future negotiations include Abdullajonov's movement.

A NEW CEASE-FIRE

A planned meeting between Rakhmonov and Nuri, delayed since September, finally took place on 10 and 11 December in northern Afghanistan, and the two men agreed on a new cease-fire—which, unlike many previous cease-fires, actually went into effect, and held for the remainder of the month. The second meeting between the two, in Moscow on 20 December, produced a long-awaited agreement on the formation of a "reconciliation council," as well as promises from both sides to release all prisoners of war and to institute a general amnesty. The council, with an opposition representative as head, is to oversee amendments to the constitution and introduce greater political freedoms in anticipation of parliamentary elections to be held in 12 to 18 months. However, Rakhmonov retains the right to veto the council's proposals, which may prove a sticking point along the road to real peace.

If December 1996 is remembered for a cease-fire that actually held, it will also be remembered as the month United Nations observers in Tajikistan had the most difficulties. In two separate incidents, government soldiers stopped UN teams, verbally and physically abused them, and threatened to kill them. Later, former opposition field commander Rezvon Sadirov's soldiers captured a UN convoy and held seven UN observers and 16 representatives of a joint government-opposition cease-fire committee hostage. Worries that the situation would derail the peace process were alleviated when the group freed all but two representatives from the Tajik opposition. The group also managed to get Sadirov's brother freed by opposition field commander Mirzo Ziyoyev in Tavil-Dara. Their other demand, for the safe return of comrades who had fled to Afghanistan through a corridor created by Russian border guards, was not met.

Economically, the announcement of the peace agreement could not have come at a better time. Tajikistan's economy barely functions, excepting the narcotics trade. The large aluminum factory in Tursun Zade, for example, was under the control of Ibodullo Baimatov after his return from Uzbekistan, but, by year's end, Baimatov was fighting with local gangs for supremacy in the city and no one was sure who was in control. The Darvoz gold-mining operation, a joint venture between the Tajik government and the British firm Gold and Mineral Excavation, located 350 kilometers southeast of Dushanbe, was overrun by an opposition group, its management held hostage for nearly a month, and much of its equipment disassembled and taken away. Tajikistan has great mineral wealth, but such stories have scared away most potential investors.

If a genuine peace can be reached, it may lure some back. But even with great foreign investment and technical aid, Central Asian countries such as Kazakstan and Kyrgyzstan have had a difficult time turning their economies around in more than five years of independence. Peace in Tajikistan would at least bring a chance to begin that process, but with the economic situation as it is and tens of thousands of firearms unaccounted for in Tajikistan, peace would be but the first step in a long process of national reconstruction.

Sidebar: CENTRAL ASIAN LEADERS MEET IN WAKE OF TALIBAN SEIZURE OF KABUL

by BRUCE PANNIER

The presidents of four Central Asian states (Kazakstan, Kyrgyzstan, Tajikistan, and Uzbekistan) and Russian Prime Minister Viktor Chernomyrdin congregated in the Kazakstani capital, Almaty, on 4 October to formulate a joint response to the Afghan Taliban movement's capture of Kabul and subsequent advance northward. At a press conference that followed the one-hour meeting, Kazakhstan's president Nursultan Nazarbayev stated that "We believe the conflict is moving toward the north of Afghanistan and the borders of the Commonwealth of Independent States. We condemn the executions and violations of human rights. . . and call upon the warring sides, especially the Taliban movement, to stop fighting and begin a political dialogue to resolve their differences."

Viktor Chernomyrdin simply expressed his agreement with Nazarbayev. Shortly after the press conference, it emerged that the participants had also agreed that the security of the southern borders of the CIS needed to be looked into and that, should the Taliban reach the border and attack, "commensurate measures" would be taken, but that there was unanimous agreement that no good would come from interfering in events within Afghanistan. Subsequent statements suggest, however, that far from presenting a common front, Central Asian leaders intended to pursue individual strategies vis-a-vis Afghanistan.

The most glaring example of the lack of unity was the absence of Turkmen President Saparmurat Niyazov at the meeting. The official reason given by Ashgabat was that Turkmenistan wished to preserve its image of neutrality, and that "The events in Afghanistan do not represent a threat to neutral Turkmenistan."

Uzbek President Islam Karimov suggested that by supporting General Abdul Rashid Dostum's forces in northwestern Afghanistan, as the then secretary of the Russian Security Council Aleksandr Lebed advocated, the CIS could create an effective buffer zone, but this proposal was rejected by the other participants. (Dostum is an ethnic Uzbek; he has several times been a guest of Tashkent, and has long been rumored to receive aid from the Uzbek government.) While stressing that Uzbekistan only provides Dostum with humanitarian aid, Karimov added that his country would "do everything possible so that he (Dostum) will prevent the Taliban militia" from advancing north.

Nazarbayev announced before the meeting that he was prepared to mediate in the Afghan fighting, reasoning that since Kazakstan does not border on Afghanistan and has never been in conflict with that country, it is the perfect mediator. Kazakstan has often proposed Almaty as the site of peace talks in several disputes, including the Tajik conflict.

Kyrgyz President Askar Akayev was categorical in stating that the CIS should not meddle in Afghan affairs, and that no support should be extended to General Dostum. Akayev was also the only Central Asian leader to pledge humanitarian aid to the population of Tajikistan and northern Afghanistan. However, despite the "common" pledge to strengthen security along the Afghan border, Akayev announced only that Kyrgyzstan's border with Tajikistan would be tightened. While this certainly considers the inevitable flow of more refugees into Kyrgyzstan, it could also be seen as a no-confidence vote in the abilities of border forces to confine refugees from Afghanistan to the Tajik border area.

Tajikistan's President Imomali Rakhmonov hailed the decision to take resolute measures in the event of a threat to the southern CIS border. Tajikistan is still living through its worst year since the full-scale civil war of 1992, and how much of the country was really under government control is debatable. Prior to the 26 September fall of Kabul, battles were reported daily between Russian border guards and Tajik opposition fighters attempting to cross from Afghanistan into Tajikistan. An agreement made with the Rabbani government, which was holed up in the Panjshir Valley with Ahmed Masoud's troops and facing attack from the Taliban, on establishing a 25–kilometer buffer zone in northern Afghanistan to distance Tajik opposition forces from the actual Tajik border soon collapsed.

The Almaty conference participants failed to respond to the proposal by Russian Federal Border Troops Commander Gen. Andrei Nikolaev that Kazakstan and Kyrgyzstan increase from the present 500 the number of their troops currently serving in the CIS peace keeping force in Tajikistan. (Uzbekistan, which has only 300 soldiers in the force, was apparently not asked to augment its strength.) Rakhmonov and Russian Foreign Minister Yevgenii Primakov, in Almaty on route to a meeting in China, subsequently agreed on unspecified measures to to step up the the defense of the Tajik-Afghan border, although Russian Defense Council Secretary Yurii Baturin said that the 25,000 men of the Russian border guards and the 201st motorized rifle division, already in Tajikistan, were sufficient. Border positions have been steadily reinforced since the beginning of this summer when intelligence reports indicated a buildup of Tajik opposition forces along the border.

The success of a religiously based movement in Afghanistan bodes ill for religious and opposition organizations in the former Soviet Central Asian states. Long suspected as harboring anti-government sentiment, these groups are in danger of being targeted on the (highly dubious) grounds they are Taliban sympathizers.

Kyrgyzstan

Population:	4,698,108
Capital:	Bishkek (pop. 650,000)
Major cities:	Osh (pop. 220,000), Jalalabad (pop. 75,000)
Area:	198,000 sq. km.
Major ethnic groups:	Kyrgyz 52.4%, Russian 21.5%, Uzbek 12.9%,
	German 2.4%, other 8.3%
Economy:	GDP growth: 6%
. . . .	Inflation rate: 35%
. . . .	Average monthly income: $20–$30
. . . .	Unemployment rate: 4.5%

PRESIDENT ACQUIRES MORE POWER IN KYRGYZSTAN

by BRUCE PANNIER

President Askar Akayev pushed through a new constitution that ensures his dominance over Kyrgyz politics. But except for numerous foreign loans and the opening of a major gold-mining operation, Kyrgyzstan made little political or economic progress in 1996.

"I'm open to cooperation with everyone." That was the quote attributed to Kyrgyz President Askar Akayev on the front page of *Vechernii Bishkek* on 2 January 1996. Akayev had reason to sound hopeful and generous at the start of the new year. Just one week earlier, he had become the third Central Asian leader in 1995 to be confirmed in his post until the beginning of the next century. Unlike the other two, Kazakstan's Nursultan Nazarbayev and Uzbekistan's Islam Karimov, Akayev had managed to retain some semblance of democracy by holding a competitive election and not a referendum.

But Akayev wasted little time after his election moving in the same direction as Nazarbayev and Karimov. Comparing himself to the Queen of England, Akayev complained that he didn't have enough power as president to get things done and requested that a referendum be held to amend the constitution. The Kyrgyz parliament accepted his request, and in February the referendum—consisting of a simple "yes" or "no" vote to some 50 constitutional amendments—was held. Of 2.3 million eligible voters in Kyrgyzstan, 2.2 million reportedly took part in the referendum, with more than 94 percent approving it. Most of those asked about the election admitted they had little idea what was involved.

The new constitution cemented the president's position as the dominant political force in Kyrgyzstan, giving him the power to nominate his choice for prime minister and appoint the government and head of the state bank. (The government formed after the new constitution was adopted, however, was virtually the same as the old.) According to an Amnesty International report released in May, the move toward a presidential state was part of a general trend toward a more repressive form of rule in Kyrgyzstan. The report mentioned in particular Akayev's use of the court system— ostensibly as a private citizen suing for libel—as an instrument in silencing two journalists at the country's only independent newspaper, *Res Publica*.

There was also grim news on the social and economic fronts. The fighting that broke out in central Tajikistan in May and June sent some 20,000 to 30,000 additional refugees into southern Kyrgyzstan. At the start of the year, the government press service announced that 25,000 of the country's investors had lost a combined $3.6 million by investing in companies that misused their funds. (The average monthly wage in Kyrgyzstan is between $20 and $30.) Privatization vouchers were offered as compensation.

Kyrgyzstan's largest state bank, Kyrgyzelbank, collapsed in February, threatening the deposits of about 2 million people—nearly half the country's population. The government promised compensation, but it was slow in coming and some depositors were still waiting at year's end. By summer, letters from hungry pensioners were regular items in many of Kyrgyzstan's newspapers. Some received basic goods, such as 50–kilogram bags of flour, in lieu of money; they were expected to keep what they needed and sell the rest to be able to purchase other essentials.

When wage and pension arrears and the promised compensation to Kyrgyzelbank depositors were finally paid in October, the outlays led to a 30 percent rise in the money supply. The Kyrgyz som, which had been the most stable currency in the Commonwealth of Independent States, dropped from 12 to 17 against the dollar in one week.

Business in Kyrgyzstan got a potential boost when the country was admitted to the customs union with Belarus, Russia, and Kazakstan in late January. But lack of adherence to the agreements and vague language employed in them kept the union from realizing its potential in 1996.

While the official economy stagnated, the underground economy flourished. In November, Omurbek Suvanalyev, the head of an anti-corruption parliamentary commission, said the shadow economy in 1996 was worth 4 billion som ($235 million), while the state budget totaled 6 billion som ($353 million).

LOANS KEEP COMING

Despite Kyrgyzstan's numerous political and economic problems, loans from foreign organizations continued to pour into the country. Akayev had previously established a reputation for Kyrgyzstan as a pioneer among the former Soviet republics that willingly adopted the International Monetary Fund's reform package. In June, the Asian Development Bank contributed $30 million for upgrading the country's heating and power sector, Japan gave $55 million for improving Bishkek's Manas Airport, and the World Bank awarded $100 million in loans to promote health-care reform and agricultural development. At the beginning of November, a conference of donor nations held in Japan promised to provide Kyrgyzstan with another $540 million.

The loans helped to offset Kyrgyzstan's poor attempts at privatization. Though many companies went on the auction block, there were few interested parties. Kyrgyzstan tried to wipe out its debt to Russia by offering enterprises to Russian investors as payment for past debts totaling nearly half a billion dollars. But interest among Russian investors was modest. Instead, the Russians agreed to reschedule Kyrgyzstan's debt payments over a 10–year period ending in 2009.

With the approach of winter, Kyrgyzstan faced a crisis stemming from the large bill it had again run up for natural gas from Uzbekistan. Residents of southern regions had long since found other means to cook food and heat their homes, but industry still relies on Uzbek gas. Uzbek President Karimov has never hesitated to punish Kyrgyzstan for moves that displeased him; in 1993, for example, Uzbekistan responded to Kyrgyzstan's unexpected introduction of the som by turning off the power, citing unpaid bills. However, this time Akayev and Karimov were able to work out a deal exchanging Uzbek natural gas for Kyrgyz hydroelectric power.

In one of the more bizarre events of the year, the speaker of the Kyrgyz parliament, Mukar Cholponbayev, was caught diverting the equivalent of $200,000 from parliament funds to a firm partly owned by his wife. One month after that information became public, it was suddenly decided that Cholponbayev had not been legitimately elected as speaker. In the vote 18 months earlier that had made Cholponbayev speaker, he had received 17 votes from the 29 deputies present in the parliament's upper house, a majority of those present but one vote short of a majority of the full 35–member house. A new vote was held and Cholponbayev was replaced.

THE 'SWITZERLAND OF CENTRAL ASIA'?

The best news for Kyrgyzstan came at the end of the year. After three years of preparations, the Kumtor gold-mining operation was completed and ready to begin work. Kumtor is said to contain the eighth largest deposit of gold on the planet, with an estimated 514 tons of gold reserves. The government has pointed to the project time and again as the savior of the country's economy. Akayev is fond of referring to his country as the potential Switzerland of Central Asia.

As 1997 dawned, Akayev had four more years to achieve his goals and much greater powers with which to achieve them. But if the Kyrgyz economy does not improve, Akayev will have few to blame but himself. Although Kumtor is scheduled to only recover its investment costs in 1997, if it can do that much it will still be a welcome sign.

Sidebar: WHATEVER HAPPENED TO TOPCHUBEK TURGUNALIYEV?

by BRUCE PANNIER *and* NARYN IDINOV

Though little attention was paid to the case, one of Kyrgyzstan's most outspoken government critics narrowly escaped a lengthy prison term at the end of 1996. The case involves Topchubek Turgunaliyev, the chairman of the Erkin [Freedom] Kyrgyzstan Party and co-founder of the For Deliverance from Poverty Movement.

Turgunaliyev faced a ten-year term in prison for embezzlement, which his lawyers claimed was a politically motivated attempt to silence this outspoken critic of the Kyrgyz government's policies. Both the conduct of the trial and the sentence Turgunaliyev initially received suggest this may well be true.

Topchubek Turgunaliyev was taken into custody by authorities on 17 December in the immediate wake of a rally he helped organize to demand better living conditions. He was charged with embezzling $10,000 from the Bishkek Humanities University in 1994, a charge he had been summoned to court over earlier in the month and for which his lawyer had requested, and received, an extension. The day before the rally, Turgunaliyev came to court expecting to answer routine questions but discovered he was to stand trial, which he refused to do in the absence of his lawyer. In any event, law enforcement authorities took Turgunaliyev into custody after he held discussions with government officials about the demands of the demonstrators.

This was not the first run-in with the authorities for Turgunaliyev. Indeed, it was the second time in two years he spent New Year's Day in jail. In late 1995 he was taken into custody on charges of insulting the president, Askar Akayev. However, when he arrived at the court room he was tried on charges of fomenting ethnic hatred by claiming Akayev was, in fact, a Kazak not a Kyrgyz. Prior to his 1995 arrest he had been acting as manager of Medetken Sherimkulov's presidential campaign. His arrest took place two days before the election, which Akayev won easily.

The 1996 charges against Turgunaliyev stemmed from a loan he approved for Timur Stamkulov while Turgunaliyev was the rector of the Bishkek Humanities University and Stamkulov was the Commercial Director of the university. Stamkulov borrowed the $10,000 promising to pay it back with interest. However, Stamkulov was robbed and lost all the money shortly afterward. Still an initial $2,300 was repaid and later an attempt was made to return an additional $3,000. By this time formal charges had been leveled against the two and the university refused to accept the money. No one seemed interested in the fact that Stamkulov had been robbed.

It is noteworthy that the Kyrgyzstan State Prosecutor's office brought this case to criminal court five times since the loan was made claiming embezzlement—although the university's witnesses, which should have been the plaintiff in the case, claimed to have no complaint against the two men. Likewise, in earlier incarnations, the court informed the State Prosecutor's office the case should be tried in civil, not criminal court. Nevertheless, this latest, sixth, trial went ahead in criminal court.

On 8 January 1997, the court found both Turgunaliyev and Stamkulov guilty of the charges. For authorizing the loan Turgunaliyev received 10 years in jail and confiscation of all his property while Stamkulov, for his part, received 6 years. Given the apparent harshness of the sentence, Human Rights Watch dispatched a letter to President Akayev requesting him to examine the merits of the case.

The Supreme Court of Kyrgyzstan changed the verdict handed down by a Bishkek municipal court to Turgunaliev on 18 February. The Supreme Court reduced his sentence from 10 to 4 years; while Stamkulov's sentence was cut from 6 to 3 years. Turgunaliev's lawyers declared their intention to appeal the decision to Kyrgyzstan's Constitutional Court. The Turgunaliyev case further tarnished Akayev's earlier reputation as the most democratic leader of Central Asia.

Turkmenistan

Population:	4,460,000
Capital:	Ashgabat (pop. 400,000)
Major cities:	Chardzhou (pop. 164,000), Tashauz (pop. 114,000)
Area:	490,100 sq. km.
Major ethnic groups:	Turkmen 77%, Uzbek 9.2%, Russian 6.7%, Kazak 2%, other 6.1%
Economy:	GDP growth: not available
	Inflation rate: 400% (est.)
	Average monthly income: $15–$30
	Unemployment rate: not available

MORE ECHOES OF THE PAST IN TURKMENISTAN

by LOWELL BEZANIS

Lack of progress toward democratization and economic downturn were once again features of the year in Turkmenistan. President Saparmurad Niyazov, the lone man at the helm for more than a decade, has given no indication of any significant changes in the course he's charted.

Five years after the collapse of the USSR, stability and continuity with the recent past remain the hallmarks of independent Turkmenistan. No visible change can be observed in the country's quiet—if impoverished—domestic life, or in the modest international profile it has adopted. The source of that continuity can be traced to the enduring problems besetting Turkmenistan: economic underdevelopment, a geographical location far from markets for its vast hydrocarbon reserves, and the authoritarian character of the country's present leadership. All three work in tandem to make and keep Turkmenistan a bastion of the past.

President (and Prime Minister) Saparmurad Niyazov, also known as Turkmenbashi (leader of all Turkmen) continued to rule Turkmenistan as he has for a little more than a decade—by brooking no opposition and regularly reshuffling, or sacking, his ministers and governors. True to his oft-repeated promise, Niyazov continued to reject rapid change in the name of stability. In an uncharacteristic display of apparent modesty, Niyazov announced in late September that he would forego accepting the title "president for life" in favor of deciding "together" (with the populace) who shall govern the country after his term expires in 2002.

Predictably, the lack of press freedom, effective limitations on speech, movement, and assembly, and the absence of any political opposition made Turkmenistan once again the subject of strong criticism by Western human-rights groups. In 1996, Turkmenistan had the dubious honor of being ranked among the 17 most repressive regimes in the world by the human-rights group Freedom House, and was branded "secretive" and "oppressive" in a report by Amnesty International.

AN ECONOMY ENCHAINED

Turkmenistan's failure to register any progress toward democratization is mirrored by its failure to liberalize the Turkmen economy, though the country did move modestly toward macroeconomic stability thanks to its success in restraining inflation. Despite promises in late 1995 to move aggressively forward on that front, Turkmenistan's largely hydrocarbon- and agriculture-based economy remains firmly in the hands of the state.

While Turkmenistan's vast oil and gas reserves may cause envy, the challenges connected with exploiting and marketing them assuredly don't. Despite hopes of increasing exports in 1996, and again in 1997, Turkmenistan's gas exports, estimated at 25 billion cubic meters, were down from the preceding year and far below the country's 1980s annual capacity of 110 billion cubic meters.

Turkmenistan's fundamental post-independence problems continued to hamper the search for prosperity. On one hand, Turkmenistan continues to depend upon Russia—its giant ally as well as its commercial competitor—to move its gas to the over-indebted markets of the Commonwealth of Independent States (CIS) in the Transcaucasus and Ukraine, which together owe Turkmenistan roughly $2 billion. On the other, Turkmenistan lacks alternative routes—being hemmed in by war-torn Afghanistan and pariah-state Iran. While progress was reported in moving gas (as well as train cargoes) via Iran, and onward to Europe through Turkey, it is still unclear where things actually stand or when the much-needed gas revenues might reach Turkmenistan's treasury.

Likewise, the late-September seizure of Kabul by the allegedly Pakistani-backed Taliban militia was widely interpreted by observers as a bid to realize a multi-billion-dollar plan to export Turkmen gas to Pakistan via Afghanistan. The scheme, initially favored by Argentina's Bridas (which in 1996 became embroiled in a legal conflict with Ashgabat over mutual rights and obligations) and subsequently the U.S. firm Unocal and Saudi Arabia's Delta, remains hostage to the ongoing military standoff between the Taliban and General Abdul Rashid Dostum and his allies, Shah Massoud and Burhanneddin Rabbani.

The consequences of the Niyazov government's statist approach to the economy came home to roost in 1996 when the cotton and grain harvests were only one-third as much as were called for. Turkmenistan had hoped to end grain imports and increase exports of cotton, a crop that earns the country hard currency. But disgruntled, long-unpaid agricultural workers and bad weather ended those hopes. To protect the populace from additional suffering because of food shortages, and presumably to head off social unrest, the Turkmen government pledged to increase social spending and undertake agricultural reform at year's end.

When harvest quotas were not reached, Niyazov sacked several governors for their "serious shortcomings and errors" in delivering on the plan. That mirrored a rash of sackings in 1995 when quotas were not reached (and likewise, sackings in the ministries of justice and defense for corruption during 1996). None of those changes, nor the announced limited privatization, is likely to significantly raise output until the serflike position of the peasantry is ended.

Contrary to the expectations of some observers, the government's harshness and general privation did not result in popular unrest during the year. Although there were unconfirmed reports of sporadic protests over food shortages in 1996 and violent prison unrest in Mary in late summer, there were no publicized anti-government demonstrations as there were in July 1995. Reports of a united, social-democratic opposition front being clandestinely formed in August remained just that. Since then, there has been no credible evidence of the front's existence, let alone activity.

MORE ENGAGED ABROAD

In its foreign relations, Turkmenistan broke new ground in 1996 with neighboring Uzbekistan. Relations between Ashgabat and Tashkent had been chilly since 1991 due to a variety of concrete problems ranging from traditional Uzbek-Turkmen antipathy and conflict over water-use rights to the differing personalities and foreign-policy agendas of the two countries' leaderships. While little can be seen behind the curtain, the exchange of official visits and large number of agreements signed at the beginning and end of 1996 appeared to signal the onset of a more pragmatic, if not amicable, bilateral relationship, presumably based on mutual need, as well as the hope of developing the emerging Central Asian-Transcaucasian Transport Corridor.

The rapprochement with Uzbekistan, Niyazov's visits to the Transcaucasian capitals and France, and repeated trips to Tehran and Moscow demonstrate that Ashgabat was marginally more engaged with the world than in past years. Otherwise, Turkmenistan's foreign relations remained significantly unaltered in 1996, with Ashgabat remaining a reluctant participant in the CIS and cool toward the efforts of its immediate neighbors to strengthen bonds among Central Asian states. While it is noteworthy that Ashgabat served as the venue for various efforts to resolve the Tajik conflict, it was probably an attractive site precisely because it represented—compared with Tashkent, Moscow, or Tehran—neutral ground.

As in the past, Turkmenistan's principal allies remained Russia and Iran, in that order. In both cases, Ashgabat's deference stems from the country's weakness and dependence upon those two regional powers for survival. In the ongoing argument over the legal status of the Caspian Sea, Turkmenistan remains firmly aligned with Russia and Iran against Azerbaijan and Kazakstan.

Incremental change in the positions of some of the players did not add up to significant change in 1996: while Turkmenistan remained the loyal junior partner of Russia in a potentially high-profit, high-stakes geopolitical tug-of-war centered on the Caspian basin, it also dreams of reducing Moscow's stranglehold over export pipelines and reaching foreign markets via Afghanistan or Iran.

Document: TURKMENISTAN'S EX-FOREIGN MINISTER ON NIYAZOV'S RULE

Former Turkmen Foreign Minister Avdy Kuliev gave a series of interviews to Elizabeth Fuller and Lowell Bezanis in which he argued that "There is only one way out" for Turkmenistan: "getting rid of this leader and this government." With a doctorate in linguistics, Kuliev worked in the Soviet diplomatic service from 1971 to 1990. Turkmen President Saparmurad Niyazov invited him to be-

come Foreign Minister in May 1990. In July 1992 he resigned from that post because of "repeated disagreements with Niyazov over policy" and returned to Moscow, where he played a leading role in Turkmen opposition activities.

ON NIYAZOV'S LEADERSHIP

"Niyazov has begun to lead the people back into the Middle Ages. Beginning in 1991, when we achieved independence, we began to slip backward from the level of development that we attained under Russian hegemony to the 19th century of possibly even the 18th.

Niyazov was counting on the country being able to survive on the proceeds of our oil and gas, which would generate enough wealth that everyone would have a Mercedes, no one would have to work, and the population would lie around drinking tea and thinking of nothing. Even the intelligentsia was taken in by this; they realized that if only they praised the president, they would be rewarded with material benefits. It was this stupid system of governing, where everyone is guaranteed enough to eat, or is given a car or an apartment, that led the country into the terrible impasse we find ourselves in today.

There is only one way out, by getting rid of this leader and this government. The way to do this is to hold free democratic elections. We have to follow the path of southeast Asia and draw on the experience of countries that know what democracy is. We have to train specialists, to teach people both how to use contemporary technology and how to think along contemporary lines.

Unfortunately, the present government, and Niyazov in particular, is not capable of taking such a step. They want to take a different approach: they are selling oil and gas concessions to the Argentineans and anyone who makes an offer, instead of beginning negotiations with one of the big companies with experience in this field and concluding an agreement on terms that do not infringe on our interests. The Bahrain government wanted to help, and they have good relations with the United States. Representatives of the crown prince traveled to Ashgabat six times while I was still minister. They offered to cooperate with us; they would take 15 percent of the profits, and Turkmenistan would keep the remaining 85 percent. Niyazov wouldn't agree—he clearly wanted to keep the entire sum himself. If he had agreed to this proposal then the state would have been rich. . . . As it is, he has $3 billion, and there isn't a single kopeck in the state treasury.

If you compare Turkmenistan with Azerbaijan (where the West is happy to invest), the political culture, the political consciousness of the Azerbaijanis and of their leadership is far higher than in Turkmenistan. And therefore corruption, theft, [and] bribery assume a more sophisticated form, which is acceptable to a Western observer. The level of corruption in Azerbaijan is no less than in Turkmenistan, but the Azerbaijani leadership gives something to the people while appropriating huge amounts for themselves. In Turkmenistan, there is blatant corruption: if you look at people's standard of living, the average salary per month is only $5 or $6. The Turkmen cannot understand where the national wealth is disappearing to. All the businessmen who flocked to Ashgabat to open offices from Russia, Turkey, and Iran in the hope of making a quick profit are shutting up shop because they realized that everything is controlled by one man, and one day he could say "No," and then they'll be left with nothing. Local businessmen who were beginning to make a success of things got caught in the same way. Niyazov imposed new taxes, confiscated their foreign currency and property.

Niyazov does these things spontaneously; he still thinks according to Soviet stereotypes. We are all still creatures of the Soviet system, whether we like it or not. He doesn't think in terms of the population or in terms of responsibility. Instead, he robs the people and accumulates wealth for himself. He knows that sooner or later he will have to leave the country. He has a large mansion in Belgium—his wife, son, and daughter live half of the year in Belgium and half in Russia—so neither he nor his closest associates have any deep links with . . . Turkmenistan. That is why they transfer money to Western banks and don't give a damn what happens in Turkmenistan.

ON CLANS/REGIONALISM

The social structure of Turkmen society was deformed during the Soviet period, and the clan system disappeared, although when a young Turkmen marries he chooses a bride from his own clan. Even though this tradition is now starting to die out, a man from the Tekke clan, for example, will never marry a girl from the Yomut clan, whose members are not considered worthy of them. It would be wrong to think that animosities still exist among the various clans, but our president, in order to secure his position has resurrected the divide and conquer approach and appoints a certain number of officials from each tribe. The hakims [administration heads] of each of the five oblasts belong to the clan that is predominant there—a northern Yomut in Tashauz, an Akhal-tekke in Akhal, a western Yomut in Balkhan Oblast, a Tekke in Mary, and an Erszari in Levab. He does this deliberately to play one off against the other.

It's the same within the government and ministries—but the power ministries are dominated by Tekke people, the minister for state security is a Tekke; so are the minister of internal affairs and the procurator general. This is all artificial in order to create tension within the leadership apparatus.

ON TURKMENISTAN'S RELATIONS WITH RUSSIA

At first, Niyazov wanted to do without Russia and played the anti-Russian card. Historically, the Turkmen were the only nation who offered resistance to Tsarist Russia; they always aspired to independence even if it meant they would starve. In 1881, the Tsarist army slaughtered 30,000 Turkmen at the battle of Geok-tepe, and the Turkmen have been anti-Russian ever since. So Niyazov began playing the anti-Russian card. First he decreed that Turkmen should be the state language, which people approved of, and which increased his authority.

I warned him against [the anti-Russian policy]. There are 400,000 Russians in Turkmenistan, of a total population of 4.5 million. They are politically the most sophisticated section of the entire population. Most of the Turkmen, by contrast, never had any interest in politics and are virtually politically illiterate even today. Niyazov initiated discriminatory policies toward these unfortunate Russians, which they didn't dare to utter a word of protest about. And this politically active part of the population simply retreated into itself and abandoned politics, which was a considerable loss for the country and has had a significant impact on Turkmen politics, present and future.

At the beginning, Niyazov was in a state of euphoria and started coming up with all sorts of anti-Russian statements, especially when the first $200 million landed in the state treasury—not that they did actually land in the state treasury but in Niyazov's own pocket. But after Niyazov quarreled with Moscow, Russia stopped providing food supplies. Bilateral trade was reduced to a minimum, and that had an effect on the people, who are now destitute; there's no meat, there's no flour, there hasn't been milk for a long time. Iran will not help us, and you can't import anything from Afghanistan or Uzbekistan, as both those states are also poor. Niyazov couldn't find common ground with Kazakstan, even though it has grain and meat—we could have bartered gas and electricity. Turkmenistan supplies Kazakstan with enormous amounts of electricity and receives nothing in return. In the end, Niyazov realized that he couldn't survive without Russia, and now he's prepared to sign any treaty, any agreement, and he doesn't stop to consider how it might affect Turkmenistan in the future. There is a secret treaty on military affairs that is not in Turkmenistan's interests, but he signed it all the same. I don't know the specific details, but I know that Russia has military facilities on the territory of Turkmenistan that it is keen to maintain."

Sidebar: IRAN-TURKMENISTAN: "THE MOST IMPORTANT TRANSPORTATION JUNCTION ON THE PLANET"

by BRUCE PANNIER

The rail-line linking Iran and Turkmenistan was officially opened on 13 May. The ceremony marking the opening was attended by 12 heads of state with an additional 700 "dignitaries and journalists" also present at the border town of Saraks. While statements in Turkmen newspapers about the link providing "the most important transportation junction on the planet" may be somewhat exaggerated it certainly is one of the most important economic developments in the area.

The line, which runs from Meshhed, Iran to Tedzhen, Turkmenistan is not only a source of pride and hope for the two countries, it also gives them more control over the shipping of their products. The newly-independent countries of

Central Asia have been economically hampered by Russian policies which still uphold ideas that have made the former Central Asian republics of the Soviet Union dependent on Moscow for import and export trade routes as the new line gives a fresh outlet to other countries. Transportation routes, for obvious strategic reasons, were not developed with the purpose of linking Central Asia with it's neighbors outside the Soviet Union. Since independence, few of these republics have been in a position to invest the money needed to open up new, reliable routes of trade. The establishment of this new railway not only greatly facilitates transport in terms of time and money but also gives the governments of countries such as Kazakstan and Uzbekistan new leverage in dealing with Russia. Kazakstan's President Nursultan Nazarbayev used his visit as an opportunity to seal an oil swap agreement with Iran which will permit Kazakstan to economically benefit from its huge oil reserves—without using an existing Soviet era, Russian-controlled pipeline—by transporting 2–5 million tons of oil across the Caspian to Iran.

For Turkmenistan the new route helps consolidate its position as a neutral political entity. Under the leadership of Saparmurad "Turkmenbashi" Niyazov the country has attempted to distance itself not only from its former masters in the Kremlin but also from its neighbors who were part of the Soviet Union. The arguments in favor of forming some sort of Turkic confederation to offset European or other outside influence have fallen on deaf ears when preached in Ashgabat. Niyazov has not expressed any desire to be one among equals in his area of the world. The completion of the new railroad further distances him from reliance on traditional routes and gives his country much more influence in the area. Turkmenistan is more the master of its own destiny when it comes to shipping many of its products, oil and natural gas notably. If other parties are interested in shipping through Turkmenistan to the Persian Gulf, thereby avoiding ever-changing rules and routes through Russian territory, they will be subject to Turkmen tariffs.

For Iran it is a demonstration that despite embargoes encouraged by the United States the Islamic Republic continues to have good relations with other countries and will play a major role in the area, particularly in trade. The benefits of outwitting "the great Satan" (the United States) will not be not lost on the representatives of the Economic Cooperation Organization who meet in Ashgabat this week.

Estimates are that in the first year the line will carry a half a million passengers and two million tons of freight and hopes are that soon the volume will be one million passengers and eight million tons of freight annually.

REGIONAL
ECONOMIC
DEVELOPMENTS
VII

CENTRAL, EASTERN, AND SOUTH-EASTERN EUROPE: A YEAR OF RECOVERY

by MICHAEL WYZAN *and* BEN SLAY

By 1996 almost all of Eastern Europe was recovering from the transformational recession of the early 1990s. The recoveries differed, however, in pace and depth. Bosnia-Herzegovina joined Albania, Poland, and Slovakia as one of the region's fastest-growing economies, while Bulgaria's record showed that misguided policies can nip a growing economy in the bud.

Economic developments during 1996 suggest a division of Eastern Europe into three regions. In the Central European core, consisting of Poland, Hungary, the Czech Republic, Slovakia, and Slovenia, integration within the region and with Western Europe has been the fastest and deepest. Hungary, the Czech Republic, and Poland were invited to join the Organization for Economic Cooperation and Development in 1996, and their prospects for full European Union membership brightened during the year. In the Baltics, with the partial exception of Estonia, stabilization has yet to be translated into strong growth, and relations with Russia are still at least as important as relations with the West. Lithuania shed its role as the Baltic economic laggard in 1996: its growth and dollar wage rates caught up with Latvia's, while Lithuania's inflation rate was lower than Latvia's and Estonia's. The Balkans continued to be the worst off. While some countries, like Bosnia-Herzegovina and Albania, experienced rapid growth in 1996, it was clearly growth from a very low level. Other countries, like Croatia and Macedonia, maintained low inflation but did not experience strong recoveries. And Bulgaria experienced a financial meltdown that could lead to hyperinflation in 1997. While the legacies of the Yugoslav wars of succession are responsible for some of those problems, hesitant reform efforts also played a major role.

CENTRAL EUROPE'S STEADY COURSE

The Polish economy emerged in 1996 as the region's most dynamic and attractive for foreign investors. While the 6 percent growth in gross domestic product forecast for the year was one point below the rate recorded in 1995, Poland was still one of the fastest-growing Eastern European economies. Investment grew by some 18 percent to 19 percent, and despite the growth slowdown in the EU and Germany (Poland's largest trading partners), dollar exports (not counting border trade) are likely to have increased by some 6 percent. However, consumption growth, which had lagged behind the growth of exports and investment during 1994–1995, shot up to between 9 percent and 10 percent in 1996. The increases in domestic demand produced a booming trade deficit, as dollar imports increased by some 30 percent during the first eight months of the year, but Poland's current accounts did remain in balance through the first three quarters.

There were problems, of course. While inflation in Poland fell below 20 percent in 1996 for the first time since the mid-1980s, it remained above the levels recorded in Croatia, the Czech Republic, the Baltic states, Macedonia, Slovakia, and Slovenia. And although unemployment has fallen considerably from its 1993 peak of 16.4 percent, the 13.2 percent rate recorded in October 1996 was still the highest in Central Europe. Those problems did not scare off foreign investors, however, who poured $4 billion–$5 billion in direct foreign investment into the country.

The approach of parliamentary elections in 1997 will test the ability of the government and the National Bank of Poland to keep fiscal and monetary policies on course. Personal income-tax rates for 1997 became a political football in October 1996, when attempts by both governing and opposition political parties to curry favor with the electorate resulted in a series of spontaneous tax cuts that put the government on a collision course with the National Bank. A compromise budget averted a conflict, but the bank and government are likely to be at loggerheads over monetary policy again in 1997. While the government wants pro-growth policies leading up to the elections, the National Bank of Poland is likely to raise interest rates to slow the growth in consumer debt (which doubled in 1996) and spending. Fortunately, investors and entrepreneurs seemed to have learned to live with Poland's political instability.

The bloom came off the Czech economy's rose in 1996. The problems were not so much with the macroeconomic numbers: inflation and unemployment remained essentially unchanged (at about 8.8 percent and 3.5 percent, respectively) from 1995 levels, industrial production for three quarters stood at 10.3 percent above 1995 levels, and the state budget remained roughly in balance. Instead, the Czech economy found itself facing two unfamiliar problems in 1996: political uncertainty and financial instability. The center-right coalition government lost its majority in the May–June parliamentary elections, and while the coalition parties did better in the senatorial elections in November, the coalition had by then lost much of its internal cohesion. The Social Democratic Party, which emerged as a contender for power in the second half of the year, vacillated between playing constructive and destructive opposition roles. Some spectacular bank failures, such as Kreditni Banka's collapse in August, provided plenty of ammunition for the opposition and threw fresh light on the Czech financial system's problems. The perennial complaints about the Prague Stock Exchange's illiquidity and lack of transparency seemed to resonate more strongly in the second half of 1996 and helped make the exchange the laggard of the Central European markets. The Czech Republic's external balance also deteriorated in 1996: the trade deficit for the year is expected to hit $6 billion, while the current-account deficit is forecast to hit $3.7 billion, or 6.9 percent of GDP.

The Czech consumption boom that began in 1995 continued in 1996 and seemed to push those troubling issues from most Czechs' minds. Real wages in mid-1996 were nearly 10 percent above mid-1995 levels, and retail sales grew by 11 percent. Unfortunately, annual labor productivity was forecast to grow by only 3.5 percent, so that real wage growth significantly increased unit labor costs. That slowed export growth to a crawl and caused GDP growth forecasts to be continually reduced, from 5.4 percent in early 1996 to 4.5 percent by the end of the year. Meanwhile, the government seemed more concerned about arguing over the trade deficit than about implementing regulations to increase the Prague Stock Exchange's transparency and liquidity.

An important year for the Czech economy will be 1997. The absence of elections could increase politicians' resolve to deal with the financial system's problems, make the stock exchange more transparent, and increase pressures on enterprises to restructure. While unemployment might rise as a result, so would labor productivity; that would reduce inflation, make Czech exports more competitive, and help attract foreign capital. Events in 1996, however, did not bode well for the Czech polity's abilities to deal with such problems.

While the Central European economies have a great deal in common, Hungary's macroeconomic trends in 1996 differed in important ways from those of its neighbors. GDP growth was forecast to be an anemic 1 percent; and real wages, consumption, retail sales, and investment all registered declines during the first three quarters of 1996, the latter by 7.5 percent and 4 percent (over September 1995 levels), respectively. Hungary had to strain to keep fiscal policy under control: inflation in 1996 was around 20 percent, and Hungary was the Central European economy most dependent on funding from the International Monetary Fund (IMF). On the plus side, however, Hungary's external balance continued to improve markedly in 1996.

Those developments can be traced to the effects of the March 1995 stabilization program, which raised interest rates, devalued the forint by 30 percent, and choked off Hungary's economic recovery. When combined with debt-servicing payments, the fiscal burden associated with Hungary's "premature welfare state"—which provides pensions to a third of the population—also contributed to the anemic growth. Still, the stabilization program was in many respects successful in 1996. The consolidated budget deficit was held to 4 percent of GDP during the first three quarters, a particularly impressive record in light of the fact that the social security deficit was forecast to end the year 60 billion forints higher than planned. The current-account deficit at the end of September had been reduced to $1.11 billion, which was less than half of the $2.27 billion registered during the same period of 1995. Disbursements from the IMF's $309 million standby credit have proceeded without a hitch. And both Moody's and Standard & Poor's had given Hungarian government debt investment-grade ratings by the end of the year.

Consumer prices in 1996 seemed likely to rise by 20 percent, below the 1995 surge (when consumer prices rose 28.3 percent), but high enough to make Hungary Central Europe's high-inflation country. Still, falling inflation did allow the National Bank to cut interest rates, which in turn reduced debt-servicing costs and fiscal pressures. The official inflation forecast of 17 percent to 18 percent for 1997 will be difficult to meet, however.

On the other hand, the recovery can be expected to accelerate in 1997, largely on the strength of growing exports and labor productivity, which increased by nearly 10 percent from January to July 1996. Slow (or negative) growth in real wages and rapid productivity growth suggest that the large declines in unit labor costs recorded in 1996 will also continue into 1997. Corporate profits should therefore continue to increase, and the Budapest Stock Exchange's sterling performance in 1996 (the BSE index had registered 121 percent growth in dollar terms through mid-December) could be repeated in 1997. Still, Hungary is likely to approach the 1998 parliamentary elections with the slowest growth, and the largest fiscal imbalances, in Central Europe.

Slovakia's excellent macroeconomic performance, one of Central Europe's biggest surprises during 1994–1995, continued in 1996. In contrast to the other Central European economies, actual GDP growth in Slovakia exceeded official forecasts for most of the year and is likely to record an annual increase of between 6 percent and 7 percent. Slovakia also seems to be cementing its position as Central Europe's low-inflation country: consumer prices in September were increasing at only a 5.2 percent annual rate. On the other hand, Slovakia's trade and current-account deficits rose steadily throughout 1996, and by the end of the year they were forecast to reach $1.7 billion and $1.5 billion, respectively. Unlike Poland and Hungary, Slovakia's dollar exports may have actually declined in 1996. Slovakia's export-led growth of 1994–1995 thus seems to be ending, as consumption is now pulling GDP along. (Retail sales increased by 14.3 percent in the first half of 1996.) In contrast to Poland, the Slovak trade deficit is clearly not the inevitable consequence of foreign investment: only $70 million in direct foreign investment found its way into the country during the first half of 1996; and the cumulative stock of such investment reached only $800 million. Moreover, growing consumption did not seem to be pulling industrial production along with it: industrial output only grew by 2.9 percent during the first eight months of 1996 (compared with the same period in 1995). And although unemployment continued to fall from the 14.8 percent rate recorded at the end of 1994, the 12.3 percent rate Slovakia recorded in August remained above the Hungarian and well above the Czech rates. The persistence of high unemployment is somewhat surprising, given Slovakia's torrid GDP growth as well as the country's small size, well-trained labor force, and relatively good transportation infrastructure.

Indeed, the inconsistencies in Slovakia's macroeconomic data—apparent in the combination of 7 percent reported GDP growth on the one hand and declining industrial production and dollar exports on the other—raise questions about their veracity. The obvious politicization of many of Slovakia's economic-policy institutions (such as the National Property Fund's supervising the transfer of state property to private firms owned by groups tied to the ruling Movement for a Democratic Slovakia and its coalition government partners) does little to dispel doubts about the Statistical Office's objectivity. And as long as Vladimir Meciar's government is able to hold on to the reins of power by keeping its opponents off balance, proponents of a less contentious approach to economic policy are likely to be frustrated. Still, Slovakia's foreign-exchange reserves seemed to end the year at adequate levels, and the country's small external-debt burden affords Slovakia advantages that Poland and Hungary do not enjoy. Even if Slovakia's reported macroeconomic performance were to undergo some slippage, it would still remain impressive.

BULGARIA COLLAPSES, ROMANIA, ALBANIA RECOVER

For the Bulgarian economy, 1996 was catastrophic. The lev fell from 70.72 to the dollar on 2 January to 487.35 on 30 December, as the Bulgarian National Bank's foreign reserves fell to $525 million on 30 November from $1.43 billion a year earlier. Consumer prices rose by 310.8 percent for the year; GDP is forecast to have declined by 8 percent to 10 percent, and industrial production by 12 percent in 1996. The average monthly wage had fallen to $50–$60 in December from $127 in December 1995, while unemployment rose to 12.5 percent and the budget deficit was 8.9 percent of GDP (vs. 6.7 percent in 1995). The deterioration results from declining production and from the high interest rates (peaking at 25 percent monthly) set by the Bulgarian National Bank to try to support the lev. Exports and imports in January–September fell by between 14 percent and 15 percent relative to January–September 1995; the trade surplus over the first nine months was $131.8 million and the current-account deficit $33.7 million.

Amid that turmoil, Zhan Videnov's socialist government endeavored to heed IMF demands for accelerated structural reform as much as its leftist inclinations and anti-reform constituency would allow. That was sufficient to win a $580 million IMF standby credit in July but insufficient to prevent the fund from halting disbursements after the first one. Toward the end of 1996, the government agreed to introduce a currency board. Such a step would replace the Bulgarian National Bank's role in controlling the money supply by a mechanism converting foreign-currency flows into leva and vice versa at a fixed rate and backing all leva in circulation with foreign reserves.

Behind the turmoil lie two facts. Bulgaria's large foreign-debt-service obligations (about $1.2 billion in both 1996 and 1997) and unattractiveness to foreign investors necessitate frequent injections of funds from international financial institutions in order to keep Bulgaria from defaulting on those obligations. And those institutions will lend only if Bulgaria progresses on structural reform, which governments of both right and left have been unwilling to do.

The government did make progress with structural reform, agreeing to close 64 money-losing enterprises, while the Bulgarian National Bank declared 13 banks bankrupt. But those attempts to close banks were resisted by the courts. And there was backtracking, as when parliament in November passed changes to the foreign-investment law discriminating against small investors and tightening provisions against foreign land ownership. Mass privatization started in January, leading to voucher auctions in October and the creation of investment funds. One big cash privatization occurred—the sale of 60 percent of Sodi Devnya to General Chemical. But the deal brought in only $30 million by year's end. Rover, one of the few large investors, announced the closure of its Varna plant in April.

If 1997 brings political stability and a currency board, there will be grounds for optimism. However, Videnov's resignation at a party congress on 21 December, that congress's rejection of radical reforms, and the fact that the next general elections are not scheduled before 1998 do not bode well.

Hopes were raised in Romania by the election of a pro-reform parliamentary majority and president in November. Macroeconomic performance deteriorated in the second half of 1996, and structural difficulties remain profound, so the new government has its work cut out for it.

The leu's official exchange rate declined by 32 percent over the course of the year. The difference between the official and black-market rates also grew during the year, reaching a record 30 percent. Four state banks—all others having lost the right to trade in foreign currency in March—ration such currency to enterprises, and the government periodically (as in August) confiscates foreign currency from enterprises, forcing them to buy it back at disadvantageous rates.

Faster monetary growth and a widening budget imbalance in the pre-election period caused some aspects of economic performance, already affected by energy shortages and a poor wheat crop, to deteriorate further. While consumer prices were initially projected to grow by 20 percent in 1996, they rose by 7.5 percent in July alone—as fuel and electricity prices increased—and are forecast to have increased by about 45 percent for the year. The budget deficit will end the year at between 5.5 percent and 6 percent of GDP, compared with the 3.45 percent target.

Still, economic growth remained robust in 1996: GDP and industrial production grew by 4.5 percent and 8.7 percent, respectively, during January–September. The official unemployment rate dropped dramatically, hitting 5.9 percent in October, compared with 8.9 percent in December 1995, while dollar (about $145) and real leu wages have changed little since the end of 1995. The output growth resulted from buoyant domestic demand, especially consumption spending, since exports fell by 5.5 percent during January–September, relative to the same period in 1995, and imports dropped by 11.1 percent over that period. However, as in Slovakia, the data may not be entirely reliable, since rapid output growth is difficult to reconcile with a precipitous decline in imports.

The trade and current-account deficits through September were lower than a year earlier, and the gross foreign debt, while growing, was a manageable $6 billion. Foreign-exchange reserves were augmented by a number of international-bond placements underwritten by investment banks, the result of a strategy of reducing dependence on the IMF, which withheld tranches of a standby credit over displeasure with Romanian economic policy.

A mass-privatization program resulted in 90 percent of those eligible exchanging their vouchers for shares in 3,900 state enterprises, and in the creation of five regional Private Ownership Funds. However, the program excludes many important enterprises, while allowing the state to retain 40 percent ownership of firms. The national bank withdrew support from two commercial banks in July and will now allow them to fail.

The year ended with an IMF delegation urging the new government of Prime Minister Victor Ciorbea to cut budget expenditures (especially subsidies), liberalize prices and the foreign-exchange regime, and accelerate the restructuring of energy-intensive sectors and privatization.

Albania experienced another year of good economic performance and substantial international support, despite indignation in the West over irregularities in the general elections in May. Albania had the second-fastest (after Bosnia-Herzegovina) growth rate in Europe: real GDP is expected to have risen by 8.5 percent (after an 11 percent rise in 1995) and industrial production by 6 percent (up from 5.5 percent in 1995), with the leading sectors being copper and chromium ores. Economic growth continues to be led by agriculture—which will experience double-digit growth for the second consecutive year—and services.

However, inflation rose to about 17 percent in 1996 from 8 percent in 1995, due in part to the removal of price controls on bread and fuels and to the introduction of a value-added tax in July. The lek gyrated wildly during 1996, falling to 120 to the dollar in May and then strengthening to about 98 to the dollar in November, before finishing at about 103. Although the strengthening currency kept inflation down, pyramid schemes were partly responsible for the lek's strength. Such schemes tempted Albanians to convert foreign exchange into lek in order to earn monthly interest rates of up to 50 percent. The IMF in November warned of the macroeconomic implications of the likely collapse of those schemes.

Albania's fiscal and external imbalances grew in 1996. The budget deficit was forecast to reach 15 percent of GDP (up from 9.4 percent in 1995), the current-account deficit was expected to double to $225 million, and the trade deficit was expected to grow to $580 million (vs. $416 million in 1995). However, unlike in Bulgaria and Romania, both exports and imports increased in 1996, the former on the strength of rising textile and shoe production. Much of the $200 million in cumulative foreign direct investment in Albania has been in tourism, although in October, Germany's Preussag committed $53 million to upgrading the country's chromium mines.

RESPECTABLE, UNSPECTACULAR BALTIC ECONOMIES

Estonia recorded a solid economic performance in 1996, with rather high inflation and modest economic growth. Aggregate production growth fell from last year's 3 percent to between 1.8 percent and 2 percent in January–August (relative to that period in 1995), while industrial production grew by 1.5 percent in January–June (the same as in 1995). Observers trace the slow growth to the aftereffects of Estonia's wide-ranging privatization program during 1994–1995 (under which the privatization agency must use the assets of privatized firms to pay off their debts) and to the migration of economic activity underground.

Although Estonia's currency board contributed to macroeconomic stability by forcing the government to keep the budget in balance, the fixed exchange rate may have contributed to inflation by preventing nominal appreciation in the exchange rate or the sterilization of capital inflows. Still, the growth in consumer prices slowed markedly following rapid increases in the first quarter to only 14.8 percent, quite a decline from the 28.9 percent recorded in 1995. Unemployment was 4.1 percent of the working-age population in April–June, compared with 4.2 percent the year before. Although Estonia's monthly dollar wage ($246 in September) was the highest in the Baltics, it was less than the $277 it had been in December 1995.

Exports through September were $1.4 billion and imports $2 billion, while the current-account deficit in January–June was $152 million (vs. $123 million in January–June 1995). The IMF has agreed to a $20 million standby facility in case official financing is needed. Although Estonia had attracted $700 million in foreign investment by 31 March (the equivalent of 20 percent of GDP), the net inflow fell during January–June. Fears that the Coalition Party would enter a coalition with the rural-based Center Party, potentially leading to increased protectionism, eased following the formation of a government that excluded the latter in December.

Privatization, featuring cash sales (including those to foreigners) forged ahead in 1996, so that only 4 percent of Estonia's companies were left in state hands at the end of the year. The emphasis in late 1996 and 1997 had shifted to selling infrastructure and public utilities.

Latvia's economic performance in 1996 was rather similar to Estonia's. That represented quite a turnaround for Latvia, since banking and political crises in 1995 had taken a toll on the economy. As in Estonia, GDP in Latvia is expected to have grown by 1 percent to 2 percent in 1996 after rising by 1.5 percent in January-June. Industrial production rose by 2 percent during the first nine months. Those results are impressive coming on the heels of the sobering 1995 statistics (GDP and industrial output in 1995 declined by 1.6 percent and 9.5 percent, respectively), and they supported those who favored taking a tough line toward the country's failing banks.

Although it is the only Baltic economy that does not have a currency board, inflation in Latvia in 1996 (which may have been as low as 13.5 percent) was lower than in Estonia. That resulted in part from budgetary discipline, as the fiscal deficit fell from 3.3 percent of GDP to 2 percent at the IMF's urging. On the other hand, Latvia's monthly dollar wage ($179 in December vs. $213 in December 1995) is lower than Estonia's, and the Latvian unemployment rate, which increased to 7.1 percent in December (compared with 6 percent a year earlier), is much higher.

The lats appreciated in real terms during 1996, which helped push the trade deficit to $510 million by September and the current-account deficit to $156 million at mid-year. Latvia has attracted only $400 million in foreign investment, a low figure reflecting financial instability and the opaqueness and alleged corruption of privatization procedures. Through 1994, Latvian privatization focused on selling money-losing enterprises to buyers who were required to cover enterprise debts and maintain employment. But cash privatization accelerated in 1995 and 1996, involving some of the biggest and most profitable firms; a mass-privatization program is also under way.

Similarly, Lithuania's GDP is forecast to have grown by 3.6 percent in 1996, although industrial production (which in October was 7.5 percent above the

October 1995 level) seems to be growing most rapidly. While Lithuania remains the poorest of the three Baltic economies, its gross dollar wage of $173 in September (vs. $163 in December 1995) has caught up with Latvia's, and its unemployment rate (6.2 percent in November 1996) remains below Latvia's. Moreover, inflation was only 13.1 percent, meaning that Lithuania will record one of the lowest inflation rates in the region. On the other hand, the budget deficit (projected to be 3.4 percent of GDP) remains very large for a country with a currency board. Fortunately, Lithuania has successfully launched Eurobond offerings and syndicated loans, and in September it became the first former Soviet republic to obtain a credit rating.

Lithuania's $430 million trade deficit during January–June was below the level recorded in the first half of 1995, although a $407 million current-account deficit was forecast for 1996. Happily, relations with the IMF improved in July when the fund agreed to resume disbursements of a 1994 credit, despite concern over generous bank bailouts. Lithuanian's economic recovery should continue, barring major policy reversals by the new government formed after the center-right Homeland Union's victory in the October parliamentary elections.

RECOVERIES VARY ACROSS FORMER YUGOSLAVIA

For Slovenia, the wealthiest post-communist country, the first half of 1996 saw a continuation of a slowdown that began in 1995, but the second half witnessed invigorated economic performance. Slovenia on 10 June signed an association agreement with the EU and by year's end had agreed on its share of the former Yugoslavia's debt with the IMF, World Bank, and Paris and London Clubs.

Although the macroeconomy remained stable in 1996, Slovenia's GDP growth is projected to fall to 3.5 percent (from 5 percent in 1995), largely because GDP only grew by 1.6 percent in the first half of 1996. Industrial production will be largely flat, and exports are forecast to increase by a meager 1.6 percent. GDP growth has therefore been led by domestic demand, which grew by about 4.5 percent. The annual inflation rate of 8.8 percent made Slovenia one of Eastern Europe's low-inflation countries, however, and the government budget was virtually balanced. Privatization moved slowly and generally favored insiders, while attitudes toward foreign investment remained ambivalent. Still, Slovenia's strong performance should improve further as EU countries recover from their recessions and trade ties with other former Yugoslav republics deepen.

The official unemployment rate declined from 14.5 percent in December 1995 to 14 percent in October 1996, while labor-market surveys conducted according to international standards found a 7.3 percent unemployment rate in May. Wages remain high (net wages were $615 and gross wages $966 in September) and real wages grew strongly during the second half of the year. Those wage trends posed an increasing threat to Slovenia's international competitiveness, especially since the tolar's strength keeps the domestic price level at about three-quarters of Austria's. Fortunately, the tolar weakened in 1996 in real terms, falling to 140.85 to the dollar from 125.99 at the end of 1995, so that export competitiveness rose by 7 percent (it had fallen by 11.9 percent in 1995). Even so, the trade deficit in January–September was $851 million, up from $628 million for that period in 1996. Fortunately, Slovenia's current-account deficit for the first nine months was only $197 million, which was small compared with $2.3 billion in national-bank foreign reserves.

Croatia's economic performance was mixed during 1996, the first year without military conflict. The impressive macroeconomic stability of 1994–1995 was maintained, and GDP growth rose to 4.1 percent but exports fell somewhat. Strained relations with the EU and the United States slowed integration with Western bodies; Croatia ended 1996 as one of the few Eastern European countries that had yet to sign an association agreement with the EU.

Industrial production rose by 2.5 percent in January–September relative to that period in 1995. Officially, unemployment is high and rising, reaching 15 percent in December (vs. 13.9 percent one year earlier), although according to international definitions, the rate is between 9 percent and 10 percent. Wages rose in the first eight months by 18 percent relative to the same period the previous year. With a stable exchange rate and little inflation, labor costs rose: average monthly dollar wages reached $397 in August.

Croatia continued its impressive record of price stability in 1996: the 3 percent to 4 percent price rise recorded in 1996 came on the heels of 1994's 3 percent deflation and the 3.7 percent inflation rate registered in 1995. In fact, since late 1993, Croatia has had the lowest inflation rates of all reforming economies. After a significant loosening in fiscal and monetary policies in mid-1996, fiscal policy tightened again in the autumn, leading to a modest budget deficit of 0.5 percent of GDP.

Weak demand in the EU and the strong kuna produced a $1.3 billion trade deficit in January–June 1996 (the same as a year earlier), although the current-account deficit fell to $662 million from $815 million. Those numbers are not worrisome, since the World Bank is providing $330 million in balance-of-payments support and a Eurobond issue will provide another $250 million. Croatia in April joined Slovenia in having agreed with the London Club on its share of the former Yugoslav federal debt.

There was some good business news: pharmaceutical manufacturer Pliva in April became the first company in the region to offer shares on the London Stock Exchange, while Zagrebacka banka has obtained several syndicated loans from international investment banks. Still, the enterprise and banking sectors remain largely unreformed: enterprise losses totaled 5 percent of GDP in 1995; and inter-enterprise arrears had reached 9 percent of GDP in August 1996.

The Macedonian economy turned around in 1996, with social product growing by between 1.5 percent and 2 percent for the entire year (after declining by 2.2 percent in 1995) and industrial output rising by 4 percent during January–September. Inflation was essentially zero for the first 11 months, giving Macedonia the best inflation performance of all economies in transition. However, unemployment continued to rise, reaching between 25 percent and 30 percent.

The denar weakened from 37.98 to the dollar at the end of 1995 to 41.38 to the dollar on 24 December, an 8.2 percent decline which should have boosted competitiveness, in view of the low inflation. However, Macedonia has rather high dollar wages (around $220 per month), so the denar's decline may have been insufficient to reduce the current-account deficit, which stood at $229 million in mid-year, up from $195 million during the same period in 1995. Exports were $448 million in January–June, vs. $640 million in the same period in 1995, while imports were largely unchanged at $668 million.

A number of developments in 1996 indicated that Macedonia was breaking out of its international isolation. Those included initialing a cooperation accord with the EU in June, agreeing in October to reschedule $644 million in London Club debt, reaching an accord with the World Bank in September on a $45 million structural-adjustment loan, eliminating all tariffs in trade with Federal Yugoslavia in October (mutual recognition between the countries had occurred in April), and agreeing with the IMF on an $80 million enhanced structural adjustment facility in November. Still, Macedonia's economy continues to face daunting structural problems. The leveraged buyouts that dominate privatization activities seem impressive on paper (870 firms with 133,000 employees have gone through the process), but they bring in little foreign capital or expertise and reinforce insider control of enterprises.

Federal Yugoslavia's hopes in early 1996 for better economic performance financed by warming relations with international institutions may have been dashed by Western reaction to political developments in Belgrade at the end of the year. Milosevic's unwillingness to accept that Federal Yugoslavia is but one of socialist Yugoslavia's successors continued to block agreements with the London and Paris Clubs and membership in the IMF, although the government did make concessions on that score late in 1996.

Preliminary reports forecast GDP growth of 5 percent (for the second straight year) and a 6 percent increase in industrial output, but the forecasts were based on possibly unjustified optimism about the economy's performance in the autumn. Unemployment is high and rose through mid-year, while the decline in real wages is slowing (average monthly dollar wages are around $116). Inflation will be about 100 percent, up from 79 percent in 1995. The trade and current-account deficits were projected to be $1.85 billion and $1.4 billion, respectively, highlighting the need for rapprochement with international institutions.

Bosnia-Herzegovina's 1996 GDP growth was projected at 35 percent, with foreign trade and construction booming in the larger cities. But overall economic conditions remained desperate: the unemployment rate was 50 percent; 75 percent of the population survived off charity; and the average monthly wage was $70. Foreign assistance helped finance a projected $1.1 billion trade gap. About $500 million in aid has been disbursed, out of $2 billion pledged; the World Bank-led reconstruction effort envisages $5.1 billion in assistance over three to four years. Even those large amounts may not be enough to rebuild Bosnia's shattered economy.

Note: The data cited in this paper are drawn from a wide variety of official and unofficial sources, including Country National Bank and Statistical Office bulletins, PlanEcon and WEFA reports, *The Wall Street Journal*, *Financial Times*, and *Business Central Europe*. Most of the 1996 data are preliminary and may undergo substantial revision.

MOSTLY STABLE IN THE CIS

by NATALIA GURUSHINA, MICHAEL WYZAN, *and* BEN SLAY

The region sometimes referred to as the Commonwealth of Independent States saw most inflation rates fall, nearly all currencies stabilize, and some economies grow. Foreign capital continued to bypass most of the region, however, and several countries were still plagued by energy shortfalls. Inflation rates fell, currencies stabilized, while Armenia, Georgia, Kyrgyzstan—and perhaps Kazakstan and Turkmenistan—recorded economic growth. That growth occurred from a very low base, however, and foreign capital continued to bypass most of the region. Worst of all, Belarus and Tajikistan could be headed for economic disaster in 1997. Economic performance in the rest of the region was generally similar to Russia's—financial stabilization was attained or consolidated, but economic recoveries did not materialize. Whether gross-domestic-product growth resumes, or whether low inflation will continue to be unaccompanied by economic recovery, is a key question in 1997.

WESTERN CIS

The year 1996 was a turning point for financial stabilization in Ukraine, where declining inflation was combined with the introduction of a new currency. Tight fiscal and monetary policies limited consumer price inflation to 40 percent during 1996, was well below the 181 percent rate recorded in 1995. Financial stabilization was accompanied by the exchange of the temporary karbovanets for the hryvnya in September. The hryvnya retained its real value against the dollar until the end of the year, while the karbovanets actually had appreciated earlier in 1996. Progress in financial stabilization in turn played a key role in the successful flotation of Ukraine's $100 million Eurobond issue in November.

But the stabilization occurred against a backdrop of persistent fiscal problems. Weak tax discipline meant that the government had to control the budget deficit largely by trimming spending, which often translated into no funding for expenditures authorized by parliament. Budget sequestrations, combined with growing inter-enterprise and fiscal debts, produced an arrears crisis. Enterprises' accounts payable rose sharply in real terms and had reached the equivalent of two-thirds of GDP in July 1996, while the government itself owed 3 billion hryvnyas (around $1.67 billion) in wage arrears. Despite this sequestration, 41 percent of the deficit (4.9 percent of GDP) during January–August had to be financed by inflationary national-bank credits. The progress on stabilization in 1996 may therefore have been borrowed from 1997. Moreover, financial stabilization definitely did not translate into an economic recovery. Ukraine's real GDP shrank by an estimated 10 percent and industrial output by 12 percent during the first three quarters, while unemployment climbed to 12 percent of the economically active population.

Ukraine's 1996 privatization program showed mixed results. The government announced the completion of the small-scale privatization program for the entire country (except Crimea) in mid-September, but the privatization of medium and large industrial and agricultural enterprises lagged behind schedule. The slow pace of privatization and a lack of restructuring of privatized and state enterprises restricted direct foreign investment, the cumulative value of which totaled slightly more than $1.2 billion by October 1996. By contrast, Poland received almost $5 billion in new direct foreign investment in 1996.

Ukraine's mixed economic performance in 1996 increases the importance of the government's 1997 economic program, which was announced in mid-October. The program calls for new subsidies, tax breaks, and national-bank support for large state enterprises and farms, all of which is difficult to reconcile with the government's promises made to the International Monetary Fund (IMF) and foreign investors to deepen economic reform. While those points could be tactical concessions designed to obtain parliamentary approval, they could undermine confidence in Ukraine's commitment to economic reform. That in turn could hurt prospects for the release of a $3.1 billion IMF loan.

Deepening international isolation and the growing authoritarianism of President Alyaksandr Lukashenka affected Belarus's economic development in 1996. While falling inflation during the first nine months was a hopeful sign, it probably resulted less from market forces than from the administrative measures introduced to stem declines in production. Those measures included the introduction of industrial-production targets, restriction on the foreign-exchange market, new restrictions on private business (Belarus's private sector accounts for only 15 percent of GDP), and artificially maintaining the Belarusian ruble's overvaluation against the dollar.

The IMF and foreign investors responded by largely withdrawing from Belarus. By September 1996, cumulative direct foreign capital in the country totaled a meager $85 million. In particular, foreign investors were scared off by the halting of the privatization process in the second half of 1996, following a corporate reregistration scheme ostensibly aimed at fighting corruption and tax evasion. The lack of external finance, combined with a persistent current-account deficit (which could reach $750 million in 1996, triple the 1995 level) and Belarus's shrinking foreign-exchange reserves (which fell from some $200 million to $45 million from November 1995 to June 1996) could send the Belarusian economy into free fall in 1997.

Belarus may have been saved from economic collapse in 1996 by Russia's decision in April to write off Belarus's $775 million debt for energy supplies and $470 million in intergovernmental debt. (In return, Belarus waived a $914 million claim regarding Russian troops stationed on its territory, and a $250 million claim for Belarusian companies' assets frozen in the former Soviet Foreign Trade Bank.) The agreement may help Russia's Gazprom to begin constructing a new gas pipeline through Belarus to Western Europe.

Like Ukraine and Belarus, Moldova recorded a large decrease (around 10 percent) in GDP in 1996. That was due in part to a 37 percent decline in the 1996 grain harvest, resulting from bad weather conditions and the unusually severe winter, which devastated the roughly 50 percent of Moldovan GDP and 60 percent of export revenues produced by agricultural and food-processing activities. Tight monetary policy and the government's strict adherence to IMF recommendations may have kept output from growing faster, but they did keep the leu stable against the dollar and helped to reduce inflation from 24 percent in 1995 to an estimated 12 percent in 1996 (except for the Transdniestr region, where the monthly inflation rate reached 20 percent to 30 percent).

Along with growing imports of investment goods, falling exports due to the poor harvest doubled the first-half current-account deficit ($158 million) over the same period in 1995. Moldova's external position in 1996 also reflected its continuing dependence on energy imports from Russia. Moldova owes more than $400 million to Russia for gas supplies, although the Transdniestr region accounts for 60 percent of that figure. The "gas" part of Moldova's debt was increasingly converted into equity positions by Russian companies and investment funds in Moldovan firms. While Moldova's cash-privatization program began in 1996, weak domestic demand and uncertainty over the future of the Transdniestr region continue to deter foreign investors: only $29 million in new direct foreign investment was recorded in the first half of 1996. Still, Moldova's inflation numbers in 1996 were the best in the western CIS.

TRANSCAUCASUS

Armenia's economic recovery continued at a slightly slower pace in 1996, despite the controversy over the alleged rigging of the September presidential election, which damaged the country's democratic credentials and highlighted popular dissatisfaction with the economy. Annual GDP growth was projected at 6 percent, which would be slightly down from the 1995 figure of 6.9 percent. The recovery was not evident in the unemployment rate, however, which stood at 9.2 percent in December, up from 8.1 percent in December 1995. The average monthly wage did climb, however, from $15 in 1995 to $23 during January–September. Inflation fell to 8.7 percent from 32 percent in 1995, while the 4.4 percent of GDP absorbed by the budget deficit was an improvement over 1995's 11.1 percent. The dram remained stable against the dollar in real terms.

The trade deficit was $344 million during January–September (compared with $403 million for all of 1995), as exports grew by 19 percent and imports by 36 percent (relative to that period in 1995). The current-account deficit was $271 million at mid-year (vs. $483 million for all of 1995). External balances of those magnitudes will only be manageable if international institutions and Armenians abroad continue to provide support. Although privatization progressed, most larger firms either remained in state hands or were privatized in ways that brought in little revenue or expertise. At year's end, the IMF warned that the projected 1997 inflation rate and budget deficit (both of which are considerably higher than the fund had earlier agreed to), coupled with the slow pace of banking reform, could jeopardize further disbursements of the $148 million credit approved in February 1996.

Although Georgia's fiscal and foreign-indebtedness problems are worse than Armenia's and its economic recovery started later, Georgia's recovery was stronger. GDP rose by 14.3 percent during January–September; 10 percent growth was expected for the year. However, a February labor-market survey found an unemployment rate of 15.5 percent, and underemployment is widespread. Monthly public-sector wages have been low but rising (about $34 in September), and poverty and income inequality are unusually severe.

Price stability improved in 1996: a 15 percent to 18 percent inflation rate was forecast (down from 57.4 percent in 1995), despite the liberalization of bread prices in June. The lari remained quite stable, depreciating by only 2 percent since its October 1995 introduction. Tax revenues in 1996 were only 6 percent of GDP, forcing the government to cut expenditures to the bone in order to hold the 1996 budget deficit at about 5 percent of GDP. The trade and current-account balances also remain in deficit, the former to the tune of $155 million during January–September. Foreign indebtedness reached $1.58 billion by September. Although serious structural reform has just begun, voucher privatization and the privatization of housing and small enterprises are complete. If political stability and international support (the IMF made two disbursements from the $246 million credit agreed to in February 1996) can be maintained, Georgia's outlook is bright. Azerbaijan trails its neighbors in economic reform and performance and in political democratization. Still, 1996 ended optimistically, with an agreement with the IMF on new credits and projections of an economic recovery in 1997.

Azerbaijan's GDP grew by about 1 percent in 1996 (after declining by 17.2 percent in 1995) and industrial production declined by 7 percent (vs. 21.4 percent in 1995), although production in the oil and timber sectors rose. Official unemployment is negligible, but monthly wages averaged only $19 in March. Inflation declined from 85 percent in 1995 to 20 percent due to tighter monetary and fiscal policies, as the budget deficit fell to 1.4 percent of GDP. The manat's 7 percent nominal appreciation during 1996 contributed to lower inflation but also to a growing ($250 million) trade deficit. Azerbaijan's future depends on foreign investment in its oil sector, which is projected to grow to $23 billion by 2010. It also depends on relations with the IMF, which released the third tranche of an $85 million credit in July and agreed in December to provide new credits totaling $219 million.

CENTRAL ASIA

While the roaring growth in Armenia and Georgia was not matched across Central Asia in 1996, Kyrgyzstan seemed to experience a strong recovery, and GDP growth was forecast in Turkmenistan and perhaps Kazakstan. Uzbekistan seemed likely to report a slight decline in GDP, while civil war plunged Tajikistan further into economic chaos. Inflation fell in four of the five Central Asian economies, while currencies (except for the Tajik ruble) generally retained their real value against the dollar. On the other hand, energy shortages plagued

Kazakstan and Kyrgyzstan, and the region's debts allowed Russia to press its claims on Central Asian assets.

Some of Central Asia's best economic news in 1996 came from Kazakstan, where the 55 percent decline in GDP recorded during 1991–1995 seemed to have come to an end. Consumer-price inflation was running at 30 percent at the end of the year (about half of the 1995 rate), and the tenge remained roughly stable in real terms against the dollar. As Kazakstan opened its doors more widely to foreign investment, the value of direct foreign investment committed in 1996 is likely to match the $860 million attracted in 1995. The progress made in stabilizing the country's finances and attracting foreign capital was capped by Kazakstan's oversubscribed $200 million Eurobond issue in December.

On the other hand, most Kazakstani households experienced worsening shortages of heat and electricity. The government apparently did not have sufficient foreign exchange to finance power imports from Russia, Uzbekistan, and Turkmenistan and to service the debts incurred from previous years' energy imports. While foreign investment in Kazakstan's energy and power sectors should eventually help to resolve those problems, foreign investors may have made matters worse in 1996 by forcing cutoffs to nonpaying users.

No major economic surprises were noted in Uzbekistan in 1996. Inflation was forecast to fall to 55 percent from the 1995 triple-digit level, while GDP seemed likely to remain flat or decline slightly. Overall macroeconomic and (authoritarian) political stability continued to be Uzbekistan's strongest attributes. But foreign investors seemed to find Kazakstan a more attractive venue in 1996, largely because of Uzbekistan's weaker interest in privatization and liberalization. That was brought home by the IMF's mid-December decision to halt further disbursements of its $185 million standby credit in response to the government's reimposition of foreign-exchange controls. Still, if its economic numbers can be believed, President Islam Karimov's government should not be judged too harshly in light of the relatively small decline in GDP (about 20 percent) reported during 1991–1996.

Official data for the first 10 months of 1996 portray Kyrgyzstan as one of the most rapidly growing CIS economies. GDP increased by 11 percent over the same period in 1995; industrial output was up 11 percent and agricultural output 15 percent. Production of consumer goods grew by 19.8 percent, while inflation was projected at 40 percent. Kyrgyzstan continued to follow IMF and World Bank orthodoxy, pursuing privatization and restructuring with the greatest vigor of any country in the region. As was the case in Kazakstan, however, Kyrgyzstan's macroeconomic numbers were offset by persistent shortfalls in electricity caused by restricted energy deliveries from Kyrgyzstan's neighbors, especially Uzbekistan. And, as also was the case in Kazakstan, the Kyrgyz government had to surrender to the Russian government and private Russian investors controlling equity packets in Kyrgyz enterprises in exchange for reductions in Kyrgyzstan's $470 million state debt, most of which is owed to Russia.

The official economic news from Turkmenistan and Tajikistan was good and bad respectively; but in neither case was it credible. GDP growth in natural-gas

Table 1. Economic Performance by Country in 1995–96

	GDP growth*		Inflation*		Unemployment rate*	
	1995	1996	1995	1996	1995	1996
Czech Republic	4.8	4.4	8	9	2.9	3.5
Slovakia	6.8	6.9	7	6	13.1	12.8
Hungary	1.5	0.5	29	20	10.4	10.5
Poland	7.0	6.0	22	19	14.9	13.6
Lithuania	3.0	4.0	36	13	7.3	6.2
Latvia	−1.6	2.5	23	13	6.6	7.2
Estonia	2.9	3.5	29	15	5.0	5.6
Belarus	−10.0	3.0	244	39	2.7	4.0
Ukraine	−11.8	−10.0	182	40	0.6	1.5
Slovenia	3.9	3.5	9	9	14.5	14.4
Croatia	1.7	4.4	4	3	17.6	15.9
Bosnia-Herzegovina	n.a.	35**	34	3	n.a.	50**
Yugoslavia	6.0	4.3	111	60	24.7	26.1
Macedonia	−2.9	1.6	11	0	37.2	39.8
Albania	8.6	8.5**	6	17**	13.1	12.1
Bulgaria	2.1	−10.0	33	311	11.1	12.5
Romania	7.1	4.1	28	57	9.5	6.3
Moldova	−3.0	−8.0	24	15	1.4	1.5
Russia	−4.2	−6.0	131	22	8.9	9.3
Georgia	2.4	11.0	57	13	3.4	3.2
Azerbaijan	−12.0	1.0	85	7	1.1	1.1
Armenia	6.9	4.0	32	6	8.1	9.7
Kazakstan	−8.9	0.5	60	29	2.1	4.1
Uzbekistan	−1.2	2.0	144	55**	0.3	0.4
Kyrgyzstan	−5.4	6.0	32	35	3.0	4.5
Tajikistan	−12.4	−17.0	382	41	1.8	2.4
Turkmenistan	−16.0	n.a.	n.a.	n.a.	n.a.	n.a.

*annual change, percent. Unemployed is registered unemployed, except Russia.
**OMRI estimate
Source: Econonomic Survey of Europe in 1996–97, United Nations Economic Commission for Europe, New York and Geneva, 1997, p. 60.

powerhouse Turkmenistan was forecast at 4.5 percent, while inflation may have fallen as low as 336 percent, down from the 2,400 percent recorded in 1995. However, the absence of external controls over the authoritarian government of Saparmurad Niyazov reduced the credibility of these numbers. Neither the IMF nor the World Bank was active in Turkmenistan in 1996, and virtually no Turkmen enterprises were privatized last year. Likewise, Tajikistan's forecast 10 percent decline in GDP and rising (to 700 percent) inflation rate are probably no more than rough approximations, although they do suggest that the Tajik economy is unlikely to improve until the guns fall silent.

Note: Some of the data cited in this article are drawn from reports of the EU program, TACIS. Other sources include the National Bank and Statistical Office bulletins, PlanEcon and WEFA reports, and Business Central Europe. Most of the 1996 data are preliminary and may undergo substantial revision.

NEW IMF LENDING TO THE POST-COMMUNIST WORLD IN 1996

by MICHAEL WYZAN

The International Monetary Fund (IMF) continued to play the dominant role in providing financial support for the balance of payments of post-communist and developing countries. The fund has the dual role of providing financial support and encouraging economic reform through the conditions attached to its loans. Such reform has generally been in the realm of macroeconomic policy, although the IMF is increasingly working together with the World Bank, conditioning its credits on progress on privatization and financial restructuring as well.

In 1996, the IMF approved new credits for Armenia, Georgia, Hungary, Russia, Tajikistan, Ukraine, Moldova, Latvia, Kazakstan, Bulgaria, and Estonia.

There are five groups of post-communist countries in terms of their relations with the IMF. The first group has stabilized to a satisfactory degree and no longer seeks credits from the body; that small group includes the Czech Republic and Poland. The Czech Republic of its own accord came up with an adequate stabilization program and did not inherit large domestic or foreign imbalances when communism fell, so the IMF's role there has tended to be relatively small. In Poland, the IMF played a major role in 1990–1991 and 1993–1994.

The second category of countries are ones that carried out successful macroeconomic stabilization programs without financial support from the IMF. That group includes Slovenia and Croatia, neither of which was eligible for IMF credits at the time they launched their stabilization efforts (largely due to unresolved issues related to the liabilities of former Yugoslavia).

The third set of countries seek and receive IMF loans, but do not draw down the funds, using the fact that the loans were approved as a seal of approval for their relations with private financial institutions. Such countries include Estonia and Hungary, both of which have witnessed sizable levels of (private) foreign investment. Hungary has had fairly severe macroeconomic problems, especially with respect to fiscal policy and foreign debt. However, private capital inflows there have frequently been so large as to make IMF balance-of-payments support unnecessary.

The fourth category of nations includes those for which IMF support is critical for the success of reform efforts and which have generally fulfilled the conditions of their loans, leading to larger and longer-term forms of credits. That category includes Albania, Armenia, Georgia, Kyrgyzstan, and Moldova. These countries tend to receive IMF support to cover large fractions of their budget and current-account deficits; the fund will tolerate the former only if they are the result of external circumstances and if there is a clear program for their reduction.

A fifth group of countries is also made up of those for which IMF support is vital, but which tend to have rocky, on-again-off-again relations with it and other international financial institutions. They periodically are awarded large credits, but the release of tranches of those credits is frequently delayed and there may be extended periods without IMF support. Countries in that group include Bulgaria, Romania, Russia, and Ukraine. Economic performance in that category tends to be disappointing, and the blame for that situation does not lie largely with external circumstances, as in the fourth group.

The first new IMF loans of 1996 to post-communist countries were to its two Transcaucasian "favorites," Armenia and Georgia. The IMF Executive Board on 14 February approved a three-year enhanced structural adjustment facility (ESAF) to Armenia worth $148 million, while Georgia received board approval for an ESAF worth $246 million on 28 February.

The board approved a 23–month, $387 million standby credit to Hungary on 15 March. The three-year, $10.087 billion extended fund facility (EFF) awarded to Russia on 26 March is one of the largest credits in the fund's history. Tajikistan assumed its first debt to the IMF on 8 May, when the board approved a $22 million first tranche under a standby facility. Two days later, the board approved a nine-month standby credit for Ukraine worth $867 million.

Moldova received approval for a three-year EFF worth $195 million on 20 May, while four days later it awarded Latvia a 15–month, $43 million standby credit. Kazakstan was awarded a three-year, $446 million EFF on 17 July, and Bulgaria received board approval for a 20–month, $582 million standby credit two days later. Finally, the IMF board approved a 13–month, $20 million standby credit for Estonia on 29 July.

The IMF has played an enormous role in the recent economic histories of most post-communist countries and even governments formed by former communist parties are loath to ignore its policy advice, as the Bulgarian case shows. A serious concern for several countries is the buildup of large debts to the IMF itself—debts that are never rescheduled or forgiven.

POVERTY, INEQUALITY ACCOMPANY ECONOMIC TRANSITION

by MICHAEL WYZAN

The post-communist years have seen increases in income inequality and poverty ranging from modest in the Visegrad countries to enormous in Central Asia. Yet the steps some governments are taking to promote equality may prove counterproductive by slowing the transition to a market economy.

A widely discussed side effect of the transition to market economies in Central and Eastern Europe and the former Soviet Union is a widening of inequality in income and wealth among households. Although the existence of such a tendency is indisputable, it may not be as universal or as dramatic as often imagined.

In the relatively developed and reformed Visegrad economies (those of the Czech Republic, Slovakia, Hungary, and Poland), measured-income inequality—although higher than when communism fell—remains at or below that in developed market economies. Moreover, no reliable data or accepted methodology exists for comparing the wealth and privileges of the upper echelons of the communist nomenklatura of the old days with those of today's nouveaux riches.

The post-communist world's mobile-phone-toting, Mercedes-driving business people are probably more numerous than the upper nomenklatura was, and wealth disparities are more obvious now than under communism. Moreover, except in a few unusual cases, such as in Turkmenistan, no one wields the sort of absolute political power the communist leadership enjoyed in the old days.

An outside observer might view those changes as reflecting improvements in social welfare. But the new transparency of income and wealth, occurring simultaneously in most cases with political democratization, has produced a sense of relative deprivation that seems more palpable than under communism. That feeling is especially strong in countries such as Bulgaria and Romania, where the new rich are often former members of the Communist Party or the secret police. Their wealth derives substantially from exploiting both the connections they developed during their previous employment and the privileges they enjoyed, such as access to an elite Western postgraduate education.

Income disparities have also increased in more noticeable ways; for example, the wage dispersion across economic sectors has risen. Sectors such as energy and banking that paid relatively high wages under communism have expanded their leads at the expense of such branches as agriculture and culture. However, the dispersion in wages actually received differs from the dispersion in wages that are supposed to be paid, since some sectors that pay relatively well (such as the energy sector) have a particularly high prevalence of wage arrears.[1]

Poverty trends are easier to track than income inequality. The percentage of the population characterized as "poor"—measured relative to some absolute standard—is higher in all countries in the region than it was under communism. The social groups that tend to be poor are largely the same as in developed market economies: members of single-parent households, the unemployed, and those with low educational attainment. The elderly are probably more heavily represented among the poor than in Western countries, as pensions in most countries have fallen relative to wages, which were themselves eroded by inflation during the first years of the transition. Moreover, that inflation wiped out the real value of pensioners' private savings.[2]

The usual life-cycle pattern is for elderly people to live in retirement on accumulated savings from their working careers. Their children save little early in their working lives, knowing that higher earnings lie ahead, and become net savers in mid-career. That pattern has been broken in the post-communist world, as pensioners have little to show financially for their years of work, and their working-age children's ability to save money is curtailed by the need to support them.

If that situation persists indefinitely, it will jeopardize the children's ability to support themselves in their own retirement, creating a cycle of self-perpetuating poverty. Such an outcome is especially likely in the poorer post-communist countries—Albania and the Transcaucasian and Central Asian countries—and in those, such as Bulgaria, that have been experiencing repeated economic crises.[3]

Poverty has an important regional dimension in large countries such as Russia, where the percentage of the population so afflicted ranges from as low as 10 percent in Moscow to 70 percent in the Altai Republic.[4] Even in smaller countries, the incidence of poverty is typically much higher in municipalities other than the capital city.

That is especially so when employment in a city is dominated by enterprises in declining industrial sectors—or even by a single enterprise in such a sector—or heavily populated by a disadvantaged ethnic minority. Examples of municipalities suffering from both problems are Kardzhali, Bulgaria, with its substantial ethnic Turkish population, and Narva, Estonia, inhabited largely by ethnic Russians.

The incidence of poverty varies greatly across post-communist economies. With a poverty line set at $120 per month, based on household survey data, only 1 percent of Czech households were poor in 1993, compared with 33 percent in Bulgaria, 38 percent in Russia, and 76 percent in Kyrgyzstan. There is evidence that poverty rates stabilize in countries such as Poland, where growth of gross domestic product has resumed, while no such trend is discernible in nations such as Belarus, where economic decline continues.[5]

Families' survival mechanisms in transitional economies are similar to those employed in the Third World. Families rely on consumption of home-produced products and work in the informal sector. However, the degree of social dislocation associated with a given poverty rate may be higher in post-communist countries, since most of those poor are new to that status. Thus, for example, only 2 percent of Bulgarian households found themselves in poverty in 1987–1988, and even Poland's relatively modest poverty incidence of 12 percent in 1993 is twice that of 1987–1988.[6]

Table 1. Gini Coefficients for Household Income, During and After Communist Rule		
	1987–88	**1993**
Belarus	na	21.6**
Bulgaria	23	34
Czech Republic	19	27
Estonia	23*	39
Hungary	21	23
Kazakstan	na	32.7**
Kyrgyzstan	17*	50
Latvia	na	27**
Lithuania	na	33.6**
Poland	25	30
Russia	24*	48
Slovakia	na	19.5**
Slovenia	24	28
Turkmenistan	na	35.8
Ukraine	na	25.7

Note: Figures are based on survey data unless otherwise indicated.

*Based on data from Goskomstat (the former Soviet and current Russian statistical committee) obtained on a census, rather than a survey, basis. Second figure for Estonia is 1995.

**Based on personal income data. Data for Slovakia and Ukraine are from 1992.

Source: World Bank, *World Development Report: From Plan to Market* (New York: Oxford University Press, 1996).

On the other hand, the fact that households frequently go in and out of poverty, consistent with their varying fortunes during the turbulent transition era, probably mitigates poverty-related social problems to some extent.

MEASURING INEQUALITY

Table 1 provides information on inequality in household incomes during 1987–1988 and 1993 for several formerly communist countries, based on the Gini coefficient, the measure most commonly used by economists to describe dispersion of income or expenditures. The Gini coefficient is scaled between 0 and 100. It equals zero in the hypothetical case where all units of observation—generally, households—in a society have the same income, and it equals 100 when one such unit receives all of the society's income.

The coefficient is estimated by ranking the surveyed units in ascending order by their incomes and dividing those households into equal-sized groups—typically, into five such groups, known as "quintiles." One then compares the shares of total income accruing to the bottom 20 percent of households with the hypothetical case in which those households receive exactly 20 percent of the income, compares the income share of the bottom 40 percent of households with the case where they receive precisely 40 percent of the income, and so on.

It has proved difficult to come up with data on household incomes for the world's countries that would allow calculation of Gini coefficients on a comparable basis. Not surprisingly, doing so is particularly challenging for the post-communist and poorer developing countries.

Higher-income households in transitional economies underreport their incomes in order to avoid paying taxes and drawing attention to themselves. Although such behavior is commonplace throughout the world, the inexperience of the tax authorities in the post-communist countries makes high-income households likelier to get away with underreporting there than elsewhere. Underreporting tends to lead to underestimation of the extent of inequality. That tendency, however, is countered to some extent by the failure to measure those components of poorer-household incomes derived from nonmarket activities, such as home food production.

POST-COMMUNIST INEQUALITY IN PERSPECTIVE

Data concerns notwithstanding, examining measured income or expenditure inequality across countries can yield important insights about the unfolding socio-economic processes in post-communist countries. Table 1 indicates that measured inequality has risen in a variety of transitional economies. There is evidence that the increase results from an increase in the income shares of the richest households, especially in Bulgaria and Russia.[7]

World experience suggests that poorer countries generally have higher income dispersion than richer ones, although countries in some regions have either low inequality (the Indian subcontinent) or high inequality (Latin America) seemingly regardless of their standard of living.[8]

Moreover, ethnically diverse countries in which certain occupations are commonly associated with given ethnic groups tend to be relatively inegalitarian in income distribution. That would partly explain relatively high Gini coefficients for Brazil (56.5), Honduras (52.7), Malaysia (48.4), and South Africa (58.4), among others.

To what extent do these general patterns apply to the post-communist world? And how does measured inequality compare between transitional economies and others at similar levels of development?

In the Visegrad countries and Belarus, Latvia, Romania, Slovenia, and Ukraine, inequality remains well below the level typically encountered in developed countries. In Bulgaria, Kazakhstan, Lithuania, Moldova, and Turkmenistan (along with China, Laos, and Vietnam), it appears to have reached the degree prevailing in much of the industrialized world. And in a number of cases in members of the Commonwealth of Independent States (CIS), such as Kyrgyzstan and Russia, inequality is already at the high levels typical of countries in Latin America and sub-Saharan Africa. Such is apparently also true for Armenia and Georgia, for which recent household surveys have revealed Gini coefficients in excess of 50.[9]

The sketchy information available on inequality in East-Central Europe and the former Soviet Union suggests that a complex pattern is emerging. The Visegrad countries as well as Slovenia seem headed for Gini coefficients of around 30, on a par with the more egalitarian European member states.

VISEGRAD vs. THE REST

Low Gini coefficients in Visegrad reflect both the high level of social spending—especially in the Czech Republic and Hungary—and government policies aimed at reducing inequality, such as flat-rate unemployment benefits in Hungary and Poland.[10] Buoyant social expenditures are as much the result of the relatively modest economic declines in the Visegrad countries as of those countries' recessions. Healthier economies produce fewer have-nots. Another Visegrad characteristic that may foster equality is the relative ethnic homogeneity of all the countries. (Slovakia's Hungarian minority makes it a partial exception to that rule.)

In the Czech case, the country's extraordinarily low unemployment rates—2.9 percent in December 1995, compared to the low- to mid-teens elsewhere in the region[11]—have played a significant role in keeping poverty negligible. The relatively large increase in the Gini coefficient in the Czech Republic is perhaps because inequality there was so insignificant under communism, although that appears not to apply to Slovakia.

The Visegrad experience suggests that countries with strong reform orientations have rising but modest levels of inequality. Elsewhere, such a pattern is not discernible with the available evidence, perhaps because the data quality deteriorates as one moves eastward.

Estonia, one of the region's leading reformers, has a higher and apparently more rapidly rising Gini coefficient than any other country in the region, with the possible exceptions of countries for which data is unavailable (Albania and several former Yugoslav republics). That may be due to its relatively high ethnic heterogeneity, in particular the disadvantaged position of ethnic Russians in its eastern regions. Still, Latvia, which also has many ethnic Russians, has an unusually low Gini coefficient.

In the CIS, Armenia, Georgia, Russia, and Kyrgyzstan have seen explosive increases in income inequality, to approximately Latin American levels. The increases reflect the severity of the economic decline in those countries and the emergence of tiny groups of extraordinarily rich people.

The low measured inequality in Belarus and Ukraine, also members of the CIS, is difficult to explain. Those countries' relatively slight progress on economic reform by 1992–1993 may have meant that neither had seen the increases in inequality experienced elsewhere. Perhaps disparities were so low there under communism that the figures already reflect substantial increases. Finally, their low Gini coefficients may simply reflect the poor quality of the data behind those calculations, so that Belarusian and Ukrainian statistics miss a higher fraction of incomes in the upper ranges than the statistics of other countries.

SOME POLICIES HAMPER REFORM

There are two types of problems associated with attempts to alleviate the inequality-increasing aspects of the transition era. Any policy measures are likely to be expensive relative to the capacity to find them, since countries with widespread poverty typically also have great difficulty raising budget revenue.

In addition, many policies aimed at assisting the disadvantaged have side effects that reduce the economy's ability to function under market conditions. For example, increased budget deficits may result from spending on social assistance.

In the post-communist world, such social transfers as pensions and unemployment benefits are typically paid for by employers. That discourages new employment and creates incentives for workers and managers to collude in defrauding the government, and for workers to work under the table.[12]

Moreover, equality-enhancing policies tend to have adverse effects on incentives. Any form of wage leveling discourages workers from leaving declining jobs, enterprises, and regions and moving toward ones with better prospects. The same is true of programs that redistribute revenues from the central government and the wealthier municipalities to the poorer ones.

In addition, unemployment benefits that replace a high fraction of earnings, depend closely on one's earnings while employed, or last a relatively long time—or all three—discourage people from seeking new employment. Encouraging enterprises to keep redundant workers because those enterprises provide social benefits that the state cannot afford also hampers labor mobility.

A debate rages over the role of minimum wages in transitional economies. The minimum wage frequently plays a more important role in such economies than in ordinary market ones, because the entire wage structure—plus many social benefits—is often scaled to it. Many economists, including those at the International Monetary Fund and the World Bank, argue that setting such a wage and protecting its real value against inflation results in higher unemployment among low-paid workers.

The International Labor Organization (ILO) disagrees, claiming there is little evidence from developed countries that the minimum wage has such an effect, except perhaps for young workers and those in extremely low-paying sectors. The ILO argues that the reduction in real minimum wages to symbolic levels may in fact harm economic efficiency by discouraging workers receiving it from working hard and upgrading their skills; such is especially true when those wages fall so low that workers' nutrition and health are endangered.[13]

Pension reform has proved particularly vexatious. Attempts to raise the retirement age have met with great resistance, and the failure to do so is another seemingly equality-promoting policy that hampers economic reform. The numbers of contributors per pensioner are very low in East-Central Europe and the former Soviet Union, ranging in 1993 from 1 in Albania to 2 in Romania, compared with an average for member states of the Organization for Economic Cooperation and Development (OECD)—the Paris-based group of developed nations—of 2.6.

The unusually heavy burden of supporting the elderly reflects early retirement ages, especially for women; the small percentage of the employed who make pension contributions; and—to a much lesser extent—some countries' relatively elderly populations. The overwhelming importance of the first two factors is illustrated by the case of Poland in 1993, where there were 1.9 contributors per pensioner but 4.6 persons of working age per person over 60, vs. the OECD average of 3.6.[14]

WHAT GOVERNMENTS CAN DO

Since well-intentioned efforts to alleviate the inegalitarian consequences of the economic transition are so prone to backfiring, the international financial institutions counsel governments to concentrate on measures that enhance economic efficiency. If high rates of economic growth can be maintained, the living standards of those at the lower end of the income distribution may improve without resort to actions that impede improved resource allocation.

Hungary and Poland have introduced flat-rate unemployment benefits, and all transitional countries now pay relatively low benefits and do so only for limited periods. Some countries, especially the Czech Republic, have adopted active labor-market policies, including measures to retrain workers and enhance labor mobility. In an attempt to foster such mobility, efforts are being made to decouple such services as day care and housing from enterprises and assign them to local governments. And Latvia and the Czech Republic have taken steps to reform their pension systems.

It is largely the more developed and reformist (and egalitarian) transition economies that have promulgated those reforms. Whether such efficiency-enhancing measures will be sufficient to prevent the creation of extremely inegalitarian societies in some of the region's other countries is an open question. Third World experience suggests that explicitly redistributive and poverty-reducing policies may also have a role to play.

[1] Penny Morvant and Peter Rutland, "Russian Workers Face the Market," *Transition*, vol. 2, no. 13, 28 June 1996.

[2] World Bank, *World Development Report; From Plan to Market* (New York: Oxford University Press, 1996), pp. 70–71.

[3] See Michael Wyzan, "Renewed Economic Crisis May End Foot-Dragging on Reforms," *Transition*, vol. 2, no. 17, 23 August 1996.

[4] World Bank, *World Development Report*, p. 70.

[5] Ibid., pp. 67–69.

[6] Ibid.

[7] Ibid.

[8] Gini coefficients for countries not covered in Table 1 were calculated by the author on the basis of data from the World Bank, *World Development Report: From Plan to Market* (New York: Oxford University Press, 1996).

[9] See Michael Wyzan, OMRI Analytical Brief, no. 173, 17 June 1996.

[10] Mitchell Orenstein, "The Failures of Neo-Liberal Social Policy in Central Europe," *Transition*, vol. 2, no. 13, 28 June 1996; World Development Report, pp. 69, 79.

[11] Daniel Munich and Vit Sorm, "The Czech Republic as a Low-Unemployment Oasis," *Transition*, vol. 2, no. 13, 28 June 1996.

[12] World Bank, *World Development Report*, pp. 75–76.

[13] Guy Standing and Daniel Vaughan-Whitehead, eds., *Minimum Wages in Central and Eastern Europe; From Protection to Destitution* (Budapest: Central European University Press, 1995).

[14] World Bank, *World Development Report*, p. 79

AGRICULTURAL PRIVATIZATION IN EAST-CENTRAL EUROPE

by ERIK MATHJIS *and* JO SWINNEN

In the former communist countries of Central and Eastern Europe, collective farms have been undergoing the complex process of privatization. A wide variety of farm structures is emerging, with many countries still favoring large-scale cooperative farming.

Agricultural privatization, land reform, and farm restructuring have taken a prominent place in the transition of Central and Eastern European markets after communism. The process has been difficult and lengthy, and it is still not finished after six years of reform. Agricultural reform includes two distinct processes: a change of ownership of land and capital assets (privatization of farm assets) and a change in farm organization. There are differences in how these countries have dealt with those processes. Some countries, such as the Czech Republic, Slovakia, and Bulgaria, created large-scale successors to the former state and collective farms—a method that still dominates agriculture there. In others, such as Albania, Romania, and some of the Baltic states, smaller-scale family farms use most of the agricultural land.

The governments of the post-communist countries of Central and Eastern Europe—Albania, Bulgaria, the Czech Republic, the former East Germany, Hungary, Latvia, Lithuania, Poland, Romania, Slovakia, and Slovenia—have chosen different ways to privatize agricultural assets.[1] In Bulgaria and the former Czechoslovakia, land is being restituted to former owners. Poland, on the other hand, has put its state land up for sale. Hungary is using a voucher scheme for privatizing a major part of the land, and Albania distributes most property rights on an equal per capita basis. However, with the exception of Poland, Albania, and Russia, a large share of the land has been restituted to its former owners (see Table 1). Countries have restituted the land to former owners within historical boundaries when possible. Otherwise, they have received property rights on a plot of land of comparable size and quality. That is the main form of land privatization in these countries.

Exceptions to land restitution are Hungary's voucher privatization and distribution of two-thirds of the land to collective farm employees, Poland's sale of state farm land, and Albania's land distribution to the rural population. In countries that did restitute land, major groups of former owners excluded include religious organizations in the Czech Republic; noncitizens in the former Czechoslovakia and Slovenia; owners in Romania who lost their land prior to 1947; and those in the former Czechoslovakia who lost property prior to 25 February 1948. Also, the sale or lease of assets often is restricted: foreigners cannot own land, restituted land cannot be resold for a certain time period, and there are upper limits to sale and leasing arrangements.

Table 1. Privatization Methods for Nationalized and/or Collectivized Assets		
Country	**Land**	**Other assets**
Albania	Distribution to workers	Distribution to workers
Bulgaria	Restitution	Mixed
Czech Republic	Sales and lease	Mixed
East Germany	Restricted sale and lease	Restricted sale and lease
Hungary	Restricted sale	Mixed
Poland	Sale and lease	Sale and lease
Romania	Restitution/distribution to workers	Restitution/distribution to workers
Slovakia	Sale and lease	Mixed
Slovenia	Restitution	Mixed

Note: Mixed refers to a blend of methods, including selling assets and distributing shares.

Source: Agricultural Privatization, Land Reform and Farm Restructuring in Central and Eastern Europe (London: Avery Publishers, 1996).

Whereas land is mostly restituted in kind, this is not the general rule for other assets. Some countries restitute non-land assets—such as farm machinery and buildings—but in many cases they have been privatized using vouchers that can be turned into capital shares in a new cooperative farm or used for purchasing non-land assets for private use. The distribution of such vouchers was the subject of much debate. In general, the principle was that cooperative farm members (or their heirs) who had contributed land, labor, or other assets during the 45 years of the farms' existence should receive some share of the remaining assets. To implement that plan required an inventory of the cooperative's assets and their value, and a formula to determine each contributor's shares. Both aspects posed great difficulties. The solutions chosen varied substantially, largely because they were influenced by political considerations and often became very complicated.

Governments usually privatized the non-land assets using a mixture of methods, including selling the assets and distributing shares to active and/or retired members. Distributing shares has been a widespread privatization method for non-land assets, mostly because of the indivisibility of some capital assets, such as a building or a combine-harvester. Distribution to farm workers was mostly based on a formula that evaluated the labor and capital contributions of all members—present and former—of a collective farm. (As a result, a great deal of the assets were left to pensioners no longer active in the sector.)

Active members received only 20 percent of non-land assets in Slovenia, compared with 40 percent in Hungary and 100 percent in Lithuania. In Lithuania, farm equipment could be purchased with investment vouchers, which everyone received; money; or "green vouchers," which only agricultural workers received. Rural pensioners thus obtained a disproportionate share of the non-land assets. In Czechoslovakia, vouchers were distributed according to a 50/30/20 scheme: 50 percent for former land owners, 30 percent for former non-land assets owners, and 20 percent for "labor contributors." In contrast, Bulgarian and

Romanian "labor contributors" received 50 percent and 60 percent, respectively, of the non-land assets.

Privatizing assets encompasses either the transfer of property rights on assets that were state owned, or the restoration of property rights on assets that private individuals officially owned but lacked the authority to make decisions on their use or exchange. The latter refers, for example, to land brought into a cooperative. In many countries, individual members retained legal ownership of the land, even though they did not retain property rights.

Each country chose its own process of privatization and land reform based on the legal and historical characteristics of its agricultural assets.[2] That includes the nature of post-collectivization asset ownership, the pre-collectivization asset ownership distribution, and the ethnicity of the former owners. Those characteristics had an effect on the mix of the various options and on the political consequences.

The choice in most cases was determined by the ownership status at the time privatization began: nationalized assets were handled differently from collectivized assets or assets that always had been privately owned, albeit only formally. In the latter case, restoration of full property rights to former owners was inevitable. Private ownership rights, after surviving 40 years of collectivization and state control, could not be confiscated by democratically elected governments supporting a market economy. The extent to which land was privately owned differs among countries, but is in general quite high: land was only nationalized in a limited number of cases, mostly large estates owned by foreigners, aristocrats, or churches. A notable exception was in Hungary, where owners who had been forced to sell their land cheaply to a cooperative were treated differently. That scenario concerns two-thirds of Hungarian cooperatives' land: part of it was distributed to farm workers on an equal per capita basis and part of it was sold at auction in exchange for vouchers, which were distributed to all victims of communism as a means of indemnification. Those who benefited from that compensation also include large feudal landowners who had lost their land just after World War II in a land reform approved by the nominally democratic government that was already dominated by communists. When land restitution to former owners would have meant giving land to foreigners—Sudeten Germans in the Czech borderlands, Germans in western Poland, Italians in Slovenia—or restoring large feudal estates, as in Albania, the governments chose other privatization policies. The difference in formal ownership is also the main reason non-land assets were typically privatized through different procedures than were used for land.

PRIVATIZATION AND PROPERTY RIGHTS

It is not clear whether all private individuals will receive their property rights through the privatization processes. Property rights include the right to consume, to obtain income from, and to dispose of those assets.[3] For example, in the case of land restitution to former owners, the land often underwent important changes: roads were built and plots were consolidated, for example, in some instances. In many cases, former owners have not been restituted their original land, but rather were given "comparable" plots of land of equal size and quality. However, because that determination was left to the discretion of collective farm management, the former owner needed to fight to make sure he got a plot of equal size and quality.

In Slovenia, state land is being restituted to former owners, but remains in "co-ownership" between the former owners and the current users (the state farms) in order to minimize disruption. That means the former owners, now co-owners, cannot sell their land or even change its use. In Hungary, although cooperative members are the legal owners of the land they contributed to a cooperative, they are not allowed to withdraw it. Instead, they have received financial compensation.

One should be careful in interpreting the data on assets called "private" in Central and Eastern European agriculture since 1989. In some cases, neither legal (ownership) rights, nor property rights are private; in some other cases, land titles have not yet been distributed, but new owners are already determining what to do with the assets and have acquired some property rights. In still other instances, ownership rights have been transferred to individuals, but private property rights are incomplete as they have only limited power over the use and transfer of the assets.

Land redistribution programs typically have five steps: first, individuals submit claims; second, the government issues ownership certificates, indicating rightful claims; third, the precise value of the asset is calculated and/or land parcels are redrawn and precisely identified; fourth, surveys are completed; and fifth, the government issues land titles. The uncertainty on property rights is only solved by finalizing the fifth step: the issuing of the land titles.

While in most countries the majority of the claims have been processed and people have been informed of the decision about their property, the issuing of land titles is far from complete. For example, in 1994, Romania often claimed that land was fully privatized, but in fact 70 percent of total agricultural land was reported as "acknowledged" property—property designated to be privatized. Individuals had "possession certificates" on only 50 percent of all acknowledged land and full ownership titles on only 20 percent. State farms have not been de-collectivized: they were renamed "commercial companies" of which private individuals own shares.

In general, the resulting property-rights distribution is affected by the choice of the privatization process. However, the effective property rights are also influenced by technical factors and transaction costs in the reform implementation, and by how affected agents—the farm management—can influence the reform implementation. Often, additional government regulations, determined by the political influence of the affected agents and by political coalitions, have restricted the use and exchange of assets. That has restricted the transfer of property rights to the new owners.

THE TRANSFORMATION OF FARM ORGANIZATION

Transformation refers to the conversion and restructuring of the collective and state farms into enterprises following the rules of a market economy. This is in part a legal conversion and in part an organizational restructuring of the farms into viable business units. The available options are specified by law and typically include conversion of collective and state farms into joint-stock companies, limited-liability companies, or producer cooperatives. De-collectivization refers to a specific form of farm restructuring—the breakup of the collective and state farms into individual (family) farms.

The decision as to the method was in most cases left to the state or collective farm itself. In Bulgaria, however, "independent" liquidation councils were installed at the beginning of the reform to oversee the complete breakup of the collective farms. Most state farms were transformed into companies, most collective farms into genuine producer cooperatives. Only a few collective farms decided to liquidate or were declared bankrupt.

In general, there is a wide variety of emerging farm structures. Often the definitions of the various terms, such as "joint-stock companies" or "private cooperatives," are not clear. Moreover, the importance of individual farming varies strongly among countries—in several, very large-scale agricultural production organizations have played an important role.

Table 2 shows that cooperatives and state farms are still dominant in the Czech Republic, Slovakia, Bulgaria, and Hungary. Private farms seem important in the Baltic states, Poland, Slovenia, Romania, the Czech Republic, and Hungary. However, the category of "private farms" in Table 2 is very heterogeneous: it includes both large-scale successor organizations of collective farms, some of which still cover thousands of hectares, and household plots that are in general smaller than one hectare.[4] Other studies[5] show that large-scale farms use 85 percent of total agricultural area in Slovakia, 80 percent in the former East Germany, 76 percent in the Czech Republic, and 75 percent in Hungary. On the other end of the spectrum is Albania, where large-scale farms use only 5 percent of total agricultural area—all collective farms have been de-collectivized into small family farms and only a few state farms remain.

Based on the data in Table 2, the de-collectivization of Central and Eastern European agriculture seems successful. However, the facts are sometimes misleading—the transformation of collective farms often was more a legal conversion than an effective change of management and organization. Many new-style cooperatives or joint-stock companies do not differ at all from their communist predecessors. The privatization of farm assets and the transformation of state and collective farms were necessary—but not sufficient—conditions for the de-collectivization of the agricultural sector. De-collectivization is the result of the actions of collective farm members and/or management that are influenced to a great extent by economic factors.[6]

Many observers suggest that these large-scale farm organizations are an optimal way for farmers to survive the severe conditions of transition.[7] More specifically, they argue that collective farms are better able to deal with risk. Even where collective farms have been de-collectivized, individual farmers have established new forms of cooperation. However, the advantages of that cooperation can be limited: it does not apply to production activities or risk management, but only to marketing, servicing, and purchasing of supplies.[8]

Table 2. Farm Organizations' Share of Total Agricultural Area
(in percentages, before and after reform)

	State farms		Cooperatives*		Private farms**	
	pre-reform	post-reform	pre-reform	post-reform	pre-reform	post-reform
Bulgaria	90	40	—	41	10	19
Czech Republic	38	3	61	48	1	49
Estonia	96	—	—	33	4	67
Hungary	14	7	80	55	6	38
Latvia	96	2	—	17	9	64
Lithuania	91	1	—	35	4	81
Poland	19	18	4	4	77	78
Romania	14	14	61	35	25	51
Slovakia	26	16	68	63	6	13
Slovenia	8	7	—	—	92	93

Source: European Commission, *Agricultural Situation and Prospects in the Central and Eastern European countries,* summary report (Directorate-General for Agriculture Working Document, 1995)

*Collective farm pre-transition; producer cooperative or association after reform.

**Household plots and small individual farms pre-transition; individual farms and business entities (companies, partnerships, etc.) after reform.

FACTORS AFFECTING FARM RESTRUCTURING AND DE-COLLECTIVIZATION

De-collectivization implies a tremendous change of production technology and a major restructuring of human capital. A modern farmer in a Western country possesses many skills, while members of collective farms often have very narrow skills. Newly established independent farmers must learn a wide variety of skills and knowledge. Some of these skills cannot be learned quickly from books but only through long accumulation of experiences. Therefore, important incentives for individuals are necessary to stimulate them to set up their own individual farms.

Farm restructuring depends on the pre-reform farm structure, on the design of the privatization and transformation policies, on the implementation of those policies, and on a series of additional factors, including the economic environment, affecting the outcome of the reform process.

First, the pre-transition farm structure differed quite importantly among Central and Eastern European countries. Agricultural production was mostly collectivized, except in Poland and former Yugoslavia, where even under the communists, the majority of farm production was from the private sector. The other extremes are Albania and the former Soviet Union, where private farming was less than 2 percent of output. In Bulgaria, all collectivized farms were consolidated with food-processing enterprises and the rest of the agro-industry into huge agro-industrial complexes in the early 1970s. These structures were abolished in 1986.

Evidently, this pre-reform structure is affecting the emerging farm structure. The most obvious examples are the small-scale family farms still dominant in Poland and Slovenia, due entirely to the existence of pre-reform family farms.

Second, privatization and transformation policies are not independent. Both policies will affect the resulting production organization and allocation of assets. Without transaction costs, the privatization process—as long as it returns all ownership rights to private individuals—might not affect the farm structure and the transformation process beyond the transformation from a socialist to a capitalist mode of production. However, in a world with transaction costs and imperfect markets the impact of the privatization process on restructuring will be important.

Third, the government has tried to influence transformation, and in particular de-collectivization—the creation of individually operated farms—through additional regulations that provide explicit rules for the design of the transformation. Facilitating the withdrawal of farmers from agricultural production cooperatives can be done through various incentives, such as providing individual private farmers with such preferential credit arrangements as low interest credit and loan guarantees, by canceling their share of the collective farm debt, or by the provision of training and extension facilities to support the development of individual farming. However, some countries have included regulations that tend to discourage farmers from leaving the cooperatives.

Key characteristics of de-collectivization policy include the role it provides for the management of the collective and state farms, as well as the incentives it offers for leaving the collective farm. For example, the 1992 Union of Democratic Forces government in Bulgaria decided to throw out the old management of the collective farms and replace it with special institutions—appropriately called "liquidation councils"—to effectively liquidate the collective farms. Similarly, the 1991 Sajudis government in Lithuania removed existing management from its controlling positions and created new institutions, the Municipal Agrarian Reform Services, chaired by outsiders. Not surprisingly, in both countries the role and the composition of these institutions was changed when the ex-communists came back to power.

Other Central and East European countries have opted for a less radical approach, emphasizing the need to minimize further disruptions. They have done so by giving the members and old management important roles in the transformation of their collective and state farms. For example, in Hungary, Slovakia, and the Czech Republic, former management plays an important role in the transformation of the collective farms: they are the main agents in the "transformation boards" that have to draw up a plan for transforming the organization. Individuals are discouraged from leaving the collectives by the imposition of the administration costs of parceling out the land in case they want to leave the transformed collective farm and start up their own individual farm. In both the Czech Republic and Hungary such policies have been criticized as being "in favor of the former communists" by the farmers' parties.

Fourth, the economic environment will affect the opportunities and risks for emerging private farmers and, thus, the incentives for individuals to set up their own farms or to stay with a reformed cooperative or state farm. The economic environment since 1989 has been characterized by lower agricultural prices relative to industrial prices, depressed farm incomes, high inflation, a lack of inputs (especially credit), technology and human resources ill-suited to modern production methods, production declines, and widespread uncertainty. Would-be private farmers face unfavorable market conditions and problems with access to supplies as well as processing and marketing facilities. These problems can come from the hostile attitude of the old-style management of agro-industrial enterprises or shortages. These factors reduce the incentives for collective farm members and employees to start up their own private farms.

The attitudes of farmers are further affected by the lack of a credible legal framework. Individuals are not inclined to start investing unless the legal framework is sufficiently stable. The most important issue is the uncertainty of property rights. As long as property rights are uncertain, de-capitalization of agriculture continues. However, the establishment of strong and stable property rights and institutions is taking time. Informal contracts have partially replaced formal contracts in agriculture during the transition.

A special case is the capital market. Investment requires capital, which in turn usually requires credits and loans. If private farmers have access to credit at all, they often do not possess the collateral needed to actually obtain loans. With low overall profitability in farming, the poorly developed banking system refuses to lend to agricultural producers unless substantive and well-defined collateral can be provided. As land titles have not been assigned, producers cannot obtain credits for investment or for purchasing basic materials.

Fifth, a key factor explaining de-collectivization is the relative productivity of the collective farm versus the collective farm members' productivity in individual farms. Knowledge of the production process and the inherent skills are highly separated in the agricultural production systems of Central and Eastern European countries rather than being concentrated in one person. Entrepreneurship among farm workers is negatively influenced by the absence of capabilities and norms that are adjusted to the peculiarities and the heterogeneity of decision-making problems in family farm operations.[9] Human capital cannot be reorganized or privatized like other assets and may therefore be the most "conservative" factor in the restructuring process. Furthermore, many of those employed on collective and state farms are elderly people, who are generally less responsive to incentives and more averse to risk.

The relation between productivity on the collective farm and productivity on an individual farm depends also on the technology and the degree of labor specialization in the collective farm before the reform. The impact of the existing capital stock is hard to assess ex ante, because it is influenced by a number of other factors. First, it depends on the availability of alternative, smaller-scale machinery and other capital assets. This is not only determined by the situation and the extent of restructuring in down- and upstream industry, but also on the extent to which farmers have access to credit for purchasing new machinery.

Second, it depends on the nature of the machinery and of the privatization process. For example, if machinery is not too large and if privatization allows for indivisibility of sales, this might stimulate the creation of institutions for custom use of such equipment. Examples from Western European agriculture show that organizational innovations in production—such as service cooperatives in Germany and France and custom workers in the Netherlands and Belgium—and the existence of cooperatives for processing and input purchasing, allow the realization of economies of scale without having to move to a large-scale production system. The development of such institutions surrounding the production system depends not only on the privatization of nonland assets but also on the restructuring of the up- and downstream industry. A key issue is whether reformed collectives can contribute to an efficient transition by gradually transforming themselves into service cooperatives.[10]

FUTURE DEVELOPMENTS

Early studies indicate a widespread lack of entrepreneurship as well as enthusiasm by farm workers for a return to an independent farmer status, a problem that is widely argued to be a serious impediment to agricultural privatization.[11] Most pre-1994 surveys indeed indicate that a large share of collective farm workers prefer to remain in now-privatized cooperative farm organizations. These studies focus on the uncertain and negative economic environment, the reported lack of human capital, and on the informal institutions.[12] They present a very pessimistic picture on de-collectivization and the emergence of new farms. This is inconsistent with reality in a number of countries. While successor organizations to the collective and state farms still dominate agricultural production in several Central and Eastern European countries, we also notice that family farms have become quite important in others, and that in some they are already using most of the land. Therefore, it appears that many of the early studies underestimated the incentives individuals perceived in gaining income from moving out of the collective and state farm framework. This in turn reflects the massive inefficiencies that were and still are present in the organization of these farms and their successor organizations. When macroeconomic stability and the functioning of markets for inputs and outputs improve, one can expect the de-collectivization of large-scale farms to continue.

[1]Jo Swinnen and Erik Mathijs, "A Comparative Analysis of Agricultural Privatization, Land Reform and Farm Restructuring in Central and Eastern Europe," in Jo Swinnen, Allan Buckwell and Erik Mathijs (eds.), *Agricultural Privatization, Land Reform and Farm Restructuring in Central and Eastern Europe* (Aldershot: Avebury Publishers, forthcoming).

[2]See Swinnen, "The Choice of Privatization and Decollectivization Policies in Central and East European Agriculture," Ibid.

[3]Y. Barzel, *Economic Analysis of Property Rights* (Cambridge: Cambridge University Press, 1989).

[4]Hungarian statistics include all plots of at least 400 square meters. See country studies in Swinnen et al.

[5]Swinnen, Buckwell, and Mathijs, *Agricultural Privatization, Land Reform*.

[6]See Mathijs and Swinnen, "The Economics of Agricultural Decollectivization: Theory and Empirical Evidence from Central and Eastern Europe," unpublished manuscript, 1996.

[7]Michael R. Carter, "Risk Sharing and Incentives in the Decollectivization of Agriculture," *Oxford Economic Papers*, 39, 1987, pp. 577–595; Y. Machnes and A. Schnytzer, "Risk and the Collective Farm in Transition," in C. Csaki and Y. Kislev, *Agricultural Cooperatives in Transition* (Boulder, Colo.: Westview Press, 1993).

[8]Karl Deininger, "Collective Agricultural Production: A Solution For Transition Economies?" *World Development*, vol. 23, no. 8, 1995, pp. 1317–1334.

[9]Konrad Hagedorn, "Transformation of Socialist Agricultural Systems," *Journal of International and Comparative Economics*, vol. 1, 1992, pp. 103–124.

[10]See Deininger, "Collective Agricultural Production."

[11]Karen Brooks, "Decollectivization and the agricultural transition in Eastern and Central Europe," Working Paper, Agricultural and Rural Development Department (World Bank: Washington DC, 1991); Frederick L. Pryor, *The Red and the Green: The Rise and Fall of Collectivized Agriculture in Marxist Regimes* (New Haven: Princeton University Press, 1992).

[12]Bulgarian Agriculture Ministry, Sofia, 1993; Dinu Gavrilescu, "Agricultural Reform in Romania: Between Market Priority and the Strategies for Food Security," and J. Kraus, T. Doucha, Z. Sokol and B. Prouza, "Agricultural Reform and Transformation in the Czech Republic," both in: Jo Swinnen (ed.), *Policy and Institutional Change in Central European Agriculture* (London: Avebury Publishers, 1994).

THE ENVIRONMENT: A TERRIBLE COMMUNIST LEGACY

by COLIN WOODARD

Socialist central planners left behind a staggering array of severe environmental problems. From the Black Sea to the Siberian taiga, entire ecosystems are collapsing, with potentially dire consequences for the future.

Humans killed the Aral Sea for cotton. In its death throes, the sea is exacting a terrible revenge. The rivers that fed the Central Asian sea were diverted to turn arid steppes into irrigated cotton plantations, and the Aral began to shrink; it's now half its original size. Salt-laden sea-floor dust has been carried far and wide by the winds, while the steppes are turning to deserts. The salts have destroyed the Uzbek cotton fields, where chemical fertilizers were already killing off the local population. Meanwhile, the desert is expanding. Dust is blown as far as the Pamir Mountains in the east and Moscow to the north, "a harbinger of the impending invasion," writes Russian geographer Ze'ev Wolfson, "as inescapable and ruthless as the Mongol horsemen."[1]

It's hard to blame experts on the Central Asian environment for speaking in apocalyptic terms. Shortsighted engineering and industrial projects have reduced the steppes in Kazakstan, Kalmykia, and the north Caspian basin to sand deserts. Overpasturing in the Kalmykia region created a 70,000–square-kilometer desert that is growing by an estimated 10 percent each year.[2] Intensive agriculture and pesticide use have forced 600,000 hectares of northern Caucasus pastures to be abandoned. The loss of the Aral Sea and pesticide use in Uzbek cotton fields weakened ecosystems bordering on the Kara and Kyzyl deserts, which swallow an estimated 1 million hectares of land each year.[3]

"If the current process of environmental pollution and desertification is not stopped or at least slowed down," Wolfson concludes, "then the expansion and merging of old and new deserts over the next decade may actually lead to the formation of an Asian Sahara. The belt of deserts and semideserts starting at the eastern outskirts of Europe—the lower Volga and the northern foothills of the Caucasus—will envelop virtually all of Kazakstan and Central Asia, possibly spreading as far as central China."[4]

Ecosystem collapse is not confined to Central Asia and southern Russia. Polar deserts are overtaking the Siberian tundra, while the tundra is replacing the Siberian taiga—the second largest terrestrial source of oxygen after the Amazon rain forests. The Black Sea and the Sea of Azov are becoming virtually lifeless, their fish species suffocated by declining levels of dissolved oxygen. The Baltic Sea and the Volga, Vistula, and Danube rivers suffer from acute industrial pollution, while the Chornobyl disaster has irradiated large areas of Ukraine and Belarus. Eastern Europeans will live with the legacy of central planning for generations to come.

CENTRALLY PLANNED DESTRUCTION

Environmental pollution is a serious problem everywhere, but communism was particularly dirty. By combining massive subsidies of energy and raw materials with an overriding emphasis on increased industrial production, economic planners created a system plagued by waste and inefficiency. The obsession with achieving centrally planned production targets meant that environmental concerns were never properly addressed.

The communist countries of Central and Eastern Europe never used resources as efficiently as the West, but the gap grew far wider after the oil crisis of the 1970s. In the West, steep increases in energy prices encouraged rationalization of energy and raw-material consumption, and a shift toward service-industry products. New information, construction, and production technologies were introduced with impressive results. Per-unit energy requirements in the member countries of the Organization for Economic Cooperation and Development (OECD) dropped by 25 percent between 1970 and 1989, a period of continued economic growth.[5] U.S. gross national product increased by more than 45 percent from 1973 to 1992, but energy consumption increased by only 7 percent.[6] New environmental regulations and technologies allowed OECD countries to register environmental improvements. Sulfur dioxide emissions dropped by 40 percent between 1970 and 1989, while carbon emissions remained stable until 1987 (when energy prices finally fell).[7]

Meanwhile, energy subsidies and the continued availability of low-cost Soviet supplies insulated Eastern Europe from the global trend toward greater efficiency. To make matters worse, as the region's economic crisis deepened, maintenance and housekeeping was deferred; so too was the replacement of aging and obsolete equipment. While the West improved efficiency, the Soviet-bloc countries used resources more wastefully. In 1991, Poland used two to three times as much energy per unit of production as did OECD countries, while Romania used three to five times as much.[8] They also produced more pollution. In 1989, Czechoslovakia and Poland each released twice the nitrogen oxides and four to five times as much sulfur dioxide as OECD countries with populations of comparable size; pollution-control equipment was rarely installed at factories and power plants and in many cases had outlived its usefulness. Budapest hospitals generate 5,700 tons of hazardous medical waste each year, while the city's five incinerators together have an annual capacity of only 200 tons. Most communities discharge untreated wastewater directly into the environment—sewers in Bucharest; Bratislava; Szeged, Hungary; Cluj, Romania; and half of Budapest release directly into local rivers. Poor agricultural practices and poorly maintained feedlots compound the problems.[9]

LOST RESOURCES

The results have been tragic. Ninety-five percent of Polish rivers are polluted, a third of them so badly that the water cannot be used for industrial purposes because it corrodes metal.[10] Water from two-thirds of residential wells in Polish villages is undrinkable, mostly due to contamination from community sewage.[11] The Baltic Sea and Black Sea ecosystems are under serious threat from river-borne pollution, unmanaged fishing, and the dumping of toxic wastes: 20 of 26 commercial fish species have disappeared from the Black Sea since the mid-1960s.[12]

Air pollution is widespread. Many countries rely on low-quality brown coal for heat and electricity generation, and the fallout taints the air, land, and water. Eighty-two percent of Polish forests and 73 percent of those in Slovakia and the Czech Republic show signs of acid-rain damage. Krakow's historic stone build-ings have melted under decades of acidic fallout from the Nowa Huta steel mill. Lead, zinc, and copper smelters release huge quantities of poisonous dust, which fall on nearby towns such as Plovdiv, Bulgaria; Copsa Mica, Romania; Ajka, Hungary; and Konstantinovka, Ukraine. Krivoi Rog, Ukraine, and Kosice, Slovakia, suffer from dust and particulate emissions from local steelworks, which lack proper emissions safeguards.

Cleaning up after the Cold War may cost as much as the arms buildup itself. Soviet military bases abandoned in Poland, Hungary, the Czech Republic, East Germany, and Slovakia will cost hundreds of millions to clean up, while the cost within the former Soviet Union is at present impossible to assess. In addition to petrochemical and heavy-metals contamination of soil and water at most of these sites, some 715 nuclear weapons were detonated between 1949 and 1990—most at Novaya Zemlya in the Arctic Ocean and Semipalatinsk, Kazakhstan. (No-madic tribesmen near Semipalatinsk were encouraged to pasture their animals to provide scientists with statistical data on radiological health problems.)

Norway's Bellona Foundation released a comprehensive report on radiologi-cal contamination in Russia's Murmansk and Arkhangelsk oblasts, which have the highest density of in-operation nuclear reactors (most of them military) in the world. Bellona found that one-fifth of Soviet underground detonations resulted in accidental radiation releases; 13 nuclear reactors, including six with their fuel assemblies still installed, were dumped into the Kara Sea. The USSR also dumped between 3.1 million and 9 million curies of radioactive waste into the Pacific Ocean and the Kara, Barents, and Baltic seas—twice as much as the rest of the world combined.[13] Russia's current leaders seem less than eager to face up to the problem: after Bellona released a report in October 1995 exposing particu-larly appalling conditions at one nuclear-waste dump, Russian authorities banned the report and launched a criminal investigation of the foundation. A former Russian naval officer employed by Bellona, Aleksandr Nikitin, was arrested in February by the Federal Security Service (the KGB's successor) and charged with treason.[14] Nikitin, who continues to be held in a high-security prison while his case is prepared, could face the death penalty if convicted.

Human health has been dramatically affected by pollution. In inner Budapest, nearly 60 percent of children have dangerous blood-lead levels. Public health authorities in Decin, Czech Republic, advise people to avoid going outdoors during winter atmospheric inversions; the town doctor avoids performing surgeries at these times because he is concerned about reduced oxygen levels.[15] Studies of children between the ages of 7 and 12 in Romania's notorious industrial town of Copsa Mica and neighboring Medias found that many demonstrated signs of mental retardation, two-thirds were underweight, and 30 percent of the boys and nearly half of the girls had abnormally high blood pressure.[16] From 1979 to 1989, overall mortality in Uzbekistan rose by 50 percent, cardiovascular disease by 60 percent, and stomach cancer by 1,000 percent. Infant mortality in Uzbekistan is 20 times that of Japan; contaminants from the Aral Sea debacle are believed to be the principal factor.[17]

WHAT IS TO BE DONE?

National governments and international organizations have taken significant steps to improve air and drinking-water quality and reduce pollution levels. But for the largest problems, it may already be too late. Again, the Aral Sea catastrophe provides an ominous case in point. Since 1988, Soviet and post-Soviet authorities have tried to redirect used irrigation water back to the seabed, but the water is so severely polluted by salts and fertilizers that it may only make the problem worse. Since there still isn't enough water flowing into the sea to prevent it from evaporating further, the toxins may end up blowing into the atmosphere.[18] The geographer Ze'ev Wolfson suggests that salt-resistant plants be planted on the former seabed to serve as ground cover, which leaves the greater problem of securing potable water for the region's 32 million people. But where to get the water?

According to Polish journalist Ryszard Kapuscinski, Soviet authorities first considered using nuclear weapons to melt the glaciers of the Pamir and Tien Shan mountains (where the Aral's headwaters are found).[19] Later, Soviet planners worked on another seemingly outlandish "solution": redirecting the course of the great Siberian rivers to flow south instead of north. The massive diversion project was expected to change ice-pack and current conditions in the Arctic Ocean and perhaps alter the global climate.[20] Although the project was abandoned under Mikhail Gorbachev's leadership in 1986, Uzbek President Islam Karimov has made repeated calls for its implementation, most recently at a 1995 Aral Sea conference in Nukus.[21] An earlier conference called for increased investment in local infrastructure (including water purification and sewage plants), the abolition of cotton monoculture "through the termination of mandatory state orders," and the improvement of irrigation systems and water use regionwide.[22] Since the Uzbek leadership relies on the cotton crop for its wealth, the implementation of such measures is difficult without outside support.

The prognosis for the Black Sea is only slightly less apocalyptic. Here the water remains, but it is rapidly becoming lifeless. Technical innovations over the past 40 years industrialized fishing and agriculture in the Black Sea basin, home to 160 million people—most of whom dump their sewage, fertilizers, and industrial wastes into the sea and its tributaries, which include the Danube, Dniester, Dniepr, and Don rivers. Fish and sea mammals are rapidly dying off—the anchovy harvest fell by 95 percent from 1984 to 1989—replaced by monstrous blooms of plankton that feed on human waste. Photoplankton concentrations are so high that light penetration on the coastal shelf has fallen by between 40 percent and 90 percent, wiping out mollusks, crustaceans, flatfish, and pastures of sea grass.[23]

"As a weakened man easily succumbs to disease, so damaged ecosystems readily fall victim to attacking forces," writes Aleksei Yablokov, Russian President Boris Yeltsin's environmental councilor.[24] As the Black and Azov seas weakened, a foreign invader took over. Discharged from the ballast tanks of a passing ship, the North American Mnemioposis jellyfish found a niche for itself in the now predatorless seas. Its population exploded in the late 1980s, devouring zooplankton (the main food of small fish) and furthering the explosive photoplankton boom. At 1 billion tons, the mass of Mnemioposis is now thought to exceed the seas' entire fish mass.[25]

Like the dust of the dry Aral sea floor, the Mnemioposis is spreading. Having exhausted its food supply, the jellyfish has been turning up in greater numbers in the Sea of Mamara and the eastern Aegean Sea, raising the specter of a wider invasion of the weakened Mediterranean. The governments that share the sea are taking urgent action but appear powerless against the profligate jellyfish. Meanwhile, some scientists fear the anoxic, hydrogen sulfide-charged sea may "turn over," as anoxic lakes regularly do, and release a cloud of toxic hydrogen sulfide gas. The difference: the Black Sea could emit such an enormous quantity of toxic gas that it could kill millions of people and irreversibly alter the composition of the atmosphere. Most scientists do not believe this will take place, but a debate continues in scholarly circles.[26]

[1]Ze'ev Wolfson, *The Geography of Survival* (Armonk: M. E. Sharpe, 1994), p. 71.

[2]*Ecos*, January 1990, pp. 18–21.

[3]*Environmental Policy Review*, vol. 4, no. 1, Winter 1990, pp. 37–39.

[4]Wolfson, *Geography of Survival*, p. 71.

[5]1991 OECD figures.

[6]Ian Torrens, paper delivered to International Conference on the Clean and Efficient Use of Coal, Budapest, February 1992.

[7]1991 OECD figures.

[8]*Romania Environmental Strategy Paper* (Washington, DC: World Bank, 1992); *The Economist*, 17 February 1990.

[9]*Environmental Action Program for Central and Eastern Europe*, (Washington, DC: World Bank, 1993).

[10]Polish Ministry of Environment data.

[11]1991 *Yearbook of the Polish Central Statistics Office* (statistics are from 1989).

[12]*Romania Environmental Strategy Paper*, p. 42.

[13]*Sources to Radioactive Contamination in Murmansk and Arkhangelsk Counties* (Oslo: Bellona Foundation, 1994), pp. 94–106.

[14]*OMRI Daily Digest*, 7 February 1996.

[15]*Prognosis,* January 1992.

[16]*Romania Environmental Strategy Paper;* Institute of Public Health of Cluj-Napoca.

[17]See Wolfson, *The Geography,* pp. 41–42.

[18]Ibid., pp. 54–58.

[19]Ryszard Kapuscinski, *Imperium* (New York: Alfred A. Knopf, 1994), pp. 262–264.

[20]Philip Micklin, "The Status of the Soviet Union's North-South Water-Transfer Projects Before Their Abandonment in 1985–1986," *Soviet Geography,* vol. 27, no. 5, May 1986.

[21]*Moscow News,* 6 October 1995.

[22]"Summary of Discussions at the Conference, 'Aral Sea Crisis: Environmental Issues in Central Asia'; Indiana University, Bloomington, Indiana; July 14–18, 1990," *AACAR Bulletin,* Spring 1991, pp. 4–5.

[23]*The Independent,* 18 June 1995; see also Neal Ascherson, *Black Sea* (New York: Hill and Wang, 1995).

[24]*Environmental Policy Review,* vol. 4, no. 1, Winter 1990, p. 2.

[25]*The Independent,* 18 June 1995; Wolfson, *The Geography,* p. 69.

[26]*The Independent,* 18 June 1995.

BUILDING DEMOCRATIC INSTITUTIONS

VIII

CHOOSING DEMOCRACY AS THE LESSER EVIL
by RICHARD ROSE

The 20th century has been distinguished by two contrasting processes: the spread of democracy and the creation of new types of undemocratic regimes. In Central and Eastern Europe, 20th-century history is a record of too many alternatives to democracy. Every post-communist country has been subject to undemocratic governments longer than democratic rule. Moreover, each country has had at least two different forms of undemocratic governance.

The demise of communist regimes in Central and Eastern Europe creates the opportunity for democracy—but is no guarantee that democracies will become established. The 1990s are a long way from 1913, 1938, or 1948. We cannot forecast the future of Central and Eastern Europe by extrapolation from the past, for the region's modern history is full of discontinuities and reversals of political direction.

Since democracy allows people to choose governors in free elections, a stable democracy cannot be created without the support of public opinion. But why should people support democracy when its introduction has been marked by rising crime rates, galloping inflation, job insecurity, and political instability?

Shortly after World War II, Winston Churchill offered a realist justification for democracy, defending it in relativistic terms: "Many forms of government have been tried and will be tried in this world of sin and woe. No one pretends that democracy is perfect or all wise. Indeed, it has been said that democracy is the worst form of government, except all those other forms that have been tried from time to time."[1]

In other words, democracy is a second-best form of government, or even a lesser evil. By definition, people in post-communist countries have tried other forms of government, and older people have lived under as many as half a dozen regimes. When the people of Central and Eastern Europe are asked to compare democracy with alternative regimes, a majority endorse the Churchill hypothesis.

REAL VERSUS IDEAL DEMOCRACY

Because of increased freedoms, we can find out what people in post-communist societies think by surveying public opinion. Surveys avoid both the totalitarian assumption that everyone in post-communist societies ought to think alike and the historicist fallacy that all people think alike if they share a national history and language.

The answers that Central and Eastern Europeans give in surveys about democracy—and the interpretations that are made of those answers—depend upon the questions that are asked. At the root of the differences is a fundamental conflict between idealist and realist definitions of democracy.

Idealists discuss how democracy ought to work in the best of all possible worlds. The best-known idealist definition of democracy is offered by the American political scientist Robert Dahl, who delineates eight conditions that a democracy should meet, including freedom of speech, the right to form and join non-state organizations, the right to vote, free and fair elections, and the accountability of the government to the governed. But using numerous and demanding criteria makes it unlikely that a country can fulfill all eight. Dahl recognizes this, concluding that "no large system in the real world is fully democratized." Attention is then concentrated on "real-world systems that are closest" to this ideal.[2]

The realist approach defines democracy in relation to the world as it actually is. Joseph Schumpeter, a political economist and Harvard professor who was born under the Habsburgs, defined democracy as government accountable to parties chosen through free, competitive elections.[3] Political competition gives opposition parties an incentive to generate dissatisfaction with the way the country is governed. Free elections give voters the opportunity to express dissatisfaction by turning governors out of office. For this reason, the replacement of Lech Walesa by an ex-communist as president of Poland is an example of democracy at work.

Most studies of public opinion in post-communist countries are idealistic, asking people whether they endorse every democratic value and regard their current system of government as ideal or less than ideal. Charles Gati goes further, interpreting survey evidence of dissatisfaction with the development of democracy as indicating that voters in ex-communist countries are ready to forsake democracy for semi-authoritarian rule.[4] Such an approach ignores the fact that in a free society, there will never be 100 percent endorsement of democratic values.

The data presented here come from the fourth annual New Democracies Barometer survey, conducted by the Paul Lazarsfeld Society in Vienna and sponsored by the Austrian Federal Ministry for Science and Research and the Austrian National Bank. The survey asks the same questions from the Czech Republic to the Black Sea. In each country, an established national research institute conducts approximately 1,000 face-to-face interviews with a stratified nationwide sample of adults aged 18 and above. Field work took place in November and December 1995; a total of 7,441 persons were interviewed.[5]

The survey includes Bulgaria, the Czech Republic, Slovakia, Hungary, Poland, Romania, and Slovenia, countries that differ in their histories before, during, and after communist rule. Collectively, they are the best test case for democratization, because their histories have been shaped by the European tradition, authoritarian as well as democratic. They are also all in association with the European Union.[6]

Because individuals' evaluations of regimes are relative, the survey first asks people to evaluate the former communist regime on a "heaven or hell" scale that ranges from plus 100 to minus 100. People are then asked to evaluate the current system of governing, with its free elections and many parties. The two responses can then be compared to arrive at a realistic assessment of democracy.

A relativistic approach does not expect government to be perfect. It evaluates democracy in comparison to known alternatives. Rather than ask, "Do you feel perfectly free?" people are asked whether they feel more or less free today than in communist times. Replies to the New Democracies Barometer surveys, which use a relative scale, show that Eastern and Central Europeans feel more free today than before.[7]

A relativistic approach is dynamic. In the mid-1980s, no communist regime was democratic, but there were differences in the extent to which they were unfree. Bulgaria and Romania ranked at the bottom of the Freedom House's seven-point scale for democracy, along with the whole of the Soviet Union. Czechoslovakia was almost at the bottom, while Poland and Hungary were on the borderline between being unfree and partly free. Since the gradual disintegration of the power of the Soviet Communist Party in the mid- to late 1980s, all the countries of Central and Eastern Europe have made major progress toward freedom. So too have the European successor states of the Soviet Union. Even countries today classified as only partly free, such as Romania and Belarus, have moved from being completely undemocratic toward a system of greater political and civil rights.[8]

CURRENT REGIME PREFERRED

NDB results show that across Eastern and Central Europe, the usual pattern is that most people view the old communist regime negatively and the current regime positively (see Figure 1). The gap between past and present is greatest in Poland and in the Czech Republic, where one-quarter endorse the old regime, while three-quarters endorse the new. More than twice as many Romanians endorse the new regime as the old. This does not mean that Poland or Romania has achieved a standard of government equal to that of Norway, or that the Czech Republic is governed like Germany. The common element in all three countries is that the communist regime is much disliked because it was identified with repression.

Hungary is the one country in which more people are positive about the old regime than the new. But to interpret this as evidence that Hungarians want the return of Soviet troops and a Marxist-Leninist regime is absurd. The old regime was the most liberal in the Soviet bloc and was cynical in its view of communism, proclaiming the doctrine, "He who is not against us is with us." Since 1990, Hungarian voters have turned out ex-communists in favor of a right-of center government, and then, as a protest against that government's failings, brought the ex-communists back—only to be highly dissatisfied again. In voting governors out of and then back into office, Hungarians, Poles, Slovaks, and Bulgarians are doing just what Schumpeter said voters ought to do in a real democracy.

The "heaven and hell" scale enables people to rate both past and present regimes negatively. Those dissatisfied with their government can rate the present regime as bad (say, –25), and yet prefer it to its predecessor, if they consider that dreadful (say, –75). Consistently, far more Eastern and Central Europeans regard the old regime as the worst possible system (–100) than regard the new regime as the best possible system (+100).

Figure 1. Approval of Democratic vs. Communist Regimes

Source: New Democracies Barometer IV (Vienna: Paul Lazarsfeld Society, 1996).

Within each of the seven countries included in the survey, people fall into four groups. The overall breakdown is:

- Democrats (average for the seven countries: 32 percent), who not only reject the old regime, but also approve of the new regime.
- Skeptics (23 percent), who disapprove of both the old and the new regimes—but usually are more negative about the old regime than the new.
- Compliant (21 percent), who are positive or neutral about both the old and the new regime.
- Reactionaries (24 percent), who approve of the old regime and reject the present one.

The Churchill hypothesis is thus supported by more than half of the people of Eastern and Central Europe today: new regimes offering free elections and greater civil liberties are considered relatively more attractive, or at least less unattractive, than the previous, communist system. Positively committed democrats are the largest group. Skeptics include idealists who give their current regime a negative rating because it falls short of democratic perfection, while giving the old regime an even lower rating because it is much further from the ideal. Whether members of the compliant group endorse both old and new regimes out of apathy or prudence, their views are unlikely to disturb ruling powers, including democratic powers.

Reactionaries can be a cause of anxiety, since they appear to have a different ideal, rating the old communist regime positively and new democratic institutions negatively. However, reactionaries are a minority in every country surveyed and make up less than one-quarter of the population overall.

Public appraisals of a fledgling democracy are especially subject to change, as new institutions demonstrate their strengths and weaknesses. Idealists demand abrupt and radical changes, whether they be "democracy Bolsheviks," who want their country to jump from a Leninist inheritance to ideal democracy overnight, or "market Bolsheviks," who want a flourishing market economy and prosperity to emerge spontaneously from the wreckage of a command economy.

However, life under communism taught ordinary people patience about everything from waiting for permission to visit relatives abroad to waiting for a plumber. Thus, most do not expect the collapse of communism to transform everything overnight. Two-thirds of the survey respondents think it will take many years for their government to deal with the problems inherited from the communists, compared with one-third who express impatience. Economic patience is also great. More people said "don't know" than gave any other answer to the question, "How long will it take for the government to deal with economic problems inherited from the past?" At the household level, most people do not expect instant gratification of their desires. Only 5 percent say they are currently economically content; the majority expect to wait indefinitely or for more than a decade before becoming materially satisfied.

When the survey asks people what they expect their government to be like in five years, most skeptics say they expect it to be closer to the positive end of the scale, and many reactionaries are moving in this direction too. But given the short time that new democratic institutions have existed and the many potential sources of instability, we must ask: What sort of government, democratic or undemocratic, do people want their country to have in the future?

DEMOCRACY FAVORED IN THE FUTURE

Introducing free elections involves risks. As Stephen White commented, "elections can delegitimate as easily as they legitimate a democratic regime."[9] Yet whether elites organize anti-democratic parties is a question of demand as well as supply. If there is little popular support for anti-democratic alternatives, this will discourage politicians from organizing parties likely to receive a derisory share of the vote and will also discourage bureaucrats and the military from plotting to introduce an authoritarian alternative.

In an established democracy, asking people about alternative regimes has little meaning, for any alternative is remote or inconceivable. By contrast, in Central and Eastern Europe, public opinion about alternatives to democracy is immediately relevant, for every adult has lived under at least two different regimes. In three countries examined here—the Czech Republic, Slovakia, and Slovenia—the state too is new.

Yet the past provides ambiguous guidance to the future. While it shows that authoritarianism can happen here, it leaves open whether Central and Eastern Europeans who have experienced authoritarian rule regard it as desirable or are reacting against it, as West Germans, Austrians, and Italians did after 1945, and

Spaniards, Greeks, and Portuguese have done in the past two decades. Hence, the New Democracies Barometer tests support for three familiar forms of authoritarian rule: a communist regime, military rule, and dictatorship by a strong leader.

Return to communist rule is often discussed, since many institutions from the communist era remain. Furthermore, former communist politicians exploit old party networks to form ex-communist parties, which are winning a noteworthy share of the vote almost everywhere in Central and Eastern Europe. In some countries, they have won office through free elections, albeit with substantially less than half the popular vote.

A return to the communist past is rejected by five-sixths of survey respondents (see Table 1). Variations among countries are noteworthy; only 8 percent say they would like a communist regime back in Poland, compared with 29 percent in Bulgaria. Opposition to the return of a communist regime is usually intense. Across all seven countries surveyed, 58 percent of respondents are strongly opposed to the return of a communist regime, compared with only 4 percent strongly in favor of bringing it back. The remainder are divided down the middle between those somewhat for or somewhat against this alternative.

Those actually wanting a return to communist rule are far fewer than those who simply have positive views of the old communist regime. Even among the sizable minority expressing nostalgia about the old days, when Soviet troops and national security services maintained order and government was stable because there was a one-party state, less than half would actually like to return to a communist regime. This is just as well, since the principal promoters of communism, the Soviet Union and the Communist Party of the Soviet Union, are no more. It appears that the key element in the term ex-communist is "ex"; those who say they favor it are not so much ideologues as opportunists, exploiting dissatisfaction with reform governments to win votes and offices.[10]

Military rule is a familiar form of authoritarianism throughout the world. There have been many prominent military figures in Eastern and Central Europe in the not-too distant past, such as Marshal Jozef Pilsudski in Poland and Admiral Miklos Horthy in Hungary. However, a military takeover requires senior military personnel to see their role as not only protecting the country from foreign threats but also guaranteeing order and good governance within it. In communist regimes, the military was subject to an unusual degree of political control. Integration of armies in the Warsaw Pact added a layer of external Soviet control. Soldiers were trained to fight an electronic World War III and defined their role as that of technicians "on tap but not on top." Separate security forces were responsible for internal order.

Only 6 percent of Eastern and Central Europeans endorse the idea of the army taking over government; in none of the seven countries surveyed do as many as one-sixth favor military rule. The level falls below 5 percent in Hungary and in the Czech and Slovak republics, which experienced invasion by Soviet forces in 1956 and 1968, respectively, as well as in Slovenia, where an example of military involvement in politics is close at hand. The rejection of military rule is particularly striking because the army as an institution inspires a higher degree of popular trust than

Table 1. Support for Alternatives to Democracy (in percentages)			
	Army should govern	Return to communist regime	Strong leader without elections
Bulgaria	15	29	23
Czech Republic	3	11	14
Slovakia	1	19	19
Hungary	3	19	21
Poland	4	8	33
Romania	12	12	29
Slovenia	4	12	29
Average	6	16	24

Source: Nationwide stratified sample surveys with a total of 7,441 interviews, reported in *New Democracies Barometer IV* (Vienna: Paul Lazarsfeld Society, 1996).

parliament or party politicians. Yet even among those who trust the army, less than one-quarter would welcome the military taking over the government.

Strong leaders are a familiar alternative to democratic governance in most member states of the United Nations, including those of Central and Eastern Europe. To test support for this, the survey asked whether or not people agreed with the statement: "Better to get rid of parliament and elections and have a strong leader who can quickly decide things." Overall, 24 percent endorsed the idea of a strong leader. The proportion varied from one in three in Poland to one in seven in the Czech Republic. It is specially noteworthy that in Slovakia, where Vladimir Meciar led the country to independence, endorsement of a strong leader is below average.

Not only a large majority but also an intense majority opposes takeover by a strong leader. Among survey respondents overall, 51 percent strongly reject the idea of a leader replacing the parliament, while only 7 percent strongly endorse a leader placing himself above elected representatives. The demand for a strong leader is not necessarily undemocratic: it can be heard in every American presidential election. In Central and Eastern Europe, it can sometimes be heard from people who want a more effective but nonetheless democratic regime, or at least a form of "delegative democracy" similar to some Latin American systems, where a ruler can do what he likes for some number of years, but then is held accountable in a free and contested presidential election.[11]

The Churchill hypothesis implies that democracy is most vulnerable when it is so unpopular that any other alternative becomes the lesser evil. In such circumstances, people would not care whether the country returned to a communist regime, or moved to a military or civilian dictatorship, or to a "red-brown" coalition. The important point would be to get rid of a fledgling democracy that a majority had come to regard as intolerable.

Adding up the number of times individuals endorse any of the three un-democratic alternatives described in Table 1—a communist regime, military rule, or rule by a strong leader—produces a scale for measuring individual authoritarianism. The scale emphasizes the commitment to fledgling democratic regimes of the majority of people in Eastern and Central Europe: 68 percent reject all three authoritarian alternatives, 22 percent endorse only one, 8 percent endorse two, and only 2 percent endorse all three.

WHO SUPPORTS AUTHORITARIANISM?

Since any endorsement of authoritarianism is worrying, we need to know why some people in post-communist countries support authoritarianism. Political, economic, sociological, and cultural theories offer competing hypotheses to explain support for or rejection of authoritarian alternatives. Analyzing the New Democracies Barometer data with standard regression statistics makes it possible to test which, among a multiplicity of potential influences, is actually most applicable. The primary conclusion is that the legacy of communism is the most important factor. Because the average adult is in his or her early forties, current political events are viewed in the light of decades of experience of life in a communist regime. But that legacy is ambiguous. Cultural interpretations of Soviet rule argued that the authoritarianism of the old regime was consistent with national traditions, implying that authoritarian attitudes should be normal today. Alternatively, past repression may create a reaction against authoritarian ways. The survey shows:

- The more negative people are about the old communist regime on the "heaven and hell" scale, the more likely they are to reject authoritarian alternatives.
- The more repressive a national communist regime was in the past, the more likely people are to reject authoritarian alternatives.
- The more people believe their freedom has increased in comparison with the past, the more likely they are to reject authoritarian alternatives.
- The greater a person's political patience, the more likely he or she is to reject authoritarian alternatives.

There is widespread popular skepticism about or distrust in the institutions of fledgling democracies, as well as criticism of their failure to act effectively or even honestly. Yet the current performance of fledgling governments has much less influence upon attitudes toward authoritarianism than does the recollection of overbearing communist regimes. An ineffectual and even corrupt government is far from ideal, but as the Churchill hypothesis emphasizes, it is a lesser evil than a strong regime that is effective in exercising coercion.

The NDB survey shows that the influence of economic factors is secondary. The great majority of Eastern and Central Europeans feel a degree of economic insecurity due to the collapse of the command economy and the introduction of a market economy. However, this does not influence their political judgments.

There is no significant influence on attitudes toward authoritarianism as a result of dissatisfaction with current family economic circumstances, or a reduction in material well-being compared to the past, or of seeing no sign that family income will rise in the future. People in countries that experienced very high inflation are not more disposed to accept authoritarianism. Attitudes toward the old command economy and the new economic system also have no statistically significant influence on support for authoritarianism.

Although they have a weaker impact than do memories of the communist past, two economic factors are significant. The longer people do without food, heat, and clothing, the more likely they are to support authoritarian alternatives. And the greater their confidence in the future of the economic system, the less likely people are to support authoritarian alternatives.

In post-communist countries, official wages are inadequate measures of poverty. The lack of basic necessities is a better measure of destitution. People who often do without necessities are more likely to support authoritarian alternatives—but most Eastern and Central Europeans are far from destitute. The average person rarely does without necessities. Just as a Leninist revolution could not be made without breaking eggs, so a market economy cannot be introduced without dislocations. Insofar as people see current costs as an investment in the creation of a healthy economic system in the future—and a majority do so—they are more likely to reject authoritarian alternatives.

Cultural interpretations that invoke national history and traditions as a reason to expect countries to be undemocratic today ignore a simple fact: Europeans now live in a post-traditional society. Communist regimes aggressively sought to modernize societies through industrialization, education, urbanization, and promoting secular over religious values. Hence, the majority of people no longer live traditional lives in isolated rural villages. The survey shows that the more educated people are, the more likely they are to reject authoritarian alternatives, and that people living in bigger cities are more likely to reject authoritarianism.

Education has a greater impact on political attitudes than economic destitution. This is encouraging for democratization, since younger people tend to be better educated. Generational turnover is likely to increase the proportion of the population that opposes authoritarian regimes. Furthermore, the old saying "Cities make for freedom" still applies in post-communist Europe. Urban dwellers are politically more active and influential, which increases their resistance to an authoritarian takeover.

Detailed and systematic statistical analyses of survey results consistently show that differences in attitudes toward authoritarianism cannot be reduced to social structure or economics. The root cause is political—the experience of four decades of communist rule and the reaction it produced. Since the experience was searing and dominated the political socialization of the great majority of today's electorate, it is likely to sustain tolerance for fledgling democratic regimes, with all their weaknesses and faults, rather than lead to demands for a strong authoritarian regime.

LIMITS OF THE CHURCHILL HYPOTHESIS

The Churchill hypothesis is not a universal "law" like those of physics; it is based on experience. In countries without any experience of democracy, people have no firsthand opportunity to evaluate that system relative to other forms of government.

If a post-communist regime has not tried to become democratic, this deprives its population of the opportunity to compare democratic institutions with other forms of governance on the basis of firsthand experience. Post-communist countries are diverse not only in past history, but also in current experiences. A number of successor states of the former Soviet Union make no serious pretense of introducing democracy: if elections are held, they are meant to rubber-stamp the position of those in power. In the Russian Federation itself; there is debate about whether or not it is desirable to hold elections. The 1993 constitution and its subsequent interpretations leave much scope for the exercise of power unchecked by the institutions of a democratic state.

To expect every country from Tajikistan to the Czech Republic to become overnight a democracy with a prosperous market economy is ridiculous. That expectation ignores the fundamental political differences among post-communist countries. Even though every post-communist country is in principle open to democracy, not all have yet experienced it. The Churchill hypothesis predicts that if a government seeks to introduce democracy, then its citizens will prefer it—and public-opinion surveys support this prediction.

[This article summarizes ideas from Richard Rose's new book, *What is Europe?* published in New York and London by Harper Collins in 1996.]

[1]House of Commons, *Hansard*, 11 November 1947, col. 206.

[2]See Robert A. Dahl, *Polyarchy* (New Haven, Yale University Press, 1971), p. 8.

[3]Joseph A. Schumpeter, *Capitalism, Socialism and Democracy* (London: George Allen & Unwin, 1952, 4th ed.).

[4]See Charles Gati, "The Mirage of Democracy," *Transition*, vol. 2. no. 6, 22 March 1996, p. 8.

[5]See Richard Rose and Christian Haerpfer, "New Democracies Barometer IV," *University of Strathclyde Studies in Public Policy*, no. 260, 1996 (Internet: http://www.strath.ac.uk:80/departments/cspp/).

[6]See Richard Rose, *What is Europe* (London and New York: HarperCollins, 1996), chapters 3–5.

[7]See Richard Rose, "Freedom as a Fundamental Value," *International Social Science Journal*, no. 145, September 1995, pp. 457–471.

[8]See Raymond D. Gastil, *Freedom in the World. Political Rights and Civil Liberties* (New York: Greenwood Press, 1987), p. 55. and "1994 Freedom Around the World," *Freedom Review*, vol. 25, no. 1, pp. 5–41.

[9]Stephen White, "Elections in Eastern Europe," *Electoral Studies*, vol. 9, no. 4, p. 285.

[10]Richard Rose, "Ex-Communists in Post-Communist Societies," *Political Quarterly*, January 1996.

[11]See Guillermo O'Donnell, "Delegative Democracy," *Journal of Democracy*, vol. 5, no. I, 1994, pp. 55–69; Richard Rose and William Mishler, "Representation and Leadership in Post-Communist Political Systems," *Journal of Communist Studies and Transition Politics*, vol. 12, no. 2, June 1996.

THE MIRAGE OF DEMOCRACY
by CHARLES GATI

Official Western optimism about the future of the post-communist transition is belied by deep discontent in the region with the course of political and economic reforms. Most of the countries in the region are not becoming Western-style democracies nor returning to totalitarianism; instead, they are choosing semi-authoritarian rule and a controlled market.

Despite vast changes since 1989 in Central and Eastern Europe and not insignificant changes since 1991 in the former Soviet Union, the public mood in most post-communist countries points to unsuccessful transitions to democracy. At least 20 of the 27 post-communist states are facing the prospect of neither democracy nor totalitarianism. While the transition has neither completely failed nor completely succeeded anywhere, the dominant trend of the mid-1990s is partial retrenchment.

Most people in the post-communist world have already made a choice between order and freedom, and their preferred choice is order. Though approving a role for market forces, large majorities are nonetheless so nostalgic for the benefits of the communist welfare state, however meager, that they are prepared to do away with what they see as the cumbersome, dissonant, and chaotic features of democratic politics. With rule by the few the familiar alternative, what they reject is not merely a leader or a party, but the very system and values of Western-style democracy.

Full restoration of the totalitarian system is not taking place nor is it likely to take place. Most people in the post-communist world are freer than they were ten years ago and will almost certainly remain so for years to come. Entirely unreformed communist politics has no significant following in Central and Eastern Europe and only some in parts of the former Soviet Union. But the transition to democracy has lost its early popular appeal and therefore its early momentum. Radicals have yielded to minimalists, the liberal impulse has yielded to a quest for egalitarianism, demands for freedom have yielded to demands for order. On the defensive, the demoralized champions of Western ways in Russia and elsewhere have already begun to reposition themselves on the political spectrum.

Thus, the transition is producing a group of semi-authoritarian, semi-democratic, nationalist, populist regimes. They may permit free enterprise so long as it is properly regulated, allow free parliamentary debates so long as they are inconsequential, and even tolerate something resembling a free press so long as it questions only specific policies rather than the semi-authoritarian order itself. Only in Central Europe (the Czech Republic, Poland, Hungary and Slovenia) and the Baltic states of Estonia, Latvia, and Lithuania are the democratic prospects promising.

This is seldom recognized to be the case because it does not fit into widely-held Western notions of politics and economics. Many Americans, in particular, tend to assume that the road to democracy and the free market may be paved with bumps and detours, but at the end of the day there is no other road to be traveled. Denial persists in the face of growing evidence of a popularly supported retrenchment. Unpleasant facts, when noticed, are seldom characterized as part of a trend; they are called instead a "temporary setback." Election results revealing the appeal of reformed or even unreformed ex-communists and demagogic nationalist parties are explained away as a "protest vote," preference for "familiar faces," or simply the return of "experienced administrators." As poll after poll shows immense and increasing dissatisfaction with the region's democratic parties, the significance of such attitudes is minimized as "understandable reactions" to initial dislocations that accompany the introduction of democracy. The disparity between the few who are rich and the many who are poor—a major source of social strife—is seen as an "inherent" problem of "early capitalism." The power of, and atrocities by, criminals are compared to Chicago of the 1920s and thus excused.

Worse yet, those who look at the facts as they are rather than as they should be are mocked as "historical determinists" for assuming, it is charged, that only a few countries with "proper democratic genes" can have a democratic future. Just the opposite is true. It is the super-optimists who seem to derive their assessments less from contemporary evidence than from the success of American history. Taking into account neither the legacy of communism nor signs of retrenchment in the post-communist world, they offer illusory forecasts based on hope, not on experience. Alas, American history as a guide to the evolution of the former Soviet Union and Central and Eastern Europe is about as helpful as an old Michelin Guidebook is to present-day Yugoslavia.

THE GOALS OF INDEPENDENCE, PLURALISM

Most Western governments and observers view the changes that have taken place since the fall of communism in Central and Eastern Europe in 1989 and in the former Soviet Union in 1991 as far-reaching and encouraging. Although the overwhelming majority of the people of the post-communist world certainly no longer like what they experience, it would be misleading to deny that the three basic goals of transition—independence, political pluralism, and free-market economics—have been pursued in some countries vigorously and successfully.

The first goal was sovereign existence, which is to say independence from Russia. Given the collapse of the Warsaw Pact together with the withdrawal of Soviet forces from Central and Eastern Europe and of Russian forces from most parts of the Soviet Union, this goal in fact has been achieved. In Central and Eastern Europe, except in Serbia and Bulgaria, not only Russian military power but Russian influence too has disappeared.

However, independence has brought with it two new disappointments and a potential threat. One disappointment is the rise of nationalist fervor—wars in the North Caucasus and in ex-Yugoslavia, tension elsewhere over the treatment of minorities, especially of Russians, Hungarians and Turks who live in inhospitable neighboring countries. The other new disappointment is the inability of the post-communist states to make use of their independence by joining the West through formal ties to NATO and the European Union. In the past it was Moscow that stood in the way; now it is the West that keeps stalling about the conditions and timetable for admission to these institutions. Finally, the threat to newly-gained independence stems from Russia's lost status as a great power. The question its worried neighbors now ask is not whether but when Russia will be strong enough to revive its imperial ambitions.

The second goal of transition was political pluralism in an environment of open societies that observe human rights and follow democratic processes and procedures. As the yearly ratings by Freedom House's authoritative surveys indicate (see Table 1), there have been far-reaching changes in the realm of political rights and civil liberties throughout Central and Eastern Europe. As Table 2 suggests, however, several countries in the former Soviet Union have actually regressed since 1991–92, and only a few advanced. On the whole, the unsurprising conclusion is that honoring political rights and civil liberties is a function of physical and presumably cultural proximity to Western Europe.

Similarly, international observer groups have regarded elections since the collapse of communism as freer in countries closer to Western Europe. In Central and Eastern Europe, including the Baltics, minor irregularities were reported in Romania and Bulgaria, but both legislative and presidential elections have been held as scheduled. Although not all political parties had equal access to television, the legislatures are broadly representative of the people. Moreover, Western norms distinguish the new constitutions. Freedom of religion and assembly too is a fact of life.

In the Transcaucasus and Central Asia, few political changes have been introduced, with deadly ethnic conflict often a major but nowhere the only contributing factor. No genuine multiparty elections have been held in Tajikistan, Turkmenistan, or Uzbekistan, which remain politically unreformed dictatorships under strong one-man rule. In Kazakstan, President Nursultan Nazarbayev, having dissolved parliament in 1995, rules by decree. In Kyrgyzstan, charges of ballot-box stuffing and intimidation of certain candidates and of the press followed the 1995 legislative elections. In Azerbaijan, opposition parties exist in the rump parliament, but effective power is held by President Gaidar Aliyev, a former KGB general and hard-line Communist Party boss. In Armenia, the July 1995 elections were described rather generously by foreign observers as "free but not fair." In Georgia, the 1992 elections were called quite fair, but in Abkhazia, South Ossetia and the country's western regions they were postponed because of persistent ethnic fighting.

In the European part of the former Soviet Union, powerful presidents—some favoring gradual economic change—face weak, often emasculated, legislators. President Alyaksandr Lukashenka of Belarus, elected in 1994, is a young, aggressive ex-communist who has returned his country to the Russian fold. In Moldova, President Mircea Snegur left the dominant Democratic Agrarian Party in mid-1995 because of what he called its attempt "to establish a one-party dictatorship" and its pro-Russian orientation. In Ukraine, the 1994 legislative

Table 1. Upholding Political Rights and Civil Liberties in Central and Eastern Europe

	Political Rights		Civil Liberties	
	1988–89	1994–95	1988–89	1994–95
Albania	7	3	7	4
Bulgaria	7	2	7	2
Czech Republic	7	1	6	2
Hungary	5	1	4	2
Poland	5	2	5	2
Romania	7	4	7	3
Slovakia	7	2	6	3
Average	6.4	2.1	6	2.5

Source: Freedom House, *Nations in Transit: Civil Society, Democracy and Markets in East-Central Europe and the Newly Independent States* (New York: Freedom House, 1995).

Note: 1 = Free; 7 = Not Free

Table 2. Upholding Political Rights and Civil Liberties in the Former Soviet Union

	Political Rights		Civil Liberties	
	1991–92	1994–95	1991–92	1994–95
Armenia	5	3	5	4
Azerbaijan	5	6	5	6
Belarus	4	4	4	4
Estonia	2	3	3	2
Georgia	6	5	5	5
Kazakstan	5	6	4	5
Kyrgyzstan	5	4	4	3
Latvia	2	3	2	2
Lithuania	2	1	3	3
Moldova	5	4	4	4
Russia	3	3	3	4
Tajikistan	5	7	5	7
Turkmenistan	6	7	5	7
Ukraine	3	3	3	4
Uzbekistan	6	7	5	7
Average	4.3	4.4	4	4.4

Source: Freedom House, *Nations in Transit: Civil Society, Democracy and Markets in East-Central Europe and the Newly Independent States* (New York: Freedom House, 1995).

Note: 1 = Free; 7 = Not Free

elections produced a fragmented and therefore weak parliament. In the most familiar case of Russia, the 1995 legislative elections produced a Duma packed with strong opponents of democratic reform. Old-fashioned communists and their allies—agrarians and communists parading as independents—obtained a majority of the seats. The upcoming presidential elections offer little or no hope for advocates of genuine reform either.

To sum up, political pluralism is now a fact of life in Central and Eastern Europe, while the former Soviet states east of the Baltics have experienced modest political change. However, public opinion has become decisively and increasingly negative. True, governments and politicians do not fare well any-where these days: the single-digit approval rating of Russian President Boris Yeltsin is matched by the single-digit approval rating of British Prime Minister John Major.

But poll results in the post-communist states must be taken more seriously. There, more often than not, negative attitudes signify not a protest against this party or that politician but a systemic challenge to the essential features of Western-style democracy. The choice there is not between liberal democrats and conservative democrats or between Democrats and Republicans, but between democrats on one side and authoritarian or semi-authoritarian nationalists, nativ-ists, populists, and communists on the other. While in theory most people appre-ciate such features of democracy as free speech, a just legal system or even the more abstract notion of separation of powers, in practice they reject the way democracy is working and long for a strong, paternalistic leader who would presumably look after their welfare.

The trend lines of post-communist public opinion point to rapidly growing majorities rejecting Western-style democratic politics. These trend lines indicate that whatever popular support there once was for a Western-style democratic political order has all but disappeared. There are exceptions, of course, but the trend is unmistakably clear.

Although professional pollsters consider some of the survey's questions too general, the highly regarded "Eurobarometer" public opinion survey conducted for the European Union is cited here (see Table 3). Its results are confirmed by countless local polls that are far more comprehensive but less comparative. As it is, complete results are available from 1991 through the fall of 1994 only for European Russia and ten countries in Central and Eastern Europe. The key political question was this: "On the whole, are you very satisfied, fairly satisfied, not very satisfied, or not at all satisfied with the way democracy is developing in your country?"

The survey shows that popular satisfaction with democracy in the countries of Central and Eastern Europe has dropped by a factor of 150 percent between 1991 and 1994 (from minus 16 to minus 40). In 1994, for Central and Eastern Europe as a whole, more than twice as many people were dissatisfied (66 percent) than satisfied (26 percent). In Russia, the absolute minus 75 percent figure for 1994 is a product of only 8 percent noting satisfaction with democracy and a stunning 83 percent indicating that they were not satisfied. Even in the Czech Republic—the

Table 3. Public Satisfaction With Development of Democracy (net results in percentage of respondents*)			
	1991	**1994**	**Trend**
Czech Republic	−25	−9	+16
Estonia	−21	−26	−5
Slovakia	−55	−62	−7
Albania	−17	−33	−16
Poland	−21	−40	−19
Hungary	−19	−43	−24
Romania	−11	−36	−25
Latvia	−9	−42	−33
Lithuania	+23	−31	−54
Bulgaria	−6	−87	−81
Average	−16	−40	−24
European Russia	−51	−75	−24
Georgia	NA	−56	NA
Belarus	NA	−62	NA
Kazakstan	NA	−62	NA
Ukraine	NA	−53	NA
Armenia	NA	−77	NA
Russia	NA	−75	NA

Source: Eurobarometer Survey (Brussels: European Commission, 1994).

*Results are expressed as the percentage of positive responses minus the percentage of negative responses.

+ = Satisfaction

− = Dissatisfaction

only country where the trend is still positive—only 44 percent said they were satisfied while 53 percent were dissatisfied.

As public opinion in the post-communist world has soured on democracy, why do Western governments and observers continue to see considerable progress? They note and appreciate, it seems, that most political laggards of the former Soviet empire are led by nationalists who are moving their countries away from Russia, and that some of these political laggards have shown some interest in economic experimentation. Yet the main reason for the difference between Western and post-communist perceptions is that different questions are being asked. The people there ask: "What have I gained from the changes that have taken place since 1989 or 1991?" The questions asked in the West are: "Compared to the communist era, do the governments respect political rights and civil liberties? Are the elections unfettered and competitive and is the press free? And is there a reasonable legal order based on constitutional principles?"

What the West wants to know is whether the processes of governance have improved since the fall of communism. What people in the former Soviet Union and Central and Eastern Europe expect from democracy is security, stability, and prosperity; they expect to benefit from their governments' substantive achievements. And that, more than anything else, means economic achievements. This is not to say that they do not want to practice the religion of their choice; that they do not favor freedom of assembly; that they do not want to read different views in their newspapers; or that they do not prefer electoral choice to one-party rule. But governments must also and above all deliver the economic goods.

This is why the vast majority of the people in the post-communist world feel cheated. Cynicism about politics and politicians prevails—even more than elsewhere—because of the empty promises made both by the West prior to the collapse of communism and by most vote-hungry politicians immediately after. In the euphoria that followed the changes of 1989 in Central and Eastern Europe and the changes of 1991 in the former Soviet Union, most people underestimated the inherent problems of transition and overestimated Western interest in lending a helping hand.

Of course, an economic upturn producing higher living standards would not transform Tajikistan, Turkmenistan, or Uzbekistan into pluralistic societies. Political democracy does not stem from economic well-being alone. But, as a Hungarian saying has it, one cannot sing the national anthem on an empty stomach. By extension, one cannot sing the praise of political democracy while living standards decline. In short, under conditions of economic decay, democracy cannot take root.

THE GOAL OF FREE-MARKET ECONOMICS

The third goal of transition was to transform the planned, highly centralized, so-called command economies of the communist era by decentralization and privatization into modern, Western-style market economies. That goal enjoyed almost universal support. After all, most communist leaders, including Mikhail Gorbachev, had considered the introduction of some market mechanisms if not large-scale privatization even before the fall of communism. They recognized too that the old command economies had failed, and while a few old-fashioned communist publications still spoke of the sins of capitalism, most people certainly believed otherwise. What they knew of capitalism through Western movies and occasional visits to Western Europe by friends and relatives convinced them that free-market economies represented a superior form of economic organization, and that they would benefit from adopting it.

In the West, the economic progress made since the fall of communism, and especially since 1994, has received fairly high marks. The received wisdom is that, in many countries, several important economic indicators show signs of improvement. Although the figures and ratings given by the European Bank for Reconstruction and Development should be treated with care, it is indeed the case that the private sector has made impressive gains. Throughout the post-communist world, retail trade and the service sector are now in private hands. When it comes to medium-size and large firms, a distinction should be made between genuine privatization (the sale of state-owned companies to individuals and groups who raised the necessary capital, or the open and fair auctioning of assets to the public who were issued vouchers for that purpose) and pseudo-privatization (the putative transfer—on the cheap—of valuable state-owned firms to "closed stock companies," generally controlled by the old nomenklatura or criminal elements). In any case, the pace of privatization is slowing down because remaining state assets are less attractive to potential buyers; there is no market for the unprofitable plants still for sale. The slower pace is also due to the growing appeal of populist agitation against capitalism, especially foreign investments.

Taking into account not only the scope but the quality of privatization, then, the leaders are the Central European states of the Czech Republic, Estonia, Hungary, Latvia, Poland, and Slovakia. In the middle of the pack, Russia—a case of both genuine and pseudo-privatization—has rid itself of about half of its assets and has done so in less time than was available to the Central Europeans. Having done little or nothing are Belarus, Moldova, and the eight states of Central Asia and the Transcaucasus.

Another important indicator—economic growth—began to show signs of improvement in Central and Eastern Europe in 1994; until then the figures were thoroughly discouraging even there. In 1990 Kazakstan, Kyrgyzstan, and Moldova still reported positive growth figures. In 1991 no country did. In 1992 only Poland moved ahead. In 1993 Poland was joined by Albania, Romania, and Turkmenistan, and the average for Central and Eastern Europe as a whole was once again in the plus column (showing a modest gain of 0.8 percent). In 1994 growth resumed in all of the states of Central and Eastern Europe, with Poland leading the way, but comparable data about the Soviet successor states remained very negative. The precipitous decline of previous years (an average of minus 8.1 percent in 1991, minus 23.2 percent in 1992 and minus 10.8 percent in 1993) continued in 1994 (when the average was minus 14.3 percent) despite favorable trends in the three Baltic states.

Overall, the post-communist economies have shrunk by at least a third since the collapse of communism. Even if some of them have indeed "bottomed out" or "turned the corner" in 1994–95, as several Western specialists maintain, it will be long before they reach 1989 or 1991 levels. (And neither, of course, was a very good year.) Moreover, the consequences and byproducts of negative growth include high unemployment, an often dramatic drop in living standards for most, and inflation. Irrespective of whether the changes have been fast (as in Poland) or gradual (as most everywhere else), the transition from the command economies to market mechanisms has benefited only the enterprising few—largely old comrades dressed in new capitalist clothes.

Indeed, as seen by the results of the "Eurobarometer" survey, the market economy is rapidly losing its once considerable popular appeal. The key economic question—one that prompted very positive responses in 1991 everywhere except in Romania—was this: "Do you personally feel that the creation of a market economy that is largely free of state control is right or wrong for your country's future?" As Table 4 shows, the market economy as an ideal still attracts more supporters than opponents in most though no longer all of the Central and East European countries. But in Russia (and presumably most every-

Table 4. Public Belief in a Market Economy
(net results in percentage of respondents*)

	1991	1994	Trend
Romania	−5	+50	+55
Albania	+45	+41	−4
Estonia	+32	+14	−18
Poland	+47	+26	−21
Czech Republic	+39	+11	−28
Slovakia	+29	0	−29
Hungary	+52	+20	−32
Lithuania	+55	+9	−46
Bulgaria	+45	−2	−47
Latvia	+43	−5	−48
Average	+38	+16	−22
European Russia	+8	−44	−52
Georgia	NA	−24	NA
Belarus	NA	−29	NA
Kazakstan	NA	−30	NA
Ukraine	NA	−18	NA
Armenia	NA	−45	NA
Russia	NA	−41	NA

Source: Eurobarometer Survey (Brussels: European Commission, 1994).

*Results are expressed as the percentage of positive responses minus the percentage of negative responses.

+ = Right

− = Wrong

where else in the former Soviet Union) the trend points to a substantial decline in popular acceptance of the capitalist experiment. The 1994 Russian response, showing almost three times as many people rejecting (63 percent) than approving (22 percent) the changes that have been introduced, suggests no public concurrence with, and thus a very dubious future for, further Russian market reform. The pain being felt exceeds the gains being promised and once expected.

Pro-Western economists in the region used to advocate comprehensive, even radical, reform entailing a vigorous program of privatization, strict control over the money supply, full currency convertibility, and toleration of unemployment. But because it was too painful, the so-called "shock therapy" lost whatever political support it once enjoyed. On the other hand, the old-fashioned command economies of the past have few champions left either. The dilemma of choice is acute. How can these countries cope with the strong egalitarian backlash against private ownership and with the growing resentment toward foreign businessmen, who are seen to be looking for a quick buck by taking advantage of poor, inexperienced natives?

Under the circumstances, many post-communist politicians find it expedient to advocate a middle ground between the "excesses" of capitalism and socialism and between free trade and protectionism. The course that most post-communist leaders have come to promote mixes the economic tenets of West European social democracy with a small dose of nationalist semi-protectionism.

The popular appeal of such a neo-egalitarian course is beyond dispute. In theory, it combines the dynamism of free enterprise with efforts to ease the pain of change for pensioners, teachers, state employees, and everyone on fixed incomes. In practice, however, poor countries in particular cannot afford to pay the high cost of social support structures; even the rich countries of Scandinavia, Western Europe, and North America have had to cut social expenditures in recent years. As for the incipient protectionist impulse, it can only produce stagnation because of the lack of sufficient domestic resources, including capital, for investment.

In the absence of alternatives, a varied lot of former communists has become the dominant force in the post-communist world, except in the Czech Republic. Ex-communist parties and politicians—appearing as social democrats, socialists, reform communists, populist-nationalist demagogues, or unreformed apparatchiks—have returned to join those who never left. On the whole, most see market reform as a necessary evil to be pursued in a perfunctory fashion. Their lack of enthusiasm for the "chaotic" market—combined with the lack of an appealing alternative to it—reflects the popular mood and indeed the post-communist reality.

Yet the basic economic feature of that reality is that the remaining problems are too serious and too pressing to be put off. Huge state bureaucracies are unwilling to give up their old prerogatives, and industrialist lobbies and trade unions waste no effort in defending their old turf. While a few of the region's parliaments have passed bankruptcy laws, their implementation, even in the case of clearly insolvent and unsalvageable firms, is subject to interminable delays. State-owned enterprises continue to produce goods no one needs or buys and keep their storage facilities full of unsold products. Concern about unemployment, however understandable, stands in the way of the structural overhaul of not only individual companies but the post-communist economies as a whole.

Moreover, inflation and monetary indulgence remains an unresolved problem. Hyperinflation is no longer as rampant as it was in 1992–1994 (it peaked at more than 1,400 percent in Russia in 1992; at 3,500 percent in Belarus in 1994; and at a stunning 4,790 percent in Ukraine in 1993). Double-digit inflation remains, however, because most of the reasons for inflation still exist. Prominent among them is the practice of printing money in an effort to pretend living standards have not plunged as much as they have. Similarly, several post-communist governments make things worse by excessive borrowing, reinforcing inflationary pressures, and indeed mortgaging the future.

Conversely, the essential political feature of post-communist reality is that no government can stay in power for long if it fails to be indulgent. Indeed, all post-communist governments must try to square the circle by steering a course between what should be done economically to move ahead and what can be done politically to maintain a modicum of domestic stability. Leaders of the less open and less pluralistic regimes, especially those in Central Asia and the Transcaucasus, shy away from market reform because they expect income differentiation and other features of capitalism to foment social tension and provoke public defiance. Leaders of the more open and pluralistic regimes, such as those in Central and Eastern Europe where elections are now taken for granted, delay austerity measures because their choice is between easing the burden of market reform or turning into critics of the next government. (In these countries, as in the West, pensioners vote in great numbers. And although they suffered longer than the young under communist dictatorships, they are now among the most tenacious advocates of neo-egalitarianism.)

The parameters of the course ahead are, and will continue to be, defined by two seemingly contradictory tendencies: the popular rejection of radical transformation and the popular rejection of full economic and political retrenchment. This is why the transition in most countries will produce neither a retreat to the totalitarian past nor a great leap forward to Western-style free-market democracies. Indeed, both the logic of the situation and prevailing sentiments point to the prospective imposition of minimal economic reforms by strong leaders claiming to act on behalf of the public interest.

FACING UP TO THE TREND

Consider the replies to the third question posed in the "Eurobarometer" survey: "In general, do you feel things in your country are going in the right or wrong direction?" Consider, too, the results of a "Eurobarometer" survey of five former Soviet states, including Russia, supplied for 1994 only (see Table 5). They show that negative views about democracy, the market, and the country's "direction" in 1994 were far more dominant in these states than in Central and Eastern Europe, and that prevailing perceptions in Russia were even more negative—except among completely dejected Armenians—than in other post-Soviet countries.

Taken as a whole, these polls reflect more than "unhappiness" over the "expected problems" of transition, more than "uncertainty" about "initial dislocations" caused by economic change, more than "disappointment" in the present performance of the region's "fledgling democracies." They certainly reflect far more than opposition only to specific policies enacted since the collapse of communism or to some of the politicians who advocated them.

What these polls indicate is discontent so acute and so pervasive as to invite comparison with public sentiments that prevailed prior to the fall of communism. As vast majorities consider the post-communist course to be a failure, they are bent on checking its direction and arresting its development. Fueled by demagogues appearing in different political colors, the angry voices seeking retrenchment express the new consensus that sees the present to be worse than the past—and expects the course being followed to produce a future that would be worse than the present.

Under similar circumstances, equally critical publics in the established Western democracies would call for a change of parties and leaders. In the post-communist world, the publics challenge the basic elements of the system, because the

Table 5. Public Agreement With the Direction of the Country
(net results in percentage of respondents*)

	1991	1994	Trend
Albania	+45	+41	−4
Czech Republic	+37	+25	−12
Estonia	+30	+17	−13
Hungary	−19	−34	−15
Romania	+26	−6	−32
Poland	+13	−29	−42
Slovakia	+13	−39	−52
Latvia	+47	−9	−56
Bulgaria	+38	−39	−77
Lithuania	+28	−49	−77
Average	+26	−12	−38
European Russia	−12	−51	−73
Georgia	NA	−39	NA
Belarus	NA	−32	NA
Kazakstan	NA	−33	NA
Ukraine	NA	−55	NA
Armenia	NA	−60	NA
Russia	NA	−52	NA

Source: Eurobarometer Survey (Brussels: European Commission, 1994).

*Results are expressed as the percentage of positive responses minus the percentage of negative responses.

+ = Right

− = Wrong

only alternative they know to rule by the many is rule by the few, and the only alternative they know to a private economy is the state-run economy. While retrenchment need not go all the way, of course, the prevailing nostalgia for the past and skepticism about the future point to a fundamental correction ahead.

Before commenting further on the form that correction is likely to take, it is important to distinguish among the leaders, laggards and losers of the post-communist world.

The seven leaders are the still-promising democratic states of Central Europe (the Czech Republic, Poland, Hungary, and Slovenia) and the Baltics (Estonia, Latvia, and Lithuania), an area where despite popular backlash both political and economic reforms continue to be carried on for now.

The twelve laggards, placed far behind the leaders, are the semi-authoritarian regimes of Slovakia, seven countries in the Balkans (Albania, Bulgaria, Romania, Croatia, Serbia, Bosnia-Herzegovina, and Macedonia), Russia, Ukraine, Moldova, and Belarus. In these countries, reorganization and retrenchment coexist; leaders reluctantly pursue modest market reforms, tolerate a press that is partly free, and legitimate their rule by seemingly fair but manipulated elections.

The eight losers are the authoritarian though no longer totalitarian dictatorships of Central Asia and the Transcaucasus, an area that is essentially unreformed and oppressive.

Because uneven development will surely persist in so diverse a region, the reluctance to identify a general pattern and especially a future trend is understandable. Still, while existing differences must be neither ignored nor disavowed, and uncertainties about the future must be frankly acknowledged, generalizations must still be made. And there is a general, pervasive, underlying trend that can be discerned: the trend of retrenchment. The question is not whether such retrenchment is taking place or not, but how far back it will take the post-communist world. Indeed, what is a likely outcome of the transition? If it is neither something akin to a Western-style political democracy and free-market economics nor a totalitarian political order combined with a centralized command economy, what? If neither Sakharov nor Stalin, who?

There is reason to suppose that the post-communist world finds a suitable option in a semi-authoritarian order—one that incorporates features of tsarist Russia, the so-called "petty dictatorships" of interwar Eastern Europe, and the Third World's "guided democracies." Although it is premature to anticipate the precise qualities of such semi-authoritarian regimes, they will of course all center around a dominant executive. The countries of the former Soviet Union can be expected to develop somewhat milder and less centralized political practices than those that once characterized totalitarian states, while the countries of Central and Eastern Europe may embrace somewhat harsher and more centralized political practices than can be found in Western democracies.

In such a semi-authoritarian order, the authorities would get their way by intimidation, not by massive terror. Several parties would compete for power, though only those that accept the self-styled rules of the game could win. Legislatures would function, though the critical decisions of state would be made by the chief executive and his acolytes. The press would be free, though it would apply self-censorship to forestall state censorship. Private enterprise would be tolerated, even encouraged, but through taxation, control over the banking system, and strict regulations the government would make sure its priorities are observed. Trade unions would be allowed to organize, though their right to strike would be circumscribed. And if massive popular discontent should still surface—as it would—a few cabinet ministers might resign, but the system would remain in place.

By so manipulating rather than fully controlling the levers of power, the semi-authoritarian regime would try to cultivate a tolerant and benevolent, if somewhat paternalistic, image. It would dominate public affairs while leaving people alone to practice their religion, attend the schools of their choice, or even travel abroad. Its leaders would be at pains to confide in Western interlocutors how difficult it is to make their "democracy" work. ("Our people are not quite ready for that yet, you know; we're not like the Swiss," they would whisper.) Indeed, they would desperately seek acceptance by the West, particularly the United States, because Western recognition of their "fledgling democracy" would help legitimate their authority at home. If accepted by the West, what is left for the domestic opposition to say?

Would the West notice—would it want to notice—that this is not democracy but a mirage? Many Western groups and individuals would notice, and they would also try to do what they can to make a difference. But they will find few supporters, because the semi-authoritarian regimes would always present their best side to the outside world and conceal the rest. After all, "Potemkin village" was a Russian invention. In any case, Western "realists" and geopolitical minimalists would ask: Isn't a semi-authoritarian regime also semi-democratic? If so, is it realistic to expect Romania to behave like Switzerland? With concern for promoting democratic values on the wane, Western governments may prefer to believe things are not so bad and look the other way. They may proceed on the assumption that these nondemocratic but nationalist regimes will resist Russia and thus contribute to Western security. Weren't Franco's Spain and Salazar's Portugal useful allies once?

The case of Russia, however, differs from the other states of the old bloc. The future of post-communist transition there is obviously a serious foreign policy concern for the West, because a semi-authoritarian Russia would be more widely recognized to be not only a challenge to Western values but a threat to Western security interests as well. It would be compared to Weimar Germany, a country confused about its past, uncertain of its future, shocked by its lost status, haunted by a sense of humiliation, full of resentments, itching for revenge—and potentially a great power. Russia may not repeat the German pattern, but it is already legitimate to ask: What outlet is it going to find for the political passions its humiliated condition has unleashed? Who will be blamed for the country's blight—foreign or domestic scapegoats, or both? All that can be said for now is that the example of Weimar Germany does not bode well for Russia's future.

While Western foreign policies can certainly shape Russian behavior abroad, they cannot counter those almost elemental political passions clamoring for retrenchment at home. The received wisdom in the West notwithstanding, no Western money or investment, no summit meetings or conciliatory gestures, no invocation of the common struggle in World War II, no joint space exploration, no arms-control treaties or cultural agreements, and no catering to its so-called legitimate security interests in the Baltics, the Balkans, or Central Europe can make Russia a democracy or even help it become one—unless and until the passions in Russia itself subside.

Alas, many Western russophiles seem to assume that the West can influence Russia's most basic domestic political choices by, say, canceling NATO's plan to admit new members (but not Russia) to its ranks. In making that assumption, they overestimate both Western influence and the popular appeal of Russian democracy, and they vastly underestimate the appeal of a semi-authoritarian resolution of Russia's current time of troubles. Needless to say, agreements and deals that are fair to both sides, and thus take no undue advantage of Moscow's weak hand at this juncture, can help improve Western relations with Russia. In exchange for something Russia wants from the West, it may do something the

West wants from it. But it is simply naive to believe that fancy Western hopes for democracy can take precedence over harsh Russian realities.

If the West chooses to do so, the place it can make a difference in advancing democratic values is among the seven "leaders" of post-communist transition, all in Central Europe and the Baltics, all relatively small. Although their trials are certainly not over either—they are also under pressure to retrench—their democracies and especially their market economies are still in place. Closest to Western Europe both physically and culturally, and thus both more exposed and more receptive to Western influences, this is the area where with some luck the promise of 1989—the promise of extending freedom's frontiers—may yet be won.

[This article is abridged from a chapter of the book *Four Perspectives on Post-Communism*, edited by Michael Mandelbaum and published by the Council on Foreign Relations, 1996.]

EXECUTIVE-LEGISLATIVE RELATIONS
by MATTHEW SOBERG SHUGART

The constitutions in post-communist Europe with the best outlook for promoting stability provide for a clear delineation of authority over cabinet ministers and the primacy of the legislature over the president in the passage of laws.

Of the many factors that influence whether a new democracy will function smoothly or be conflict-ridden, a prominent one is constitutional form. Constitutions may provide incentives to actors to cooperate and find solutions, or they may tend to exacerbate conflicts and drive actors farther apart in times of crisis. Knowledge of a country's regime type permits predictions of, for example, what is likely to happen if the country's president is of one party and its assembly majority of another party. Will the president prevail over the choice of cabinet ministers, or will the assembly majority? Can the president dissolve the assembly and try to get a majority more to his or her liking? Will the president or the assembly majority prevail in enacting its legislative program, or will the outcome have to be either a compromise between the two or else deadlock and policy stasis? The key to answering such questions lies in knowing the regime type. Constitutional forms vary considerably across post-communist Europe. They also differ from the typical patterns found among the more established democracies of Europe, particularly in the tendency to give greater powers to elected presidents.

Several post-communist systems have high potential for instability built into their constitutions. In Armenia, Croatia, Russia, and Ukraine, either the president or the parliamentary majority can dismiss cabinet ministers, making high turnover in government ministries likely. Other constitutions establish clearer lines of accountability, stipulating that cabinets are clearly dependent only upon the "confidence" of the president (as in Georgia) or upon the parliamentary majority (for example, in Moldova, Poland, Romania, Slovenia, and the "pure parliamentary" constitutions in which there is no popularly elected presidency, as in the Czech Republic and Hungary). Powers over legislation are also important. Where the president holds decree powers, as in Russia, conflicts over legislation are likely to be especially intense—possibly threatening regime stability—as presidents may try to impose policies for which there is no support among a majority of elected representatives.

Constitutions are commonly divided into two broad categories: presidential and parliamentary. That dichotomy, however, defines only one of four variables that affect formal executive-legislative relations: cabinet accountability to either the parliamentary majority or to a popularly elected president. The other variables are whether there is a popularly elected president (even if that person is not the head of government), whether terms of office for the president (if any) and assembly are fixed, and whether a presidency functions as a "veto gate," meaning that its consent is required to pass laws.

A "pure" parliamentary system has a cabinet accountable to the assembly majority; no president, or one who is neither popularly elected nor more than ceremonial; no fixed term for the executive (because of the possibility of votes of no confidence and often the possibility of early dissolution of the assembly); and no veto gate besides the lower (or sole) house of parliament (meaning no other actor whose consent is required to pass laws). Because the parliamentary majority is sovereign over both government formation and legislation, the main issue confronted in such regimes is whether the party system is capable of sustaining stable coalitions or whether parties are so polarized as to breed instability.

A "pure" presidential system combines a cabinet accountable to a president who is popularly elected, sits for a fixed term, cannot dissolve the legislature, and usually holds veto power or other legislative authority that makes the president a player in shaping legislation. Many regimes, however, have an elected president with some but not all of those powers; wherever such a presidency exists, the assembly majority must share authority with the president over government formation, legislation, or both. Precisely how that authority is shared makes a difference in the definition of regime type and in the prospects for cooperation or conflict.

GOVERNMENT TYPES IN GREATER EUROPE

Table 1 shows all the pure presidential and parliamentary systems in the "greater European" area, as well as those regimes that do not fit either ideal type. Parliamentary systems, many of them constitutional monarchies, predominate in Western Europe and the Mediterranean region, comprising 12 of 19 cases. In the Eastern European-Caucasus region, however, parliamentary systems are slightly outnumbered by presidential and other types, with 9 of 20 cases. Pure presidential systems along the model of the United States and most Latin American countries are rare in both regions. Systems with elected presidencies, however, are very common, comprising all the "other" systems, except Switzerland (where the assembly elects a fixed-term executive council that is effectively accountable to no one). Some of these "other" regimes that have popularly elected presidencies are "president-parliamentary" in the sense that cabinets must maintain the simultaneous confidence of both the president and the assembly. Many others, for instance Finland, France, Poland, and Romania, are "premier-presidential" regimes that combine an elected president with exclusive cabinet accountability to parliament and usually the possibility of presidential dissolution of the assembly.

There are two dimensions on which regimes with elected presidencies vary, as defined in Table 2. The first dimension, the vertical axis in Figure 1, defines how much power a president has over the cabinet. That power may range from zero, in which case the choice of the prime minister and other ministers is left entirely to parliament (whether or not there is indeed a popularly elected president), to a maximum, in which the president may appoint whomever he wants to the cabinet and may dismiss ministers at any time. Intermediate steps are identified in Figure 1.

The second dimension defines the degree of each branch's separation of sur-

Table 1. Parliamentary, Presidential, and Other Regime Types in Greater Europe		
Parliamentary	**Presidential**	**Mixed System**
Belgium[a]	Cyprus	Austria
Denmark[a]	Belarus	Finland
Germany	Georgia	France
Greece		Israel
Ireland[b]		Portugal
Italy		Switzerland
Netherlands[a]		Bosnia-Herzegovina
Norway[a]		Croatia
Spain[a]		Lithuania
Sweden[a]		Macedonia
Turkey		Moldova
United Kingdom[a]		Poland
Albania		Romania
Bulgaria[b]		Russia
Czech Republic		Ukraine
Estonia		
Hungary		
Latvia		
Slovakia		
Slovenia[b]		
Yugoslavia		

[a]Constitutional monarchy.

[b]Popularly elected president with few constitutional powers.

vival in office vis-à-vis the other—that is, whether terms are fixed, or whether one branch can "attack" the survival of the other and thereby shorten its term. At the minimum degree of separation (zero on the horizontal axis), the assembly can oust the cabinet at any time on a vote of no confidence, and the popularly elected president can dissolve parliament at any time. At the maximum (a score of four on separated survival for both the assembly and the executive), neither branch can shorten the mandate of the other, as both have fixed terms.

Intermediate cases are indicated in Table 2. A score of four is given when survival in office of the other branch can be jeopardized only at specified times. An example is France, where the assembly's survival in office is subject to a presidential dissolution power that can be exercised only once a year. The score is two when the term of the cabinet or parliament may be shortened only in the context of "mutual jeopardy." For instance, the Polish and Russian presidents' dissolution power may be exercised only in response to censures of the cabinet by the assembly. There is, therefore, more separation of survival than in France because the parliament, in Russia, can avoid dissolution by not exercising cen- sure or, in Poland, by "constructively" electing a new government on the same vote by which it expresses no confidence in the incumbent one.

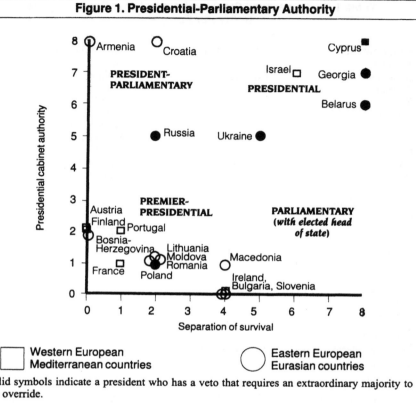

Figure 1. Presidential-Parliamentary Authority

Western European Mediterranean countries

Eastern European Eurasian countries

Solid symbols indicate a president who has a veto that requires an extraordinary majority to override.

Source: Author.

Finally, either branches' or both branches' separation of survival from the other is scored three when the term of office can be shortened only if the branch initiating the shortening of the other branches' term also stands for re-election. For instance, in the new Israeli system, a parliamentary censure of the executive (including the directly elected chief executive as well as the rest of the cabinet) necessitates a new parliamentary election, and an executive order to dissolve parliament means there must be a new election for the head of government as well as for parliament.

The scoring of the constitutions in greater Europe is shown in Table 2, and the countries are depicted graphically in Figure 1, showing a wide variation in presidential powers in the area. In Figure 1, the two points at which presidents have maximum power over cabinets are the upper left and the upper right. However, those two extremes are diametrically opposed in the degree of separation of executive and legislative survival.

Table 2. Regime Characteristics in Greater Europe

Country	Presidential powers over cabinet		Separation of survival for . . .	
	Cabinet formation	Cabinet dismissal	Assembly	Executive
Armenia	4	4	0	0
Austria	1	1	0	0
Bosnia-Herzegovina	2	0	0	0
Bulgaria	0	0	4	0
Belarus	3	3	4	4
Croatia	4	4	2	0
Cyprus	4	4	4	4
Finland	2	0	0	0
France	1	0	1	0
Georgia	3	4	4	4
Ireland	0	0	4	0
Israel	3	4	3	3
Lithuania	1	0	2	0
Macedonia	1	0	4	0
Moldova	1	0	2	0
Poland	1	0	2	0
Portugal	1	1	1	0
Romania	1	0	2	0
Russia	1	4	2	0
Slovenia	0	0	4	0
Ukraine	1	4	4	1

Scoring system

Powers over cabinet

Cabinet formation

4 President appoints ministers without need for assembly confirmation
3 President appoints ministers with consent of assembly
2 President appoints ministers who need confidence of assembly
1 President nominates prime minister who needs confidence of assembly; prime minister appoints other ministers (possibly with consent of president)
0 President cannot name ministers except on recommendation of assembly

Cabinet dismissal

4 President dismisses ministers at will
3 President dismisses ministers with consent of assembly
1 President dismisses ministers, but only under certain restrictions
0 Ministers (or whole cabinet) may be removed only by assembly on vote of censure

Separation of survival in office (scored for both assembly and executive)

4 No provisions compromising separation of survival (i.e., fixed terms)
3 Survival can be attacked, but attacker must stand for re-election
2 Survival can be attacked only in situation of mutual jeopardy
1 Survival can be attacked, except at specified times
0 Survival can be attacked at any time (i.e., unrestricted censure or dissolution)

Source: Author.

In the upper left, a full president-parliamentary regime gives the president discretion to dissolve parliament at any time as well as the right to appoint and dismiss cabinets freely. That form of regime is probably inherently unstable because the president cannot keep in office a cabinet of his liking against the wishes of the parliamentary majority, but he can always respond to a vote of no confidence by appointing another cabinet of his own choosing or by dissolving parliament. That is exactly the situation that bred repeated parliamentary elections in the latter years of the Weimar Republic in Germany, until Adolf Hitler was finally appointed *Kanzler* in a tragically ill-fated attempt to create a cabinet that could maintain parliamentary confidence.

Unfortunately, there are some constitutions in post-communist Europe that exhibit such dual responsibility of the cabinet. Armenia has full president-parliamentarism, and Croatia, Russia, and Ukraine all have important elements of it. The only reason Croatia is not a full president-parliamentary regime is the restriction on dissolution power: parliament can be dissolved only if it fails to pass the budget within 30 days. In both Russia and Ukraine, presidents have somewhat less authority over the appointment of cabinet ministers because, unlike in Armenia and Croatia, the president may appoint the prime minister only with the consent of the assembly and he indirectly appoints the other ministers through the prime minister. The fundamental point about those constitutions is that the president may freely dismiss any minister and the cabinet maybe dismissed by the assembly majority. Thus there is no clear line of authority over cabinets.

The entire left side of the figure contains regimes that are sometimes called semipresidential or are said to follow the "French model" of combining an elected president with cabinet accountability before parliament. But many of those regimes are not in fact following a crucial feature of the French model whereby, in a conflict between the president and the assembly over the composition of the government, the parliament prevails. The importance of that feature has been revealed already in both Moldova and Poland. In the former, President Mircea Snegur attempted to dismiss the defense minister but was forced to reinstate him when the parliament argued (and the Constitutional Court agreed) that ministers needed only the parliament's and not the president's confidence. Similarly, in Poland, President Lech Walesa found he had to accede to the opposition majority's preferences for cabinet positions after the opposition won the 1993 parliamentary elections. Only those regimes in the lower-left region— the premier-presidential systems such as Moldova and Poland—are, in fact, close cousins of the French system. With an important twist, Bosnia-Herzegovina has such a constitution. The twist, of course, is that the presidency is a three-person institution, and there are safeguards to prevent one ethnic group from being outvoted in either the presidency or the assembly by a majority constituting the other two groups.

The upper-right region contains presidential regimes, in which cabinets are accountable only to the popularly elected president and the term of office for the assembly as well as the presidency is fixed. Moreover, presidents in those countries have vetoes that require more than a majority to override. Those are the only presidential systems of the greater European area, notwithstanding the careless use of the label "presidential" to apply to such regimes as Russia's or Ukraine's, which lack separation of survival for cabinets, the assembly, or both. Israel's new system is an innovative and promising form of government, although it seems thus far not to have been considered seriously in the former communist countries. Although terms can be shortened in Israel and hence that country violates the fixed-term component of the definition of presidentialism, neither branch can attack the survival of the other without shortening its own term, too. Thus it is fundamentally different from those other regimes with nonseparated survival shown in the left half of the figure, and Israel can be classed as a hybrid variant of presidentialism.

The Polish system also deserves special comment. Although fundamentally premier-presidential, it does have an unusual hybrid appointment process. First the president nominates a candidate for prime minister. If that candidate fails to get a majority of all members of the Sejm to vote for confirmation, then the Sejm can try to elect a prime minister by the same majority. If it fails to do so, the president may try again, this time with a majority of those voting sufficing. If that attempt also fails, the Sejm again tries to elect a prime minister by a majority of those voting. If this last attempt also fails, the president may dissolve parliament or appoint an interim government for a six-month period. The interim government remains in office unless a majority of all members vote against it; the president may in such cases dissolve parliament unless the parliament elects a successor government at the same time that it passes the no-confidence vote. The alternating appointment process is important because it provides an "escape valve" against the threat that the president and parliament may not be able to agree on a new government. However, the crucial bottom line of the process is that, ultimately, a unified majority of the assembly can determine the composition of the government.

Finally, the presidencies of three countries are so weak that the systems there are effectively parliamentary: Bulgaria, Ireland, and Slovenia. Macedonia is almost in the category as well, although there the president has some discretion in the choice of a prime minister.

MULTIPLE VETO GATES

Figure 1 also depicts those presidents who have veto powers, found in Belarus, Cyprus, Poland, Russia, and Ukraine. The Polish presidency stands out in Figure 1 as being unique in having a veto while holding only limited authority over the cabinet. (In Armenia, Lithuania, and Portugal, vetoes of most types of legislation can be overridden by a majority of all members—meaning a unified majority can prevail, but some vetoes may be sustained.) Not depicted in Figure 1, the Russian president has another important source of legislative power: the power to issue decrees that establish new laws in areas where there is no current law—and in the process of establishing a new market economy, there are many such areas. Moreover, due to the veto power, the president's decrees are difficult to rescind.

With the support of only one-third of the legislators in either house of the assembly, the Russian president can be assured that his decrees stand as law regardless of the preferences of legislative majorities. That kind of decree power is unprecedented in democratic institutions; elsewhere, for example Brazil and Colombia, presidential decree-laws are subject to rescission by a majority of the legislature, meaning that presidents must negotiate with the assembly majority.

If the presidency is a veto gate—and even more obviously if the president holds decree powers—the assembly majority cannot always prevail in the legislative process. The give-and-take can be an advantage in that it increases the range of interests represented in policymaking. Both the interests of the president and of the assembly must be accommodated, implying a more consensual form of lawmaking and less hasty decision making (except, as noted, in Russia). On the other hand, it can be a disadvantage in the sense that conflict sometimes erupts over whose conception of voter preferences is more valid. In the extreme, the president, especially if supported by the courts, the military, or the police, may be tempted to flout the constitution. At a minimum, policy stalemate may prevail, which is not necessarily a bad thing but might leave pressing problems unresolved.

Partisan support in the assembly and the kinds of powers that the president holds in reserve are important factors determining whether compromise or dangerous interbranch conflict is the most likely outcome. Electoral systems that promote numerous or factionalized parties (such as those in Georgia, Russia, and, to a lesser degree, Poland), or where there is no nationalized party system (for example, in Russia and in Ukraine), are likely to have presidents with minimal legislative support. Where the terms of the two branches are of different lengths (for example, in Armenia, Georgia, Poland, and Ukraine, but not Romania), elections will sometimes occur in the latter portion of the president's term. Such elections frequently result in a sharp reduction in the president's co-partisan legislative contingent, as in France in 1986 and 1993 and Poland in 1993. If the constitution clearly requires the president to cede authority over the cabinet in the event he lacks legislative support, such situations are less likely to threaten the regime. If the president has a veto, he is unlikely to be marginalized in the policy process and thereby be tempted to resort to unconstitutional measures. However, worst of all is a situation of little partisan support but an ability to issue decree-laws. Then, a "war of laws" may result, with each side attempting to overturn the other's actions, with possibly dangerous consequences.

PRESIDENTS IN PARLIAMENTARY SYSTEMS

Parliamentary systems may be divided into monarchies and republics. In the established constitutional monarchies of Europe, it is safe to assume that the monarch is a purely ceremonial head of state who does not exercise any authority over the composition of cabinets or the passage of legislation. But the same cannot necessarily be said about the heads of state in parliamentary republics, some of whom are granted genuine constitutional powers and may be less restrained in using them than a monarch would be. And some do have potential for exercising independent powers.

Presidents in parliamentary systems are usually elected by parliament itself, but the German and Italian presidents are elected by electoral colleges that consist of parliamentarians and delegates from state or regional legislatures. Often, as in Greece, Hungary, Italy, Slovakia, and Turkey, constitutions prescribe an extraordinary majority—at least at the first ballot—in order to elect a president. If the initial balloting fails to produce the requisite majority for any contender, usually a second ballot can be held with new candidates; but if there is still no winner with the required majority, the necessary majority is reduced. Thus, for example, ultimately a relative majority among the two highest vote-getters from the second ballot can be elected in Germany and Hungary.

The president in most parliamentary systems serves for longer terms than parliament (Latvia is an exception). So the majority that elected the president will not always be the majority that currently controls parliament. Some presidents may serve only a limited number of terms (two in Greece) or a limited number of consecutive terms (two in the Czech Republic, Estonia, and Israel). The Turkish president is limited to a single term. All of those measures—attempts to ensure an extraordinary majority, lengthy terms, and limits on re-election, along with the fixed term for which all of them serve—are means by which presidents are afforded some independence from the day-to-day parliamentary majority that sustains a cabinet in office. They give presidents some possibility of exercising a check on the governing majority. A president elected by parliamentarians may have less potential for independence than does one elected by the voters at large, but, even so, such presidents sometimes play a politically relevant role. Of course, their ability to do so depends not only on how they are elected but also on what faculties are assigned to them constitutionally.

Some parliamentary presidents have considerable authority over formation and reshuffling of cabinets—more than some popularly elected presidents. For instance, the Czech, Italian, Latvian, Slovak, and Turkish constitutions all say that the president alone appoints the prime minister. Of course, the president's discretion is limited because cabinets require the confidence only of parliament, but the power of appointment gives the president potentially more leverage than if he merely recommends a prime ministerial candidate who must receive parliamentary approval prior to forming a government, as in Estonia, Germany, and Hungary. The Greek president is the only one in a European parliamentary system who has no constitutional discretion in nominating a prime minister. Most parliamentary presidents have an effective veto over the prime minister's recommendations to head other ministries (but the German and Hungarian presidents do not). Presidents in Estonia, Slovakia, and Turkey may refuse the prime minister's request to dismiss a minister. The Italian president even has discretion in dissolving parliament.

A few parliamentary presidents have minimal legislative power. Most can delay legislation by sending it back for reconsideration. In the Czech Republic and Greece, a vote to reconsider must receive a majority of all members (as opposed to a simple majority of members present and voting) in order to require that the law be promulgated.

Presidents in parliamentary systems are generally assumed not to exercise their powers. Indeed, there are few scholarly analyses of the institution, which suggests that political scientists think there is nothing to study. Yet there are occasional cases in which presidents enter the political fray. They can be expected to do so more in cases in which party systems are fluid and presidents therefore have the opportunity to use divisions among the parties in the governing coalition to their own advantage. On the basis of formal powers, then, which presidents should we expect to be able to successfully insert themselves into the political process in times of political division? The ones that most come to mind are those of Italy, Slovakia, and Turkey, because those presidents have greater power over government formation than most of their colleagues in other countries. The active presidencies of Vaclav Havel in the Czech Republic and Michal Kovac in Slovakia have shown that the office of president in a parliamentary system need not be purely symbolic.

A tentative conclusion is that the more poorly institutionalized the party system, the more opportunities the president has to exploit divisions among the parties and exercise influence, even if his or her formal powers are weak. Presidents who lack a direct connection to the electorate may be even more dependent on party-system characteristics in order to exercise authority. Even constitutionally weak presidents must be reckoned with if popularly elected, in part because their ability to claim a mandate might imply electoral costs for legislators who attempt to ignore them.

Certain regimes are more likely than others to promote smooth executive-legislative relations. Most propitious among those regimes with popularly elected presidents are those that provide clear primacy to the parliament in terms of government formation and legislation. Examples are the premier-presidential systems of Lithuania, Moldova, and Romania. Poland could also be included, although the existence there of a strong presidential veto makes for an odd and potentially conflictual situation in which the parliamentary majority is ultimately sovereign over government formation but not over legislation.

The regimes that have the greatest potential for executive-legislative conflict are those that have president-parliamentary cabinet accountability, especially if combined with unrestricted dissolution authority, as in Armenia. Croatia, Russia, and Ukraine also have features of president-parliamentarism, and the Russian president has preponderant legislative powers. As for the parliamentary systems, the main threat to stability is not in executive-legislative relations per se, given that the legislature is always free to remove a cabinet, but in interparty relations: if the party system is fragmented, it may be difficult to form governments. Most of the parliamentary systems of the post-communist region, however, have exhibited fairly stable patterns of coalition formation, at least so far. Some risk of instability exists if the head of state is elected for a lengthy term and has some legislative or other powers—as in Slovakia, for example.

Many factors influence interbranch conflict and impinge on the prospects for stable democracy; constitution design is only one of those factors. Nonetheless, some countries of the region are better equipped constitutionally than others to manage inevitable political disagreements.

HOW FREE ARE THE MEDIA IN THE CIS?
by LAURA BELIN

Ten years ago Mikhail Gorbachev's *glasnost* policy was just beginning to change the environment for the media in the USSR. Unfortunately, a report issued on 3 May 1996 by the U.S.-based Freedom House found that none of the 12 former Soviet republics in the Commonwealth of Independent States could be said to enjoy genuine freedom of the press. Four countries—Armenia, Kyrgyzstan, Russia, and Ukraine—were rated "partly free." The rest of the CIS fell into the "not free" category.

The Freedom House report placed Turkmenistan and Tajikistan in a group rated "worst of the worst," where the practice of journalism is extremely restricted. All publications in Turkmenistan must be screened by a state committee for the protection of state secrets. In Tajikistan, every legal newspaper is state-controlled, and dozens of journalists have been killed since the civil war started in 1992. Mehitdin Olimpur, a Tajik correspondent for the BBC, was shot on 12 December 1995 in Dushanbe; the crime had all the markings of a contract killing.

Six other CIS countries were rated "not free" by Freedom House. Moldova was downgraded from its 1995 "partly free" press rating. In late April, the Moldovan parliament voted unanimously to cancel an article in the Criminal Code making it a crime for journalists to insult the president or parliament speaker. However, this move should be seen not so much as reflecting concern for the freedom of the press, as part of a competition between leading politicians to appear more liberal, both to improve Moldova's image abroad and to win media support during the upcoming presidential campaign.

In Belarus, President Alyaksandr Lukashenka has created one of the most repressive environments for journalists in Europe. In October 1995 three independent newspapers were banned, two of them are currently printed in Lithuania and smuggled over the border. More recently, the government banned live TV and radio coverage of a 26 April demonstration against an agreement signed earlier that month forming a new community between Russia and Belarus.

Independent journalists in Uzbekistan are often harrassed. A steady stream of foreign journalists, mostly working for Russian news organizations, have left the country as President Islam Karimov makes it more difficult for them to practice their profession. In Kazakstan, more opposition voices find their way into the press than in Uzbekistan, but journalists must still exercise caution. In March 1995, the offices of the independent newspaper *Karavan* burned down days before President Nursultan Nazabayev was to hold a referendum on extending the president's term. When the paper reopened, it was much less critical of the government.

Finally, Freedom House also placed Azerbaijan and Georgia in the "not free" category. In Azerbaijan, the authorities have indeed imposed strict censorship. Last fall, five young journalists with the unofficial Azeri journal *Chesme* were sentenced to prison terms of 2 to 5 years for publishing caricatures that allegedly insulted President Heidar Aliev. Aliev demonstratively pardoned them on the eve of the November parliamentary elections. However, the Freedom House rating for Georgia is at odds with the conclusions of a March report by the European Institute for the Media. An EIM team monitored election coverage during the November 1995 parliamentary campaign in Georgia and found "a laudable plurality of opinion" represented in both the official and independent media.

Freedom House rated four CIS countries as "partly free." Most newspapers in Kyrgyzstan are subsidized by the government, but the independent *Res Publika* has not hesitated to criticize President Askar Akaev. But even in Kyrgyzstan, journalists have occasionally faced reprisals. Last year two *Res Publika* correspondents were put on trial for slander and eventually banned from practicing journalism for a year and a half.

In other CIS countries rated "partly free," direct censorship is a thing of the past, but the authorities may still wield considerable leverage over the media. Most publications and electronic media in Ukraine are at least partly dependent on state funding. As a result, the media are less critical of President Leonid Kuchma than what might be expected given the poor state of the Ukrainian economy.

In Russia, the Moscow-based media are essentially unrestricted and have been quite critical of President Boris Yeltsin in recent years, especially over the war in Chechnya. However, in the spring they rallied in support of Yeltsin fearing a victory by Communist candidate Gennadii Zyuganov in the June presidential elections. The Russian regional press often practices self-censorship to avoid running into trouble with powerful governors. At least 17 journalists have been killed in Chechnya since fighting escalated in December 1994. Most of these have been accidental deaths. However, in April *Obshchaya gazeta* correspondent Nadezhda Chaikova was severely beaten and shot execution-style. Her killers have not been found, nor are they likely to be.

In Armenia, the authorities appeared to be cracking down on the opposition press in late April. The registration of one daily newspaper was revoked, and the Central Electoral Commission took a weekly paper to court for publishing results of a July 1995 referendum on the new Armenian constitution that contradicted the official results.

Aleksei Simonov, director of the Moscow-based Glasnost Defense Foundation, has defined *glasnost*, as opposed to freedom of the press, as follows: in conditions of *glasnost*, you can say anything you like, but I can smack you in the face for it. In the four "partly free" CIS countries named by Freedom House, journalists effectively live under *glasnost*: they do not face direct censorship, but they may be denied funding or access if their reporting displeases the authorities. With the exception of Georgia, journalists in the countries labeled "not free" have yet to achieve even *glasnost*, let alone press freedom. For them, journalism remains a difficult and even dangerous profession.

ISSUES IN
FOREIGN
POLICY

IX

EVERYBODY NEEDS RUSSIA— INCLUDING EASTERN EUROPE

by J.F. BROWN

No longer a superpower, Russia demands and deserves to be treated as a European power. East European countries will have to understand and accommodate Russian interests to some extent, even as they look to the West.

"About face, Eastern Europe!" It may not have been an order, but it was certainly the drill after 1989. After more than 40 years of subjection to the Soviet Union, looking eastward with Comecon and the Warsaw Pact, the East European states suddenly turned westward. "Joining Europe"—or rejoining it— became the order of the day. But it was, of course, not quite as neat as that. Détente had already partially opened up some East European states to the West long before 1989. And immediately after the revolutions of that year, some states were not as ready as others to cut their eastern ties. For one thing, some were not as "post-communist" as others; some were hardly "post-communist" at all. For another, with Germany reuniting, the future of the continent looked so clouded that some states initially preferred to hedge their bets. Perhaps the devil they knew was safer than the one they didn't.

But soon the Soviet Union and the whole communist system was to collapse. Six European successor states to the old Soviet Union—Estonia, Latvia, Lithuania, Belarus, Ukraine, and Moldova—emerged between Russia and its former Cold War satellites with just the Russian exclave of Kaliningrad remaining as a reminder of Russian power. In the years after 1989, the political map of Europe changed more than it had since 1918, as new countries were born or reborn and Yugoslavia and Czechoslovakia disintegrated. The Soviet collapse shattered all hopes of either revival or survival for Eastern Europe's communists. Their lodestar and their sustaining power were gone. For some, it was the beginning or the acceleration of evolution toward social democracy; for others, it was sauve qui peut, through adaptation to the new order; for still others it was simply a dead end and stagnation. But for virtually everybody, the pull was westward.

At first that seemed to be the case with the new Russia, too. The pace in Russian politics was being set by a largely Moscow-based group of personable, democratic, internationalist, market-oriented, pro-Western, learn-from-America intellectuals. Russia at last seemed on the right train on the right track. Not only the West's political victory but also its ideological victory seemed complete. But the euphoria was not to last. Soon the real Russia stood up—a murky muddle of all types and trends, with just about the only common denominator a proud, bewildered, and aggrieved nationalism. While there were different degrees of intensity in that nationalism, it was now the Russian mainstream.

That is the Russia that America, Western Europe, and Eastern Europe must now accept and cope with. The summer election in 1996 removed the threat that old-style communism might return, but Russian nationalism will survive and

---

become more coherent. Eastern Europe will be directly affected by it, and the East European response will also help shape it.

Historically, East Europeans have had varied attitudes toward Russia. They have by no means been as uniformly hostile, fearful, or contemptuous as some now try to make out. In general, the southern Slavic nations—Serbs, Bulgarians, and Montenegrins—saw Russia as liberator and protector. Subsequently, though, Serbia became a satellite of Austria for much of the later 19th century, and Bulgaria in the 20th century fought on the German side in both world wars (but, significantly, it did not declare war against Russia in the second). Until 1917, Orthodox Christianity was a powerful religious and cultural bond between those nations, strengthening their mutual ethnic ties; at times, intellectual pan-Slavism was strong.

Among the non-Slavic Balkan nations, Russia was indeed seen as the historic enemy. For the Romanians, non-Slavic and right next door, the Russians were alien invaders who periodically trampled them underfoot in the drive toward Constantinople and the warm-water ports. For the Balkan Muslims, whatever their ethnic provenance, Russia was the enemy of the Ottoman empire under which they enjoyed superior status over their Christian neighbors.

Moving northward into what was once the Habsburg Empire, there was little but dislike and fear of the Russians. That was especially the case in Hungary. Its 1848 revolution was crushed by Russian troops acting on behalf of Austria; it fought against Russia in both world wars, had a revolution crushed again by Russians in 1956, was then garrisoned by Soviet troops for nearly four decades and was forcibly kept inside Moscow's ideological and imperialist system. Croatia and Slovenia, adjuncts and now aspirants to Central Europe, brushed against Soviet Russia while they were part of communist Yugoslavia, but they were seldom involved with it. Farther north, in the Czech lands, there was always considerable popular, intellectual, and national-level sympathy with Russia, something most Czechs now try to forget. That sympathy was only finally exorcised in August 1968, when the Russians' ideas of "deliverance" were brutally at variance with those of the Czechs.

Finally, there are the Poles, who have hated, despised, and feared the Russians for three centuries. Russia helped partition the Polish state out of existence at the end of the 18th century, tried to strangle the reborn state after World War I, partitioned it with Nazi Germany in 1939, and then incorporated it into the Soviet empire after 1945. But with Poland doomed to lie in perpetuity between Germany and Russia, a strong body of "nationalist-realist" opinion emerged during the brief interlude of independence between the wars that saw Russia as the lesser evil and advocated that Polish foreign policy be made accordingly. The policy experienced a brief flicker of revival after 1989, when some influential Poles saw the newly reunited Germany as the main potential danger. With the demise of the Soviet Union and communist imperialism, Josef Stalin's tenet of international relations—that conquest meant imposing not just your will but also your ideological system on the territories you took—was gone. When East Europeans now talk about the "revival of the Soviet Union," what they mean is the revival of the Russian empire, or the re-emergence of the Russian imperialist urge, not Soviet ideology.

THE RUSSIAN INTEREST

Before World War I, Russia saw Eastern Europe as little more than a wasteland peopled by nations in different stages of definition, to be fought or haggled over with imperial Prussia (later Germany), imperial Austria, and imperial Turkey. Independent statehood for any of the smaller nations was something to be resisted, undermined, or exploited for influence. The other three imperial powers held the same view. All four expired as a result of World War I. Two of them, though, were to bounce back under new ideological guises: Nazism for Germany and communism for Russia. German Nazism collapsed as a result of World War II, but Russian communism, emerging victorious from that war, now claimed the whole of Eastern Europe. And along with control came the attempt at forced ideological conversion.

Russia has now lost most of the empire it took four centuries to accumulate. Now Russians refer to the severed parts of the old Soviet Union as the "near abroad," the connotations of which are not entirely clear but are generally regarded as ominous by the successor states—despite Russia's generally correct behavior toward them. But how does Russia view the East European states, the "new empire" it gained in 1945 and then lost a half-century later? There is virtually no serious hankering to "regain" them, but most Russians—including some of the best and the brightest in Western eyes—put Eastern Europe in a special category as far as their national security, interests, and sense of self-esteem are concerned. Russia may no longer be a superpower, but Russians of all persuasions still regard their country as an unbowed, great European power with legitimate interests that should be respected.

Eastern Europe matters to Russia; it is special. Not the near abroad, certainly, but perhaps the "intermediate abroad," seen as independent but not unrestrainedly so, sovereign but not uninhibitedly so, free but not irresponsibly so. The Russians' perception of their security and power interests in Eastern Europe is reflected in their determination not merely to keep Kaliningrad, but to keep it bristling with men and weapons. That policy may not be designed specifically to intimidate Poland, Belarus, and Lithuania, but it is certainly aimed at reminding them of Russia's continuing presence and power. Similarly, in Southeastern Europe, Russia seems to be looking at part or all of the self-declared Dniester Republic as a counterpart to Kaliningrad. Former Security Council Secretary Aleksandr Lebed himself said that the region was crucial for Russian influence in the Balkans. And the conviction is firmly held in Moscow, among both the political class and the military, that history ordained the Balkans as a region of Russian influence and concern. Not surprisingly, therefore, there is bitterness and humiliation over what Russians regard as American exploitation of their current weakness by "moving into" parts of the former Yugoslavia and the southern Balkans. What they want, they insist, is a droit de regard; the Americans they accuse of having filched a droit du seigneur.

RESPONDING TO RUSSIA

Such Russian responses to the momentous changes in what they used to call the "correlation of forces" have yet to cohere into a consistent policy. (How long that will take depends on when recognizable and consistent leadership emerges.) But the West, as well as the East European countries, would do well to take the responses seriously. The West, in particular the United States, will play an important role in how Russia's East European policy unfolds and how flexible, rigid, or predictable it becomes. It is essential, therefore, that American policy does not become the stomping ground of megalomaniacs, confrontationalists, triumphalists, exceptionalists, right-or-wrongers, conditioned Russophobes, time-warped diasporas, or cap-in-handers to the military. What is needed now is diplomacy—a diplomacy tempered by firmness and breadth, that has nothing to do with appeasement. American global diplomacy was born and bred in the confrontation of the Cold War, and the zero-sum habit of mind engendered by it (and reinforced by victory in it) has not yet been entirely flushed out.

It is essential, too, for East European leaders, no matter how Western-oriented they might aspire to be, to act with an understanding of the long-term implications, opportunities, and restrictions of their geopolitical situation and to see their national interests not as provincial, short-term imperatives, but as part of a wider, even global interplay of interests. That does not mean surrender, but it does demand modesty and perspective. A touch of statesmanship, which is in short supply everywhere, also wouldn't hurt.

It is not necessary here to dredge up the continuing controversy about NATO enlargement; the arguments are well known. One thing, however, should be kept in mind: Russia, despite its vagaries and its testiness, has been a rational and restrained player in international relations. It is in everybody's interest to keep it that way. Russia must, therefore, be treated with the respect it needs and deserves. It must not be treated as a beast to be humored; it cannot be treated as a weakened enemy to be spurned.

Most East European countries genuinely fear a revival of what in effect would be the Soviet Union. Just as Russia dominated and drove the Soviet Union, so, they contend, it now seeks to make a reality of, and then to dominate and drive, the Commonwealth of Independent States (CIS). The near abroad would then melt into the new imperial power, and what was once the intermediate abroad would become the near abroad. The fear is understandable, as is its corollary: get into the European Union and especially NATO as quickly as possible and pull up the drawbridge behind you. It sounds simple and final, but it is neither.

The United States and Western Europe have constantly assured Russia that it has an important place as a partner in any new European or international arrangement. And that means a substantial degree of Russian-East European interaction. If Russia were to feel excluded, it would most likely only strengthen its efforts to control the CIS. Some East European states, therefore, might feel formally secure behind NATO's perimeter fence, but the tension throughout the region could become more palpable than ever. Life would become more, not less, complicated.

In addition, normal relations with Russia, especially economic relations, would be beneficial for all the East European countries, even those, like the Czech Republic, Poland, and Hungary, that are first in line to join the EU. Those countries have had remarkable success in reorienting their trade westward, but there is still room for trade with the East, particularly in fuels and raw materials. And for those countries that are farther back in the queue for EU entry, trade with Russia remains crucial. In March, there was considerable commotion in Sofia and some Western capitals when Yeltsin mentioned Bulgaria as a possible candidate for inclusion in an economic association comprising several CIS countries. Whether Yeltsin had something specific in mind or was simply ruminating was not clear. But for Bulgaria and other Balkan states, closer association with Russia might prove to be more in their interests than dangling interminably on the West European hook.

PIVOTAL UKRAINE

Special attention must be given to Ukraine. It is, after all, Ukraine and not Russia that borders on four East European countries, and Ukraine is a major state in its own right. Its future depends on how well it gets along with Russia, with which it has a complex relationship. Sometimes the relationship has looked perilously close to breaking down; it has survived because of the good sense of both sides. For the time being at least, Ukraine's economic requirements and large ethnic Russian minority force it to gravitate toward Russia.

Ukraine's independence in the longer term, however, depends on a partial gravitation toward the West. Polish-Ukrainian relations, full of enmity in the past but now improving so much that speculation about a Kyiv-Warsaw "axis" can be heard, can play an important role. Ukraine is also intimately connected with Romania. Their relations are both complicated and difficult because Romania claims the return of territories given to the Ukrainian Soviet Socialist Republic under the Molotov-Ribbentrop pact of 1940—and the Ukrainians, selective in their repudiation of their Soviet past, refuse.

The whole tangled Southeast European web covering Russia, Ukraine, Moldova, and Romania is so potentially dangerous that it might be best to let matters rest. But it would be too much to expect that all the parties will. The East European states' relations with Ukraine will unavoidably bring them in contact with Russia. Eastern Europe will pull Ukraine away from Russia, but Ukraine will pull Eastern Europe toward Russia, at the same time acting as a buffer against Russia. Such a course of regional interaction is now set for the opening of the 21st century, and it will require skill and patience by all concerned to navigate it.

Belarus, unlike Ukraine, was always a doubtful proposition for independence and is now looking politically, economically, and psychologically increasingly unviable. Closer association with Russia is inevitable, incorporation by it quite possible. And incorporation could bring more, not less, regional stability. It need not be taken as proof that Russia is on the march.

With the Baltic republics, the matter is entirely different. But Estonia and

Latvia, with large Russian minorities that are not simply going to go away, will get nowhere if they do not treat their Russians more magnanimously and imaginatively. Tension with Russia on that score should be avoided. Their case, and their global reputation, would be helped by sticking to both the spirit and the letter of international rules and recommendations on minorities.

A CALL FOR COOPERATION

What would help strengthen the Eastern European countries in their relations not only with Russia but also with Western international institutions would be meaningful regional or subregional cooperation among themselves. In East-Central Europe there is, of course, the Visegrad grouping of the Czech Republic, Slovakia, Poland, and Hungary, but while it may have become a bit firmer and deeper recently, it remains more lip-service than practical business. Perhaps Hungary is keenest on it. Poland is now less dismissive than under former president Lech Walesa but still sees itself as a major-league team among minor leaguers. And Slovakia under Prime Minister Vladimir Meciar qualifies more for pariah than member status in any civilized association. But the real saboteur of effective cooperation is the government of the Czech Republic. Prime Minister Vaclav Klaus has said that the only Visegrad he takes seriously is the Prague cemetery of that name (Vysehrad). Vintage Klaus, that is the kind of hubris that spells damnation for the spirit Visegrad was meant to encompass. Without the Czech Republic there simply can be no East-Central European cooperation. Hungary and Slovakia, bitterly divided by the controversy over ethnic Hungarians in Slovakia, would not want to be part of a Polish-dominated trio.

Historical memories, cultural incompatibilities, and the recent unpleasant experience of fraternal togetherness would make regional cooperation difficult under any circumstances. And now there is also the lure of "Europe" and the "West," not exactly beckoning as much as magnetically attracting. And for almost all East Europeans, that "Europe" makes everything they have look inferior or provincial. How can Visegrad compete with Brussels? Their attitude is understandable enough, but it is self-defeating now and could become increasingly harmful—for none more harmful than for the Czech Republic itself, the loudest in its refusal of any "Eastward orientation." Czechoslovakia could have become as pivotal a state in Central Europe as Ukraine can be in Eastern Europe. Yet Czechoslovakia was allowed to split, partly because no one had the statesmanship or the skill to keep it together, but mainly because the Czechs did not want the bother or the risk of being internationally important. What they thought they were getting was the West. What they have become is a Western appendage—a German appendage, to be precise. In terms of Czech history, of course, German control is nothing new. The Germans are bending over backwards now to be benevolent, and they mean it. But Czechoslovakia after 1989 need have been nobody's appendage; it could have been a player, a doer—a leader, even. It would have at least been a state. The Czech Republic is beginning to look more like a business. And businesses become the target of takeover bids, however friendly.

In Southeastern Europe, the war in former Yugoslavia and the crises, or potential crises, elsewhere have made the need for cooperation all the greater, and yet the will for it is all the less. Slovenia slid off the northwest corner of the Balkans into Central Europe with little fuss. Croatia now disowns any Balkan connections and pretentiously claims Central Europe as its habitat. "Bosnia-Herzegovina" may not survive. Serbia is still in thoroughly deserved limbo. It is too much to expect the former warring nations in Yugoslavia to cooperate.

In the Balkans, neighbors, if not considered potential enemies, are seen as potential problems and better left alone. There is also an "ashamed of the neighborhood" complex: my own nation is all right, but the rest are Europe's dregs. And, of course, for the Balkans, just as for the East-Central European countries, "Europe" symbolizes freedom and progress. But the Balkans perceive Europe in another way as well. "Why combine to solve our problems when Europe will do it for us?" they ask. "These problems are too big for us anyway." The incorrigible, comprehensive disunity of Southeastern Europe is likely to persist, slowing up recovery, probably alienating the West, and perhaps presenting opportunities for the Russians. If the Russians take those opportunities, no one should cry "foul."

THE IMPACT OF CHINA

But Russia, its present (probably short-lived) weakness notwithstanding, is a world power, and early in the 21st century it will play a key role in a new world challenge: the containment of China. One need not be accused of purveying "yellow peril" hysteria by pointing to the momentous implications of China's growing power, population, and assertiveness. The Chinese challenge is likely to generate tension over a long period of time, punctuated by major and minor crises. That is a pessimistic prediction, perhaps, but not necessarily a doom-laden or apocalyptic one.

The United States and Russia, along with China, will be at the center of the tension. Russia, though, will most likely be the third party, courted by the other two as their rivalry deepens, each knowing how grave the consequences would be if Russia were to side with the other. Still, the rationality that Russia has shown so far in its foreign policy, as well as its historical awareness of the gravity of the Chinese threat, will be reflected in support for the United States—not as ready or demonstrative as the Americans would wish, and probably not in every case. And certainly not without a price! It will be a dangerous three-cornered game.

Some diplomatic moves in that game may have already started. For the past two years, Russian-Chinese relations have been improving, and President Boris Yeltsin made a much-publicized visit to Beijing in April with several Central Asian leaders in tow. There was, of course, plenty of debris from past disputes to clear away, but the visit may have marked the beginning of the new phase that will soon dominate global diplomacy. It was not a sign of an incipient Sino-Soviet alliance against America but rather a Russian signal to Washington of the possibility of one—a signal that Russia was an independent player keeping its options open and was going to play hard to get.

The basic question is how the United States will handle Russia. Some "frontalists," who claim to have won the Cold War with their approach, seem to think that there is no need to change U.S. policy. Others see Russia as so impotent that all its huffing and puffing can be ignored. But the fact is that Russia, despite disturbing behavior such as the murderousness in Chechnya, has changed remarkably for the better in a very short time. Russia is still powerful and proud. Russia is also in Europe and will want to play a key role as a European power. Finally, if the China scenario becomes reality, America will need Russia.

Times have changed. The world's sole superpower will need diplomacy and willingness to compromise. And the main compromise with Russia will have to be on Russia's position in Europe. It may take a bit of getting used to.

"Is this good or bad for us?" East Europeans might ask, echoing the historically familiar response of nations to events over which they have no control. Many might conclude that nothing could be better for them than having Russia tied up in Asia—Russia looking eastward and Eastern Europe inside the NATO perimeter and looking westward. What better security could there be? But that comfort would turn out to be illusory. In the 21st century, no matter how much Russia is involved in the Far East or in nationality conflicts within its own borders, it is going to be thinking and acting like a European power and demanding to be treated like one.

The East European states will have to come to terms with that, and the problems will not be solved just by their joining Europe's main institutions. Unless Russia is convinced that a partnership plan can be devised for Europe involving it—instead of the divisive, exclusionist arrangement now taking shape—the East European countries will find that membership in NATO or the EU, or any other Western embrace, will not give them the real security they deserve. In fact, Russia will soon be in a position to make things distinctly uncomfortable for any East European state if it so chooses. And such states need not look to Western Europe, and probably not to the United States, for continuing sympathy if their policy toward Russia were to be based on continuing rejection.

What future, then, for Eastern Europe? Zwischeneuropa, or something similar to Yalta status? Not at all. But the implacability of geopolitics cannot be ignored. Nor can the fact that Russia is European, and must become more so, and that this will be good for European stability and for world peace. The independence and sovereignty of the East European states cannot be sacrificed to that goal—they, too, are integral to European stability and world peace. But the preferences and the policies of some East European countries may have to be circumscribed to accommodate Russia if the results are to be advantageous for everybody. Eastern Europe, therefore, can become an essential part of Europe, linking its unity and cementing its stability. The price it will pay is not excessive and the role it will play by no means demeaning. "About face, Eastern Europe?" Not all the way.

CENTRAL EUROPE RETHINKS RUSSIAN TIES

by SHARON FISHER, *with* ZSOFIA SZILAGYI *and* JIRI PEHE

The Czech Republic, Hungary, and Slovakia have all recognized the importance of good political and economic relations with Russia. But only Slovakia has formed ties that seem to threaten its integration into Western structures.

Following the collapse of communism in 1989, the countries of Central Europe rushed to improve their ties with Western Europe. At the same time, they tried to introduce as much distance as possible into their relations with the Soviet Union and, later, Russia. Strong anti-Soviet sentiment was apparent in Central Europe, particularly during the first post-communist years, and maintaining good relations with both the East and the West seemed almost unthinkable.

Current Czech, Hungarian, and Slovak ties with Russia show, however, that it is possible to have good relations with both the East and the West, as long as a certain approach is followed. While all three countries have basically good relations with Russia, only Slovakia has put its westward orientation into question owing to the ambiguous rhetoric of its politicians. Slovak Prime Minister Vladimir Meciar and his ruling coalition have cast doubt over their government's sincerity in seeking membership in the European Union and NATO, not only by repeatedly disregarding Western warnings against undemocratic practices in Slovakia but also by their efforts to build a "special" relationship with Russia. Although Russia has also played up these "special" ties to some extent, it would be a mistake for Slovakia to overestimate its own importance in the eyes of Russian policy-makers. In reality, Russia's relations with Slovakia are not much, if any, better than its relations with the Czech Republic or Hungary.

PRAGMATIC CZECHS

Since 1989, the Czech Republic has gone the furthest to toss aside Russian links, at least in rhetoric. The country's top officials have made it all too clear that they see themselves historically and culturally as part of Western Europe. Still, the republic's highest officials evidently continue to recognize the importance of maintaining ties with Russia—particularly economic ones—and current Czech-Russian relations are generally trouble-free.

Russia's opposition to NATO expansion is one of the few remaining sticking points in Czech-Russian relations. Many Czech politicians, particularly President Vaclav Havel, have criticized Russia's position. They have repeatedly argued that eventual Czech membership in the Atlantic alliance is not aimed against Russia and that, at any rate, Russia has no right to veto Czech membership in international organizations.[1] Czech politicians not only have little sympathy for Russia on the NATO issue but also do not feel the need to hold back criticism of other areas of Russian policy. Czech criticism of the Russian military intervention in Chechnya was met with dissatisfaction in Moscow. The friction especially increased in May 1995 after Havel sent an official protest to Russian

President Boris Yeltsin regarding the fact that troops involved in the Chechnya conflict had taken part in the Moscow celebrations honoring the end of World War II in Europe, contrary to previous assurances that this would not be the case. Two days later, the Russian Embassy in Prague issued a statement complaining that Czech media and politicians were assailing Russia with a "vociferous campaign in the worst traditions of the Cold War."

While Slovakia and Hungary have accepted military jets from Russia as partial repayment of Soviet-era debts, the Czechs have scorned such deals, hoping instead to buy equipment from Western countries, even at a higher cost. Such plans have finally proved to be financially unrealistic. Judging by the proposal for drastic military cuts put forward in late August by the new Czech defense minister, Miloslav Vyborny, it seems that the plan to replace aging Soviet-made MiG-21 fighter planes with advanced Western aircraft will be dropped.

The level of cooperation between the Czech and Russian secret services has been minimal. Oldrich Cerny, the Czech intelligence director, visited Moscow in November 1995. The visit was reciprocated by the Russian secret-service chief, General Vyacheslav Trubnikov, who came to Prague for a two-day secret visit in late September. During Trubnikov's Prague trip, the first by the head of Russian intelligence in three years, talks focused on organized crime and international terrorism, including the diffusion of technology and components for the production of weapons of mass destruction and illegal trade in strategic materials and weapons. In its latest report, however, the Czech civilian counterintelligence agency, which is in charge of monitoring the activity of foreign spies in the Czech Republic, warned that the Russian secret service may try to discredit the country through deliberate disinformation, thereby preventing its entry into NATO.[2]

AMBIVALENT HUNGARIANS

Hungary's first democratically elected government harbored a clear anti-Soviet sentiment during its initial year in office. More than a year passed before any of the country's top political leaders paid an official visit to Moscow. The opposition strongly criticized the government for spoiling relations with what was then Hungary's largest neighbor and main supplier of raw materials and energy.

In December 1991, Russian President Yeltsin and Hungarian Prime Minister Jozsef Antall signed a basic bilateral treaty. The Russian Duma, however, delayed the ratification of the treaty because it contained a clause denouncing the 1956 Soviet invasion of Hungary. Communists refused to acknowledge the intervention as a negative political act, and liberal and nationalist forces rejected the idea of sharing responsibility for an act committed by the Soviet Union. A new parliament finally ratified the treaty in January 1995.

Today, only a few problems remain in Hungarian-Russian relations. As in the Czech Republic, the most discussed issue is NATO enlargement. The current socialist-liberal coalition government has repeatedly stressed its willingness to hold consultations with Moscow on the issue, but it has reiterated Hungary's sovereignty with regard to the actual decision to join the alliance. Another problem in bilateral relations concerns the fate of the unreturned Hungarian art trea-sures confiscated by the Soviets after World War II.

Many of Hungary's leading politicians—particularly the members of the rul-ing Socialist Party, many of whom studied in Moscow—maintain a two-faced approach toward Russia. While most Socialists distance themselves from Mos-cow in rhetoric, in practice they continue to capitalize on their political and economic contacts in Russia. The past two years have witnessed several curious developments—such as the recent "oilgate" scandal—suggesting the existence of numerous shady dealings among Hungarian politicians, Socialist-leaning busi-ness circles, and Russian partners, especially in the oil business and in matters concerning the repayment of Russia's debt.[3]

SLOVAKS FORGE "SPECIAL" RELATIONS

While official Czech and Hungarian relations with Russia have remained in check, Slovakia's political and security ties with Russia have been expanding, as Meciar has made "special" relations with Russia a key point of his political and economic agenda.[4] Analysts have expressed particular concern about the 1993 bilateral treaty, which linked the security of both states to the Conference on Security and Cooperation in Europe and called for the development of a Europe-wide security system.[5] Slovak politicians—both in the government and the oppo-sition—have been much more accommodating to Russian concerns about NATO expansion than their Czech and Hungarian counterparts. In February, Sergei Yastrzhembskii, then Russian ambassador to Slovakia, asserted that while Bratislava respects the Russian fear of NATO's eastward expansion, "Prague, Budapest, and Warsaw unfortunately do not."[6] Even so, top Slovak representa-tives have remained committed to NATO integration—at least in rhetoric—de-spite Russian attempts to persuade them to drop such plans.

The Russian secret service reportedly enjoys close links with the Slovak Information Service (SIS) and its chief, Ivan Lexa. Plagued by scandals related to his alleged involvement in the unauthorized searching of church buildings, the kidnapping of the president's son, and interference in the subsequent investiga-tion of the abduction case, Lexa has become increasingly isolated from his Western and Central European partners. The SIS's strengthened ties to Russian intelligence were underscored by a mid-January visit to Moscow by Lexa and a number of other SIS employees; a training seminar for Slovak secret agents held last May in Bratislava by their Russian counterparts; and a series of study trips to Moscow by Slovak agents. During a late-September visit of Russian security-ser-vice chief Trubnikov to Slovakia, discussions reportedly focused on deepening bilateral cooperation and the negotiation of several agreements between the two organizations.[7]

While Slovak officials have made frequent attempts over the past few months to convince the West of their country's sincere desire to join NATO and the EU, Yastrzhembskii and other Russian representatives have played up the importance of Russian-Slovak ties. In February, Yastrzhembskii said that "Moscow and

Bratislava have succeeded in becoming the first pair in the post-socialist region to create a new model of bilateral relations."[8] In August, Yastrzhembskii was rewarded for his top-notch work in Slovakia with the position of presidential spokesman in Moscow.

NO LONGER A THREAT

In contrast to their Polish neighbors, the populations of the Czech Republic, Slovakia, and Hungary do not currently perceive Russia as a realistic threat. That is partly because, unlike Poland, the other Visegrad countries do not share a border with Russia. At the political level, top Czech, Slovak, and Hungarian officials were relieved by Yeltsin's victory in the recent presidential election, as he is seen as the best guarantee that Russia's expansionist desires will be kept at bay. Some unease remains, however, over Yeltsin's health and prospects for recovery.

Most Czechs feel reasonably secure and do not believe that Russia is about to expand westward. A poll conducted earlier this year by the Slovak Defense Ministry's public-affairs office showed that only 8.8 percent of Slovaks thought the biggest security threat for their country was posed by the imperialist or expansionist ambitions of certain states, especially the great powers. In contrast, larger percentages of Slovaks were more afraid of a possible spread of conflict from other European regions, strife with neighboring countries, instability in Central Europe, and international terrorism and crime.[9] The Hungarian public, which lacks the pan-Slavic ties that link Czechs and Slovaks to Russia, is fairly indifferent about Russians and Russia.

In the Czech Republic, Hungary, and Slovakia, the desire to join NATO seems to be more symbolic (rejoining the West) than based on any great fear of being conquered by Russia. In both Hungary and the Czech Republic, support for NATO membership has recently fallen as low as 30 percent, although the latest polls put Hungarian support for NATO at 48 percent. Popular support for NATO membership has remained higher in Slovakia—which now seems to be off the list for early membership—where it has been hovering between 40 percent and 50 percent. While a poll showed that only 3 percent of respondents would favor a political and security alliance with Russia, 19.3 percent said Slovakia was growing closer to Russia. Only 29.8 percent believed that Slovakia was really headed for the EU.[10] In all three countries, support for EU membership has been higher than for joining NATO.

Hungarians' and Czechs' biggest worry about Russia concerns the presence of Russian criminal gangs—particularly in the capitals—and migration from Russia. Slovakia, meanwhile, dropped Soviet-era travel restrictions for Russian citizens in August 1995. Many feared the move would make Slovakia a center of Russian criminal activity, while the Czechs, and Hungarians protested that such a step would also increase the influx of Russian crime into their countries. Even so, in February the Czech Republic followed the Slovak lead, allowing Russian citizens to visit with only a passport.

ECONOMIC CONTACTS

During the past seven years, much has changed in terms of economic links between Russia and Hungary, Slovakia, and the Czech Republic. The Soviet Union was the most important trading partner of Czechoslovakia and Hungary before 1989. Later, a drastic drop in trade with Russia resulted from the collapse of the Council for Mutual Economic Assistance, economic difficulties and changes in the import priorities of the Soviet successor states, and the economic transformation in the Central European countries aimed at Western integration. In the first years of the transformation, as their countries tried to boost exports to the West in order to earn hard currency and shore up their economies, Czechoslovak and Hungarian companies virtually deserted the Russian market. At the same time, however, both countries continued to depend heavily on Russian raw materials and particularly on energy (mainly oil and gas).

Dependence on Russian raw materials and energy is highest in Slovakia, which, in contrast to the Czech Republic and Hungary, made few efforts to diversify its resources and continues to rely almost entirely on Russian imports. Many of Slovakia's biggest industries depend on cheap imports of raw materials from Russia, making the country especially vulnerable to price changes.[11]

While the Czech Republic is still quite dependent on Russian oil, the completion of an alternative pipeline—originating in Ingolstadt, a German port on the Danube—last March has made this more an economic problem than a strategic one. The country could switch to the Ingolstadt pipeline should there be any problem with oil from Russia, since the pipeline can carry up to 10 million metric tons of oil annually, which exceeds the Czech Republic's total demand.

Slovakia's extreme dependence on Russian raw materials and energy has resulted in a huge trade deficit with Russia. Although the Slovak government has tried to remedy the situation—going so far as to suggest the possibility of creating a customs union—it has had scant success thus far, as Russia seems to have little interest in the products Slovakia has to offer.[12]

The Czech Republic and Hungary also have large trade deficits with Russia, but their main economic concern regarding Russia has been the payment of Soviet-era debt. The Czech Republic and Russia negotiated repayment of the $3 billion Soviet debt two years ago, but Russia has failed to pay this year's 6 billion crown ($222 million) installment. Half of Russia's $1.7 billion state debt to Hungary was paid with the delivery of military hardware in 1993, but the payment of the second half has yet to be settled. In Slovakia, it was recently suggested that part of the Russian debt could be transformed into a privatization stake in Russian firms.

[1]Jiri Pehe, "The Choice Between Europe and Provincialism," *Transition*, vol. 1, no. 12, 14 July 1995.
[2]*Mlada fronta Dnes*, 27 September 1996.

[3]See Zsofia Szilagyi, "Slowing the Pace of Economic Reform," *Transition*, vol. 2, no. 2, 4 October 1996.

[4]Alexander Duleba, "Pursuing an Eastern Agenda," *Transition*, vol. 2, no. 19, 20 September 1996.

[5]Svetoslav Bombik, "O co ide Rusku?" [What Is Russia's Aim?] *Sme*, 26 August 1993.

[6]Interview with Yastrzhembskii, *Mlada fronta Dnes*, 8 February 1996.

[7]*Sme*, 26 September 1996; CTK, 27 September 1996.

[8]Interview with Yastrzhembskii, *Mlada fronta Dnes*, 8 February 1996.

[9]*Pravda*, 22 February 1996.

[10]FOCUS agency poll, reported in *Sme*, 22 January 1996.

[11]Alexander Duleba, "Pursuing an Eastern Agenda."

[12]*Sme*, 31 August 1996.

THE DAYTON AGREEMENT: THE U.S. LEADS, EUROPE PAYS

by SUSAN L. WOODWARD

The Dayton peace accord did not provide an executive authority to make policy decisions, resolve differences, or define a real strategy for peace. The intervening powers have little to work with to resolve their conflicts on major issues.

The image of the Balkans as a tinderbox of great wars focuses wrongly on the box, when the real action—taking place in great-power capitals—is the fire that can be kindled. The package for peace in Bosnia-Herzegovina, the Dayton accord and Operation Joint Endeavor, represents only the newest phase in a historical pattern in which the major powers play out their conflicts of interest, shifting power relations, and rules of international governance during periods of transition in the Balkans.

While many conclude that the Dayton accord has ended the war in Bosnia, the accord and the process of its implementation continue the disagreements within the Atlantic alliance and among the major powers that have since 1990 plagued their efforts to resolve the Yugoslav crisis. The most recent in a long series of clashes that have characterized—and frequently driven—the Yugoslav conflict was the escalating quarrel in June between the U.S. government and European officials in the Organization for Security and Cooperation in Europe (OSCE) over whether elections in Bosnia-Herzegovina should proceed as planned by 14 September.

Anyone watching the Dayton negotiations and the first six months of the implementation process would likely be drawn to the individual personalities involved and, through their conflicts, to the often raw assertion of national power over multinational cooperation. The importance of the friendship between the international community's high representative, Carl Bildt, and German Chancellor Helmut Kohl is as striking as was the antagonism between the former foreign ministers of the Netherlands and Germany in 1991. The rivalry between then-U.S. Assistant Secretary of State Richard Holbrooke and Britain's delegate to Dayton, Pauline Neville-Jones, that began at the Wright-Patterson Air Force Base has continued and even appeared in print.[1] But the conflicts within single governments, between departments of foreign affairs and defense, and between chief executives and their ministries—whether in Washington, Paris, London, Bonn, Moscow, or Rome—also have not subsided. Commanders of the Implementation Force (IFOR) on the ground have not always seen eye to eye with their national capitals or with NATO headquarters, such as on the highly publicized issue of whether the Dayton mandate to "cooperate" with the International Criminal Tribunal for the Former Yugoslavia requires IFOR to detain and arrest indicted war criminals—particularly the Bosnian Serb political and military leaders, Radovan Karadzic and Ratko Mladic, respectively.

Some national alliances have been fairly constant since the start of the Bosnian war. The Washington-Bonn axis has been in support of Croatia, the Bosnian Muslim-Bosnian Croat federation, the combat use of air power, and sanctions on Serbia and Montenegro; the British-French axis has been in favor of Yugoslav integrity, humanitarian action, and policies that treat the Bosnian conflict as a civil war. But national positions also have shifted with changes in the countries' executives, their allies' policies, and conditions in Bosnia.

Behind these myriad conflicts and mixed messages are far more fundamental questions of European security and international organization. Who should take action toward the crumbling Yugoslavia, then Croatia, and finally the ill-fated Bosnia-Herzegovina, and why? What are the implications of that decision for Balkan policy, national power, the financing and organization of European security, and the acceptable arguments for intervention in the future? These questions, first raised explicitly by NATO and the Conference on Security and Cooperation in Europe in November 1990, have not been resolved. Although it is commonplace since Dayton for Europeans to insist that American leadership was necessary to get a settlement and to end the war, the struggles over whether the United States can dominate and Europe should pay are far from over.

AMERICA vs. EUROPE

The willingness of the Clinton administration during July 1995 to be dragged by its European allies into taking leadership, after five years of vacillation by two U.S. administrations, has raised both the ante and the fever of the power struggle between the United States and Europe. Is the peace agreement the Dayton accord or the Paris accord? Which hat is the outgoing American commander of the NATO-led implementation force, Admiral Leighton Smith (or his successor, Vice Admiral T. Joseph Lopez), wearing when he makes decisions? Is the lead agency for the economic-reconstruction program the European Union or the World Bank and the International Monetary Fund? Is the decision over certification of conditions for free and fair elections and the date of those elections the U.S. government's, through U.S. diplomat Robert Frowick, who heads the OSCE electoral operation in Sarajevo but takes instructions from U.S. Secretary of State Warren Christopher, or does it rest with the OSCE's current chairman, Swiss Foreign Minister Flavio Cotti?

The answers to those questions—and the ability to find answers and agree—and the successful conclusion of the peace process in Bosnia are of no less significance than the reform of NATO, the next stage of European integration, the incorporation of Russia into the West, and the nature and status of American global leadership in the post-Cold War period. As Christopher announced in his first major foreign-policy address, "Leadership for the Next American Century," at Harvard University in January 1996 (with conscious reference to an earlier Harvard speech by Secretary of State George Marshall in 1947), the Bosnia operation has "historic implications": "Our actions in Bosnia have proven that NATO is here to stay as the guarantor of transatlantic security. As we help overcome the divisions of Bosnia, we also help overcome the division of Europe itself."[2]

Although all parties agree that the fate of Yugoslavia had ceased to be of any vital, strategic interest to the alliance or individual states by the end of the Cold War, ironically it is the Bosnia operation that is deciding the future of European security arrangements and American leadership. Direct military intervention was out of the question, any other military deployment had to be premised on the U.S. refusal to participate, and the NATO allies could not take any action that would risk serious rupture in their mutual relations and institutions. Quarrels on policy substance had to be avoided, redefined as issues of jurisdiction or procedure that were of vital national or collective interest, or relegated to multilateral organizations.

The result was, of course, the opposite of that intended. It tied the fate of intervening powers' own relations and institutions to what decisions they made in Bosnia. The fact that multilateral security interests had to be seen to be threatened to justify intervention in Bosnia in 1995 subsumed ministerial, national, and personal disagreements over Bosnia within a broader contest between the United States and Europe. But the behavior of Holbrooke's team toward the Europeans present in Dayton, Ohio (to the point of physically excluding some Europeans from negotiating rooms they were invited to), and the U.S. officials' gloating about the necessity of American leadership and what they saw as the abject failure of Europeans to agree, lead, and solve their own security issues exacerbated this contest, adding a layer of injured national pride, personal animosities, and deep-seated resentments to the disputes over policy.

Although muted by the collective hope about the war's end and the effort to make Operation Joint Endeavor work, these disagreements are liable to resurface with every difficulty on the ground. The atmosphere of mutual recrimination suggests that the NATO alliance could still become unstuck if the Bosnia operation goes seriously wrong.

THREE ISSUES OF CONTENTION

The disagreements contained within the Dayton accord and its implementation are fundamental: the political end state of Bosnia, the approach to building peace, and the best way to end the war. The Dayton (Paris) accord is the seventh or eighth peace plan written for Bosnia, depending on whether one includes the Washington agreement for a Muslim-Croat federation and if one counts all versions of the Invincible Plan as one.[3] The plan no longer has to deal with the earliest dispute regarding Bosnia—whether it was viable as an independent state. Although most Europeans remain skeptics, the United States won that round. But the point at issue with each peace plan—whether Bosnia-Herzegovina should be organized as a multiethnic federation or a confederation of ethnically drawn units—remains unresolved.

The Bush administration erased the question of Bosnia's viability as an independent state in the spring of 1992 on the basis of the European decision in December 1991, which the United States opposed vociferously at the time, to recognize the republics of Slovenia and Croatia as sovereign states. The European Community's policy of unconditional and pre-emptive recognition sanctified the borders of the federal republics as international borders, if the republics requested recognition.

The United States had insisted that Slovenian and Croatian sovereignty in their republican borders not be recognized until after the EC's Hague peace conference (set up on 7 September 1991 to find a comprehensive solution to the Yugoslav crisis), but Germany won over its European allies to the opposite position. The shoe then moved to the other foot, and the United States insisted on immediate recognition of Bosnia-Herzegovina—before the negotiations in Lisbon under Portuguese Ambassador Jose Cutileiro were completed. Those negotiations, the one remnant of the Hague conference, were held to find a constitutional settlement among the three ruling parties of Bosnia. Bosnia's independence and the sanctity of its republican borders became protected by international norm and membership (in May 1992) in the United Nations.

Negotiations to find a constitutional settlement for the Bosnian state became synonymous after March with negotiations to end the war. The NATO allies—with troops on the ground in Croatia in a UN force beginning in March and after 28 June in a UN humanitarian operation in Bosnia-Herzegovina, and because they were committed to a negotiated solution to the war—grew increasingly angry at the United States for what they said was obstruction of each subsequent peace proposal. They criticized Washington not only for blocking the Cutileiro principles of February–March 1992 for ethnic cantonization of Bosnia but also the Vance-Owen plan of January 1993 for a 10–province, decentralized yet integral Bosnia, as well as the Owen-Stoltenberg plan of August 1993 (revised as the Invincible Plan in September 1993, and then further under an EU Action Plan in November) that returned to the Cutileiro approach. They further protested U.S. unwillingness to accept Russian-French-British modifications of the American-led Contact Group plan of July 1994, which shifted the two-entity, integral Bosnia toward a two-entity, confederal Bosnia in order to win Bosnian Serb acceptance. The Americans, for their part, accused each plan (and by implication the Europeans) of appeasing the Serbs, whom they insisted caused the war and were guilty of aggression against the legitimate state of Bosnia.

The Dayton accord combines elements of all previous plans, and it refuses to choose between the de facto partitioned Bosnia of ethnic enclaves (achieved with bloodshed and plunder rather than a Portuguese pen) and the integrated Bosnia of American, Bosnian Muslim, and Vance-Owen aspirations. The accord thus prolongs the conflict over Bosnia's political end state, both for warring parties and for Atlantic allies.

The fact that the Dayton accord is a compromise and draws substantially on previous peace plans, and also that it actually offers less to the Bosnian Muslims than the other plans in spite of the Americans' claim to have taken their side at Dayton, is secondary to Europeans. They have been impatient to end the war and their military and financial commitments there. Nonetheless, this diplomatic history fosters an element of cynical resignation to the American IFOR commanders' decisions when one or another European commander does not agree with them. The original French plan to stabilize Sarajevo first and gradually transfer

Serb-held territories to federation control, based on nearly four years of UN experience commanding Sector Sarajevo, was overruled by external pressure not to deviate from Dayton-prescribed deadlines. British units in Banja Luka that sighted Karadzic but chose not to detain him because they would have risked a shoot-out were sharply criticized by many. While sectoral and divisional IFOR commanders appear in remarkable harmony considering differences in their respective governments' military doctrines and policies, they have preserved the political cohesion that is essential to the unity of military command and control on which successful peacekeeping depends by sticking to a very narrow definition of their mandate. Their refusal to take on broader tasks, however, has provoked disillusionment and criticism—in Bosnia, the foreign media, and some national capitals—that threaten the credibility of IFOR and NATO. It also sets the scene for a possible repetition of the unraveling of the UN Protection Force (UNPROFOR).

For the most part, disagreements about the Dayton accord's intended political outcome have only rhetorical significance and hide more substantive conflicts of interest. Nonetheless, the widespread view in Europe that U.S. negotiators made private deals with the Bosnian Muslims at Dayton has encouraged some Europeans to do the same on the ground, keeping their national interests primary while provoking U.S. accusations that overtures (by the British and French among others) to Bosnian Serbs undermine the accord. By defining policy positions in terms of political loyalties to one side in Bosnia, the quarrel over whether the country has been partitioned or can be reconstituted also threatens to become serious as events on the ground force new decisions. Those issues include when elections should be held; how to react if one party chooses to boycott the elections; whether to arrest Karadzic and Mladic; and what to do if Bosnian Croat and Bosnian Serb delegates to a newly elected parliament decide to create special relationships, respectively, with Croatia and Yugoslavia (which is their right according to the Dayton constitution).

The global debate about whether the country is being partitioned and who is responsible has a tendency to hide other issues of consequence, such as the role of Russia after its presidential elections if the arbitration decision or IFOR departure leads to violence at Brcko, where the Russian battalion is deployed within the American division, and the role of the Spanish Catholics in the EU's administration of Mostar.

Far more serious for the fate of the operation and for major-power relations is a second category of quarrels, over the approach to peace building. The Dayton accord contains two contradictory approaches for transforming the ceasefire into a sustainable peace. The approaches, which separate most Europeans from the Americans, are classic peacekeeping principles and mutual deterrence by military equilibrium between the two entities, the Muslim-Croat federation and the Republika Srpska. Because most European countries with troops in IFOR also participated in UNPROFOR, and many were deployed in federation territory after the March 1994 Washington agreement (of which the Dayton accord is simply an extension to Serb-held territories), they have experience in implementing ceasefires according to peacekeeping principles. This experience includes residual resentments over the damage done to UNPROFOR and its credibility by U.S. policy to end the war by creating a military balance on the ground and pressure to use UNPROFOR for this purpose (such as bombing Bosnian Serb military targets and looking the other way at arms deliveries to the federation and the offensives of the Croatian and Bosnian armies against the Serbs). Pentagon insistence on robust rules of engagement for IFOR were a direct criticism of the peacekeeping principles adhered to by the Europeans in UNPROFOR: impartiality, consent, and a minimal and proportionate use of force. U.S. calls for peace enforcement and European peacekeeping principles (personified by General Sir Michael Rose's definition of a "Mogadishu line" that could not be crossed) reflected differences in military doctrines; those conflicts should be meliorated by the fact that IFOR is in Bosnia to implement a signed ceasefire agreement, in contrast to the raging war UNPROFOR faced. But the conflicts over military doctrine have also been finessed by combining prior consensus among major troop contributors on the principle of consent with these more robust rules of engagement and equipment.

This lingering difference and European resentment at American pressure throughout 1993–1995 for a policy of "lift and strike"—lift the arms embargo and bomb the Serbs—when European countries were actively pursuing a negotiated solution and had soldiers on the ground to aid civilians (at the same time that the Pentagon insisted on unusually narrow rules of engagement for American soldiers in Croatia and Macedonia so as to prevent any casualties) are being revived by sharp differences of opinion on the contradictory programs for military stabilization in the Dayton accord. The intense European preference for arms control and a "build down" of all military forces in the region, being pursued in OSCE-formula negotiations in Vienna, is in direct conflict with the U.S. policy to "build up" Bosnian (federation) forces under a multimillion-dollar program of "train and equip" required by the U.S. Congress in exchange for approval of troop deployment.[4] An arms race in the Balkans begins to impinge directly on European national-security interests.

This bitter conflict also reflects deeper philosophical approaches at the heart of the new European identity since the Helsinki accord of 1975. Peace and stability result from democracy and economic prosperity, not from armies trained and equipped by the United States (in the minds of most Europeans who benefited from the Marshall Plan). As a potential European country, Bosnia-Herzegovina must eventually meet European conditions that require demonstrated commitment to a pluralistic democracy, a market economy, and respect for human rights. The dispute over the certification of elections is about the larger issue of how to build a sustainable peace. U.S. insistence on September elections so that IFOR can exit after 12 months reinforces the Europeans' doubts about the United States' long-term military commitment to the security of Europe. The American belief in the magic of elections—held rigidly without regard to the time required to create conditions for a free and fair outcome—brings home the irreconcilable differences over the cause and remedy of the war. Was it a civil war for which there can only be a stable, internal constitutional solution (or does the refusal to consider a change in the external borders of Bosnia-Herzegovina require it to be treated as such)? Or was it a war of external aggression for which military solutions are sufficient for peace?

Confrontation over the issue cannot easily be avoided in the second six months as the timing of elections and its tie to IFOR's exit date, on the one hand, and a sustainable peace, on the other, bring into the open discussions about a follow-on force and its composition. NATO allies refuse to continue a military presence without U.S. ground troops. The NATO reforms aimed at circumventing that problem with a European-mounted Combined Joint Task Force, although adopted in Berlin on 3–4 June, will not have been hammered out in operational and command detail before the NATO summit in December.

Dayton's long-term viability is also trapped by a third fundamental disagreement: how wars end. Western Europeans saw the American approach after World War II to combine the Nuremberg trials and military occupation with the Marshall Plan, which gave aid in exchange for European economic and political cooperation to overcome border conflicts and wartime hostility. In the Bosnia conflict, the United States has taken on the role of guardian of an existing international order and its norms, and thus it has focused its attention more narrowly on the punishment and deterrence of war crimes and aggression and on the military defense of borders. Regarding the economic assistance that is considered essential to consolidate the peace, the United States has insisted on giving to the Croat-Muslim federation alone and on isolating the Bosnian Serbs. The Europeans counter that economic reconstruction must occur throughout the country and must aim to reintegrate its parts, if the goal is peace and a single country. This dispute emerged early on in the planning stages for IFOR and at Dayton. The Pentagon insisted on a complete separation between military and civilian aspects rather than the integration that Europeans with peacekeeping experience knew was necessary, and it blamed Europeans for delays in the civilian operation. The Europeans insisted that the cause of such delays was that very separation and tardy American commitment of funds for civilian (as opposed to military) tasks and assistance. There were reportedly intense battles in the back rooms at Wright-Patterson over who would get the prize of high representative for the civilian tasks (particularly between the United States, France, and the EU, and the eventual victors, Swede Carl Bildt and German Michael Steiner) and over the U.S. statements that because it would pay a large share of the military costs, the Europeans must bear the burden of financing the civilian side. Public statements by Holbrooke and other American diplomats assigning financial responsibility for longer-term tasks of economic reconstruction to the Europeans contrasted with the curious absence of European finance ministers—who were expected to foot the bill and persuade their parliaments—from Dayton. The Europeans argued that they had been bearing heavy military and humanitarian costs alone in Bosnia since 1992.

The continuing fights over turf and budgets—between the Europeans and Americans, among EU commissioners, between the White House and Congress, between High Representative Bildt and the U.S. government, and between IFOR and the civilian operation—stalled much of the actual civilian work in the first three months. That fighting has been replaced by differing perspectives on the use of conditionality—withholding funds until parties have complied with particular obligations as opposed to using economic assistance as a positive incentive to entice cooperation, withdrawing it later if the parties do not comply—and whether instituting harsher conditions for the Republika Srpska is a counterproductive tactic in the long run. The overwhelming focus on indicted war criminals intensifies the disagreements on the role of economic reconstruction in ending the war as the separate issue of elections approaches, because of the odd position that elections will not be free and fair if Karadzic and Mladic remain free in Bosnia and the clause in the Dayton accord that economic aid must be withheld from any community that does not cooperate with the Hague tribunal. American calls at the 2 June summit in Geneva to reimpose sanctions on Serbia proper if President Slobodan Milosevic does not hand over the two men will compound the dispute. Europeans have already established diplomatic relations with the Federal Republic of Yugoslavia (the United States has not), and they now see sanctions as essentially unenforceable and counterproductive.

REAL ISSUES AT STAKE

Western policy toward Bosnia in 1992–1995 was a policy of containment: to do whatever was necessary to keep the war and its consequences from spreading over borders (through humanitarian aid to keep refugees at home; sanctions on Serbia and Montenegro that would close the border; troops in Macedonia as a tripwire; and limits on the virulence of war through an arms embargo, a no-fly zone, and economic sanctions). Equally, if not more, important was its containment of major-power conflict. By the summer of 1995, the policy had failed in the second goal. The fall of Srebrenica to Bosnian Serb forces, the rumors of horrible massacres that mobilized European public opinion to intervene directly, the challenge tossed to NATO and U.S. President Bill Clinton by French President Jacques Chirac to defend the remaining UN-declared safe areas (especially Zepa, Gorazde, and Bihac), and French and British preparations for a rapid-reaction force to withdraw their UNPROFOR units from Bosnia after the hostage crisis in May; the month of July presented Clinton with unavoidable crisis in NATO. At the same time, European impatience with the Bosnia engagement, with its financial and military costs, with the refugees unwilling or unable to return, and with the serious damage to the credibility of both the United Nations and NATO became a common denominator on which they could agree, pushing substantive disagreements into second place and acceding to the Clinton administration's position on the war.

The Dayton accord and subsequent decisions during the first phase of implementation have reinstated those disagreements, however. Major-power conflict has been dodged by not specifying one political end state in Bosnia or one coherent strategy for building peace and ending the war. While the purpose of the Dayton peace process is still to prevent the spread of war, the priority given to the goal of containing conflicts among the major powers has turned the focus to operational matters: whether they can get in and get out before their fundamental disagreements about Bosnia and peacemaking boomerang. This solution makes the conflicts over upcoming issues unusually contentious because they all affect when IFOR can leave. Those issues are: when elections should be held; whether to accept election results if there are major irregularities, boycotts, or violence; whether to reimpose sanctions on Serbia because of Karadzic and Mladic; how to address possible delays in the decision on Brcko, in the arms-control negotiations in Vienna, and in Croat-Muslim integration; and what the force structure and command arrangements of a NATO follow-on force should be.

The rhetoric of disappointment with Dayton's first six months is that the Paris accord is the parties' agreement and that it is their political will and commitment that will decide whether it works—but that is not the case. No matter how much the intervening powers would like to quit the scene, hoping to limit their engagement and leave the quarreling parties to resolve their conflicts alone, they cannot do so. They now have too much at stake. This, in turn, makes them vulnerable to manipulation by Bosnian parties that try to extract more resources and commitments from outsiders by playing them off against each other. If political cohesion begins to break down, the decision-making mechanisms of the North Atlantic Council—its painstaking process of ensuring consensus among at least the core states (the Quad Four)—is not likely to be adequate to the task. The Peace Implementation Council is an ad hoc group with no experience in resolving differences. The Dayton accord provided no executive authority for the entire operation that is able to make policy decisions, resolve differences where necessary, or define a strategy for peace.

[1]See Pauline Neville-Jones, "Don't Blame the Europeans," *Financial Times,* 17 May 1996, response to Richard Holbrooke's piece in *Time,* 20 May 1996.

[2]U.S. Secretary of State Warren Christopher, "Leadership for the Next American Century," address before the John F. Kennedy School of Government, Harvard University, 18 January 1996. (U.S. Department of State official transcript.)

[3]An extremely useful survey by the chief legal expert and author for the constitutional aspects of most of the peace plans, Paul C. Szasz, is "The Quest for a Bosnian Constitution: Legal Aspects of Constitutional Proposals Relating to Bosnia," *Fordham International Law Journal,* vol. 19, no. 2 (December 1995), pp. 363–407.

[4]See James Risen and Doyle McManus, "U.S. OK'd Iran Arms for Bosnia, Officials Say," *Los Angeles Times,* 5 April 1996.

STABILIZING PARTITION WITH SFOR
by JANUSZ BUGAJSKI

NATO's reduced mission in Bosnia has many of the same objectives as its predecessor but fewer people with which to carry them out. Ultimately, the international military presence will probably reinforce, not overcome, the ethnic division of the country.

Despite U.S. President Bill Clinton's pledge that one year would be sufficient to ensure peace and stability in Bosnia-Herzegovina, NATO has extended its mission another 18 months. The 12–month mandate was clearly unrealistic given the deep political and ethnic divisions in Bosnian society as well as the unstable and unpredictable regional climate. The NATO-led Implementation Force (IFOR) has been transformed into a Stabilization Force (SFOR) on the assumption that a prolonged international military presence will be essential in implementing the civilian and political ingredients of the Dayton accord. SFOR began operating in mid-December and has already embarked on such tasks as confiscating unregistered weapons and ammunition.

The IFOR mission was eminently successful in its military objectives: enforcing the separation of rival armies, monitoring munitions, and deterring combat. But the implementation of the civil and political aspects of the Dayton agreement left a lot to be desired. Neither NATO nor the Organization for Security and Cooperation in Europe (OSCE) nor any other international agency was able to ensure freedom of movement, the return of refugees and displaced people to their homes, or the arrest of more than a handful of indicted war criminals.

Moreover, numerous loose ends were left in attempts at the institutional re-stitching of the country. Instead of joining together the two halves of Bosnia, the elections held last September merely created a facade of unity for the benefit of the international community without fostering political or social integration. Behind the facade, ethnic homogenization and the consolidation in power of ethno-nationalist political forces were further strengthened and legitimized, thus enshrining ethnically based partition.

In such an inauspicious environment, the prolonged NATO operation seems destined primarily to maintain peace but not to restore a viable single state. The economic, diplomatic, and military levers applied so far have fallen short of the initial, optimistic predictions. There is little reason to believe that, with a much-reduced NATO contingent, the practical impact on the three protagonists will prove any greater. On the contrary, new dangers lurk for SFOR. Political instability, social unrest, and brewing military conflicts could further accentuate allied disputes over the means and ends of the NATO mission.

ALLIED DISPUTES

The IFOR mission officially expired on 20 December 1996. Numbering some 58,000 soldiers at its peak, it was scaled down gradually over the course of

1996. NATO peace enforcers have now been committed until the middle of 1998, when the next general elections in Bosnia-Herzegovina have been scheduled by the OSCE. But the SFOR contingent is substantially smaller than IFOR; NATO leaders are evidently seeking a credible exit strategy.

After some internal wrangling, NATO finally agreed to deploy between 25,000 and 30,000 troops from approximately 30 countries, with a more elaborate reserve force stationed in nearby states. NATO Secretary-General Javier Solana has said the alliance plans to review the size of the force in June, with a view to reducing it significantly during the latter part of the year.[1] SFOR will rely heavily on air reconnaissance and intelligence gathering to make up for its smaller size. NATO will also retain the capability to rapidly send troops back into Bosnia in case of emergency.

Shortly after his re-election in November, Clinton announced that the United States would dispatch troops to participate in a NATO follow-on force for an 18-month period. The mission's purpose was to help stabilize the country and maintain the security conditions necessary for rebuilding a joint state. In order to dampen unrealistic expectations, however, then-Defense Secretary William Perry was quick to point out that the new NATO operation would not in and of itself guarantee peace and stability because "the Bosnians themselves are going to have to make those changes."[2] Nonetheless, Clinton's announcement provoked some domestic criticism and sparked some disputes with the European allies who sought closer consultation with the White House.

At its peak, the U.S. force in IFOR numbered 15,600 inside Bosnia and a further 7,000 support forces in Croatia, Hungary, or Italy. In contrast, the American SFOR contingent, although still the largest of the allied contributions, numbers 8,500 and will be cut back in accordance with overall NATO reductions during the mission. An additional 4,000 to 5,000 U.S. military personnel are to be deployed to the region as reinforcements in case of an emergency.

Clinton delayed announcing his decision on SFOR until after the election. Yet, largely because of the lack of American casualties, Bosnia barely registered as an election issue. While some Republican lawmakers were critical of extending the NATO mission with a continuing U.S. presence, their voices were neither loud enough nor persuasive enough to resonate publicly following the presidential election.

In addition, most influential Republicans agreed that the NATO operation should be prolonged, even though the question of cost appeared likely to cause future disputes with the White House. As long as the American contingent in Bosnia does not sustain combat casualties, the timing and cost of NATO's planned enlargement to Central Europe will figure more prominently in policy debates than the SFOR mission.

For several months, NATO planners had debated over the Bosnian follow-on force. Four possible scenarios were considered: continuation of the IFOR mission in its existing structure, total NATO withdrawal, deployment of a small deterrence force to prevent a fresh outbreak of fighting, and deployment of a "deterrence plus" force capable of performing a broader mission. In November, it was decided to pursue the last option: continuing NATO's military tasks in ensuring a stable security environment and providing some assistance for civilian reconstruction. NATO ambassadors gave unanimous consent to the reduced multinational force in mid-November. An operational plan for SFOR was produced by the end of November; it was approved at the NATO ministerial meeting in mid-December and by a United Nations Security Council resolution.

Although in September NATO leaders had approved in principle the stationing of a new Bosnia force, the European allies were at odds with Washington over the size and longevity of the follow-on mission. Some governments expressed concern that the White House had failed to consult them before declaring plans to redeploy U.S. forces for an additional 18 months. The British Foreign Office, for example, claimed that many of the European powers that had agreed to supply troops expected the new tour of duty to last 12 months.

As a result of the American position, the NATO governments needed to adjust their planning and preparations and re-examine the length of their commitments. Britain agreed to provide the second largest contingent, 5,000 troops. Paris preferred a two-year SFOR mandate but finally committed itself to about 2,500 troops. Germany announced it would contribute a contingent of similar size, although it preferred a more restricted 12–month mission.

Transatlantic disputes have also been evident over the American-led program to equip and train the Bosnian army. Washington maintains that such a program will enable Bosnia to defend itself in the future by creating greater balance between Bosnian and Serbian forces. According to the Clinton administration, the program will also render future NATO military actions in defense of Bosnian integrity unnecessary. The "equip" part of the program finally got off the ground in late November 1996, after Sarajevo agreed to dismiss a deputy defense minister who allegedly had close ties with Iran. A $100 million arms shipment was subsequently delivered as the first part of a $400 million program.

The Western Europeans have in general been opposed to the "equip and train" policy, arguing that it will create additional instabilities and even endanger the new NATO mission. They point out that two fundamental conditions of the program have not been met: the combination of the Croatian and Bosnian armies into a single federation force and progress in regional arms reductions. Indeed, OSCE officials admit that the arms reductions are significantly behind schedule. The Europeans claim that the Bosnian Serbs are unlikely to comply with arms-reduction proposals so as not to be outgunned by federation forces.

MISSION: IMPROBABLE

Dayton promised peace with justice in Bosnia-Herzegovina. But while peace has been ensured by the NATO presence, at least temporarily, justice has clearly not been secured, and limited progress has been made toward ethnic and political reintegration. SFOR's primary mission, therefore, will be to act as a deterrent against any new outbreak of fighting. As a result, NATO troops were dispatched to the major trouble spots along the interentity boundary. While NATO planners contend that SFOR will conduct a more selective mission than IFOR did, some officials believe that it could assume a more prominent role in supporting civil and political reconstruction.

The international community's December 1996 conference in London on the implementation of the Dayton agreement set new deadlines for the numerous civil and political reconstruction tasks that had not been completed during the previous year. Arms reductions are now slated to be completed by this October, municipal elections need to be held by summer, a central bank is to be operational by early in the year, and a new all-Bosnian flag must be approved by the close of the year. The conference also pushed the Bosnian authorities to take steps toward privatization, toward formulating an integrated fiscal and foreign-trade policy, and toward establishing a viable customs service. Numerous objectives were specified in the realms of human rights, democracy building, and state reconstruction.

Among the most criticized features of the NATO operation has been its failure to apprehend war criminals on all three sides of the conflict, and SFOR looks to be no improvement over IFOR on that front. Only seven out of 74 indicted war criminals are in custody at the International Criminal Tribunal in The Hague. All the detainees are low-level alleged culprits and not the high-ranking officials who planned and organized mass murders, rapes, and evictions. Although NATO troops reportedly know the whereabouts of the major alleged war criminals, they have avoided capturing them lest casualties be sustained and the Dayton process be further undermined by public protests and political boycotts. In the Republika Srpska, several suspects continue to serve as local officials and security officers. The Bosnian Serb government rejects the authority of the Hague tribunal and refuses to extradite any of the accused.

Despite the public disappearance of Radovan Karadzic and his replacement by Biljana Plavsic as the Bosnian Serb leader, Karadzic continues to exercise some control from behind the scenes. For instance, the recent sidelining of General Ratko Mladic, the commander of the Bosnian Serb army, was reportedly orchestrated by Karadzic in order to resolve the continuing conflicts between the Serbian civilian and military leaderships. While the international community praised Mladic's replacement, viewing it as a step toward his appearance at the war-crimes tribunal, in fact his dismissal primarily served to strengthen political and police control in the Serbian entity.

Some analysts calculate that the consolidation of a more repressive police force in the Republika Srpska may prove more challenging for NATO. The police have actually been held responsible for attacks on Muslims seeking to return to their home villages. SFOR enforcement of future efforts at free movement could bring NATO troops into collision with Bosnian Serb police units.

Some NATO-country officials, including German Foreign Minister Klaus Kinkel, have urged a more robust "seek and detain" NATO policy on war crimes. But there is little consensus on pursuing that option. Carl Bildt, the international community's high representative in Bosnia-Herzegovina, has suggested that new measures might be used to arrest indicted war criminals if the former warring parties refuse to hand over suspects themselves. However, no such role has been specified either for NATO or for the international police force in Bosnia.

The European Union's external-affairs commissioner, Hans van den Broek, has emphasized that economic threats were not effective enough in pressuring the Bosnian, Croatian, and Serbian authorities to implement the civilian aspects of the Dayton agreement. He said NATO needs to take more forceful measures. But Bildt and van den Broek may be threatening policies that NATO leaders are unwilling to adopt. Indeed, President Clinton's new national-security adviser, Sandy Berger, while conceding that more effective steps needed to be taken to ensure the capture of alleged war criminals, also reiterated that U.S. troops would play a largely backup role in any effort to hunt down suspects.[3] Some officials have proposed the deployment to Bosnia of specially trained police units to capture the indicted war criminals, but such suggestions have aroused controversy within NATO ranks.

Several private organizations have also urged NATO to become more assertive. The International Crisis Group, a private monitoring commission with broad international membership, delivered a report to the London conference appealing to Western forces to actively seek out alleged war criminals. Although direct military action is probably the only sure way in which high-level indicted war criminals will be apprehended, such an approach appears unlikely given Western fears of casualties at a time when the NATO contingent is being reduced in size and resources.

Observers have contended that without the capture and trial of the major war criminals there can be no justice or reconciliation in Bosnian society. And without justice and reconciliation, neither democracy nor peace can flourish. Nonetheless, the international community has not considered the war-crimes issue its highest priority. Insufficient authority and resources have been provided to the Hague tribunal, and the tribunal itself was only afforded observer status at the London conference—an indication that concrete deeds on the war-crimes issue rarely match the stirring words of diplomats. Although there were promises of more resources for the tribunal, there can be little hope for major improvements in the court's work in the absence of strong pressure on the governments of Bosnia, Croatia, and Serbia.

NATO has also failed to ensure the return of refugees and freedom of movement for all Bosnian residents, a key ingredient of the reconstruction and democratization processes. According to UN estimates, only 250,000 of Bosnia's 2.5 million refugees and displaced people were able to return to their homes during 1996, and almost none ventured across interethnic boundaries. All three sides have blatantly hampered freedom of movement, especially in the Serbian- and Croatian-majority areas. Local authorities have effectively barred refugees from returning home, often by bombing their houses or engineering protests by current residents.

Over the past year, right under the eyes of NATO troops and OSCE observers, ethnic homogenization continued through the forced eviction of minority families and the settlement of members of majority ethnic groups in the homes of those expelled. Moreover, human-rights violations continue, including harassment of and discrimination against minorities who have no viable international protection.

The international community now has an opportunity to carefully prepare for and organize the municipal elections, which were twice postponed because of blatant manipulation, particularly by the Bosnian Serb administration. In order to help implement civil and political reconstruction, the OSCE extended its mission to Bosnia for the next year. In particular, the organization will again be responsible for the conduct of local elections scheduled for the summer.

According to some reports, OSCE officials have made an inauspicious start in preparations for the ballot. A secret deal was apparently struck with representatives from the Republika Srpska under which Serbian refugees will be allowed to vote where they choose as long as they can provide some proof of future residence, such as an invitation from a relative, a promise of housing, or an offer of employment.[4] Clearly, the registration and voting process will remain susceptible to wide-scale abuse.

SFOR will evidently be mobilized to provide security for election officials and voters in the upcoming ballot. NATO planners have also left open the option of calling in additional reserve forces for the elections. But numerous problems can already be foreseen, particularly in the absence of freedom of movement to register and vote. Potentially explosive situations could arise, particularly if Muslim voters insist on returning to their home villages to prevent them from falling permanently into Serbian hands. Robert Frowick, who heads the OSCE mission in Bosnia, believes that a smaller force will be sufficient to ensure a successful election—but that depends on how you define success.

Elections aside, the leaders of the three ethnic groups have drawn international ire for failing to establish the joint political institutions required under Dayton, including a functioning council of ministers at the interentity level. Concerns are regularly voiced that deliberate institutional delays will obstruct integration and jeopardize the prospects of rebuilding a common state. The three members of the Bosnian presidency have found it difficult to agree on the composition and powers of the new government, partly because of Serbian obstructionism and partly because of the intricate attempts at ethnic balance between and within each ministry. Even when the new central government becomes operational, it may remain gridlocked and essentially paralyzed.

Participants at the London conference warned the three protagonists that further reconstruction assistance would be dependent on significantly greater cooperation. It was hoped that such warnings would persuade the Serbs in particular to be more cooperative, as the Republika Srpska only received 2 percent of the approximately $900 million in international aid to Bosnia during 1996. Failure to hand over war criminals or to permit refugees to return home would evidently delay any planned reconstruction work and could plunge the Republika Srpska deeper into poverty. Scheduled World Bank assistance in 1997, to the tune of $300 million in reconstruction projects, could be shelved if donor countries insist on conditionality.

Economic pressures alone are unlikely to be a significant enough lever to foster genuine state-building and collaboration. In addition, as Western governments contemplate the extent to which conditions should be attached to financial help, division and indecision have been apparent. Such disputes will probably be exploited by the Bosnian protagonists and will neutralize any concerted new policy initiatives. Furthermore, the 18–month limit on the SFOR operation will leave little time for political reconstruction and ethnic reconciliation to become an enduring reality.

MILITARY AND POLITICAL CHALLENGES

The SFOR contingent will also face additional security challenges during its mission. Military observers complain that insufficient progress has been achieved in the arms-reduction program. Indeed, over the past few months, a number of illicit arms caches have been detected and destroyed, especially on Serb-held territory. And that may be only the tip of the iceberg, particularly as clandestine shipments of weapons continue to find their way into the country. Although the traffic in arms may not directly endanger the SFOR contingent, the monitoring of it could preoccupy the new mission as all three sides endeavor to raise their combat readiness in preparation for the NATO departure.

Of more immediate concern is the unresolved issue of Brcko and the Posavina corridor. Renewed armed conflict could erupt if the arbitration committee's decision on the status of the region, postponed until mid-February, is not acceptable to the Republika Srpska. If the area around Brcko and the city itself is placed under Sarajevo's administration or under some international mandate (similar to the situation in Mostar), and if Muslim refugees are slated to return to the area, presumably SFOR would be called upon to enforce those decisions. NATO troops might then face conflicts with Serbian residents and even with Bosnian Serb soldiers or police officers. Alternatively, the agreement could remain on paper only and would not prevent the consolidation of ethnic partition.

In the longer term, renewed military action can be expected once NATO speeds up the withdrawal of its forces. Indeed, some analysts have speculated that the Muslim side may become increasingly emboldened during the next year as a result of its acquisition of new weapons and training. The morale of the army of Bosnia-Herzegovina is reportedly higher than that of the Republika Srpska's army, and a number of prominent Muslim leaders are evidently committed to regaining the Muslim-majority territories in eastern Bosnia that were lost to the Serbs at the outset of the war.[5]

The international community also needs to contend with the Slobodan Milosevic and Franjo Tudjman factors in the Bosnian imbroglio. The Serbian and Croatian leaders have been generally viewed as stabilizing players, not because they are committed peacemakers (as both claim to their domestic and international audiences) but because they possess the capacity to diminish armed conflicts and influence their compatriots within Bosnia. However, it is evident that they are not fully committed to the integration process and continue to favor some form of partition once the ethnically homogeneous territories are stabilized by the international community. Furthermore, neither Milosevic nor Tudjman has been cooperative in surrendering indicted war criminals.

As the democratic credentials of the Serbian and Croatian presidents come under increasing international scrutiny as a result of growing unrest within their own borders, the Western powers may conclude that alternative political leaders in both states may be more favorably disposed toward fully implementing the Dayton agreement. While both Belgrade and Zagreb were reasonably quiet, significant internal leeway was given Milosevic and Tudjman by the international community. But the last few months have starkly exposed the autocratic and repressive basis of their governance as well as the widespread public opposition to their policies.

Clearly, Western governments must seriously rethink the intricate relationships among politics in Serbia, Croatia, and Bosnia. If either Milosevic or Tudjman is incapacitated or ousted during the coming months, new political forces may take control over whom the West could exert more influence and fully revoke any claims to a "greater Serbia" or a "greater Croatia."

The replacement of either Milosevic or Tudjman would have reverberations in the Republika Srpska and the Herceg-Bosna quasi-state. It is too early, however, to see whether that would lead to power struggles and social instability and whether it would actually strengthen or weaken the nationalist and separatist option in either para-state. Nevertheless, NATO planners have to be prepared for significant political changes in Serbia and Croatia that could directly affect the mandate in Bosnia-Herzegovina.

[1] Reuters, 4 and 9 December 1996.

[2] Ibid., 27 November 1996.

[3] See R. Jeffrey Smith, "Push on Bosnia War Crimes Pledged," *The Washington Post*, 9 December 1996.

[4] Reuters, 5 December 1996.

[5] David L. Bosco, "The Coming Bosnia Breakdown," *The Washington Post*, 8 December 1996.

NEW THREATS TO NATIONAL SECURITY
by CHRISTOPHER ULRICH

With the Soviet Union and the Warsaw Pact consigned to history, the former communist states have found themselves ill-prepared for the new threats to their security posed by organized crime, ethno-national conflicts, and militant religious fundamentalism. Especially in the former Soviet Union and the Balkans, deeply entrenched corruption and the largely unchecked use of violence for criminal as well as political ends are undermining the establishment of democracy and civil society.

During the Cold War, the possibility of armed conflict between the military forces of NATO and the Warsaw Pact was seen as the main threat to security in Europe. The second major security issue was the socialist states' periodic use of their armed forces to suppress popular uprisings. With the end of the Cold War, the retreat of the Soviet army from Central Europe, and the breakup of the Soviet Union and the Warsaw Pact, those traditional security issues receded in importance.

The wars in the former Yugoslavia and Chechnya showed that the capacity of state-sponsored armies to wage war has not diminished. At the same time, however, a host of new challenges to public order have arisen, many of them stemming from nonstate actors, from criminal gangs to nationalist movements. Social scientists have been rather slow to realize the scope and seriousness of these phenomena and to analyze the threat they pose to the coherence of civil society.

The threats are not in fact new, for the most part, but were merely suppressed or hidden during the communist period. They are also not unique to the post-communist world. In recent years, established democracies from France to the United States have faced attacks on public order from terrorists, militant fundamentalists, and criminal gangs. They, too, have found that the wealth and expertise they poured into developing large, high-tech armed forces are not of much use in dealing with the new security problems.

Initially, it was optimistically assumed that once the institutions of the communist state were overthrown and the foundations of a market economy were put in place, democratization, civil society, and the rule of law would steadily develop in the post-communist states. In practice, in many of the countries in transition, those processes have been undermined by the resurgence of formerly hidden or ignored threats to public order. Those threats include organized crime, corruption, criminal-related violence, terrorism, piracy, separatism, political extremism, and militant religious fundamentalism. Many of those categories overlap—for example, the line between criminal activity and ethno-nationalist conflict is often blurred, as in the case of Chechnya, where kidnapping for ransom by bandit groups has been a prominent feature of the conflict with Moscow.

Organized crime and institutionalized corruption are persistent and entrenched features of many of these societies, with widespread implications for regional and international stability. The domination of the old Communist Party of the Soviet Union, according to Louise Shelley, has been partly replaced by the controls of organized crime, which have penetrated most of the newly independent states of the former Soviet Union at all levels of government.[1] Many of the old communist elites or their offspring have been able to reinvent and assimilate themselves into the new environment. Those elites had very little understanding of, or commitment to, the concepts of civil society or the legitimate side of a free-market economy. As a result, organized crime, corruption, the black economy, the state bureaucracy, and the legitimate economy have become intermingled and consolidated.

Thus, the current transition has brought about the growing interdependence of security, democratization, and economic liberalization. Criminal groups can enrich themselves through the new quasi-market environment and use their wealth to buy themselves into the democratic process. In Russia and in the states of the former Yugoslavia, organized crime has supplanted many of the basic functions of the existing state structures and has helped finance the elections of new members to parliament.

Deteriorating social conditions, a depressed economy, rising crime rates, widespread corruption, discontent within the military, internal subversion, and ethno-national tensions are a potent brew weakening public confidence in democratic regimes and facilitating retrenchment toward authoritarian rule. Charles Gati wrote this year that "at least 20 of the 27 post-communist states are facing the prospect of neither democracy nor totalitarianism."[2] Samuel Huntington warned in 1991 that there is always a danger that new democracies, with relatively weak traditions of democratic values, may slip under the control of authoritarian or semiauthoritarian rulers offering simplistic solutions to the mounting social insecurity, the breakdown of order, and the political polarization that usually accompanies rapid socioeconomic change.[3]

The security challenges unleashed by the end of communism are themselves a product of market reform, democratization, and the emergence of independent countries in the wake of a single superpower. Ironically, they in turn threaten the very processes that gave rise to them; they undermine national sovereignty, legitimate economic liberalization, and the development of democratic institutions and values. The new security challenges eat away at the foundations needed for the introduction or establishment of democratic practices and a coherent market economy.

Those processes are most seriously advanced in the countries of the former Soviet Union and the Balkans. Most of Central Europe will probably escape the vicious circle of instability that has gripped many of the countries farther east. In Russia, despite the verbal commitment of Boris Yeltsin's administration to reform, the economy continues to shrink, while the social fabric is falling apart and political institutionalization is fragile.

GROWING TOGETHER: TERRORISM AND ORGANIZED CRIME

In a speech to the November 1994 World Ministerial Conference on Organized Transnational Crime in Naples, Italy, United Nations Secretary-General Boutros

Boutros-Ghali remarked: "A sociologist recently posed the question, 'What does a market without a state and without rules of law resemble? The jungle. And what organization is born of the jungle? The mafia.' "

Media coverage of the more sensational features of organized crime in Russia and its international activities have brought it to the attention of the Western public.[4] Organized crime and institutionalized corruption are not new phenomena to the former Soviet Union and East-Central Europe. They have existed in the region since the days of the Austrian emperors and Russian tsars but were suppressed or hidden from view during the communist era. However, particularly in parts of the Soviet Union, corruption and criminal activity became firmly institutionalized beneath the surface during the rule of Leonid Brezhnev, from 1964 to 1982.

According to Graham Turbiville, members of the communist elite and the security services cooperated with organized criminal groups and used the illicit economy as a parallel system to further their personal interests.[5] Such connections have expanded and strengthened in the post-socialist transition to such an extent that it casts into doubt the very integrity of democratization and market reform. Criminals operating on a national and transnational level rely on a spectrum of networks, including those currently or formerly within the state structure (such as government bureaucracies, the armed forces and veterans' organizations, the security services and informal networks of former agents, and state banks and trading companies) and other kinds of connections (such as ethnic ties or sports clubs). Particularly worrying is the criminalization of parts of the armed forces.[6]

Greatly increased opportunities to travel and trade internationally have allowed many of these criminal networks to expand far beyond their original scope. According to John Deutch, director of the U.S. Central Intelligence Agency, criminals from the former Soviet Union were operating in about 30 countries in 1994, rising to 50 by 1996.[7] The parameters of their activities are virtually unlimited—government corruption, drug trafficking, weapons proliferation, terror, embezzlement of state property, contract murder, bank fraud, extortion, money laundering, organized prostitution, vehicle theft and smuggling, alien smuggling, counterfeiting, illegal exportation of cultural objects and strategic material, and, at least potentially, theft and trafficking of low-grade radioactive material and nuclear technology.

Particularly where order is severely disrupted by ethno-national conflicts, organized crime and political terrorism tend to intertwine. In 1994, a UN document observed that "in considering the activities of transnational criminal organizations, both the use of terror tactics and links with terrorist and guerrilla organizations are recurring themes. The motives of terrorist groups and criminal organizations may differ, but the strategies they adopt to achieve their objectives are increasingly indistinguishable."[8] According to Turbiville, in "new or reinvigorated centers of interethnic conflict, insurgency and various forms of terrorism have acquired an organized-crime content that in many cases blurs the distinction between political and criminal agendas in and out of governments."[9]

Tactics used in criminal violence and terrorism in the former Soviet Union, East-Central Europe, and the Balkans in the post-communist era include assassination, hostage taking, arson, bombings of cars and buildings, air and maritime hijacking, and kidnapping (where ethnic cleansing has been carried out, add to that list rape, sniping, and attacks on homes and communities by neighbors, mobs, and paramilitary squads). Among the violent incidents this summer in Moscow were a bomb blast on the subway on 11 June that killed four people and two bombings on trolleybuses the next month. On 6 August, a bomb exploded beside a Moscow highway minutes before Prime Minister Viktor Chernomyrdin drove by. No one claimed responsibility for any of those attacks; suggested perpetrators included criminal groups, radical communists, the Russian military, Chechen separatists, rogue politicians, and even elements within the Russian government intent on postponing the presidential election.[10]

Hijacking and kidnapping have been integral parts of the Chechen war. Indeed, aircraft and bus hijackings were common even before federal forces invaded the republic in December 1994. In June 1995 (in Budennovsk) and January 1996 (in Kizlyar and Pervomaiskoe), Chechen forces took hundreds of civilians hostage. In the wake of the Pervomaiskoe crisis, a Turkish ferry was seized en route from Trabzon to Sochi by hijackers who supported the Chechen cause. Then-Chechen President Dzhokhar Dudaev threatened to carry out terrorist acts against "the West" in retaliation for its support of the Russian government, although with his death and recent moves toward peace that threat seems to have receded.

Apart from ethnicity-based separatist movements, possible perpetrators of violent acts range from quasi-fascist groups and radical communists to millenarian sects of various religions.[11] For example, Aum Shinrikyo, the cult that carried out the sarin nerve-gas attacks in the Tokyo subway on 20 March 1995, spent large amounts of money advertising its presence in Russia in the early 1990s and claims 30,000 members in that country.

Terrorism, like organized crime, is not new to the former Soviet Union or East-Central Europe. It dates back at least to the 19th century, when nationalist, anti-imperialist, and revolutionary groups or individuals conducted campaigns of violence. Feliks Gross wrote in 1972 that the "theory of tactical, individual terror developed, perhaps even originated, in Russia," and it became a prominent feature of political life in Russia and the Balkans.[12] Elements of the state in those regions also launched campaigns of violence and terror against the populace in general as well as against specific sociopolitical movements.

To some extent, the upsurge in violence since 1989 can be seen as part of a broader historical pattern. Ethnic, religious, and territorial rivalries in the region could easily give birth to separatist or nationalist groups like the Irish Republican Army or the Basque Liberation Army. Terrorism could also originate in communist-oriented movements that oppose market reform and democratization. Also, the post-communist region could provide a base for terrorists from neighboring Middle Eastern states.[13] Sam Perry has even speculated that the former Soviet Union, in particular Central Asia and the northern Caucasus, could eventually replace the Middle East as the main source of state-sponsored international terrorism.[14]

SEARCHING FOR A NEW SECURITY PARADIGM

Before 1991, security challenges were traditionally perceived as originating outside the boundaries of the sovereign state. Now, with democratization and marketization, national boundaries have become more porous, and the distinction between external and internal threats has eroded. Increased migration, voluntary and forced; improvements in transportation and communications; and the globalization of financial flows have contributed to the process. The rise of variable forms of security challenges has refocused national-security debates away from the international arena toward law-enforcement and domestic-security concerns. That calls for the development of a new paradigm or approach that would move away from a narrowly based focus on military issues to a broad spectrum encompassing political, economic, and social factors.

The nature of the new security challenges seems to be well understood by Russian elites from liberal to conservative—although they differ over how to tackle the problems. Minister of Internal Affairs Anatolii Kulikov has observed that at Russia's current stage of development, during "its creation as a state and the implementation of democratic reform, new factors have emerged that threaten the security of the individual, the society, and the nation."[15] Many of the law-enforcement and internal-security forces of post-communist states recognized the need to refocus their attention from external military or espionage threats to domestic and transnational security. Just as these threats became increasingly visible in the late 1980s, however, the resources available to deal with them declined, and the judicial framework atrophied in the chaos of transition to democracy.

The Russian Security Council in November 1993 approved a new national-security and military doctrine that reflected the shift toward domestic concerns. It viewed the following factors as major challenges to domestic stability: the creation of illegal armed groups; organized crime; corruption; smuggling; the illicit proliferation of weapons, munitions, explosives, and other means used for subversion and terrorist acts on the territory of Russia; the drug trade; attacks on the facilities of nuclear, chemical, and biological industries and other facilities; and attacks on arsenals, arms depots, and arms enterprises with the aim of capturing weapons.[16]

According to a publication put out by the U.S. Special Operations Command in January 1996, in the post-Cold War world one sees in many regions a "breakdown of the authority of nation-states, [the] widening of social and economic disparities, and a degeneration of traditional societal mores. It is exacerbated by the re-emergence of long-repressed ethnic, religious, and cultural hatreds, the increased acceptance of violence as a means to resolve issues, and the rise of nonnational and transnational powers that threaten traditional nation-states. Examples include the collapse of central government authority and the rise of criminal cartels and insurrection in parts of the former Soviet Union [and] the

Balkans."[17] According to Scott MacDonald, these factors have "opened the door to a new age of transnational crime, terrorism, and small and destructive wars."[18]

Since the end of the Cold War, both European and American scholars have been trying to develop new concepts for dealing with those issues. The discussion falls under such headings as "weak states," "the problem of ungovernability," "low-intensity conflict," "operations other than war," and "gray-area phenomena." French criminologist Xavier Raufer argued that "to understand this complex problem, we need to develop a new conceptual approach or paradigm that integrates information on terrorism, narcotics trafficking, arms dealing, and political and ethnic conflict."[19] U.S. specialist Max Manwaring has urged the United States to orient its security policy toward such "gray-area" phenomena, which he takes to include terrorism, insurgencies, drug trafficking, warlordism, militant fundamentalism, ethnic cleansing, and civil war.[20]

Such approaches have been generally used to examine the political and socioeconomic situation in Latin America or Southeast Asia or transnational threats to the United States. But few efforts have yet been made to systematically apply such concepts to the emerging situation in the former Soviet Union, East-Central Europe, and the Balkans.

The challenge for Western states is how to develop a strategy for containing the growing wave of instability in the post-communist world. The traditional vehicle for establishing order is the state—and yet it is precisely the state in the countries in transition that has been undermined by these developments. The wave of new security challenges shows no sign of abating and threatens to undermine the fragile coalition for democratization and economic reform within the post-communist regimes. Anarchy, rather than a return to communism, is the specter haunting ex-communist Europe.[21]

[1]Louise Shelley, "Post-Soviet Organized Crime," *Demokratizatsiya,* vol. 2, no. 3, Summer 1994.

[2]Charles Gati, "The Mirage of Democracy," this volume, pp. 340–54.

[3]Samuel Huntington, *The Third Wave: Democratization in the Late Twentieth Century* (Norman, Oklahoma: University of Oklahoma Press, 1991), pp. 290–291.

[4]See Claire Sterling, *Crime Without Frontiers: The Worldwide Expansion of Organized Crime and the Pax Mafiosa* (London: Little, Brown, 1994); Stephen Handelman, *Comrade Criminal: The Theft of the Second Russian Revolution* (London: Michael Joseph, 1994); and Brian Freemantle, *The Octopus: Europe in the Grip of Organized Crime* (London: Orion Books, 1995).

[5]Graham Turbiville, "Operations Other Than War: Organized Crime," *Military Review,* January 1994, p. 45.

[6]Graham Turbiville, *Mafia in Uniform: The Criminalization of the Russian Armed Forces* (Fort Leavenworth, Kansas: U.S. Army Foreign Military Studies Office, 1995).

[7]John Diamond, "Crime Threatens Russian Democracy, CIA Says," *The Scotsman,* 1 May 1996, p. 10.

[8]UN Doc. E-Conf. 88/2, 1994, section on Transnational Criminal Organizations and Terrorism. See also Patterns of Global Terrorism (Washington, D.C.: U.S. State Department, 1995).

[9]Turbiville, "Operations Other Than War," p. 45.

[10]Paul Goble, "Who's Behind the Moscow Bombings?" RFE/RL news wire, 15 July 1996.

[11]Vladimir Prybylovsky, "What Awaits Russia: Fascism or a Latin American-style Dictatorship?" *Transition*, vol. 1, no. 10, 23 June 1995; Penny Morvant, "Cults Arouse Concern in Russia," *Transition*, vol. 2, no. 7, 5 April 1996.

[12]Feliks Gross, *Violence in Politics: Terror and Political Assassination in Eastern Europe and Russia* (The Hague/Paris: Mouton, 1972), p. 23.

[13]James Blagg, "European Terrorism: Down, but Not Out," *Military Review*, December 1994–February 1995, p. 16; Dennis Pluchinsky, "Academic Research on European Terrorist Developments: Pleas From a Government Terrorism Analyst," *Studies in Conflict and Terror*, vol. 15, pp. 18–19.

[14]Sam Perry, "Terrorism: A Frightening New Perspective," *CJ Europe*, vol. 11, no. 5, September–October 1995.

[15]Anatolii Kulikov, "Russian Internal Troops and Security Challenges in the 1990s," in Graham Turbiville Jr., ed., *Global Dimensions of High Intensity Crime and Low Intensity Conflict* (Chicago: Office of International Criminal Justice, University of Illinois, 1995).

[16]"Basic Provisions of the Military Doctrine of the Russian Federation," Jane's Intelligence Review-Special Report, January 1994.

[17]U.S. Special Operations Command Publications, Special Operations in Peace and War, 25 January 1996.

[18]Scott MacDonald, "The New 'Bad Guys': Exploring the Parameters of the Violent New World Order," in Max Manwaring, ed., *Gray Area Phenomena: Confronting the New World Order* (Boulder, Colorado: Westview Press, 1993), p. 33.

[19]Xavier Raufer, "Background Paper: The 'Gray Areas,' " conference paper, October 1991.

[20]Dick Ward, "Gray Area Phenomena: The Changing Nature of Organized Crime and Terrorism," *CI International*, vol. 11, no. 2, March–April 1995.

[21]Aleksander Smolar, "Democratization in Central-Eastern Europe in International Security," in New Dimensions in International Security, International Institute for Strategic Studies Adelphi Paper 266 (London: Brassey's, 1992), p. 25.

Contributors

Laura Belin writes on Russian affairs for Radio Free Europe/Radio Liberty in Prague. From 1995 to 1997 she covered Russian domestic politics and media issues for the Open Media Research Institute. She is the co-author of the book *The Russian Parliamentary Elections of 1995: The Battle for the Duma*.

Lowell Bezanis was an OMRI assistant research analyst from 1995–1997 specializing in Turkish and Central Asian affairs. He previously taught in Ankara, Turkey, and has written extensively on the area. He is currently an independent consultant based in Washington, D.C.

J.F. Brown is an independent British scholar and the author of several books on Eastern Europe, including *Hopes and Shadows: Eastern Europe After Communism*. He was formerly director and research director of Radio Free Europe.

Janusz Bugajski is director of East European Studies at the Center for Strategic and International Studies in Washington, D.C. His latest book is *Nations in Turmoil: Conflict and Cooperation in Eastern Europe*.

Zlatan Cabaravdic is a journalist from Sarajevo who works and lives in Prague.

Emil Danielyan works in Yerevan as a correspondent for Radio Free Europe/Radio Liberty's Armenian Broadcasting Department. He previously was an intern at the Open Media Research Institute in Prague.

Bhavna Dave has been a lecturer in Central Asian politics at the University of London's School of Oriental and African Studies since 1996. She previously was an OMRI assistant research analyst specializing in the ethnic and linguistic politics of Kazakstan.

Sharon Fisher worked as an OMRI senior research analyst specializing i: Slovakia from 1995 to 1997. She had previously written on Slovakia for Radio Free Europe/Radio Liberty in Munich.

Elizabeth Fuller is deputy editor of Radio Free Europe/Radio Liberty's *Newsline*, where she is an analyst on Transcaucasian affairs. She is also a contributing editor to *Transitions* and was previously a supervisory research analyst at OMRI. She is a graduate of the University of London and worked as a Transcaucasian analyst for Radio Liberty from 1980 to 1994.

Charles Gati is senior vice president of Interinvest, a global money-management firm, and a fellow at Johns Hopkins University. He was a consultant and then senior adviser to the U.S. State Department's Policy Planning Staff from 1989 to 1994, and has authored several books on the former Soviet bloc.

Saulius Girnius worked as an OMRI senior research analyst specializing in the Baltic states from 1995 to 1997. He was previously a Baltic analyst at Radio Free Europe/Radio Liberty in Munich and is currently working in Vilnius for the Lithuanian government.

Natalia Gurushina is a graduate of Moscow State University and completed a DPhil in economic history at Oxford University. She was an analyst at OMRI from 1995 to 1997 and now works for an investment company in Moscow.

Naryn Idinov works for Radio Free Europe/Radio Liberty's Kyrgyz Broadcasting Department.

Dan Ionescu reports on Moldovan and Romanian affairs for Radio Free Europe/Radio Liberty's Romanian Broadcasting Department. He previously worked as an OMRI senior research analyst specializing in Romania and Moldova. From 1984 to 1994, he worked as a research analyst for the RFE/RL Research Institute in Munich.

Roger Kangas is deputy director of the Central Asia Institute at Johns Hopkins University's Paul H. Nitze School of Advanced International Studies in Washington, D.C. He previously was an OMRI research analyst specializing in Central Asia. He is the author of *Uzbekistan in the Twentieth Century: Political Power and the State in a Post-Colonial Nation.*

Jakub Karpinski is a political analyst based in Warsaw and a contributing editor to *Transitions.* He was an OMRI senior research analyst specializing in Poland from 1995 to 1997. He has published a number of books on the postwar history and political system of Poland and has been a frequent contributor to *Uncaptive Minds.*

Steve Kettle is a political analyst based in London. He previously worked as an OMRI research analyst specializing in the Czech Republic. He has worked as a journalist for Reuters, UPI, and Radio Free Europe/Radio Liberty in Great Britain, Italy, France, Germany, and Czechoslovakia.

Maria Koinova was an OMRI intern from 1996 to 1997. She recently completed a European Journalism Network program in which she reported for the Munich daily *Munchner Merkur* and took courses at the Bavarian Press Academy. She currently lives in Sofia.

Stefan Krause is an independent political analyst based in London. He previously worked as an OMRI research analyst specializing in Bulgaria, Macedonia, and Greece, and compiled and edited *Transition's* chronology of the "Balkan Peace Effort."

Chrystyna Lapychak worked as an OMRI research analyst specializing in Ukraine from 1995 to 1997. She was a freelance correspondent for The Christian Science Monitor in Kyiv and served as Kyiv bureau chief and associate editor for the New Jersey—based Ukrainian Weekly.

Stan Markotich is a political analyst based in Vancouver, British Columbia. He previously worked as an OMRI research analyst specializing in Yugoslavia and Slovenia. He has a Ph.D. in history from Indiana University and worked as a research analyst for the RFE/RL Research Institute in Munich.

Ustina Markus was a senior research analyst for OMRI from 1995 to 1997 specializing in Ukrainian and Belarusian political and military affairs. She previously worked as a research analyst for Radio Free Europe/Radio Liberty in Munich.

Erik Mathijs is a research assistant in the Department of Agricultural Economics of the Catholic University of Leuven in Belgium. He is engaged in various projects funded by the European Union and the Belgian National Fund for Scientific Research about land reform.

Patrick Moore is a senior regional specialist at Radio Free Europe/Radio Liberty and a contributing editor at *Transitions*. He was an OMRI senior research analyst from 1995 to 1997 specializing in Croatia and Bosnia, where he studied in 1973–1974. He wrote on Balkan, Central American, and Far Eastern affairs for the RFE/RL Research Institute in Munich from 1977 to 1994.

Penny Morvant is a research fellow at Sidney Sussex College at Cambridge University. She worked as an OMRI research analyst specializing in Russian social issues from 1995 to 1997. Previously she worked for the RFE/RL Research Institute in Munich.

Robert W. Orttung is a fellow at the Institute for EastWest Studies in New York and editor of the IEWS *Russian Regional Report*. He previously worked at OMRI as a senior research analyst specializing in Russian domestic politics. He is the author of *From Leningrad to St. Petersburg* and co-author of *The Russian Parliamentary Elections of 1995: The Battle for the Duma*.

Bruce Pannier studied at Tashkent State University in 1990. He traveled throughout Central Asia in 1992 and 1993 doing sociological research in rural areas for the University of Manchester. He has been a research analyst specializing in Central Asia for the Open Media Research Institute and currently reports on the region for Radio Free Europe/Radio Liberty.

Scott Parrish is a fellow at the Monterrey Institute for International Studies in Monterrey, California. He previously worked at OMRI as a senior research analyst specializing in Russian foreign policy. He has authored numerous articles in *Transition* and written for *Problems of Post-Communism*.

Jiri Pehe is a political analyst based in Prague and a contributing editor at *Transitions*. He is also the editor of Radio Free Europe/Radio Liberty's Newsline.

Richard Rose is the director of the Center for the Study of Public Policy at the University of Strathclyde in Glasgow and international scientific adviser to the Paul Lazarsfeld Society in Vienna, which conducts the New Democracies Barometer public opinion surveys. He is the author of numerous books, including *What is Europe?*

Peter Rutland is an associate professor of government at Wesleyan University in Middletown, Connecticut, and a contributing editor to *Transitions*. From 1995–1997, he was on leave as assistant director of research at the Open Media Research Institute.

Fabian Schmidt is a political analyst specializing in Albania and Kosovo and a contributing editor to *Transitions*. He was an international election monitor for Albania's June 1997 parliamentary elections.

Michael Shafir is an eastern Balkans analyst for Radio Free Europe/Radio Liberty's Newsline. He previously worked as an OMRI supervisory research analyst specializing in Romania. He holds a Ph.D. in political science from the Hebrew University of Jerusalem, previously served as chief of the Romanian Research Unit at the RFE/RL Research Institute in Munich, and is the author of Romania: Politics, Economics and Society: Political Stagnation and Simulated Change.

Matthew Soberg Shugart is an assistant professor in the Graduate School of International Relations and Pacific Studies at the University of California-San Diego.

Ben Slay is an assistant professor in the Economics Department at Middlebury College. He worked from 1996 to 1997 as a senior economist at OMRI in Prague where he was the editor of the *Economic Digest*.

Daria Sito Sucic was an OMRI analyst from 1996–1997. She currently works for Reuters in Sarajevo.

Jo Swinnen is an assistant professor in the Department of Agricultural Economics of the Catholic University of Leuven in Belgium. He is engaged in various projects funded by the European Union and the Belgian National Fund for Scientific Research about land reform, and is a consultant with several policy analysis units funded by the EU's PHARE program.

Zsofia Szilagyi is a public relations officer for the United Nations High Commissioner for Refugees in Budapest. She worked from 1995 to 1997 as an OMRI research fellow specializing in Hungary.

John B. Taht has a master's degree in Russian and Eastern European history from Indiana University. He works as a research assistant in the Landegger Program in International Business Diplomacy at Georgetown University.

Christopher Ulrich is a freelance writer who is completing his doctoral disseration in the U.K.

Oleg Varfolomeyev was an OMRI intern from 1996 to 1997 and now works for the electronic publication *Eastern European Economist* in Kyiv.

Colin Woodard is a freelance journalist in Budapest.

Susan L. Woodward is a senior fellow in the Foreign Policy Studies Program at the Brookings Institution in Washington, D.C. She is the author of *Balkan Tragedy: Chaos and Dissolution After the Cold War*.

Michael Wyzan is a research scholar at the International Institute for Applied Systems Analysis in Laxenburg, Austria, and a contributing editor to *Transitions*. He is the author of numerous articles and the editor of three books, including *First Steps Toward Economic Independence*. In 1994–1995, he was a U.S. Treasury Department adviser to the Bulgarian Ministry of Finance.

Index

www.ingramcontent.com/pod-product-compliance
Ingram Content Group UK Ltd.
Pitfield, Milton Keynes, MK11 3LW, UK
UKHW020856280225
455677UK00006B/62